IDEAS PLUS DOLLARS:
RESEARCH METHODOLOGY AND FUNDING

15.75

IDEAS PLUS DOLLARS

RESEARCH METHODOLOGY AND FUNDING

HAROLD ZALLEN
and
EUGENIA M. ZALLEN

 ACADEMIC WORLD INCORPORATED

ISBN 0 915582 00 7

5-9-77 9⅙.

IDEAS PLUS DOLLARS:
RESEARCH METHODOLOGY AND FUNDING

Copyright © 1976 by ACADEMIC WORLD INCORPORATED, Post Office Drawer 2790, Norman, Oklahoma 73069, United States of America. All Rights Reserved. No part of this publication may be reproduced, stored in a retrieval system, or transmitted, in any form or by any means, electronic, mechanical, photocopying, xerography, recording, or otherwise, without the express prior written permission of the publisher.

Adapted and enlarged from: PLANNING FOR RESEARCH AND SPONSORED PROGRAMS: A GUIDE AND RESOURCE BOOK. Harold Zallen and Richard Robl, Oklahoma State University, Stillwater, Oklahoma 74074. © 1973

LIBRARY OF CONGRESS CATALOGING IN PUBLICATION DATA:

Zallen, Harold, 1926
Ideas Plus Dollars: Research Methodology and Funding
Adapted from Planning for research and sponsored programs.

Includes bibliographical references and index.
   1. Research — United States — Methodology. 2. Proposal writing in research. 3. Research — United States — Finance. 4. State encouragement of science, literature, and art — United States.

I. Zallen, Eugenia M., 1932   Joint Author   II. Title
Q180.U5Z34   001.4'3'0973
Library of Congress Catalog Number: 75-46502

INTERNATIONAL SERIAL BOOK NUMBERS:

ISBN: 0-9-15582 -00-7 Hardcover
ISBN: 0-9-15582 -01-5 Microfiche

COMPUTERIZED PHOTOGRAPHIC TYPESET IN MELIOR MODERN TEXT BY ED-BE, INC., OKLAHOMA CITY, OKLAHOMA
COVER AND ART BY ROBERT CHECORSKI
PRINTED BY THE UNIVERSITY OF OKLAHOMA, NORMAN, OKLAHOMA
BOUND BY UNIVERSAL BOOKBINDERY INCORPORATED, SAN ANTONIO, TEXAS

PRINTED IN THE UNITED STATES OF AMERICA

7   6   5   4   0   1   2   3   4   5   6   7   8   9

CANISIUS COLLEGE LIBRARY
BUFFALO, N. Y.

Q
180
.U5
Z34

What Is Research?

"Research" is a high-hat word that scares a lot of people. It needn't. It is rather simple. Essentially, it is nothing but a state of mind — a friendly, welcoming attitude toward change. Going out to look for a change instead of waiting for it to come. Research, for practical men, is an effort to do things better and not to be caught asleep at the switch. The research state of mind can apply to anything: personal affairs or any kind of business, big or little. It is the problem solving mind as contrasted with the let-well-enough-alone mind. It is the composer mind instead of the fiddler mind. It is the "tomorrow" mind instead of the "yesterday" mind.

— Charles Kettering

This book is dedicated to:

Dr. John E. Christian
Purdue University

and

Dr. Grayce E. Goertz
The University of Tennessee

To these two people, we owe sincere appreciation for their contributions to our lives as researchers and administrators. Their words and deeds continue to influence us for they have provided examples of the finest in instruction, research and administration.

H.Z.
E.M.Z.

PREFACE

IDEAS PLUS DOLLARS is intended to meld the views of the researcher and administrator. Each will find Chapters of especial interest to their needs, yet both researchers and administrators should view the total book to gain understanding of the total research-funding matrix.

This book can serve either as a textbook or reference book. It is anticipated that both the experienced researcher and/or fund raiser as well as the neophyte can find useful bits of information. The principal goal of the authors is to present an open and candid view of the total funding process. A special effort has been made to provide assistance to the principal investigator as he or she prepares a research document.

The contents of this book have been tested in a workshop-seminar environment. Because of the successful use of the material by potential fund seekers, the authors believe a new dimension is provided in the areas of research, research administration and proposal planning for educational, industrial and general audiences.

Grateful acknowledgement is extended to Dr. Richard Robl who co-directed the workshop and co-authored the precursor to this book. Without his help and dedication this book would never have been realized. Many thanks to Dr. Robert Gumm for his assistance in developing the computer retrieval system. The authors appreciated the encouragement and endorsement given by the Oklahoma State University Committee on Educational Innovation and the Oklahoma State University Research Council for the workshop which served as a test site for the concepts in this book.

For their participation and assistance in the workshop setting which served as a testing arena for this book, the authors give particular thanks to: Dr. Harold Cannon, National Endowment for the Humanities, Washington, D.C.; Mr. John D. Colby, U.S. Office of Education, National Center for Educational Technology, Washington, D.C.; Dr. William J. Riemer, Planning Officer, National Science Foundation, Washington, D.C.; Dr. M. Thomas Wagner, Jr., National Environmental Research Center, Environmental Protection Agency, Research Triangle Park, North Carolina; Dr. Charles F. Walters, Grants Officer, Environmental Protection Agency, Research Triangle Park, North Carolina; and Dr. Gilbert Woodside, Associate Director, National Institute of Child Health and Human Development, National Institutes of Health, Bethesda, Maryland.

The authors wish to acknowledge and thank the following for permission to reproduce portions of manuscript used in this book: American Institute of Biological Sciences; Department of Health, Education and Welfare; Federation Proceedings; G. & C. Merriam Company; Dr. Bruce Ketcham; National Science Foundation; Oklahoma State University and; the late Dr. Robert Beezer.

Harold Zallen
Eugenia M. Zallen

Norman, Oklahoma
January, 1976
The Bicentennial Year

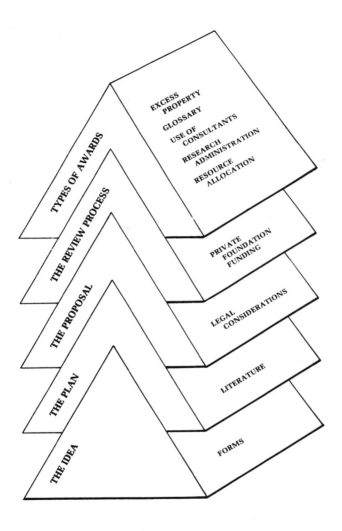

THE RESEARCH TRIANGLE

Contents

Chapter One
THE
IDEA

Chapter Two
THE
PLAN

Chapter Three
THE
PROPOSAL

Chapter Four

HOW TO PICK
A FUNDING SOURCE

Chapter Five

COMMUNICATING
WITH FUNDING SOURCES

Chapter Six

EXAMPLES OF
COMMUNICATIONS

Chapter Seven

THE REVIEW PROCESS

Chapter Eight
TYPES OF AWARDS

Chapter Nine
USE OF CONSULTANTS

Chapter Ten
RESOURCE ALLOCATION
AND MANAGEMENT

Chapter Eleven

MODELS OF RESEARCH ADMINISTRATION ORGANIZATIONS

Chapter Twelve

EXCESS AND SURPLUS PROPERTY

Chapter Thirteen

PRIVATE FOUNDATION FUNDING

Chapter Fourteen

LEGAL CONSIDERATIONS

Chapter Fifteen

LITERATURE RELEVANT TO RESEARCH
AND PROJECT FUNDING

Chapter Sixteen

USEFUL SAMPLE FORMS

List of Figures

List of Tables

IDEAS PLUS DOLLARS:
RESEARCH METHODOLOGY AND FUNDING

Chapter One

THE
IDEA

- THE IDEA
- DEFINITION OF THE IDEA
- SOURCE OF IDEAS
- DEVELOPMENT OF THE IDEA
- COMMUNICATING THE IDEA
- CONCLUSION

THE IDEA

The foundation of this book is the **IDEA.** It is from the idea that the entire creative process begins. Thus, an *idea* should be perceived as the beginning not the middle nor the end. Some people say that ideas are a *"dime a dozen."* If an idea is only generated and then it is not carried to fulfillment, perhaps the expression offered is valid. However, if an idea is transformed into reality then the mere existence of an idea becomes of prime importance. It is the latter premise, the *idea is of prime importance* which is the warp and woof of this book. Ideas are important and in any process, the idea must be carried to completion.

Ideas are considered by some as abstract, foolish and without any use. Indeed, ideas can be useless, but to treat

21

the subject properly, ideas should be looked upon as assets and not liabilities. An idea is the result of both intrinsic and extrinsic forces. The *imagination* is one of the most powerful components of the intrinsic forces. In *Figure One* the components of both the intrinsic and extrinsic forces are graphically portrayed. Albert Einstein is quoted as saying, *"Imagination is more important than knowledge."*[1] Perhaps the concept this great scientific giant meant in his statement was, *imagination is the precursor of knowledge.* He might have been telling us that the imagination should not run wild but assume an ordered and channeled posture. The message first may be imagine then acquire facts. Facts are then assimilated into knowledge.

The idea is so important to research methodology and the funding process that a great deal of emphasis is placed on both the generation of the idea and all of the intervening steps after the idea's birth. An idea is amorphous and requires the same treatment as a delicate newborn if it is to grow and acquire shape and structure.

DEFINITION OF THE IDEA

Webster's New Collegiate Dictionary gives considerable space, almost a fourth of a page to the definition of *idea*. Almost two-thirds of the space devoted to *idea* is to its synonyms.[2]

An outline for refining the original write-up of the idea may be useful. A sample outline sequence follows:

- **THE PROBLEM(S).**
- **THE PROJECT OR PROGRAM DESCRIPTION.**
- **OBJECTIVES.**
- **PROCEDURES (WITH RESPECT TO THE OBJECTIVES).**
- **ESTIMATES OF TIME — START TO FINISH.**
- **SIGNIFICANCE.**
- **ANTICIPATED RESULTS (WITH RESPECT TO SIGNIFICANCE).**
- **POSSIBLE USES TO BE MADE OF THE RESULTS OF FINDINGS.**

A proposal or project is built around an individual's idea. Ideas have been defined in the text both graphically

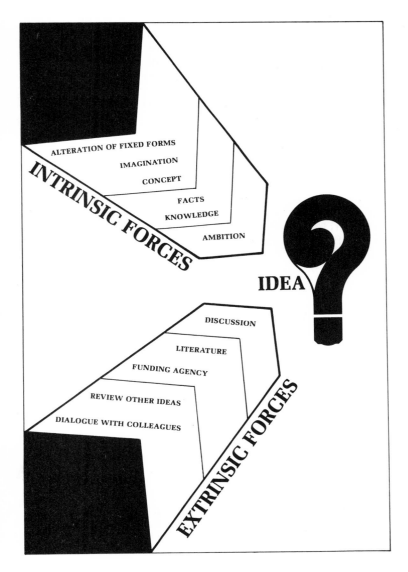

Figure 1.   •   COMPONENT FORCES OF THE IDEA

idea \ī-'dē-ə, ᵀid-(ˌ)ē-ə, *esp South* ᵀid-ē\ *n* [L, fr. Gk, fr. *idein* to see — more at WIT] **1 a :** a transcendent entity that is a real pattern of which existing things are imperfect representations **b :** a standard of perfection : IDEAL **c :** a plan for action : DESIGN **2** *archaic* **:** a visible representation of a conception : a replica of a pattern **3 a** *obs* **:** an image recalled by memory **b :** an indefinite or unformed conception **c :** an entity (as a thought, concept, sensation, or image) actually or potentially present to consciousness **4 :** a formulated thought or opinion **5 :** whatever is known or supposed about something <a child's ~ of time> **6 :** the central meaning or chief end of a particular action or situation **7** *Christian Science* : an image in Mind — **idea·less** \ī-'dē-ə-ləs\ *adj*

syn IDEA. CONCEPT, CONCEPTION, THOUGHT, NOTION, IMPRESSION *shared meaning element* **:** what exists in the mind as a representation (as of something comprehended) or as a formulation (as of a plan). IDEA is equally applicable to a mental image or formulation of something seen or known or imagined, to a pure abstraction, or to something assumed or vaguely sensed <that's not my *idea* of a good time> <try to get an *idea* of the complexity of the problem> CONCEPT in precise use applies to a generic idea conceived by the mind after acquaintance with instances of a category <the child as he grows develops such *concepts* as "chair", "dog", and "house"> but in frequent, if sometimes criticized use *concept* is applicable to any formulated and widely accepted idea of what a thing should be <we must expand the *concept* of conservation to meet the imperious problems of the new age —J. F. Kennedy> CONCEPTION. though often interchangeable with *concept* in the latter's more general use, can distinctively stress the process of imagining and formulating <too often a writer's *conception* exceeds his capacity for execution> THOUGHT is likely to suggest the result of reflection, meditation, or reasoning rather than of imagining <a child's *thought* about God> NOTION can apply to a vague, tentative, or chance idea <most of us retain the *notion* that all technical change is progress, is necessarily good —R. M. Hutchins> but in precise use it can come close to *concept* in suggesting a general or universal idea <arriving at the *notion* of law —Irving Babbitt> or to *conception* in denoting the meaning content assigned by the mind to a term <[they] have no adequate *notion* of what we mean by causation —Edward Sapir> IMPRESSION usually implies the presence of external stimulation that gives rise to an often vague idea <I had an *impression* that the door opened softly>

By permission. From Webster's New Collegiate Dictionary ⁽ᶜ⁾ 1975 by G. & C. Merriam Co., Publishers of the Merriam-Webster Dictionaries.

Figure 2. • *DICTIONARY DEFINITION OF IDEA*

and verbally and by the dictionary. Thus, an idea can be looked upon as something existing in the mind of an individual as an object of thought or knowledge. This object of thought or knowledge is usually a human want or need to be met in the near or distant future. An individual experiences a level of dissonance in relation to his environment and begins to pose questions and hypotheses. For each question or problem there can and will be numerous answers or solutions. In the context of this book, an idea for a proposal includes both a question and a possible solution.

SOURCE OF IDEAS

The first source of ideas for proposals involves an individual. We identify this person with the title project director or principal investigator. This is the individual proposing both the problem to be solved and a possible solution. The project director is the most important entity in the process. These individuals are directly involved with the project plan. The principal investigator seeks a funding source that has a mission related to his or her ideas.

Sources of ideas are many and difficult to document. However, ideas for proposals supported at the college or university level, or the city, county and state government generally come from two sources. The first being the innovative idea from a principal individual. Second, an office or agency with funds to support proposals will identify a need or problem and a *Request for Proposal* will be advertised to provide a solution to an agency's particular problem. Or guidelines will be sent to a proponent proposal writer announcing a particular grants program. The funding agency may only briefly state the problem or it may specify in detail the type of program to be mounted, the audience to be served, and other elements of the proposed solution. As you read further into the book more explanation will be given and examples of typical questions asked by the resource (funding source) will be answered.

DEVELOPMENT OF THE IDEA

As the principal investigator, you have identified an idea for a proposal. Before you begin writing a proposal it is suggested that you carefully examine your idea to determine its validity and how it can be improved.

Is your idea *evolutionary* or is it *new and innovative?* An *evolutionary* idea is an extension of existing ideas. It is usually the result of subdividing and establishing conflicts or collaborations within an environment which have to be resolved. It is probably an idea that parallels or extends your own experience. A *new and innovative* idea is the result of inputs from unfamiliar and high resistance paths in an environment. A review of the related literature and discussion with your professional colleagues will help decide the nature of an idea.[3]

A second set of questions that can be used in idea development are based on *needs analysis.* A *needs analysis* involves examining an idea in terms of local conditions and societal variables. It may be helpful first to categorize your idea by function; is it research, training, facilities, demonstration, or a service project? What population is to be served by your idea? What evidence do you have that it is a real need of that population? What are the symptoms and causes associated with the identified need? Of what importance is the need in comparison to other regional or national problems? What does the research show about some of the solutions which may be applied to the need? Do you and your institution have the resources and capabilities to carry out the proposed solution to meet the need? Finally, examine the idea in relation to the program goals of your department, college, and/or institution.

Idea development can be accomplished further by using a funding agency's guidelines for proposal development to determine the acceptability of your proposed idea. Although these guidelines will vary from agency to agency (private and Federal) similar concepts are found in most such specifications. A basic question is that of the value and rationale of an idea. This can be derived from previous research, from practical experience, or from an analysis of needs. Are the procedures suggested by the solution adequate and appropriate, and can they be accomplished in a reasonable time period? Have the constraints of the situation been analyzed and considered when deciding the solution? And finally, is the solution cost effective and reasonable in light of anticipated results?

Many other approaches to idea development could be presented but the important thing is that you develop your idea before beginning the costly task of writing a proposal. There are real dollars and human costs involved when writing and processing a proposal. A proposal is the culmination (final step) of the idea process not the initial step.

COMMUNICATING THE IDEA

The idea must be communicated in order to be utilized. The first method of communication already recommended is to commit the idea to writing. Write, write, and write until either the writer or the idea becomes exhausted. The original write-up now requires a refining process. The way to accomplish this is to design an outline in sequence of development. For example, if you were going to design a new automobile, one of the last steps in the evaluation phase would be to road test the automobile. You would not place it first in the sequence of operations. The consideration of the number of passengers and the anthropomorphic characteristics would precede the road test not follow it in the sequence.

The purpose of a proposal is to communicate the principal investigator's ideas and intentions to a potential funding office or agency. As you write, and review what you write, put yourself in the shoes of the expected reviewer of your proposal. Most writers will agree that effective communication is not easy. You become a better writer by asking questions about the fundamentals of good writing.

Write clearly, simply and with a positive attitude! To carry out this charge you must know your audience, have your subject matter well in hand and realize that writing is just clear and logical thinking. Have an organized planned sequence of steps for putting down your ideas, and use an expanding outline to prepare the draft.

Since words are the basic tools of written communication, the choice of the words used must be made carefully. Ideas are expressed best in simple language. Shorter, concrete words convey thoughts more quickly than complex, abstract words. Use positive words such as *will* instead of *may, would* or *should expect to.* Concentrate on using active verbs in the write-up and in your preliminary thinking before the write-up. An *active verb* is one which expresses action which the doer performs: a professor *teaches* or an actor *performs* on the stage. Active verbs offer the vigor and conviction so essential to a good proposal.

Use plain talk with a low "fog factor" when expressing an idea. Do not say **"give consideration to obtaining the product at the present time while postponing the actual expenditure of capital to a future period."** Rather, say, **"Buy Now and Pay Later!"** Put lengthy, involved listings, explanations, or voluminous technical detail in the appendices.[3]

John O'Hayre in his book, *"Gobbledygook Has Gotta Go"* speaks of the use of excess words in writing as *pomposity.* He considers two factors as the cause. First, an error in judgement, and second, an almost maniacal madness for using big words.[4]

Error No. 1: When you write pompously, you judge wrongly that readers appreciate elegant writing; that they expect you as an educated person to sound elegant and impressive and will think you undignified if you do not. This may have been true years ago, when five per cent of the people had social position and educational status and the other ninety-five per cent had neither. But that is not the way things are any more and readers do not like for you to write like they were. In short, parading elegant words is no longer a suitable ceremony for the educated to use to IMPRESS the less educated.

Error No. 2: The maniacal madness for big words. H. W. Fowler says that those writers who run to long words are mainly the unskillful and tasteless; they confuse pomposity with dignity, flaccidity with ease, and bulk with force.

John O'Hayre uses a fire report to illustrate what he calls evil pomposity.

Fire Report: Heavy rains throughout most of the State have given an optimistic outlook for lessened fire danger for the rest of the season. However, an abundance of lightning maintains a certain amount of hazard in isolated areas that have not received an excessive amount of rain. We were pleased to have been able to help Nevada with the supression of their conflagration.

Fire Report (rewritten from 61 pompous words to 41 simple words): Fire readings are down throughout most of the State. But a few rain-skipped areas are dry, and lightning is a hazard there. We are glad we could send some of our people to help Nevada put out their recent range fire.[4]

Excessive use of words, indirectness, insufficient exploratory information, non-precise use of words, and improper sentence structure are the most common faults of technical writing. Please note that whether the proposal is being written for the creative arts, humanities, social sciences or the performing arts and religion this format and discussion are valid. Constant awareness and remedy of these faults can improve your written work.

Word processing is becoming a commonplace word in our technological society today. Many small businesses as well as colleges and universities are moving rapidly in this direction. It was not too many years ago that the only persons who would use signs for correction of proofs or drafts would be the newspaperman, editor, book writer and printer. Today with word processing burgeoning in all areas where the written word is used, it is common to find a manager using standard signs for correcting proofs and communicating to his or her secretary or word processing center the revisions required. The state of the art in hardware is advancing so rapidly that the secretary of today will be typing on machines that will produce the printing of tomorrow. Recognizing the importance of a standard language for correcting manuscript for both word processing and the editing of professional manuscripts and proposals a table of *Signs Used in Correcting Proofs* is found in the *Appendix* of the book.

CONCLUSION

The idea has been defined as many things and yet they are all very much the same — idea, concept, conception, thought, notion and impression. Give thought to what happens to ideas? In some cases ideas are expounded to superiors as well as colleagues. They are listened to with great care and respect. Then nothing may happen to the ideas. The reason is simple. The audience that became the receptor of the idea from the donor never did anything about implementing the idea. The blame is everyone's — therefore we will avoid the pitfall of blaming it on people but blame it on poor communications. The latter is truly the reason in this case. The idea should have been committed to writing with a conceptual framework constructed to serve as a point of departure for a discussion. Considerable time will be spent in the development of the idea into a proposed plan in ensuing Chapters. It is the intent to reduce frustration or obstacles through and by development of a methodology of communicating and testing ideas.

Chapter Two

THE
PLAN

- **INTRODUCTION**
- **RESEARCH**
- **APPLIED RESEARCH**
- **ESSENTIAL ELEMENTS IN A RESEARCH DESIGN**
- **THE PLAN FOR RESEARCH**
- **PLANNING INFORMATION**
- **NATURE OF PLANNING**
- **A RESEARCHER PLANS**
- **PLANNING TECHNIQUES**
- **CONCLUSION**
- **SELECTED READING LIST**

INTRODUCTION

One step removed from the idea is the plan. An idea is without shape and dimension. The plan is ordered, with shape and dimension. The idea is generated using a thought process. The plan is a requirement for successful research, and the plan precedes a proposal.

To think is to become stimulated and to become stimulated results in motivation. Those proposals which captivate funding agencies do so by a force called interest. Interest is generated by an intriguing proposal.

An interesting idea cannot be transformed or transported directly into a proposal which will yield funds. It
must go through steps of refinement into a realistic,
plausible and viable plan. The steps of making such
a plan follow.

RESEARCH

In order to produce a plan which is founded on sound
principles, it is necessary to outline thorough and
systematic research. Figure 3 illustrates the Dimensions
of a Plan. Do not confuse a cursory look at the literature
with research.

The literature search and a written review of literature are but phases of the entire research process.
Research is defined in as many ways as the number of
people who have defined the term. Charles Kettering
defined research as follows:

> "Research" is a high-hat word that scares a lot of people. It
> needn't. It is rather simple. Essentially, it is nothing but a state
> of mind — a friendly, welcoming attitude toward change. Going
> out to look for change instead of waiting for it to come. Research,
> for practical men, is an effort to do things better and not be
> caught asleep at the switch. The research state of mind can
> apply to anything; personal affairs or any kind of business, big
> or little. It is the problem solving mind as contrasted with the
> let-well-enough-alone mind. It is the composer mind instead of
> the fiddler mind. It is the "tomorrow" mind instead of the
> "yesterday" mind.

Research is a purposeful activity aimed at the extension
of knowledge and experience. Some of the readers of this
book will not be active researchers but will be involved
with the researcher in an administrative capacity. Before
understanding can become complete for research administration personnel it would be both wise and prudent to
look at and gain a better understanding of research itself.
The research administrator cannot be of maximum assistance to the principal investigator if the research process

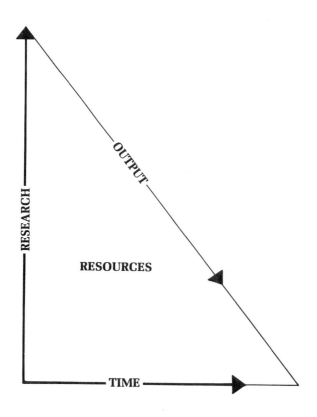

Key: Physical — space, instruments, equipment, library, computer
     Human — principal investigator, research assistants, fellows, faculty,
             graduate students
     Fiscal — grant funds, dollars, appropriated funds, gifts
     Time   — evaluation, program planning, research effort
     Output — research produced, implementation.

Figure 3 • DIMENSIONS OF A PLAN

is not fully understood. It is for these reasons some of the more important components of the research process have been included.

Research differs in mechanics among the various academic disciplines. The same basic principles apply whether it be in the creative arts; hard or exact sciences (astronomy, mathematics, physics and chemistry); social sciences (psychology, sociology); humanities (history, English, languages); and applied sciences (engineering, pharmacy, computer sciences, home economics, architecture, biological sciences).

There is agreement that research may be either *basic* or *applied* but confusion exists as to what constitutes basic research. The National Science Board, the policy making Board of the National Science Foundation, in 1973 published *"Science Indicators, 1972."*[1] In this report, *basic research* is defined.

Basic research is that portion of the total research and development effort whose primary aim is extending the fundamental understanding of man and nature. The strategy of basic research is determined primarily by the structure of science itself which indicates the opportunities and possible directions for advancing knowledge. Although potential applications underlie and ultimately justify support for basic research, such research must emanate from the conceptual structure of science itself.

While relationships between basic research and eventual applications are often complex and may involve a considerable time interval for realization, there is no doubt that modern technology is increasingly dependent upon the fundamental knowledge base. Basic science, moreover, provides a pool of knowledge and understanding which helps in determining the most efficient strategy for applied research and development, and also serves as a source of ideas for new applications and for attacking social problems as well. The contributions of basic research to the quality and variety of our lives are innumerable, and include:

- **GENETICS, which advanced the development of hybrid grains, stock breeding, vaccines, and medical diagnostic techniques;**
- **CHEMISTRY, which produced polyester fibers, pharmaceuticals, petroleum refining, and pesticides;**
- **PHYSICS, which led to the development of nuclear power generation, transistors, and radioisotope tracers;**
- **ELECTRONICS, which developed radar, magnetic tape recording, heart pacemakers, and biomedical recording techniques;**
- **MATHEMATICS, which helped in the development of computers, multivariate analysis techniques, systems analysis, and simulation models; and**
- **SOCIAL SCIENCES, which devised polling and survey methods, national income and product accounting, cost-benefit analysis, aptitude testing, and economic input-output models.**

Finally, basic research is an integral part of education. It is not only an integral element of advanced education in the sciences and engineering but its findings constitute the objective knowledge of the physical and social world which is part of the education of the population as a whole.

Whether for educational and cultural purposes, for technological and social reasons, or for the sheer intellectual understanding basic research provides, the health and vitality of such research is a matter of National significance.[2]

APPLIED RESEARCH

APPLIED RESEARCH — Applied Research is defined as problem solving or problem related systematic endeavor. Additionally it can be said that applied research utilizes principles derived in basic research and applies basic principles in solving problems which exist for people as they live in the natural world. Applied research **must** rest on a theoretical base. Applied research follows the same essential procedures for extending knowledge as does basic research. Applied research represents the research mission of many disciplines and the value of those disciplines to people is equivalent to basic research.

Basic research differs from applied research in that the problem solving for applied research is more in the focus of the public — and the public therefore expects those problems to be solved more quickly. Many basic research problems have been solved and are relatively well understood. It is another series of serious study and investigations before the basic principles can be transformed into usable devices or practical uses.

The quest for knowledge through basic and applied research must never stop or be slowed down. A myriad of live-saving devices and the spin-off for a multi-billion dollar industry are the result of the basic research discovery and the applied research studies made from the *transistor*. Today the integrated circuit, microelectronics and MOS, serve as but one example of the benefits to mankind through applied research.

The important point to remember is **good research** is **good research.** This principle applies to all research. It does not matter whether it is a basic equation for the discovery of a new energy source; the degradation of meat and its chemical analysis; the synthesis of a new compound for anti-cancer use; the statistical study of monetary habits; the design of a new dance for the creative arts; the determination of the effects of new legislation on the populace; the determination of food habits; or the effect of human sexuality on behavior patterns. Whether the study is historical, basic sciences, engineering science, or religion, it is important that fundamental research principles and tenets are adhered to without equivocation. *The rule and guide* to adhere to in the quest of good research is the adoption of the *scientific method.*

THE SCIENTIFIC METHOD — The scientific method is a system of going from *known* to *unknown* steps. One starts first with the *observation*. The *observation step* involves viewing and recording the known. Then and only after thorough observation, is the known described. Within the examination phase of the known, a thorough search for known ideas should be made. After the *known* has been described and recorded a *hypothesis* can be formulated. Here the *observation(s)* are transformed into a *hypothesis*. The *hypothesis* is the researcher's guess as to how the research will conclude. The guesses should be made on a sound firm base resulting from careful analyses of the observations. To test the stated hypothesis it becomes necessary to *experiment*. The *experimentation phase* is merely a verification of the guess (as far as possible — not absolute). This produces a degree of confidence in the answer. After great amounts of experimentation and a long time span, the above steps are culminated in the formulation of a *theory*. Theories undergo modification and refinement as a result of experimentation. The results of experimentation are disseminated through professional journals. The experimentation and specific experiments form the bases of new ideas; and thus the cycle repeats itself yielding new results with each repetitive process.

In a distant time when the experimentation has proved a *theory*, the *theory* takes on a new identification called a *law*.

In research, the researcher **never absolutely proves anything.** Evidence is gained to support a hypothesis. *The scientific method* is one way by which knowledge is acquired. There are others. Inherent in *the scientific method* are the following characteristics: *systematic organized statements of fact; procedures for gathering supportive evidence; and a rational basis which develops the open mind.*

The sources of knowledge follow:

- **CULTURE, TRADITION, AUTHORITY FIGURES AND EXPERT OPINION.**
- **EXPERIENCE.**
- **REASONING FROM OBSERVATION OR LOGICAL THOUGHT — DEDUCTION.**

- **EXPERIMENTATION.**
- **REVELATION, INTUITION.**

Dr. Robert Beezer has analyzed many research proposals. As a result, he devised thirty-four steps which he called *"Essential Elements in a Research Design."*[3]

ESSENTIAL ELEMENTS IN A RESEARCH DESIGN

A research proposal should be so written that any competent researcher, who is well informed about the specific subject area with which the proposed study is concerned, could use it as a basis of conducting the research without consulting the proposer. The problem, objectives, procedures, and the relationships among all three should be clearly stated in sufficient detail and be well formulated technically. When essential details are missing, a reviewer is unable to adequately evaluate a proposed project. The proposal should state specifically, yet concisely, (1) *WHAT* would be done, (2) *HOW* it would be done, (3) *TO WHOM* (all of the pertinent characteristics of the subjects should be specified), (4) *WHY* (there should be a sound theoretical and/or experimental rationale for the proposed use of each major procedural step, independent variable, and dependent variable), and (5) what the *ANALYSES* of each category of data would be. *WHEN it is appropriate*, each facet of a research design listed should be included in a proposal.

1. **THE RESEARCH PROBLEM SHOULD BE CLEARLY DEFINED.**
2. **THE SCOPE OF THE RESEARCH SHOULD BE APPROPRIATELY DELIMITED.**
3. **THE THEORETICAL FRAMEWORK SHOULD BE CLEARLY SPECIFIED.**
4. **ALL OF THE INDEPENDENT VARIABLES SHOULD BE DELINEATED.**
5. **ALL OF THE DEPENDENT VARIABLES SHOULD BE DELINEATED.**
6. **A THEORETICAL AND/OR EXPERIENTIAL RATIONALE FOR THE PROPOSED USE OF EACH MAJOR PROCEDURAL STEP, INDEPENDENT VARIABLE, AND DEPENDENT VARIABLE SHOULD BE PROVIDED.**

7. THE HYPOTHESES TO BE TESTED, THE QUESTIONS POSED, OR THE STATED OBJECTIVES SHOULD BE WELL FORMU- LATED AND CLEARLY EXPRESSED. (NOTE: NOT ALL RE- SEARCH SHOULD BE SPECIFIED.

8. ALL OF THE CHARACTERISTICS OF THE SUBJECTS PER- TINENT TO THE PROPOSED RESEARCH SHOULD BE SPECIFIED.

9. THE SAMPLING PLAN, FOR THE SELECTION OF SUBJECTS AND/OR THE MAKING OF OBSERVATIONS, SHOULD BE APPROPRIATE AND CLEARLY STIPULATED.

10. THE METHODS THAT WOULD BE USED TO MANIPULATE OR CONTROL, EITHER EXPERIMENTALLY, STATISTICALLY,OR BOTH, ANY VARIABLES SHOULD BE CLEARLY SPECIFIED.

11. ALL VARIABLES THAT VERY LIKELY WOULD BE SIGNIFICANT SOURCES OF VARIANCE, BUT WHICH WOULD NOT BE MANIPULATED OR CONTROLLED BY THE RESEARCHER(S), SHOULD BE IDENTIFIED.

12. WHEN NO GENERALLY ACCEPTED PROCEDURE OF MANIPU- LATING OR CONTROLLING A POSSIBLE SIGNIFICANT VARI- ABLE EXISTS, A METHOD DESIGNED TO ATTEMPT TO MANIPULATE OR CONTROL SUCH A VARIABLE, OR TO MINIMIZE ITS EFFECT, SHOULD BE DESCRIBED, AND A CONVINCING RATIONALE FOR THE PROPOSED METHOD SHOULD BE PRESENTED.

13. THE SEQUENCE AND KINDS OF EXPERIMENTAL TREATMENTS AND/OR MAJOR PROCEDURAL STEPS SHOULD BE DESCRIBED.

14. INDICES OR OPERATIONAL DEFINITIONS OF ALL KEY CONCEPTS AND CONSTRUCTS (E.G., CURIOSITY, VALUES, CULTURALLY DEPRIVED, AND SOCIOECONOMIC STATUS) SHOULD BE PROVIDED.

15. THE METHOD WHEREBY SOCIOECONOMIC STATUS WOULD BE DETERMINED SHOULD BE EXPLICITLY STATED.

16. THE TYPES OF DATA WHICH WOULD BE OBTAINED SHOULD BE SPECIFIED.

17. THE WAYS IN WHICH VARIOUS CATEGORIES OF DATA WOULD BE INTERRELATED SHOULD BE DESCRIBED.

18. ALL DATA-COLLECTION TECHNIQUES SHOULD BE SPECIFIED IN ADEQUATE DETAIL, AND THE QUALIFICATIONS OF THE DATA COLLECTORS (E.G., TESTERS AND INTERVIEWERS) SHOULD BE INDICATED.

19. THE PSYCHOMETRIC INSTRUMENTS TO BE USED SHOULD BE SPECIFICALLY NAMED OR IDENTIFIED, THE RATIONALE FOR THE PROPOSED USE OF EACH SHOULD BE PRESENTED, AND ALL PERTINENT AVAILABLE STATISTICAL CHARACTER- ISTICS (E.G., RELIABILITY AND VALIDITY) OF THE INSTRU- MENTS SHOULD BE PROVIDED IN QUANTITATIVE, NOT QUALITATIVE, TERMS.

20. IF ANY PSYCHOMETRIC INSTRUMENT IS TO BE DEVELOPED ON THE PROJECT, A DETAILED DESCRIPTION OF HOW IT WOULD BE CONSTRUCTED, AND OF HOW ESSENTIAL PSYCHOMETRIC DATA (E.G., RELIABILITY AND VALIDITY) ABOUT IT WOULD BE OBTAINED SHOULD BE PROVIDED. (NOTE: IN MOST INSTANCES, THE CONSTRUCTION OF A

PSYCHOMETRIC INSTRUMENT CONSTITUTES A PROJECT IN AND OF ITSELF! IF A RESEARCHER FAILS TO DEVELOP A PSYCHOMETRICALLY SOUND INSTRUMENT, THE RESULTS OF HIS RESEARCH WOULD BE INCONCLUSIVE.)

21. THE WAY IN WHICH THE RESULTS OF ALL PSYCHOMETRIC INSTRUMENT DATA WOULD BE USED IN THE ANALYSES SHOULD BE DESCRIBED.

22. HOW POSSIBLE INTERACTION EFFECTS BETWEEN ANY PRETESTING AND EXPERIMENTAL CONDITIONS WOULD BE DETECTED SHOULD BE ADEQUATELY DESCRIBED.

23. A DETAILED DESCRIPTION OF HOW REGRESSION TO THE MEAN, WHICH TENDS TO BE MANIFESTED IN POSTTEST SCORES, WOULD BE DEALT WITH STATISTICALLY SHOULD BE PRESENTED.

24. A PROCEDURE OF DETERMINING HOW THE SUBJECTS PERCEIVE ANY TREATMENT OR INTENDED REINFORCERS (THEIR PERCEPTION IS THEIR REALITY) SHOULD BE ADEQUATELY DESCRIBED.

25. HOW THE TREATMENT CONDITIONS AND THE USE THAT WILL BE MADE OF DATA OBTAINED ABOUT THE SUBJECTS WOULD BE DESCRIBED TO THEM SHOULD BE SPECIFIED.

26. WHEN QUESTIONNAIRES WOULD BE USED, THE AREAS OF INQUIRY (E.G., EDUCATION AND WORK EXPERIENCE) SHOULD BE DELINEATED, THE RATIONALE FOR THE IN-CLUSION OF EACH AREA OF INQUIRY SHOULD BE STATED, SAMPLE ITEMS MOST DIRECTLY RELATED TO EACH AREA OF INQUIRY SHOULD BE PROVIDED, AND PLANS FOR A PRETEST AND VALIDATION OF THE QUESTIONNAIRE SHOULD BE ADEQUATELY DESCRIBED.

27. TRAINING TO BE GIVEN TO SUBJECTS (E.G., TEACHERS) SHOULD BE ADEQUATELY DESCRIBED, AND A RATIONALE FOR THE PROPOSED USE OF EACH MAJOR TRAINING ELEMENT SHOULD BE PRESENTED.

28. THE METHOD THAT WOULD BE USED TO DETERMINE HOW WELL THE SUBJECTS (E.G., TEACHERS) HAD LEARNED WHAT THEY WERE SUPPOSED TO HAVE LEARNED DURING TRAINING DESIGNED TO PREPARE THEM FOR IMPLEMENTING AN EXPERIMENTAL PROCEDURE SHOULD BE ADEQUATELY DESCRIBED.

29. THE OBSERVATION PLAN THAT WOULD ENABLE THE RESEARCHER(S) TO DETERMINE HOW WELL SUBJECTS (E.G., TEACHERS), TRAINED TO IMPLEMENT AN EXPERIMENTAL PROCEDURE, WERE ACTUALLY PERFORMING SHOULD BE DESCRIBED IN DETAIL.

30. METHODS THAT WOULD BE USED TO BRING ABOUT AN ACCLIMATIZATION TO AN EXPERIMENTAL PROCEDURE, BEFORE THE DATA TO BE USED IN ANY ANALYSES ARE COLLECTED, SHOULD BE ADEQUATELY DESCRIBED.

31. METHODS THAT WOULD BE USED TO DETECT, MINIMIZE, OR PRECLUDE A POSSIBLE HAWTHORNE EFFECT SHOULD BE DESCRIBED.

32. HOW A POSSIBLE ORDER EFFECT WOULD BE CONTROLLED OR MINIMIZED SHOULD BE ADEQUATELY DESCRIBED.
33. ALL APPROPRIATE DETAILS ABOUT MODEL BUILDING AND THEORY DEVELOPMENT SHOULD BE CLEARLY AND ADEQUATELY DESCRIBED.
34. ALL STATISTICAL ANALYSES THAT WOULD VERY LIKELY BE USED SHOULD BE DENOTED AND RELATED TO THE SPECIFIC DATA TO WHICH THEY WOULD BE APPLIED.

THE PLAN FOR RESEARCH

The design for research or a creative endeavor should be a comprehensive, detailed plan which includes everything from justification to budget. Accountability has always been a factor in successful research and today accountability has become the theme of all institutions in which research is conducted. The successful researcher is one who can see problems and needs, can envision the total series of steps to complete research and is able to partition a plan for research into fundable and time possible units.

In other Chapters of this book, the proposal for requesting funds is extensively discussed. The plan for research is the basis for such a proposal and all information contained in the proposal is abstracted from the plan. Steps for developing the research plan include:

1. Identification

In basic research or creative endeavor, a need for the knowledge required should be established. In applied research, a problem is identified. Identification is based on observation, serendipity, reading the literature, and/or research which has been completed. For a productive researcher the last mentioned will frequently identify further study.

2. Definition

In defining a possible area of research, information which relates to the topic is collected. Data are compiled from all sources which will influence the possible outcome of the selected research. Possible relationships are derived which will provide meaningful variables. The literature is studied to see what other researchers say.

Additional definitions which are needed include skills which will be needed to accomplish the research — available skills and skills which are possible to acquire. The research should be defined in relation to the institution in which it is to be conducted. The institutional framework has inherent goals, personnel and resources which must be considered by the researcher.

The size of the study should be defined. How many variables are present which require solutions? How large a sample is needed? Of what units is the sample composed? How many hands and minds are needed? How many replications are recommended? How long will it take to complete the project? What physical facilities are required? How much money is needed for the project?

3. Review of Research Conducted

In every step of research, the literature is a vital component. When deciding on an area of study, when planning the study, and when preparing the results of the study, the literature is cogent and necessary. In the plan itself, the literature is used to determine what is actually already known or suspected, to identify current research, to provide the researcher with a broad background and to ascertain research techniques which have been used successfully.

4. Statement of Specific Purpose

To do something is the researcher's purpose. The key word is the one which follows *to* in the stated objective. If that word says the purpose is to measure, then data collection methods must reflect the meaning of *to measure.*

The ultimate purpose of any research study is to test hypotheses and to express a degree of confidence in the outcome. Hypotheses are statements which move from a *known* fact to a *conceptual* element. A thorough treatment of hypotheses with relation to the *Scientific Method* is discussed in detail earlier in this Chapter. The hypotheses may be stated as a question, as a declarative sentence or in quantitative terms as a null hypothesis. Hypotheses in any form should be: (1) specific as to conditions; (2) testable, usually by statistical procedures; (3) logical for testing; (4) brief, clear and concise; (5) plausible; (6) adequate in scope; and (7) simple to explain.

The collection of data is only one dimension of research. A key to meaningful results is to identify relationships and to measure the significance of relationships. Differentiation of research from other systematic activities is based upon the testing of hypotheses.

5. Specification of Variables and Controlled Conditions

Every experiment has two variables. Few research studies have only two. Economy of time and money preclude the luxury of only two. Each variable is specified with care and those which are part of the experimental plan are identified. Non-experimental variables must be recognized and either controlled by holding them constant or manipulated by techniques of experimental design.

6. Population and Sample

A *population* is the aggregate of all elements, cases or observations which conform to a designated set of specifications. The *population* should be clearly and precisely defined. A *sample* is a subset of a population which may or may not be representative of the *population*. If all units of a defined population are studied, the data collected are called *parameters*. *Parameters* truly describe the *population*. For reasons of cost, time or availability, all units of a population are not commonly studied. Thus, the population is sampled and inferences are made from the sample to the population.

Sampling may be *non-probability* in nature which includes *accidental, quota* and *purposive*. Sampling may be *probability* when there is a known chance of an element appearing in the sample. When *probability sampling* is used, generalizations from the sample to the larger population can be made. A sample of adequate size must be used to warrant the generalization. The sample size will be based upon the size of the population, presence of uncontrolled variables, size of the expected differences in the variables measured, stratification of the sample, and statistical tests to be used.

7. Collection of Data

To measure a variable, to make quantified observations, or to collect data from a sample, an instrument capable of measurement is a necessary requirement. Essential characteristics of an adequate instrument are that it be objective, valid and reliable. Desirable characteristics are that it be simple, cost-related to the data obtained, and requires a reasonable length of time for data collection.

Types of instruments which have been successfully used include:

- Humans
- Questionnaires
- Interview Schedules
- Observation of activities with recording by checklist, rating scale, occurrence in time

sampling, or mechanical devices such as videotape.

- Instruments which are based upon chemical, biological and physical principles.

Instruments for data collection can be stock items or can be created by the researcher. If created, the instruments must be *validated*.

The process of data collection requires detailed explanations. After careful justification and description of the instruments to be used, a plan should include the forms on which data will be recorded.

8. Research Design

In the selection of a research design, the researcher refers to the *purpose* of the study. He also should refer to the variables in the study. On the basis of these factors, a research design is developed.

The research may be *exploratory, descriptive, historical* or *experimental* in design. Within experimental research, there are designs differentiated by the degree of control imposed. No researcher should state that his research design was selected by a statistician and that was his reason for using a particular design. Every researcher should study research methodology to the extent that he or she clearly understands the limitations, usefulness and pertinence of the design selected.

The purpose of this book is to demonstrate how good research methodology leads to funds for accomplishing the projects chosen. The authors have not included detailed specifics in regard to various research designs, but urge the readers to study several of the research design books available. A list of suggested reading in this area has been included at the end of this Chapter.

9. Analysis of Data

Once decisions are made with regard to purpose,

population, sample, size, and research design, the method of data analysis must be decided. Again, it can be noted that the collection of data is one component of research, but for the process to be complete, data collected must be analyzed and conclusions drawn from the relationships that have been identified. The time to decide upon the method of data analysis is when *the plan* is constructed. The time *not* to decide the method of data analysis is after the study has been completed. *(Authors' Note: The experienced researcher and reviewer of proposals can detect the after-the-fact data analysis quite readily).* Manipulation of data collected by the choice of analysis method yields research results and conclusions of **doubtful value.**

10. Budget

The budget aspect of the research study is often difficult but of necessity. A complete listing of **all** costs anticipated should be included. Some cost components may be absorbed by existing budgets and programs at your institution. Others may represent a **cost-share** commitment as extramural funds are sought. Other costs will be clearly identified as needing a source. **All** costs will become an accountable part of the research study. A sampling of items which must be given a value includes: secretarial support, laboratory technicians, interviewers, publication page costs, foreign and domestic travel, instrument purchases, maintenance and repair, postage, shipping costs, printing costs for questionnaires and the like, chemicals, subjects (human or animal), construction materials, etc. Identifying all items and determining the costs will insure a smoother flow of data and a smoother research project experience.

The parts of *The Plan* should all fit together at this point. Planning is the process of taking individual components and fitting them together so that the whole picture evolves into a microcosm of work to be accomplished. The developed plan should be viewed as a dynamic view of a dynamic process — research.

PLANNING INFORMATION

Planning we may now agree is examining situations, formulating objectives and deciding what is to be done in the future. Decision making can be done only when solid, hard data (information) are available. If one is to forecast, information to make assumptions must be available. Forecasting is more commonly associated with management and business; however, science policy and research and development are likewise forecast.

In a smaller sphere, perhaps less complex, the researcher, the research administrator, the teacher, the professor and the professional can likewise forecast. Technological changes dictate forecast changes. For example, take the professor of electrical engineering who is expert in the area of solid state switching devices. The *integrated circuit* has markedly changed the size, capability, function and performance of all its predecessors. Today the *monolithic chip* has dramatically changed computers, calculators, household consumer electronics, and soon will revolutionize the watch and clock industry. The changes in this area of technological evolution dictate new markets, research, development and acquisition.

It is not the intent of the authors to delve deeply into *Delphi, Monte Carlo* or other think tank forecasting techniques — there are an adequate number of treatises, scientific research papers and textbooks readily available on this subject. It is the authors' intent to call attention to the existence of these techniques, and to the importance of being aware of them when considering extramural funding in *technology transfer and science policy.*

Recently the United States Government published a *"Directory of Technology Transfer."*[3] This treatise on technology transfer points to the importance of good planning and forecasting. There are a few theoretical based research administrators who attempt to use the aforementioned sophisticated techniques to predict future needs, and plan with their peers proposals to stay ahead of the competition. This is a worthwhile exercise if resources, personnel and time allow for the luxury of such planning. This is normally a very expensive model and requires both sophisticated personnel as well as much computer time.

NATURE OF PLANNING

As we have discussed in other parts of the book, planning is an intellectual process. The plan is not the proposal. Planning charts a course of action for the future. One of the components of the planning process is decision-making. For some this is very difficult to comprehend. Yet for others it will be quite easy and logical. Since the plan follows the idea phase, it requires the manipulation of abstract ideas.

Planning is a primary function. The researcher must plan before other functions can be intelligently treated.

A RESEARCHER PLANS

The researcher is concerned with what will happen in his or her endeavor or professional interest. Thus, the researcher may be said to be concerned with the future. Planning is a process which deals with the future. The periods of planning vary from *short, medium* to *long range. Short term* plans usually encompass a period of six to twelve months; *medium range* a period of one to five years; and *long range* covers a period of five, ten or as much as twenty years.

The objectives when defined should include within each time period the *short, medium* and *long range* plans. This is also true for the proposal writer. The funding agencies need to see beyond the immediate and assimilate what the writer intends to do in the future with the project or what the writer perceives may be the results of the research or project for the professional discipline or society in general.

PLANNING TECHNIQUES

Planning for some projects is a relatively simple task, that is when compared to the planning of a supersonic aircraft, a polaris submarine or an integrated energy system. As the authors have already stated, the principles of planning are very much the same whether the project is relatively simple or extremely complex. As the number of variables increases and the number of persons and organizations requiring interaction, so does the need for improved techniques for both graphic presentation and decision making.

Henry Gantt in the early 1900's developed a graphic systems approach for the display of planning information. A sample chart is found in Chapter Sixteen. Using the Gantt approach, tasks, personnel (resources) and the time to accomplish each task can be graphically portrayed with the utmost of simplicity. The Gantt approach allows for a multitude of modifications in the planning process and fits well as a valuable tool for both researcher and administrator.

Drucker[5] says that the Gantt charting, although developed during World War I, is still one tool we have to identify the process needed to accomplish a task, whether making a pair of shoes, landing a man on the moon or producing an opera. As the data become more complex, so does the decision making process. Simple decisions as to when one step should start and another end have always been difficult for planners. New tools and techniques along with the computer have simplified and increased the accuracy of predictions and forecasting.

A technique which is widely used today is called *network analysis.* In the family of *network analysis* two techniques are most widely used in research and research planning. They are, *Program Evaluation Review Technique* (PERT) and *Critical Path Method* (CPM). Both are extensions and elaborations of Gantt's original work. They are both process flow diagrams. PERT became known for its success in the Fleet Ballistic Missile program of the United States Navy. In 1958, the Polaris Missile Program of the Navy employed some 2,000 contractors — it was here that job components critical for completion and single time estimates were made. The cost-effectiveness and the savings of time which made the Program such a success have been given to the PERT techniques employed in its overall administration.

One year prior to the Navy's adoption of PERT the counterpart for industrial applications was announced by Morgan I. Walker of E.I. du Pont de Nemours Company and James E. Kelley Jr. of the Remington Rand Corporation. They called their system *Critical Path Method (CPM).* Here single time estimates are determined for the accomplishment of various tasks. CPM is commonly used today in the construction industry.

Because it is not the intention of this book to go into quantitative planning techniques such as PERT, CPM, Monte Carlo, and a host of other excellent methods for quantitative planning, the authors have included a selected reading list for those who wish to learn more about the subject at the end of this Chapter. Should the occasion arise that expertise is needed in quantitative planning techniques, persons who are normally conversant and knowledgeable come from the following areas of expertise: industrial management; industrial engineering; computer science; operations research; planning engineers; and consultant groups and firms.

CONCLUSION

The development of a comprehensive plan for research is a sequential step between the idea and a proposal which will be submitted for funding. A proposal which is to be submitted should rest on a sound, well organized plan. Any research plan identifies the area of study; defines it; reviews pertinent research; states a purpose; specifies all procedures for collection of data, the research design and analysis of data; and specific costs associated with the project. A number of planning techniques are available to assist the researcher with the compilation of a plan.

SELECTED READING LIST

Anthony, R.N. *Planning and Control Systems*, Harvard Business School, Cambridge, Massachusetts, 1965.

Argyris, Chris. *Organization and Innovation*, Yale University Press, New Haven, Connecticut, 1963.

Campbell, D.T. and Stanley, J.C. *Experimental and Quasi-Experimental Design for Research*, Rand McNally and Company, Chicago, Illinois, 1966.

Champion, D.J. *Basic Statistics for Social Research*. Chandler Publishing Company, Scranton, Pennsylvania, 1970.

Cochran, W.G. and Cox, G.M. *Experimental Design, 2nd. Edition.* John Wiley and Sons, New York, New York, 1955.

Compton, N.H. and Hall, O.A. *Foundations of Home Economics Research*. Burgess Publishing Company, Minneapolis, Minnesota. 1972.

Conant, J. *Science and Common Sense*, Yale University Press, New Haven, Connecticut, 1951.

Fayol, Henri. *General and Industrial Management*, Pitman, New York and London, 1949.

Federer, W.T. *Experimental Design*. Macmillan Company, New York, New York. 1955.

CANISIUS COLLEGE LIBRARY
BUFFALO, N. Y.

Gantt, Henry, *Gantt on Management*. Edited by A.W. Rathe, American Management Association, New York, New York, 1961.

Joseph, M.J. and Joseph, W.D. *Essentials of Research Methods and Evaluation for Home Economists*, Pylcon Press, Fullerton, California, 1975.

Maslow, A.H. *Motivation and Personality*, Harper and Row, New York, New York, 1954.

McGregor, D. *The Human Side of Enterprise*, McGraw-Hill Publishing Company, New York, New York, 1958.

Meyers, L.S. *Behavior Research: Theory, Practice and Design*. W.H. Freeman and Company, San Francisco, California, 1974.

Chapter Three

THE
PROPOSAL

- **BACKGROUND**
- **THE PRELIMINARY OR PREPROPOSAL**
- **ANATOMY OF THE PRELIMINARY PROPOSAL**
- **THE PROPOSAL**
- **PROPOSAL FORMAT GUIDELINES**
- **THE UNSOLICITED PROPOSAL**
- **THE SOLICITED PROPOSAL (REQUEST FOR PROPOSAL)**
- **COST OF A REQUEST FOR PROPOSAL (RFP)**
- **COMPONENTS OF A REQUEST FOR PROPOSAL (RFP)**
- **REQUEST FOR QUOTATION (RFQ)**
- **ASSEMBLY OF THE PROPOSAL**
- **SUBMITTING THE FORMAL PROPOSAL FOR FUNDING**
- **CONCLUSION**

BACKGROUND

Each agency, private or governmental, responsible for the disbursement of funds is normally busy with numbers of people coming in and out of the doors. This is not hard to understand when one envisions the number of requests made upon private and governmental funding sources and the small percentage of monies that are awarded. Do not be deceived when visiting the action office to find it looks much like a one man operation. There may be as many as twenty-five persons behind the scenes responsible for clerical and staff work for a program. This is required to process proposals and develop guidelines.

Because competition for the dollar is so great, anything the writer of a proposal can do to sharpen up his or her communications (written and/or verbal) with the potential funding agency becomes a definite advantage over the competitor. The principles and methodology proposed here should bear more fruit than your current *modus operandi.* Whenever a contact is made try to keep the purpose in mind. There is an added burden placed upon the action officer by the large number of visits made to the agencies. It is to the proposer's advantage to be succinct and to the point in anything that is sent to the action officer or given to him in person not to add further pressure.

THE PRELIMINARY OR PREPROPOSAL

Today, there are large numbers of people comprised of both administrators and principal investigators who believe preliminary proposals are not the sensible route. That segment of the population which adheres to this belief may be spending inordinate amounts of money, enormous amounts of energy and wasting valuable time to later find their proposal was denied because of inadequate preparation. Within the funding agencies there will be some programs that will accept the preliminary or preproposal and there will be others that will not. If a program will accept your preliminary proposal this is the safest and best of all avenues to pursue. It will provide the writer of the project with successive dialogue through an iterative process of either written communication through letters, or oral communication through visits or a combination of the two. In addition to the communications it provides, a higher degree of probability toward receiving an award may be the result.

In May, 1975, the National Science Foundation multimillion dollar RANN (Research Applied to National Needs) Directorate formally announced it would accept preliminary proposals. Those seeking funds from RANN programs were asked to first submit preliminary proposals. In the National Science Foundation Publication 75-21, the specifics (in the form of questions) are listed.[1]

- **IS THE TOPIC OF IMPORTANCE TO THE PROSPECTIVE USERS AND TO THE NATION?**
- **IS THE IDEA OR APPROACH PRESENTED TECHNICALLY SOUND?**
- **ARE THE QUALIFICATIONS AND RESEARCH RESOURCES OF THE PROPOSED TEAM APPROPRIATE TO THE TASK?**
- **ARE THERE OTHER SOURCES OF SUPPORT FROM FEDERAL, OTHER PUBLIC OR PRIVATE ORGANIZATIONS?**

There are program officers within agencies and organizations who have elected not to accept preliminary proposals. Those in this category have stated that the preliminary proposal gives an advantage to the writer over the person submitting a formal proposal without any prior dialogue with the action officer or his staff. This is indeed true. That is why a great deal of emphasis has been placed upon the preliminary proposal. Attempt to take advantage of every opportunity which will allow you to take trial or practice runs. The formal proposal is a *go* or *no-go* situation. Discussion or communication pertaining to the project is not permitted after submission of a formal proposal. Some agencies go so far as not to permit supplemental material to be added either by letter or other means to a formal proposal once it has been submitted, received and logged (assigned a number) by that agency.

Although grant applications may be submitted at any time and on any subject to most agencies, it is strongly advisable to those seeking support to first contact the agency and particular program of interest before writing the proposal. It is essential to the writer that he obtain details about the program's current objectives. The writer also must have as much information as available about the current priorities or those which have been deferred. A letter or telephone discussion often will save valuable time and prevent wasted effort both for the applicant as well as for the funding agency. The letter or telephone action can serve to highlight the subject areas most likely to receive favorable consideration.

Two actions taken prior to the submission of a formal grant application (Formal Proposal) will be helpful to the writer and the goals and objectives of the funding program. First, determine whether the stated goals and objectives match the applicant's research capabilities and interests. Another, submit a simple preliminary proposal rather than a voluminous document.

The preliminary proposal outlining the proposed research concept should be sent to the cognizant program official or action officer for informal review.

ANATOMY OF THE PRELIMINARY PROPOSAL

A *preliminary proposal* normally consists of a three to five page narrative outlining the project concept and containing the following information:

- COVER SHEET
- ABSTRACT
- INTRODUCTION
- OBJECTIVE(S)
- PROJECT PLAN
- BUDGET
- RELEVANT REFERENCES
- VITA
- LETTER OF TRANSMITTAL

COVER SHEET — The *cover sheet* of the preliminary proposal should contain the name of the funding agency, name of your organization, principal investigator, principal investigator's title, department head's name, title and signature and the next higher person in the administration along with his or her signature. The reason should be obvious. The potential funding agency immediately knows that the "idea" in the preliminary proposal has received sanction of the institution. This is a plus for an initial contact. In addition, it invariably speeds communication between the institution submitting the plan and the funding agency. Other items should appear on the *title page* or *cover sheet* of the preliminary proposal. They are: date of submission, title of the project, duration of the project and cost for the project. The latter is usually referred to as the "amount requested."

ABSTRACT — The *abstract page* should immediately follow the title or cover page. The abstract should be typed in single space and cover from one-half to three quarters of the page. The abstract should be written after the preliminary proposal has been finished. The danger of writing the abstract in the beginning of the process is the abstract may not be coherent or tell the whole story. It is quite important to the outcome of the preliminary proposal that the abstract not be written hastily. At a recent workshop of proposal writers, the attendees were polled as to what was the most difficult part of the proposal to complete. In almost every case the abstract was chosen as the most difficult.[2]

INTRODUCTION — Following the abstract the *introduction* is written. The introduction should be approximately one-half of double spaced typewritten page. The introduction should serve as a lead-in for the remainder of the proposal. Do not let the introduction dangle or drift from the lead-in that it is intended to accomplish.

OBJECTIVE(S) — The *objective* is a clear statement what the project seeks to accomplish. If the objective is designed

A
PRELIMINARY PROPOSAL
SUBMITTED TO
THE UNITED STATES DEPARTMENT OF SCIENCE
DIVISION OF PLANETARY ENERGY
HEXAGON BUILDING
MOUNT VERNON, VIRGINIA 34578

TITLE: EFFICIENT USE OF HEAT FROM SATURN TO HEAT EARTH

PERIOD OF THE STUDY:　Five Years
AMOUNT REQUESTED:　$ 500,000.
AMOUNT MATCHED:　　$ 500,000.

PRINCIPAL INVESTIGATOR:　　　　　　APPROVED:

Alberto Einsteino, Ph.D.
Master Progress Professor
Department of Thermal Energy
Telephone: 555 — 555-1000
Social Security Number: 444-56-7890

George F.J.H. Hockock, Ph.D.
Dean and Director
College of Energy
Telephone: 555 — 555-1006

APPROVED:　　　　　　　　　　　　ENDORSED:

Harvey J. Sing, D.Sc.
Chaired Professor and
Head of Division of Thermal Energy
Telephone: 555 — 555-1001

Harvey H. George, J.D.
Governor and Chairman of
the Tri-State Energy Commission
January 30, 1976

SUBMITTED JOINTLY BY THE

Minnesota College of Energy and Science
and the
Tri-State Energy Commission
St. Paul, Minnesota 56789
January 30, 1976
Proposal No. 76-09

Figure 4　•　PRELIMINARY PROPOSAL COVER SHEET

to fulfill a specific task, or tasks, these should be identified as potential accomplishments within a specified time period. If the objective cannot be associated with any specific tasks, some statement of the presumed value to the program of attaining the research objective should be made.

PROJECT PLAN — The *project plan* is a brief description of the research, development, or demonstration concept. It is also a plan for execution of the proposed project, including a projected time line — schedule for accomplishment of intermediate project meterstones and the final objective.

BUDGET — The *budget* in the preliminary proposal should be a sound estimate of total project costs. Include an indication of the share of project costs which will be provided by the applicant (i.e., summer salary for the principal investigator in the case of a nine or ten month academic type of appointment, graduate assistance, equipment, travel, publication costs, etc.). It may be prudent to adopt a policy which is not commonly used which is to send one figure for costs of the project to the funding agency. This is the figure which can be placed in the amount requested block on the cover page if no further explanation is required by the potential funding agency. The one figure for the preliminary proposal allows you at your own institution to compute all costs. Do keep a good record should any questions arise from the funding agency. Some agencies require a separate figure for indirect costs and others such as the National Institutes of Health do not. There are several private funding agencies which do not allow indirect costs. Some of the private sources often allow costs for rental and lease of equipment and space not allowed in the Federal sector. It is important to have accurately computed all of your costs at the time of submission of the preliminary proposal. Check again and be sure budget figures that were developed are both accurate and realistic. Also check to see that they are kept on file for immediate recall. Some agencies have the authority to take the preliminary proposal which is attractive and timely to that agency's requirements and with very little modification make the document into a "single source" contract or award. The Office of Naval Research is one agency which has been known to use this methodology. The National Institutes of Health have been known to take preliminary proposals and on the basis of what has been submitted make the proposals "single source" contracts.

How embarrassing for the project leader and the submitting institution if a preliminary proposal with an unrealistic budget which was merely a guess or "shot in the dark" became a funding reality. What would be the consequences if the project idea was enticing enough and the requested funds were sufficiently low to receive an award by an interested agency? Even more embarrassment would come when the project was to begin and inadequate resources existed at the home institution to properly carry out the project because the budget was put together as an after thought without much thinking. Thus, budgets should be made up with assistance and know-how of an administrative officer of your institution. Coupled with the proposed investigator's input, the administrative officer can come up with a reasonable budget. The agency receiving the proposal whether it be preliminary or formal, assumes that some serious dialogue has taken place between the investigator and his administrative leadership.

It is wise to develop a standard format and adhere to this format for all future proposals. This will help in both record keeping at the home institution as well as giving the reader agencies the benefit of a sophisticated appearing proposal. Should the necessity arise for more explanation than that included on the cover sheet for the budget, limit yourself to a quarter of a page in a preliminary proposal. Unless specifically required do not give any more information than is requested. Irreparable damage can be done by giving out too much information at this time in the proposal life-cycle.

RELEVANT REFERENCES — A half page or a maximum of three quarters of a page of timely and *relevant references* from the literature which will support the project is of extreme importance. This adds credence to the project. If the subject area under investigation is controversial, it is wise to choose references from both sides of the argument. Often times persons cited from the literature in the relevant reference section are asked to serve as reviewers. Remember the reviewers ultimately pass judgment on your project. Do not pad this section. Use only relevant references which support both need and scientific direction.

VITA — The *vita*, c.v. (cee-vee), curriculum vitae also called resume is the one place a superior proposal can be easily killed. Readers of proposals do not want to be entertained, nor do they care what high school you attended or what civic activities you engage in. Church activities and speeches made to Kiwanis, Sertoma or Boy Scouts are not going to get an award. The vita in a preliminary proposal should not exceed three quarters of a page. The important facts to the reader are your five most recent publications and the journals they appeared in. The publications should be related to the project you are submitting. If they are not, do not include them. Tell the reader you have "x" number of publications in assorted or whatever journals but this project is new. Cite expertise in the vita which gives you credibility to perform the work outlined in the proposal. Do give your academic credentials but in very brief form. Do not take the vita out of your file which may have been used for a recent job interview. Revise and use a vita for each occasion. Do not try to impress the reader with all of your Who's Who in a preliminary proposal. Use the strongest and the fewest items. This is a preliminary proposal and the space is very limited. The document by necessity must be limited in size and content. In the vita confine your background to items which directly impinge on the project.

LETTER OF TRANSMITTAL — The *letter of transmittal* is a very important component of the proposal process and should always accompany a preliminary proposal, formal proposal, periodic reports, or supplemental data which may be sent from time to time to a funding agency. The content of the letters of transmittal will vary. Samples of letters of transmittal are found in this Chapter. There are several points to consider but always leave a professional impression. This should be the watchword in seeking funds for sponsored or extramural activities. Typing in a preliminary or formal proposal should be professional and not be sloppy with erasures and errors.

Make final checks to be sure the contents of the proposal are technically correct and up to date. Make a trip to the library and check references from the most recent literature to make absolutely sure that nothing of importance has been overlooked. Re-read and re-write your draft copy of the preliminary proposal many times until you are satisfied that it expresses your thoughts and intent in an unambiguous manner. Ask a friend or professional colleague in a discipline other than your own to read the proposal and then ask for criticisms. The other person reading the preliminary proposal may not be expert in the particular subject but may have general knowledge of principles and be able to point out what needs to be clarified. Correct any grammatical errors. You are not being graded on grammar, but rest assured that these kinds of errors in judgement give rise to a "questionable" proposal. One reviewer recently said, "I compare the grammatical error to sloppy weighing on an analytical balance or taking too fast a reading on a spectro-

THE GREAT AMERICAN UNIVERSITY
CAPITOL AVENUE
ANYWHERE, USA 55555

OFFICE OF THE VICE PRESIDENT
FOR RESEARCH AND GRADUATE STUDIES

January 31, 1976

Dr. Harry Orewel Jones
Deputy Director for Grants
The United States Department of Science
Division of Planetary Energy
Hexagon Building
Mount Vernon, Virginia 34578

Dear Doctor Jones:

I am pleased to transmit to The United States Department of Science, Division of Planetary Energy, our proposal Numbered 76-09, entitled "Efficient Use of Heat from Saturn to Heat Earth," by Doctor Alberto Einsteino.

We would appreciate receiving your consideration for support for this project. Please note that fifty per cent ($500,000) will be matched by the submitting agency to support this project.

This proposal has not been submitted to another funding agency, private or public.

Please feel free to communicate directly with me should you have any questions pertaining to this proposal.

Thank you for your interest.

Cordially,

John G. Ogar, Ph.D.
Vice President for Research and
    Graduate Studies

em

Enclosure

Figure 5   •   LETTER OF TRANSMITTAL

photometer."[2]

Following the review and evaluation of the preliminary proposal, the prospective applicant is normally advised whether (a) an application should be submitted for review formally, (b) submission of a modified preliminary proposal is suggested, or (c) further pursuit of the particular topic is discouraged.

THE PROPOSAL

The *formal proposal* is the document which when transmitted with appropriate signatures of approval provides the whole story from program to budget. The document called the *proposal* or *formal proposal* becomes a binding contract should an award be made. Each agency differs in philosophy regarding its proposals. Although there are differences in procedure, all agencies follow a formal logging (receipt and assignment of a number) procedure for the proposal. Acknowledgement may be by a simple form postal card, or letter. After the mechanics of logging and acknowledgement, proposals are referred to individuals in academic circles, industry, institutes, foundations and other Federal government agencies for relevance and scientific and/or technical merit review.

The proposal should be flawless. If it is an evolution of dialogue between an agency and the principal investigator as a result of a preliminary proposal — be sure to include all of the material generated in the preliminary proposal. If the formal proposal is not a result of dialogue between the funding agency and the prospective grantee, it is essential that certain fundamentals be followed. Content-wise the following are required for most if not all formal proposals. Note the similarity between the following list and what has already been discussed about the preliminary proposal. One difference to keep in mind is the detail and the size of the preliminary proposal versus the formal proposal.

- COVER SHEET
- ABSTRACT
- INTRODUCTION
- STATEMENT OF THE PROBLEM
- OBJECTIVE(S)
- PROJECT PLAN (PLANNED PROCEDURES)
- TECHNICAL FACILITIES (SPECIALIZED EQUIPMENT; INSTRUMENTS, ETC.)
- JUSTIFICATION
- BUDGET (COST TO DO THE PROJECT — ALL DIRECT AND INDIRECT COSTS)
- CURRICULUM VITAE (RELEVANT TO THE PROJECT)
- LIST OF PUBLICATIONS (FIVE MOST RECENT RELEVANT TO THE PROJECT)
- LIST OF REFERENCES (BIBLIOGRAPHIC)

Another example of an agency receiving proposals is the National Aeronautics and Space Administration (NASA). NASA receives two kinds of proposals. They are classified as the technical (type) and management (type) of proposals.[3] NASA requires different kinds of information for each type of proposal. Some of the elements have been taken from the NASA guide and others added to more closely fit a family of proposals rather than one in particular.

Technical Proposal

COVER LETTER (LETTER OF TRANSMITTAL) — Each proposal is to be submitted under a covering letter signed by an official of the investigator's organization who is authorized to commit the organization to the proposal and its contents.

COVER PAGE (COVER SHEET) — The cover page should contain the following elements:

- SHORT DESCRIPTIVE TITLE FOR THE INVESTIGATION.
- NAME OF THE PROPOSING ORGANIZATION.
- NAMES, ADDRESSES (FULL), TELEPHONE NUMBERS, AND ORGANIZATIONAL AFFILIATIONS OF ALL OF INVESTIGATORS AND OFFICIALS SIGNING THE PROPOSAL.
- DATE OF SUBMISSION.
- DURATION OF THE PROJECT. (GIVE THE BEGINNING AND ENDING DATES.)

- **DOLLARS REQUIRED TO PERFORM AND COMPLETE THE PROJECT. (INDICATE THE $ REQUIRED FOR EACH YEAR AND THE TOTAL $ REQUIRED FOR THE ENTIRE PROJECT).**

SUMMARY — A concise statement of what the proposed investigation is, how it will be performed, and the anticipated results should be part of the summary.

BACKGROUND AND JUSTIFICATION — A description of the research work that motivates the proposal should be included in the justification. It is essential that a statement demonstrating need for the proposed investigation be included. This section should specifically describe how the investigator expects to solve his experimental problems in his field of interest.

OBJECTIVES AND MAJOR REQUIREMENTS — A brief statement of what the proposed experiment is designed to accomplish and what technical requirements must be met to insure the success of the experiment is appropriate for the proposal objectives.

APPROACH — The approach taken often dictates whether the proposal is acceptable or not to the various funding agencies. That is not to say the approach must be strictly traditional. Do not innovate just for the sake of innovation. The innovative approach should have a deep rationale and plausible justification for turning away from the traditional. The approach should contain the following elements:

- **CONCEPT OF THE INVESTIGATION.**
- **METHOD AND PROCEDURES FOR CONDUCTING THE EXPERIMENT.**
- **PERFORMANCE CRITERIA FOR SUCCESS OF THE EXPERIMENT.**
- **SUPPORTING STUDIES INVOLVED IN THE INVESTIGATION.**
- **PLANS FOR EVALUATION OF EXPERIMENTAL SAMPLES.**

EXPECTED RESULTS — An indication of the expected results from the investigation, if successful, and the implications to the investigator's field of study will be expected by the funding agencies.

Management Proposal

COVER LETTER — Each proposal should be submitted under a cover letter signed by an official of the investigator's organization who is authorized to commit the organization to the proposal and its contents.

WORK PLAN — The work plan is **not** just a brief statement indicating that the work for the project has been planned. It is essentially an exact time-table which will be read with great scrutiny. The essential elements of a work plan follow:

- **PROGRAM MANAGEMENT PLAN, GIVING THE NAMES OF PERSONS RESPONSIBLE FOR CARRYING IT OUT.**
- **NAMES, ADDRESSES AND EXPERIENCE AND EDUCATIONAL RESUMES OF THE PROGRAM'S KEY SCIENTIFIC AND MANAGEMENT PERSONNEL.**
- **PERFORMANCE SCHEDULE INDICATING MANPOWER REQUIREMENTS AND LENGTHS OF TIME NEEDED TO COMPLETE SPECIFIC PHASES OF THE PROPOSED WORK.**

COST PLAN — The cost plan is intended to portray to the reader costs for the project. Manpower costs should fit well with the program plan. Do not include in the cost plan any proposed expenditures that are not fully justifiable. A test for justification that can be used is to match program elements with manpower needs. One simple test used very often by the funding agencies is to see how much secretarial help is required based upon the project planning shown in the technical portion of the proposal. Those who pad the budget in the cost plan section will find that the technical portion was out of balance with the requested monies and personnel shown in the cost plan. TEST: THE EFFORT DESCRIBED IN THE TECHNICAL PORTION OF THE PROPOSAL MUST BALANCE THE EFFORT REQUESTED IN DOLLARS IN THE COST PLAN OR BUDGET REQUEST FOR THE SAME PROPOSAL. Some key elements of the cost plan follow:

- **COST ESTIMATES FOR DIRECT LABOR TO INCLUDE INDIVIDUAL MAN-HOURS AND RATES FOR PERSONNEL INVOLVED IN THE PROJECT ARE NECESSARY ELEMENTS OF A COST PLAN.**

- ESTIMATED COST FOR MATERIALS.
- TRAVEL COSTS FOR CONDUCTING THE PROJECT. BE ESPECIALLY CAREFUL TO ITEMIZE PLANNED TRAVEL. SEGREGATE AND GIVE SOME DISCUSSION TO THE NATURE OF TRAVEL COSTS. CATEGORIES OF TRAVEL NORMALLY INCLUDE, (A) TRAVEL TO PROFESSIONAL MEETINGS FOR THE DISSEMINATION OF TECHNICAL INFORMATION RELATIVE TO THE PROGRESS OF THE PROJECT, (B) TRAVEL FOR CONSULTANTS TO ASSIST IN THE PROJECT AND (C) TRAVEL TO SURVEY WHAT OTHERS IN THE FIELD ARE DOING AT OTHER LABORATORIES OR LOCATIONS. TRY TO AVOID THE "TRAP" OF REQUESTING FUNDS FOR A PROFESSIONAL MEETING IN A PROJECT WHICH HAS NOT BEEN IN OPERATION LONG ENOUGH TO FINISH ITS START-UP PHASE. THIS ONE "TRAP" HAS BEEN KNOWN TO KILL MORE PROPOSALS THAN SEVERAL OTHER LARGE REQUESTS IN THE BUDGET.
- OVERHEAD AND GENERAL ADMINISTRATIVE COSTS ACCOMPANIED WITH A DETAILED DESCRIPTION OF THE COSTS. THE METHOD FOR THE CALCULATION OF APPLYING THE COSTS TO LABOR AND OTHER CHARGES FOR THE PROJECT IS EXPECTED IN THE PROPOSAL.
- OTHER COSTS IS A CATEGORY COMMONLY USED FOR ALL COSTS NOT INCLUDED IN THE GENERAL COST SECTION. IT WOULD BE WISE TO USE THE OTHER COSTS CATEGORY FOR UNUSUAL PROPOSED EXPENDITURES. EACH OF THESE KINDS OF COSTS SHOULD HAVE AN APPENDED EXPLANATION JUSTIFYING THE INCLUSIONS.
- A QUARTERLY SPENDING CURVE KEYED TO THE WORK SCHEDULE SHOULD BE INCLUDED IN THE COST PLAN.
- THE TOTAL COST OF THE PROJECT.

PROPOSAL FORMAT GUIDELINES

The first question that should come to mind is what should a proposal accomplish? A proposal must answer basic questions about an idea submitted for support. Every proposal must include several basic elements, each possessing distinctive characteristics and serving a specific purpose. A proposal may range in scope and format from a short letter to a more formal and detailed presentation. The following discussion is designed to provide some basic information about the components of a "typical" proposal.

If a funding source or agency requires the use of specific forms or guidelines in preparing a proposal, then these directions should be followed step by step without deviation. If directions are general, the suggestions offered in this book will serve as a guide for producing a proposal that is complete and professional in its presentation.

TITLE PAGE — The *title page* provides the funding agency with such information as the title of the project, and the name(s), title(s), department(s) or division(s), institution, and signature(s) of the project director and the official(s) authorized to commit the college, university, foundation, firm or state government to the project. Information concerning inclusive dates of the project, total budget requests, and the name of the agency receiving the proposals also may be included on the title page. To avoid confusion, you should know the title page has more than one identity. It is also known as the cover sheet and cover page. In addition to items already cited, more and more funding agencies are adding the requirement that the principal investigator provide the agency with his Social Security Number and residence telephone number. A sample *title page* is found in this Chapter.

ABSTRACT — The *abstract* is a concise, accurate, *birds-eye view* of the entire proposal condensed to approximately 200 to 250 words. Great care should be taken in writing the abstract. The action officer, his staff and sometimes reviewers read only the abstract. Since this may be the only part of the proposal that is carefully read, we repeat, great care should be taken with it. Another reason, not widely known, is what is actually done with the abstracts by the agency. Some private funding sources as well as Federal funding agencies take the abstract and place it on their own forms then distribute the abstracts for staff information and review. Others place the proposal abstracts on computer along with other data provided on the title page. This should be enough of a reason to make the abstract tell the story and tell it well. It is suggested that the abstract still in its draft form be read by one or more of the writer's peers. The reader should react both to content as well as smoothness of "telling the story". The abstract should coherently include a statement of the problem (the need), the objectives, procedures, evaluation, and dissemination plan for the project.

TABLE OF CONTENTS — The *table of contents* may be used to list the various sections of the proposal, illustration(s), table(s) and appendix(es). The table of contents is a tremendous aid to the reader and is a time-saver in panel review sessions. It will be an additional time-saver to the reader if the proposal table of contents is keyed to any color-coding of the proposal. Following the page number simply indicate yellow colored page(s).

The reader of this text will note that a great deal of repetition appears throughout the various chapters focusing on saving time for the reviewers of the proposal. This is quite intentional. For those who have had the experience of evaluating proposals for funding, you already know how pressed for time each reader is whether it be at his or her home, a conference room or in a panel review session. The readers appreciate time-saving devices. None of these devices in themselves will substitute for a well planned rational proposal — but they help.

Text

The elements within the text of a proposal may vary considerably depending upon the nature and scope of the project proposed. The text of a proposal may typically include the following sections:

STATEMENT OF THE PROBLEM — The statement of the problem defines and delimits the project and indicates significance of effort. It states the need and why something should be done to meet the need. Reference to related research or previous projects also supports the need for the project.

OBJECTIVES — The objectives will structure selection of procedures and evaluation. They will determine the resources required to accomplish the project. An objective is a concise and precise statement of what is to be accomplished. Objectives should be measurable and contain a time frame. There may be an objective for each need identified in the statement of the problem.

PROCEDURES — This section describes how the objectives will be met. The reader should be walked through the project as the methodology is spelled-out for the project. Procedures may include a description of the population to be served, administrative structure of the project, technical approaches to be used, and a description of the consultants who will be used to assist with the work.

EVALUATION — Identify procedures which will be used and evidence which will be submitted to indicate the results of the project. This section must communicate how the objectives of the study have been accomplished.

DISSEMINATION — How will the results of the project be shared with others? Many sources of funding are concerned how the results of a project will be transmitted to other interested people. The term *transportable* is used a great deal today. A transportable project is defined as a project which, after completion, is of such nature that the entire project can be transported to another environment and successfully operate. This applies to projects in the physical sciences as well as the social sciences. *Transmittable* is a term which simply means the project will receive a wide broadcast to the appropriate community. The dissemination section of the proposal is becoming more important in the evaluation of the project's worth for funding. This section also should include details as to content and intervals that periodic reports will be filed with the funding source.

RESOURCES — Personnel, equipment, and facilities required for the project should be discussed in the resources section. Note which resources are available and which resources will need to be obtained to carry out the project. Include a brief listing of key project staff and their capabilities. Give a brief description of any special facilities which would contribute to the success of the project. Be sure if your institution has unique facilities to specify these in the narrative. Designate a single person who will have responsibility for planning, co-ordinating, and supervising the project. In addition identify the percentage or number of hours per week this person will devote to the project.

BUDGET — In preparing the budget for a project, care must be exercised to follow all of the funding agency and institutional requirements. In academia, some college-level offices exist to help members of the faculty prepare a realistic budget. Such assistance at the college level is found in the decentralized model for research administration. Research administration models are discussed in detail in Chapter Eleven. In the university utilizing the centralized mode for research administration, assistance can be found in a variety of locations depending upon organizational structure. It could be at the research foundation, research institute, grants and contracts office, graduate college, office of sponsored research, office of the president, development office or foundation, or at a host of other locations. It may not exist at all.

In industry one is more likely to find budget assistance for a proposal in a proposal development office. Companies which engage in sub-contracting research and development to other entities, by necessity, already possess this capability. In city, county and state governments a *potpourri* similar to the universities exists. Although some state governments are becoming more centralized, there still is a large replication between agencies within the same state. Identity is so obscured that it is often impossible to discern one from the other. This may account for the increased use of consultants within city, county and state governments assisting in development of realistic project plans for extramural funding.

Many funding sources require the use of special forms when submitting a budget. Examples of such forms are found in Chapter Sixteen. A budget should include wages and salary items, fringe benefits for employees, purchase of equipment, space allocations, travel costs, publication costs, overhead or indirect costs, secretarial costs, and other special costs involved in accomplishing the project. The budget page will be scrutinized by the action officer and the staff of the funding agency. A good practice (if not contraindicated by funding agency guidelines) is to use a color (other than white) for the budget page(s). This will help the action officer by saving time in thumbing the pages or looking up a particular page in the table of contents. Another practice to aid the action officer is to send five to eight extra copies of the cover sheet (title page) fastened together with the budget. One additional cover sheet bearing original signatures also should be sent. If an abstract is included make extra copies and insert them with the budget and cover sheet packet as described above. The action officer is then free to compare amounts requested on the budget page with the text without turning pages back and forth.

APPENDICES — Additional or supplementary material, having supporting value but not essential to completeness and understanding, is included as the appendix. Examples of material that may be appended include:

- **REFERENCE OR BIBLIOGRAPHIES.**
- **FACULTY OR COMPANY RESUMES.**
- **DETAILED OR LENGTHY SUPPORTING TECHNICAL DATA.**
- **LISTING OF ACCOMPLISHMENTS AND/OR PROJECTS IN RELATED AREAS.**
- **GENERAL SUPPORTING INFORMATION ON THE APPLICANT'S RESOURCES.**

THE UNSOLICITED PROPOSAL

The unsolicited proposal is a document initiated and formally submitted by a prospective grantee (called contractor in the case of contracts) to a funding agency (usually an agency of the United States Government). The person or group submits an unsolicited proposal with the prime objective of obtaining funds either through the grant mechanism or awarding of a contract. United States Government Agencies have somewhat different methods for handling (development, receipt and processing) of unsolicited proposals.

Contracts may be awarded on the basis of unsolicited proposals which meet the sole-source requirements for the Federal Management Procurement Regulations. Unsolicited contract proposals always should be addressed to a specific agency. The unsolicited proposal may be transferred within an agency to the contracts area from the grants area of responsibility. (i.e. National Institutes of Health, National Cancer Institute). The problem dealing with the National Institutes of Health is that too few understand the difference between the granting area of responsibility and the contract area of responsibility. The Associate Director of the National Cancer Institute is usually a Ph.D. scientist who is responsible for the administration of grants for extramural activities. Until very recently that person was a biochemist by discipline. The Contracting Officer of the National Cancer Institute does not need to be a scientist and contracting officers rarely are. They are usually auditors and accountants with business college backgrounds. There are many that also have come up from the procurement side of the house. Contracts are developed through a process of needs arising from the scientific community and scientists within the National Institutes of Health and the National Cancer Institute.

The *idea* in an unsolicited proposal could result in

the writing of a solicited proposal such as the Request for Proposal (RFP). There is no guarantee to the writer of the *idea* that he will become the recipient of a contract. The Request for Proposal receives a wide broadcast as established by Law. In rare instances, an unsolicited proposal results in a single-source (sole-source) contract. The expertise of the proposer and need of the funding agency would have to be so unique that the agency could stand the scrutiny of both the scientific community as well as the United States Congress. The investigator should use the unsolicited proposal route whenever possible. Advantages of the unsolicited proposal outweigh disadvantages. The unsolicited proposal should generally contain items delineated below, although no specific format is required.

- **PROJECT OBJECTIVES**
- **NEED (UTILITY AND SIGNIFICANCE OF THE PROJECT).**
- **SCOPE OF THE WORK (PROJECT PLAN).**
- **EXPERIMENTAL DATA PREVIOUSLY DEVELOPED.**
- **COMPLETED FEASIBILITY STUDIES.**
- **ESTIMATED DURATION OF THE PROJECT.**
- **TECHNICAL CAPABILITIES (PERSONNEL, FACILITIES AND SPECIAL RESOURCES).**
- **PROJECT COSTS.**

THE SOLICITED PROPOSAL (REQUEST FOR PROPOSAL)

Request for Proposals (RFP) for all planned contracts are advertised in the COMMERCE BUSINESS DAILY. Information how to obtain the COMMERCE BUSINESS DAILY is found in Chapter Fifteen. RFP packages are obtained from the agencies expecting response. Information as to how one obtains the "package" is found in detail in the Commerce Business Daily. The advertisements give the details, format, content, time required, and place of submission for the RFP.

A major concern associated with the Request for

Proposal (RFP) is commonly referred to in the vernacular as *wired-in*. Agencies have vehemently denied such accusations. Yet statistics and follow-up procedures show otherwise. **(U.S. CONGRESS PLEASE TAKE NOTICE.)**

Take for example an RFP which calls for a chemical synthesis of a particular compound or a group of compounds. The RFP was answered by a university professor who would serve as the project's principal investigator. This university professor has devoted his entire professional life to the study of the specified group of compounds in the RFP. There is little that he does not know about the chemical behavior and synthesis of this group. Another group answering the RFP is an industrial based medium-size manufacturing firm employing 200 persons. The firm has a chemical division which has been somewhat idle because of the delay of approvals from the Environmental Protection Agency for the release of several agricultural pesticides. This division of the manufacturing company does possess some expertise for the synthesis of the compounds listed in the RFP. They have already in the company inventory sufficient scientific equipment to synthesize any of the chemicals in the group specified in the RFP. However, the deep expertise and experience of the university professor is not by any stretch of the imagination present with the idle pesticide group. These are the kinds of competition which come about because of the widespread audience RFP's enjoy.

Should the dollars requested in the contract bid make any difference in who may be the awardee? One would assume so. The fact that widespread coverage is given to RFP's and a competitive quality is intended as part of the contracting award process should and must be encouraged and preserved. This is the good part of the RFP process. The discouraging part of the RFP process to most, if not all, is the tardiness in receiving in-hand the RFP documentation. Response is often imposed with deadlines that are impossible to meet. Many times the response is a week from the date received. The RFP copy usually is produced by xerography and the copy received is not in the most readable fashion. Take for example a one-week response as a case in point. The only way humanly possible to complete the RFP (and it is a voluminous document) is to work twenty-four hours a day for that entire week. The document will require that typing and duplication be done on a "crash" basis. Production of the RFP would demand the efforts of additional secretarial services and a great deal of overtime. Someone would be required to hand-carry the document to the funding agency contract officer's desk since the due date is rigid. The RFP by Law must be received by a specified time designated in the RFP at a designated location. Some confuse this with a postmark date. The postmark date is useless. Although the next example pertains to an actual proposal not an RFP, the basic principles still hold relative to mailing and dispatching proposals in general.

The classic that comes to mind to illustrate postmark dates and proposal deadlines is a true story. It is, however, a sad commentary on the operations of the United States Postal Service. A package of proposals were sent from Charlottesville, Virginia to the National Science Foundation, 1800 "G" Street N.W., Washington, D.C. This is a relatively short distance between the two cities. In fact it could have been driven in less than a day round-trip. The applicant institution assumed it took all of the necessary precautions. They wrapped the package with the U.S. Postal Service recommended brown wrapping paper, used the brown gummed tape and placed several extra windings of rope about the package. One would think that the package was going around the world rather than to a local delivery which crossed only Virginia into the District of Columbia. They attempted to cover all bets by sending the package **REGISTERED MAIL-SPECIAL DELIVERY-RETURN RECEIPT REQUEST-**

ED. The package arrived sixteen weeks after the program deadline. The postmark from Charlottesville revealed the date of dispatch was one week before the deadline date. The panel review had already been completed for the program at the National Science Foundation. The in-house analysis for recommendations of awards was already in progress. At this time in the process a mutilated package beyond imagination was delivered by the United States Postal Service to the Foundation seventeen weeks later to the day. The University in question was duly notified of the late arrival and condition of the contents. The University president was furious, the calls from the Congressional leadership were even louder. Yet, the Foundation had no communication except for the letter of transmittal tucked away in the same "Special Delivery" package. No knowledge of the proposal was transmitted or followed-up by the University. If they had checked the return receipt record the incident may have had a different outcome. This story has been told to emphasize the due date or deadline. As a result of this incident, The National Science Foundation changed its postmark deadline to read, ". . . proposals must be received by ＿＿＿＿＿ Program no later than 5:00 P.M. on ＿＿＿＿＿ date in the Central Processing Section located in Room 223, National Science Foundation, 1800 "G" Street N.W., Washington, D.C. 20550."

Another discouraging area of concern with the Request for Proposal process is what may be called unilateral treatment. Unilateral in the sense the contracting officer can exercise certain procedures. For example, the contracting officer may have not received an RFP proposal from a particular source he desired or expected. Unbeknown to the other writers of RFP's who responded in a frenetic manner — respondents to the RFP each receive a note from the contracting officer extending the time of the RFP by three additional weeks. Experience should tell the writer that his RFP has been sentenced to "death". It also should be a warning that the RFP might well have been *wired-in.* Why? Simply the writer can be asked, did that writer ask for an extension? The answer will be invariably no. Either the number of respondents to the RFP were so small or there may have been one or more particular organizations who were expected to reply but just did not. The extension, thus provides a mechanism for adding to the list above those who responded in good faith within an unreal time period.

Still another discouraging point is the dollar request. You recall we left this subject in-limbo at an earlier point in the Chapter. Dollar requests whether too high or too low should have a bearing on the outcome — there are cases that this is not so. The following true case is somewhat of a contradiction to the rules. These contradictions indeed do exist in the RFP process. Most of us would logically agree that all things being equal in an RFP evaluation, the lower cost dollar figure bid would prevail. This is not always so. In one case there were six respondents to a chemical synthesis RFP. The synthesis was extremely complex and the purity level required of the end products was very difficult to produce. The purity required would ultimately be at the level of a standard. After the award was made it was revealed that the award was not made to the lowest bidder. In fact, the *frenetic writer's* RFP was $100,000 below that of the awardee. The award was given to an Institute with a fine reputation. The Institute was a spin-off of one of our most prestigious institutions of higher learning. What about the reputation of the professor who priced his project significantly lower? In comparing the respondents to the RFP, the professor from the less prestigious state university averaged twenty publications each year in either the Journal of Organic Chemistry or the Journal of the American Chemical Society. He was recognized by his State and University as a "chaired-professor". He served on several National committees. In this area of specialty on the subject RFP he would be regarded as an expert. Regardless, the contracting officer, because he is legally empowered to choose the proposal of his choice did not act on dollars alone. There may have been valid reasons for the choice, but the other respondents would never know them. Is this bilateral or unilateral treatment?

Why all the discussion about RFP's? The answer is simple. RFP's are gaining popularity daily among the Federal funding agencies, thus RFP's need to be understood more thoroughly. The RFP document is lengthy, cumbersome, and complicated. It requires a tremendous amount of expertise to complete. In fact, much of the repetitive "boiler plate" copy is pulled out of the files by experienced submitters at a moment's notice. Those not experienced spend far too much time on "boiler plate". The major concern of those who submit is the probability of success. In this vein, there are investigators and contractors who have submitted as many proposals as one a month averaging a dozen RFP's a year. When questioned about success they say, ". . . we have never received an award." Are RFP's *wired-in* to selected investigators?

Advice to the "Federalies". Publish widely in your press releases those who applied and those who were awarded monies. Give the amounts requested for those awarded and those denied. Allow a post-mortem discussion or letter with the reasons why the award was made to one and not to the other. There is a very wide credibility gap when it comes to RFP's. It is a canyon when it comes to the university community. Why not close the gap? Information and not bureaucratic jargon will help close it. Do not force the United States Congress through pressure to the agencies to close the gap. Do it at the agency. Do it now.

COST OF A REQUEST FOR PROPOSAL (RFP)

In a recent exercise, some costs involved in writing of an RFP were examined. In this case the particular RFP chosen was a chemical synthesis project. The award made to another entity, an Institute, was made for $380,000 covering a twelve month period. The professor who has been alluded to before in this Chapter submitted the RFP at a cost of $980. The cost was for the typing, duplication, packaging, shipping (air freight) plus an airport pickup at Washington National Airport by a motorcycle messenger for delivery to a Federal agency in Maryland. This analysis did not include the principal investigator's time nor did it include the time of the administrative officials who participated in the process. Direct cost charges for labor of the staff accountant and the direct charges for paper and supplies were included. No computation was made for indirect costs. The document was very costly as all RFP's are. One should give great thought and consideration whether the current RFP route is very worthwhile to travel. Perhaps as some believe, some legislation is necessary to alter the current RFP route. The RFP route, with its complicated method of computing overhead, was evolved by the Department of Defense. The research and demonstration projects community of prospective grantees have been long influenced by the methodology which is used to procure battleships, ball bearings, fighter planes and weapons systems.

The moral to the RFP if there is one is simply to attempt to gain G-2 (seek out intelligence) about the project, capabilities of your own staff to perform the RFP, and to *psych-out* who might be the competitor(s). Then, after weighing the facts, decide what to do with the RFP.

Now let us look at some hard-core realities if you are in academe and competing for a RFP project. Your institution is relatively small. You are **Unknown College of**

Science and have just completed and submitted an RFP. The competition it turns out is three from the Big Ten, two of the West Coast "biggies" and one from the Ivy League. What do you think your chances are for the award? Compare yourself to the lot presented. **Unknown College of Science** although a superb undergraduate college with an outstanding record of its graduates completing master's and doctorates would be in the same competitive level as would Nowhere, Maine and Goodness Knows, Arizona.

Let us turn to city government improvement. The competing cities for the project included Nowhere, Goodness Knows, New York City, Dallas, Atlanta and Los Angeles. Would Nowhere or Goodness Knows receive an award?

The decision to submit or before that whether to spend the time to write-up the RFP is a difficult one to make. Nevertheless the decisions must be made. Should we actually respond to the announcement in Commerce Business Daily? Should we (if we responded to the announcement) develop a full-blown RFP? Should we bring in a consultant to assist us with developing the RFP? Is the competition for colleges, or major universities; is it for small cities or large metropolitan areas; is the RFP really written for our type of situation or is it specifically written for someone else? These decisions should not be based upon emotion but on experience of your institution and track record for success with RFP's. There is one thing certain if you have ideas and have some data to back the ideas — keep writing unsolicited proposals. Make sure that the proposals are sufficiently brief but enticing so that the agency you have directed the idea to will come back for more.

COMPONENTS OF A REQUEST FOR PROPOSAL (RFP)

The RFP is in essence more than one proposal. It is several proposals built into one. The first section referred to as the *proposal proper* is usually acceptable in the established format for any proposal previously discussed in this Chapter. The RFP *Cover Sheet (Title Page)* is followed by an *Introduction* and an *Abstract Page*. The next portions are rather lengthy proposals in themselves. First the *Technical Proposal* which is normally composed by the principal investigator and his staff. The next proposal is called the *Management Proposal* and this is normally composed with dialogue involving the administrative officers of the organization and the principal investigator. Following the *Mangement Proposal* is the *Cost Proposal.* This is where the content is found which deals with costs associated with the performance of the contract. Finally a *Summary, Appendices, References* (literature not personnel or personal), and a *Proposal Outline.* More detail will follow on the preparation and contents of the RFP.

Request for Proposal Format

PROPOSAL CONTENTS

- **TABLE OF CONTENTS**
- **INTRODUCTION**
- **JUSTIFICATION OF THE PROPOSAL**
- **RFP AND NUMBER**
- **SOURCES OF ADDED INFORMATION**

TECHNICAL PROPOSAL CONTENTS

- **OBJECTIVE(S)**
- **DURATION AND SCOPE OF THE PROJECT**
- **STATEMENT OF THE PROBLEM**
- **ALTERNATIVES TO BE CONSIDERED**
- **DESCRIPTION OF FINAL SOLUTION OR END PRODUCT**
- **TECHNICAL REQUIREMENTS**
- **ANTICIPATED RESULTS**

- STATE OF THE ART OR EVALUATION OF LITERATURE TO DATE
- ASSESSMENT OF CURRENT PROGRAM
- ASSESSMENT OF FUTURE PROGRAM VALUE
- TECHNICAL COMPETENCE
- COST EFFECTIVENESS
- SUMMARY OF THE PROPOSAL

MANAGEMENT PROPOSALS

- TABLE(S) OF ORGANIZATION
- NARRATIVE OF RESPONSIBILITIES AND PHILOSOPHY
- HIGHLIGHT OF THE ORGANIZATION OF THE INSTITUTION OR COMPANY
- EXPERIENCE
- EXPERTISE

COST PROPOSAL

- COPY OF AUDIT RATE ASSIGNMENT
- DOCUMENTATION OF BIDS FOR REQUESTED SUPPLIES AND EQUIPMENT
- LABOR COSTS BREAKDOWN
- PROFESSIONAL COSTS BREAKDOWN
- CONSULTANT COSTS BREAKDOWN
- PROPERTY INVENTORY CONTROL
- STATEMENT OF WORK

MANAGEMENT PROPOSAL — This is the portion of the RFP which normally is *not* put together by the principal investigator but is worked on simultaneously by the administration (research administration) while the principal investigator is working on the *Technical Proposal* attempting to make the deadline. The purpose of the *Management Proposal* is to convey to the awarding agency the experience, expertise, organizational philosphy and how the institution, company, or foundation operates. This is quite important because the dialogue between the funding agency and the content of the *Management Proposal* becomes the bridge of communication with the two entities when and if a contract is awarded.

COST PROPOSAL — This is the portion of the RFP which complies with the Federal Fair Labor Practices Law, Requirement of Public Law 87-653, the implementation of the Armed Services Procurement Regulations (ASPR's) if it is a Department of Defense Agency, the disposition of Government property, certification and representation, elements of cost, statement of work, work breakdown, structure, current prices, (either from current catalogs or formal quotations from vendors), audit practices and procedures employed by your organization, indirect cost data, Civil Rights Compliance, employment practices, etc.

FINAL SUMMARY — The *Final Summary* portion of the RFP should be carefully and succinctly prepared. The summarization of the cogent points of the proposal should be developed in detail. Use this section to emphasize unique points and features, specialized equipment and major thrusts which will add quality to the proposal. This section is ready by the agencies and those who review the RFP with a great deal of care.

REQUEST FOR QUOTATION (RFQ)

The *Request for Quotation* may be requested by an Agency to determine the "ball-park" costs of a particular project or program. It may award or may not award monies. The respondent should carefully read the document and keep accurate records on file relative to the figures submitted. In this type of request be sure to include indirect costs. Do not take wild guesses. The agencies have been known to award a Purchase Order for the project (usually sufficiently low to go that route) to avoid indirect cost reimbursement. This can be most costly.

ASSEMBLY OF THE PROPOSAL

REVIEW INFORMATION FROM FUNDING AGENCY — A great deal of material is mailed from the various funding agencies. It would be wise to ask your supervisor, research office, dean or department head for information concerning requirements and proposal guidelines which have been sent by various agencies. Read the material paying particular attention to the following:

- THE EXACT NAME AND ADDRESS TO WHOM THE PROPOSAL IS TO BE SUBMITTED. NOTE THE CORRECT TITLE OF THE INDIVIDUAL AND THE ZIP CODE.
- FORMAT REQUIREMENTS IF ANY IMPOSED BY THAT PARTICULAR PROGRAM WHICH IS BEING CONSIDERED. NOTE THE SPECIFICATIONS FOR THE COVER PAGE AND THE REQUIRED SIGNATURES. CHECK TO SEE THAT THE BUDGET IS NOT OF A SPECIFIC FORMAT.
- NORMALLY THE ADMINISTRATIVE ARM OF YOUR ORGANIZATION IS RESPONSIBLE FOR SPECIAL FORMS WHICH ARE REQUIRED BY MANY AGENCIES. (i.e. CIVIL RIGHTS COMPLIANCE).
- THE NUMBER OF COPIES TO BE TRANSMITTED TO THE FUNDING AGENCY IS EASILY HANDLED IF THE WRITER PREPARES A DRAFT LETTER OF TRANSMITTAL AND IN THE TEXT OF THE LETTER STATES THE REQUIRED NUMBER OF COPIES BEING SENT TO THE FUNDING AGENCY. THE ORGANIZATION SHOULD HAVE A POLICY AS TO HOW MANY ARE PRINTED FOR RETENTION BY THE ORIGINATING INSTITUTION. ALWAYS RETAIN AT LEAST ONE COPY FOR YOUR FILES AS THE WRITER OF A PROPOSAL.
- DEADLINES ARE MOST IMPORTANT AS DISCUSSED IN OTHER PARTS OF THE BOOK AND EMPHASIZED IN THIS CHAPTER. BE SURE TO READ CAREFULLY WHETHER POSTMARK DATE OR ACTUAL RECEIVED DATES ARE USED. THIS IS IMPORTANT.

FORMAT FOR TYPING THE PROPOSAL — The following is a list of the parts of a proposal in order of their appearance. Several notes on style and format are included for you information. This has been discussed in great detail in other parts of this Chapter.

- COVER SHEET. THE COVER SHEET USUALLY CONTAINS THE TITLE OF THE PROPOSAL, THE DATE, ORGANIZATION TO WHOM IT IS SUBMITTED, ORGANIZATION SUBMITTING IT, THE NAME(S), TITLE(S), SCHOOL(S) OR DEPARTMENT(S), AND SIGNATURE(S) OF THE PRINCIPAL INVESTIGATOR(S), AND THE PROJECT ADMINISTRATOR OR COORDINATOR AND THE OFFICIAL(S) AUTHORIZED TO COMMIT YOUR ORGANIZATION TO THE PROJECT.
- ABSTRACT (SEE OTHER PARTS OF THE CHAPTER FOR DETAILS PERTAINING TO THE ABSTRACT).
- TABLE OF CONTENTS. IN THE TABLE OF CONTENTS, LIST VARIOUS SECTIONS OF THE TEXT, ILLUSTRATION(S), TABLE(S), AND THE APPENDIX(ES).
- TEXT OR BODY OF THE PROPOSAL. CAREFULLY TYPE COPY IN EASILY READ FORMAT ON UNCROWDED PAGES. A TERM PAPER STYLE GUIDE IS A USEFUL REFERENCE FOR CHECKING THE SPACING OF OUTLINES, LOCATION OF PAGE NUMBERS, AND OTHER DETAILS. MANY OF YOU

HAVE WRITTEN THESES FOR GRADUATE DEGREES — LOOK AT SOME OF THOSE FORMATS ALSO.

- BUDGET. MAKE CERTAIN THAT THE BUDGET FIGURES BALANCE. MAKE AN ADDING MACHINE TAPE AND ATTACH THE TAPE TO THE FILE COPY OF THE PROPOSAL. USE A SECOND COLOR FOR THE BUDGET PAGE(S).
- APPENDICES. REFER TO EACH APPENDIX IN THE APPROPRIATE PART OF THE TEXT. NUMBER THEM IN ORDER OF THEIR APPEARANCE. ENTITLE EACH APPENDIX. DO NOT APPEND MATERIAL AS AN AFTER THOUGHT WITHOUT HAVING REFERRED TO THE APPENDED MATERIAL IN THE TEXT. THIS MAKES THE PROPOSAL WHICH MAY BE OTHERWISE FINE VERY SLIP-SHOD AND SLOPPY.
- FORMS. FORMS ARE USUALLY INCLUDED IN THE APPENDICES. MAKE SURE THAT ALL QUESTIONS ARE ANSWERED. IF FOR SOME REASON A QUESTION CANNOT BE ANSWERED, EXPLAIN WHY IT HAS NOT IN AN APPENDED STATEMENT.
- BINDERS AND FANCY COVERS. STAPLE IN THE UPPER LEFT HAND CORNER ONLY. FUNDING AGENCIES ARE NOT IMPRESSED WITH EXPENSIVE LOOKING COVERS SUCH AS SPIRAL, PERFECT, OR CASE BOUND PROPOSALS. IN MOST CASES THE BINDINGS ARE SEPARATED UPON RECEIPT.
- LETTER OF TRANSMITTAL. THIS LETTER IS ATTACHED TO THE PACKAGE OF PROPOSAL(S) SENT TO THE FUNDING AGENCY. A LETTER OF TRANSMITTAL SHOULD ALWAYS ACCOMPANY A PROPOSAL.

DISTRIBUTION OF THE PROPOSAL — The proposal is to be first routed through the proper channels within your organization for appropriate recommendations and approvals. This is normally accomplished on an internal document called a proposal routing sheet. More details and samples of proposal routing sheets are found in Chapter Sixteen. Find out how many copies are required for your internal approval system. After the proposal has been officially approved by your organization the writer should retain at least one copy for his or her records. Some items worth examining after the proposal has been approved follow:

- MAKE ADDITIONAL CORRECTIONS IN THE PROPOSAL AS MAY BE REQUESTED BY YOUR ADMINISTRATIVE OFFICERS OR SUPERVISOR.
- FIND OUT THE NUMBER OF COPIES NEEDED: THOSE TO BE SENT TO THE FUNDING AGENCY AND THOSE TO BE CIRCULATED TO OTHER PERSONNEL OR KEPT AS FILE COPIES. RECOMMEND THAT DUPLICATION BE ACCOMPLISHED BY OFFSET RATHER THAN XEROGRAPHY, SPIRIT DUPLICATOR, WET PHOTOCOPY OR MIMEOGRAPH. THE OFFSET PROCESS IS LESS EXPENSIVE AND YIELDS A MORE PROFESSIONAL AND ATTRACTIVE COPY.

- SECURE THE CORRECT ADDRESSES OF ALL THOSE TO WHOM THE PROPOSAL IS TO BE SENT. FIND OUT HOW THE PROPOSAL IS TO BE DISTRIBUTED. THIS MAY BE BY UNITED PARCEL SERVICE, UNITED STATES POSTAL SERVICE OR HAND CARRIED BY SOME ONE FROM YOUR ORGANIZATION WHO IS TAKING A TRIP TO THAT CITY, ETC. PACKAGE IT ACCORDINGLY. MAKE SURE THAT BOTH THE RETURN ADDRESS AND THE SENDING ADDRESS ARE CLEAR AND CORRECT. THE PACKAGING AND DISTRIBUTION OF PROPOSALS SHOULD NOT BE LEFT TO THE WRITER OR POTENTIAL PRINCIPAL INVESTIGATOR — THIS IS A FUNCTION THAT SHOULD BE HANDLED BY THE RESEARCH OR SPONSORED PROGRAMS OF YOUR ORGANIZATION.
- THE ORIGINAL AND ONE COPY OF THE LETTER OF TRANSMITTAL SHOULD BE IN THE MAILING PACKAGE. ANOTHER COPY OF THE LETTER OF TRANSMITTAL SHOULD BE SENT IN A SEPARATE ENVELOPE BY AIRMAIL TO THE FUNDING AGENCY. ON THAT COPY INDICATE, "PROPOSALS BEING SENT OR HAND CARRIED UNDER SEPARATE COVER." INCLUDE IN THE PACKAGE TWO ORIGINALLY SIGNED PROPOSALS PLUS THE REQUIRED NUMBER OF ADDITIONAL COPIES OF THE PROPOSAL REQUIRED BY THE SPONSOR.

SUBMIT THE FORMAL PROPOSAL TO THE FUNDING AGENCY — There are several questions which come up at the time of submission of a formal proposal. Many of these will be answered in Chapter Fourteen entitled Legal Considerations. One question becoming increasingly common is, "Can I submit the same proposal to more than one funding agency?" The answer is yes. There are some ethical and procedural considerations which should be followed. Legally the question is answered categorically yes. The best method of handling this question is to be open with the funding agencies. On the letter of transmittal and the abstract page, include a statement relative to the distribution to other agencies or sources. A statement which probably will not jeopardize your submission might be. "This proposal has been submitted to the Army Research Office, The National Science Foundation and the Ford Foundation for consideration in addition to your agency. We will keep you informed as to the decisions and status of this proposal with the other funding agencies." Another statement may be: "A similar proposal has been submitted to the Rockefeller Foundation for consideration. We will keep you informed as to its status." By using this approach you will find that your chances for funding will not be hurt. In fact if the proposal is good and the amounts requested are high it will not be the first time dual funding has taken place. Dual funding is not duplicate funding but split funds from more than one source. This is handled by the action officers at the respective agencies not by any action of the proposing organization.

Do not expect a quick response from your potential sponsor. The response may take as much as six to nine months and sometimes longer before decisions and awards are announced. You should, however, receive an acknowledgement from the funding agency indicating your proposal has been received within a two week period. The normal transmittal of acknowledgement is to the writer of the letter of transmittal unless a statement to the contrary is included.

NEGOTIATIONS — This is a dangerous subject. Negotiations are made by funding agencies primarily to reduce the amount of a request or strike an item or items requested as invalid by their funding protocol. Budgetary changes are often initiated by telephone. The inexperienced will kill the project or accept reductions to the extent of making the project difficult or impossible to complete because of enthusiasm and an over zealous wish to receive an award. When the telephone call does come and you are the principal investigator not an administrative official take the message, write down every detail and read back the request of the agency. Inform the agency that you are not empowered to act for your institution but you will have that person call either by the close of business that day or the next morning. Take the telephone number and extension and the times that individual will be at his or her desk. At the close of the conversation make an appointment immediately with the administrative official, dean, vice president,

supervisor etc. responsible for the negotiations of contracts and awards. Sit down with him or her and discuss
the terms presented and what alternatives might be. If
you cannot live with the cut, inform your administrative
official. It may be better to refuse the award than attempt
to do what is expected without proper resources.

If you are an administrative official and the reverse
of the situation should come about — weigh the importance of the project and the overall goals and objectives
of your organization. If the cut was made by the funding
source can you pick up the slack from another fund or
source? If it is salary for the summer months can that be
picked up from another source? Dialogue not monologue
should be ever present within the organization before
the outside negotiations take place. Those negotiations
are the joint concern of the administrator and the
principal investigator.

CONCLUSION

The proposal represents the device whereby the
researcher communicates his or her plan for future
research to potential funding sources. The researcher
who seeks funds should have clear ideas as to the type(s)
of proposals which will be accepted by the various
organizations who dispense funds. Preliminary proposals,
formal proposals, unsolicited proposals, solicited proposals, and requests for quotations are variations which
may be used. Regardless of the type of proposal used,
several rules remain constant. Proposals should be written
from research plans. They should be realistic in terms of
objectives, personnel and budget. They should have the
support of the institution from which they are submitted.
Visually, as well as in contents, proposals submitted should
represent the best efforts of the researcher and institution.
Potential funding sources may never see the researcher or
the institution, but money will or will not flow in response
to the proposal.

Chapter Four

HOW TO PICK
A FUNDING SOURCE

INTRODUCTION

How does a researcher choose a funding source? This question is asked by many. Those who do not have a clear picture of what is required are generally far behind the crowds hunting funds. Or perhaps, if you fall by the wayside, it is due to not knowing the right sources. This Chapter may be a most valuable Chapter to the neophyte in the business of obtaining extramural funds, as well as to the more experienced researcher.

Integrity is a most important factor in the relationships which develop in the arena of research funding. Do not try to fool persons in the business. If you do, the

probability is high that you will end up with results —
all bad.

A few anecdotal remarks might be helpful at this
juncture. Those who give extramural funds do so because
they have come to the conclusion that certain types
of projects will help society in general. For example, those
projects of a social science nature for the abatement of
crime may be funded by the Law Enforcement Assistance
Agency of the Department of Justice. The improvement of
the lot of the disadvantaged and minorities may be funded
by the Department of Labor. For those projects of a
National Security nature which might yield research
beneficial to weapon systems, the various agencies within
the Department of Defense may be appropriate.

To simplify a complex issue, one should ask oneself,
how can one person know where all of the funds are
located? The answer is simple. One cannot know where
all of the funds are to be found. The process is time
consuming, frustrating at times and not always productive.
One must examine the sources of funding just as one
studies the subject matter in which he or she professes
to be an expert. The simplest approach is to break up
the lists into categories and subcategories.

First, identify within your own organization the
sources, amounts, purposes and availability of research
funds. Some academic institutions have *seed monies* for
new faculty or new projects. With stabilizing personnel
in teaching positions, more universities are allotting
funds for *career development* and expanding or shifting
research capabilities. The shifts may be under this
aegis. Do a thorough job at home and tap every source
available. The extramural funding sources are very
interested in noting internal support when they look at
proposals.

Next, as you move to seek extramural funds, categorize
the research you have planned. Is it basic or applied? Is it
people oriented, concerned with manpower needs,

environmental quality, identification of new food sources, etc? Write the title of your research project until it focuses on the major essentials and key words. With internal support and a clear sense of the type of research you are planning, you are ready to identify external sources. The first separation is to classify the sources as to whether they are private or public.

In the private sector you may wish to include: industry; private foundations; private research organizations; universities (private); colleges (private); and consulting firms. The public sector may include: universities (publicly funded); colleges (publicly funded); Federal government; state government; county government; city government; and quasi-government agencies.

Using a previously cited example, research directly in support of weapon systems would not fit in both classifications. In fact, it would probably only fit either the Federal government or industry. This is one approach to narrow the classification of *source*. A more complex *source* is the Department of Defense. In itself it is a multi-billion dollar operation. Nearly every conceivable research project and classification is being conducted by or in a Department of Defense installation. The Army Materiel Command is responsible for research in the United States Army. This Command is responsible for laboratory complexes all over the country. To name a few: Harry Diamond Research Laboratory; Natick Development Center; Ballistics Defense Laboratory; and the Fort Monmouth Electronics Laboratories. These laboratories are responsible for research, development and procurement of clothing, food, weapons systems, missiles, tanks, and automotive materiel. The army supports *basic research* through the Army Research Office located at the Research Triangle, Raleigh-Durham, North Carolina.

Do not give up yet. There are reference materials your research administration office should have for your perusal and study. Volumes and rooms can be filled with what is available from the various funding agencies and those who sell services to assist you in making your choices. It would serve little value if there was not some way to cut down the volume and be more discerning. In another section of this book you will find relevant literature which will help in making the decision. Look at Chapter Fifteen for this assistance. The research administrator serves an important function in the culling process of the literature available and the sources which are more viable and receptive to a particular project. Rely on these people; they have had the experience and can save a great deal of anguish.

Federal agencies often refer to *Guidelines of Programs.* These are available upon request from the agencies and will be sent to the principal investigator. Many agencies maintain a mailing list and automatically send announcements and guidelines to each of the 3000 presidents of institutions of higher education, private foundation directors and chief executive officers of select industries. There are differences in the many guidelines — budget is only one. What the research will do in the sense of benefit for others should be given prime consideration. Is there a technology transfer? Is it basic research? The Federal government is awarding less and less to basic research each year.

One source in assisting in the process of *How to Pick a Funding Source* will be found in the *United States Congress Authorization Hearings.* Each Federal agency must defend its programs and give reasonably strong defense of the viability of its programs. In addition the agency must prepare a defense for new monies, continuation, or reallocation of funds to new programs. It is from the *Authorization Hearings* that one can forecast the agency's wants and desires for the future. As a matter of fact the precursor to the *program guidelines* will be for the most part found in the *Authorization*

Hearings. **CAUTION:** Remember your course in high school and college, civics and government — the *Authorization Hearings* set limits and authorize programs but do not *Fund.* It is the *Appropriation Hearings* which ultimately produce the *Bills* which are passed by the Congress. The *caution* is not to set up programs at home based upon the outcome of the *Authorization Hearings.* All one has to do is a little arithmetic and total the number of *Bills* which are actually *Authorized.* It far exceeds the availability of funds. The *Authorization* process does serve a number of purposes. The main one is that the *Authorized Bills* are very good *bench marks.* Often in a year or more the *Authorized* program becomes a funded program either in start-up mode or for full funding.The *Bills* may go through the Congress and be passed on to the President for his signature. This does not insure monies at this point. The Office of Management and Budget is empowered to impose limits on funds or outright freeze funds. This is of course in great controversy today — the impoundment of funds. But nonetheless, the reality of frozen and impounded funds does exist. Information from *Authorization Hearings* should be culled by research administrators and that information provided to researchers. In turn, researchers should inform administrators of their interest and pass on to the research administrators copies of their publications. This assists the research administrator in better understanding the area and specifics of the research staff.

PRIVATE FOUNDATIONS

The portion devoted to private foundations and private foundation funding will be found in a separate Chapter. Chapter Thirteen has been devoted wholly to this subject.

ORGANIZATION HANDBOOKS AND TELEPHONE DIRECTORIES

If one were to examine a successful research and research administration organization one will find on the shelves a battery of telephone books and organizational charts and handbooks. They should include: private foundations (Ford, Rockefeller, Kettering, Exxon, Danforth, Russell Sage, etc.); Department of Defense, Department of Health, Education and Welfare; National Science Foundation; National Endowment for the Humanities; National Endowment for the Arts; National Institutes of Health; National Aeronautics and Space Administration; Federal Aviation Agency; Department of Transportation; National Bureau of Standards; Energy Research and Development Agency, Environmental Protection Agency, Department of the Interior; Nuclear Regulatory Agency; Veterans Administration; Department of State; Agency for International Development, etc.

The telephone books, organization charts and handbooks provide valuable information as to titles of individuals, correct addresses, telephone numbers, program titles and room numbers. In addition by using previous issues a comparison of programs can be made. Programs which are expanding can be readily seen and those which are being curtailed or phased out likewise can be noted. For example, IRRPOS (Interdisciplinary Research Relevant to Problems of Society) at the National Science Foundation expanded from an Office level to a Directorate which is now called RANN (Research Applications). This could have been guessed long before the public was informed through press releases. In reality it became obvious to the attentive person when the United States Congress first *Authorized* programs and gave a great deal of favor at the Authorization *Hearings* which was carried over with increased funds to the *Appropriation Hearings*.

Telephone books and other material cogent to the internal operations of Federal agencies may be purchased at the Government Printing Office Bookstores in Washington, D.C. A store convenient to the National Science Foundation and the White House is located at the corner of 18th and Pennsylvania Avenue, N.W. in the United States Information Agency Building. Cash is accepted and previously purchased coupons from the Superintendent of Documents for the purchase of the documents in the Bookstore. Handbooks and telephone directories should be extensively used both by administrators and researchers.

LOCAL SOURCES

This is the most viable, yet the least tapped source for extramural funds. Private foundations in each State are likely sources. President Thomas Broce of Phillips University recently wrote a valuable treatise entitled, *"Foundations of Oklahoma."* Similar books are available in your libraries. If there is not one available for your State, perhaps monies could be raised within the State from insurance, legal or banking sources to finance a professor of history or economics to compile such data.

Identify trends in businesses and industries of your State and region to note sources. Banks are increasing their automation every day. Bankers are now turning to *electronic fund transfer* technology and the required supportive systems. Those in computer science, marketing, banking and commerce could no doubt be of value to a local, chain bank or State Banking Commission.

State Insurance Associations have been known to give monies to improve course content. While this manuscript was prepared a local State University gave an unrestricted gift of $5,000 for the improvement of courses for life insurance underwriters. Every organization in your community and State is a potential source of support. Examples of local industry may include Western Electric, Boeing, Friden, Control Data, etc.; local grocery chains; local organizations (Chamber of Commerce, Merchants Bureau); and local civic groups.

Professional associations also are a valuable source of information. They can serve as a clearinghouse for specific disciplines and often do. An excellent compendium is the *Encyclopedia of Associations*.[1] A number of professional organizations give grants for research and these should be identified in your area of interest.

THE BUDGET OF THE
UNITED STATES GOVERNMENT

The United States Government Budget is an astonishingly simple document covering the expenditures of Government. This document should be in every research administrator's office. It contains information which would stagger the imagination. Because of the change of the Federal government year the usual dates for release will be changed. Each institution's research office should ask their Congressman or Senator to supply this information when it is available. The same sources previously mentioned for telephone books can supply copies of the nearly eleven hundred page document. Expect to pay about thirteen dollars for a copy of the Budget. The *"complete"* Budget is one of several volumes which will be described. The *"complete"* Budget contains four parts and an index as follows:

I.   **DETAILED BUDGET ESTIMATES**
II. **SCHEDULES OF PERMANENT POSITIONS**
III. **SUPPLEMENTAL APPROPRIATION PROPOSALS FOR THE CURRENT YEAR**
IV. **ANNEXED BUDGETS AND OTHER MATERIAL**
     INDEX

With an intelligent reading of Part I for example, it would be possible to match institutional interests with budget for the various agencies. Some statutes are very specific and set rigid requirements for the use of funds — others are quite fluid.

Part I detailed Budget Estimates contains:

- **LEGISLATIVE BRANCH**
- **THE JUDICIARY**
- **EXECUTIVE OFFICE OF THE PRESIDENT**
- **FUNDS APPROPRIATED TO THE PRESIDENT**
- **DEPARTMENT OF AGRICULTURE**
- **DEPARTMENT OF COMMERCE**
- **DEPARTMENT OF DEFENSE — MILITARY**
- **DEPARTMENT OF DEFENSE — CIVIL**
- **DEPARTMENT OF HEALTH, EDUCATION, AND WELFARE**
- **DEPARTMENT OF HOUSING AND URBAN DEVELOPMENT**
- **DEPARTMENT OF THE INTERIOR**
- **DEPARTMENT OF JUSTICE**
- **DEPARTMENT OF LABOR**
- **DEPARTMENT OF STATE**
- **DEPARTMENT OF TRANSPORTATION**
- **DEPARTMENT OF THE TREASURY**
- **ATOMIC ENERGY COMMISSION**
- **ENVIRONMENTAL PROTECTION AGENCY**
- **GENERAL SERVICES ADMINISTRATION**
- **NATIONAL AERONAUTICS AND SPACE ADMINISTRATION**
- **POSTAL SERVICE**
- **VETERANS ADMINISTRATION**
- **OTHER INDEPENDENT AGENCIES**

If one wishes to have the complete story, there are companion documents to complete the several documents which relate to The United States Government Budget:

- *THE BUDGET OF THE UNITED STATES GOVERNMENT.* **CONTAINS THE BUDGET MESSAGE OF THE PRESIDENT, INFORMATION ON THE FEDERAL PROGRAMS BY FUNCTION AND BY AGENCY AND ACCOUNT, SUMMARY TABLES, AND STATISTICAL INFORMATION.**
- *THE BUDGET OF THE UNITED STATES GOVERNMENT. APPENDIX.* **CONTAINS THE TEXT OF APPROPRIATION ESTIMATES PROPOSED FOR THE CONSIDERATION OF THE CONGRESS TOGETHER WITH SPECIFIC SUPPORTING INFORMATION ON THE VARIOUS APPROPRIATIONS AND FUNDS, AND OTHER SUPPLEMENTARY MATERIAL. THE CONTENTS OF THIS VOLUME ARE FURTHER EXPLAINED AT THE BEGINNING OF EACH OF ITS FOUR PARTS.**

- *THE U.S. BUDGET IN BRIEF,* **A PAMPHLET TYPE PUBLICATION, IS AVAILABLE FOR THOSE WHO WISH A MORE CONCISE AND LESS TECHNICAL PRESENTATION THAN EITHER OF THE ABOVE TWO DOCUMENTS.**
- *THE SPECIAL ANALYSES, BUDGET OF THE UNITED STATES GOVERN-MENT* **CONTAINS 19 SPECIAL ANALYSES OF SIGNIFICANT ASPECTS OF THE FEDERAL BUDGET.**
- *THE BUDGET OF THE UNITED STATES GOVERNMENT, DISTRICT OF COLUMBIA,* **CONTAINS THE ESTIMATES FOR THE MUNICIPAL GOVERN-MENT OF THE DISTRICT OF COLUMBIA.**

Attention should be given to the volume, *Special Analyses* of The United States Government. This volume of *Special Analyses* contains facts and figures on various features of the recommendations transmitted by the President in *The Budget of the United States Government.* Its purpose is to present special analytical information about significant aspects of Government activities. This complements the detailed financial and program information which is contained in the *Budget Appendix.*

Part 1 provides analyses and tabulations which cover Government finances and operations as a whole, and reflect the ways in which Government finances affect the economy.

Part 2 furnishes Government-wide program and financial information in seven social program areas — education, manpower, health, income security, housing, civil rights, and crime reduction.

Part 3 discusses trends and developments in selected areas of Government activity — aid to State and local governments, public works, research and development, and environmental quality.

The *Special Analyses* volume includes a *Special Analysis* of all Federal Research and Development Programs. This is accomplished normally in less than thirty pages. It deals with the effects of budget on acceleration of programs. It also covers the effects of markets and new jobs as well as our country's world trade situation.

The contents of the *Budgets* can greatly assist in

choosing a Federal funding source and should not be overlooked. *The Budget of The United States* is complex, yet the presentation is quite readable. It represents many iterations before its actual release. The *Budget* is prepared by the Executive Office of the President, Office of Management and Budget.

CATALOG OF FEDERAL DOMESTIC ASSISTANCE

The material in this compendium changes nearly daily. It should not be just placed on a shelf. In spite of the changes, it is one of the few compilations of Federal Programs found in one place. Figure 6 represents a sample page from the *Catalog*. The document represents a horrendous task of compiled data. Each Federal agency is required within its own agency to submit to a central clearing house each of its programs along with pertinent financial data as shown in Figure 6. The authors heartily recommend that each research administration office have this document for reference. The update is on a yearly basis and a standing order to the Government Printing Office will insure regularly receiving the insert pages. Many that have been lax have found the document unavailable because it was sold out.

A computerized system has been developed and can be implemented using the yearly updated information from computer tapes.[2]

CONCLUSION

The *"picking"* of a funding source is in fact a culmination of the three preceding Chapters. The needs of the agency **must** be matched with the aspirations of the proposal writer. If this does not take place, the mismatch will result in no funds and much frustration. Competition

13.328   ENVIRONMENTAL HEALTH SCIENCES - RESEARCH GRANTS

FEDERAL AGENCY: NATIONAL INSTITUTES OF HEALTH, DEPARTMENT OF HEALTH, EDUCATION, AND WELFARE

AUTHORIZATION: Public Health Service Act of 1944, as amended, section 301(d); 42 U.S.C. 241.

OBJECTIVES: To support research on the phenomena associated with the source, distribution, mode of impact, and effects of environmental factors on biological systems.

TYPES OF ASSISTANCE: Project Grants.

USES AND USE RESTRICTIONS: Research grants are intended to support the direct costs of a project, in accord with an approved budget, plus an appropriate amount for indirect costs.

ELIGIBILITY REQUIREMENTS:

Applicant Eligibility: A university, college, hospital, public agency, or nonprofit research institution may submit an application and receive a grant for support of research by a named principal investigator. In exceptional cases, a grantee may be an individual in the United States.

Beneficiary Eligibility: Same as applicant eligibility.

Credentials/Documentation: Applications must be signed by appropriate officials of the grantee institution.

APPLICATION AND AWARD PROCESS:

Preapplication Coordination: None.

Application Procedure: Submission to the Division of Research Grants of PHS form 398.

Award Procedure: Grants are made on the basis of a dual review of an investigator-prepared application. The reviews are made by peer groups: The first by a study section for scientific merit; the second by an advisory council for program relevance. Final approval of these recommendations is made by the Director, NIH.

Deadlines: New and supplemental application: October 1, February 1, June 1. Renewal applications: September 1, January 1, May 1.; Continuation applications: 2 months before scheduled start date of budget period.

Range of Approval/Disapproval Time: 180 to 240 days.

Appeals: Disapproved applications may be revised and submitted for review.

Renewals: Subject to same criteria as new applications.

ASSISTANCE CONSIDERATIONS:

Formula and Matching Requirements: Current legislation requires that the grantee also participate in the cost of each research project. Cost-sharing agreements are individually negotiated with the grantee.

Length and Time Phasing of Assistance: Grants may be awarded for up to 5 years (in special circumstances 7), generally in 12-month budget periods. Funds are released primarily on letter of credit, but can be released in lump sum or on quarterly basis depending upon institution.

POST ASSISTANCE REQUIREMENTS:

Reports: Expenditures must be reported within 120 days of the end of each budget period; and reports must be submitted of any inventions accomplished under the grant. In addition, a progress report must be submitted with any application for continued support and a terminal progress report must be submitted 6 months after termination of the research project.

Audits: Grants are subject to audit by representatives of the Department of Health, Education, and Welfare to insure proper accounting and use of grant funds.

Records: Financial records, including all documents to support entries on the accounting records, must be kept readily available for examination.

FINANCIAL INFORMATION:

Account Identification: 09-30-0862-0-1-651.

Obligations: (Grants) FY 70 $7,375,000; FY 71 est $8,495,000; and FY 72 est $10,047,000.

Range and Average of Financial Assistance: $10,000 to $800,000; $92,000.

PROGRAM ACCOMPLISHMENTS: Approximately 92 research grants will be supported in fiscal year 1971, compared to 94 in fiscal year 1970. Of these, 6 are university based Environmental Health Sciences Centers. These grants support research in the following fields; pesticides, food toxicants, occupational health hazards, heavy metals, air pollution, smoking and health, toxicology, and others related to the mission of the Institute.

REGULATIONS, GUIDELINES, AND LITERATURE: 42 CFR, Part 52, "Public Health Service Grants for Research Projects," publication No. 1301, and various other related publications may be obtained from the Division of Research Grants, National Institutes of Health, Bethesda, Maryland 20014.

INFORMATION CONTACTS:

Regional or Local Office: Not applicable.

Headquarters Office: Associate Director for Extramural Programs, National Institute of Environmental Health Sciences, Post Office Box 12233, Research Triangle Park, North Carolina 27709. Telephone: (919) 549-8411.

RELATED PROGRAMS: 13.327, Environmental Health Sciences - Fellowships; 13.329, Environmental Health Sciences - Training Grants; 47.008, Environmental Sciences Research Project Support.

13.329   ENVIRONMENTAL HEALTH SCIENCES - TRAINING GRANTS

FEDERAL AGENCY: NATIONAL INSTITUTES OF HEALTH, DEPARTMENT OF HEALTH, EDUCATION, AND WELFARE

AUTHORIZATION: Public Health Service Act of 1944, as amended, section 301(d); 42 U.S.C. 241.

OBJECTIVES: To establish, expand, and operate training programs in environmental health sciences at qualified universities and other institutions of higher education.

TYPES OF ASSISTANCE: Project Grants.

USES AND USE RESTRICTIONS: Funds are made available to the institutions and may be used both for administrative expenses and for student expenses. Graduate training grants are intended to support the direct costs of a training program (including stipendiary support to named pre and postbaccalaureate trainees), plus indirect costs, currently limited to 8 percent of direct costs.

ELIGIBILITY REQUIREMENTS:

Applicant Eligibility: A university, college, hospital, public agency, or nonprofit research institution may submit an application for the support of a research training program under the guidance of a named program director. Grants are made only to qualified researchers working in nonprofit organizations on the basis of dual review of an investigator-prepared application.

Beneficiary Eligibility: Same as applicant eligibility.

Credentials/Documentation: Applications must be signed by appropriate officials of the grantee institution.

APPLICATION AND AWARD PROCESS:

Preapplication Coordination: None.

Application Procedure: Submission to the Division of Research Grants of PHS form 2499-1.

Award Procedure: The reviews are made by peer groups: the first by a training committee, the second by an advisory council. Final approval of these two recommendations is made by the Director of NIH.

Figure 6   •   CATALOG OF FEDERAL DOMESTIC ASSISTANCE

is increasing and resources to fund projects are becoming thinner. The content of the proposal and the direction the project leads when submitted to "X" funding source must not be done without careful thought, planning and decision. The researcher can identify some sources alone, but for thorough perusal, the assistance of the institution's office of research administration is required and essential.

Chapter Five

COMMUNICATING WITH FUNDING SOURCES

- INTRODUCTION
- CASE STUDY — DR. DEAN GOES TO WASHINGTON
- CASE STUDY COMMENTS
- ESTABLISHING A DIALOGUE WITH POTENTIAL FUNDING SOURCES
- WHY RESEARCH GRANT APPLICATIONS ARE TURNED DOWN
- CONCLUSION

INTRODUCTION

Just as the development of a plan is critical to the success of extramural funding so is the means of establishing contact with those who either make or assist in the decision making process of recommending funds for a particular project or program. Often times this phase of the proposal-award life cycle is overlooked.

The impression the project plan makes on the potential funding source has a great deal to do with the probability of funding. The people at the source and they are just that are not to be feared but respected. In the scenario of giving dollars for projects the funding source must be studied well. After all, they will study you, and you can be sure it will be thorough when monies are requested. There are really no second chances in this business — a poor impression may kill future chances of you and your colleagues for some time to come. You may say to yourself that this is a drastic statement — not so. The interagency, interfoundation and intergovernment dialogue is profound and constantly is going on. To be sure, not much written communication, but manifold telephone communication takes place. The cost of long distance telephone calls is never a deterrent in this business for the givers of money.

CASE STUDY — DR. DEAN GOES TO WASHINGTON

The following is a Case Study which is intended to familiarize the reader with case studies in general. In addition the reader is expected to determine in his or her mind the **do's** and **do nots** of the case. The criterion for this determination is what strengthens the case for funding **(do's)** and the converse of this **(do nots)** are what weakens the case for Dr. Dean.

Regardless of what position you occupy today, whether it be professor, research administrator, city manager, research associate or lawyer, in the first reading you are to play the role of the chief executive of Sun University — its president. As president you should write a written analysis of the Case Study being free to criticize, praise, look for incidents which you would like repeated, incidents which you would like avoided or modified in the future and a general evaluation of the expenditure Dr. Dean incurred in his visit to Washington, D.C. In addition, after completing the case study as the President of Sun University, repeat the process (each time writing an analysis) for each position listed (if you are academic based) and appropriate positions (if you are based in industry or government). Finally take your present position and do the analysis of the case study placing yourself in your everyday role.

Analyze this case with care and objectivity. This case can happen and does happen every day, although this particular case study has been contrived.

Dr. Roget Dean is a professor of biophysics and he wishes support for a project which in his own estimation will yield a breakthrough and cure for what is known today as monocytic leukemia — a blood cancer and "killer" of children. Dr. Dean holds a joint appointment at Sun University (located on the West Coast) and at the private Cloud Research Foundation located adjacent to his University. His remuneration is divided, with half coming from each source. At Sun University he teaches one graduate course per semester and directs three graduate students. Two of the three students are candidates for the Ph.D. degree. At the Cloud Research Foundation where he has his office and an assigned laboratory he engages in research, the remaining portion of his 100 per cent total load. His graduate students are housed in Sun University facilities not at the Cloud Research Foundation.

Dean said, until today he did not worry or concern himself about money. He also said, that was for the administrators to do. All he did in the past was to fill out some relatively simple forms and equipment, chemicals and space were supplied or allocated to fill his research needs. At least this was the system until today which went back fifteen years.

Dr. Dean and his colleagues were summoned to a meeting three weeks ago to first introduce the new Foundation President and second to a get acquainted coffee to introduce the newly appointed executive director. During the formal portion of the meeting each member of the research staff was given the opportunity to briefly tell what he or she was doing. At the close of the meeting the staff were told that effective, January 1, next, no less than fifty per cent of each research project was to include extramural funds.

Those projects which did not attain that level after January 1, would be critically reviewed by the Trustees, the President and the Executive Director for phasing out or termination.

The University Board of Trustees were made aware of the new policy for the Cloud Research Foundation in advance. The University would later announce that full-time faculty would not be funded for research with in-house funds without tangible evidence that the projects would yield future funding from outside sources.

Following this traumatic news, Dr. Dean thought it best to engage in discussions and prepare to fill in the gap with outside funds. He did just that, followed by submission of a travel request both from the University and the Research Foundation. Shortly thereafter, Dr. Dean was given the authority to travel with each of his organizations paying half of all of the costs incurred so that he could start dialogue with potential funding sources.

Dr. Dean flew from his West Coast Sun University to Los Angeles International Airport where he boarded a non-stop flight for Washington, D.C. Upon arriving he settled in a downtown hotel located on 16th Street, N.W. With mixed excitement and apprehension he found his way to Bethesda. To his dismay he also found that Bethesda was located in Maryland and not a walk around the block but a taxi fare of nearly twenty dollars.

Upon arriving at the information desk at the National Institutes of Health he spent about twenty minutes looking at programs, offices and titles in the latest telephone directory and decided that his research was best suited for the National Cancer Institute. Still excited and awed, he proceeded directly to the offices of the Associate Director for Grants and Extramural Support at the National Cancer Institute. He gingerly stepped into the suite which housed Dr. Elcatsbo, and quickly found that he was out of the office and testifying on the "Hill" at a Congressional Hearing. He also found that immediately after the testimony was completed, Dr. Elcatsbo was to fly to Antwerp and visit with NATO supported research directors.

After leaving the secretary's desk, Dr. Dean was walking toward the elevator and while doing so in the hall he met Dr. Smythe, Vice President for Research and Federal Programs at Sun University. After exchanging the usual amenities and each asking the other, "what are you doing here?" Dr. Smythe suggested that Dr. Dean accompany him to the office of Senator Rekaf — where Dr. Smythe was headed anyway. He did so. The meeting in the Senator's office was short as one might expect. Dr. Dean was given the opportunity to tell his research story and as expected it was long and disjointed. It was also all brand new to the smiling face of Vice President Smythe. Senator Rekaf asked if he could have a copy of Dr. Dean's abstract so that he could discuss it with his senatorial colleagues, particularly the Chairman of the Sub-committee on Health Research of the Committee on Science and Technology. Dr. Dean replied, that he did not have that material with him. The Senator confessed to the group that he did not understand one word of the technical jargon the brilliant Dr. Dean attempted to relate to him during the meeting. He further stated that the best he could do for Dr. Dean was to place a call and give him a personal note to see a friend (former college room-mate) who is now the Congressional Liaison Officer at the International Foundation for American Support in the Sciences (IFASS). After handing Dr. Dean the hand scratched note a call was placed by his assistant. Senator Rekaf then asked the two to join him for lunch. While enjoying the food in the Senate Dining Room, Dr. Dean was daydreaming about what he would do with the funds IFASS would give him after lunch. He felt elated and quite confident at this point.

Dr. Dean arrived around two o'clock at the Congressional Liaison Officer's suite and found he was unavailable because of previously scheduled meetings with the Director of IFASS. The girl at the desk (receptionist) recognized the importance of the hand scribbled note from the Senator and was especially cognizant of Senator Rekaf's constant blasts against projects funded by IFASS. She did arrange a meeting with an assistant program director in the Division of

Biological and Medical Sciences for the following morning at 9:00 o'clock for thirty minutes with Dr. Ayp. While the call was being placed Miss Mosob asked Dr. Dean for copies of his vita and proposal abstract so that she could make copies for Dr. Ayp in advance of the meeting. He was unable to give them to her nor did he offer to prepare them for the meeting.

In the intervening time from 2:15 P.M. to 9:00 A.M. the next morning, Dr. Dean entertained himself by first taking a Grey Line Sightseeing Tour of the City, toured the new FBI Building, had a superb dinner at the Kennedy Center for the Performing Arts and remained to see the International Ballet.

The 9:00 A.M. meeting was scheduled for a maximum of thirty minutes. The Assistant Program Director, newly arrived (two weeks on the job) and on a year leave of absence from Eastern University took copious notes, listened intently and interrupted from time to time asking questions about the research. Finally, Dr. Ayp asked for a copy of his proposal, a copy of his budget and a typed abstract. Dr. Dean chagrined, nodded no in each instance. He was saying to himself, "It seems that everyone in Washington has but one question — where is your typed abstract?"

As the meeting progressed and Dr. Dean repeated the technical speech as he did several times before, Dr. Ayp interrupted and said, "IFASS cannot fund such a project". IFASS is not allowed to deal with medically oriented research by Law. The only one that can fund this kind of research also by Law is the National Institutes of Health. Frustrated by this time and somewhat short tempered, Dr. Dean related the incidents which preceded his visit to IFASS which included a trip to NIH in Bethesda. Dr. Ayp said he would be happy to call a friend and colleague who funded him on the university campus who was in charge of the drug synthesis program at the National Cancer Institute — "which incidentally is the area that supports the kinds of research you have been telling me about", he added. While sitting at the desk, he called Dr. Rallod at NCI. "Tom, I appreciate your call and I would be delighted to talk to Dr. Dean, but I am just leaving for Dulles Airport to catch a plane for Stockholm for the International Meetings on Drug Abuse. Why not have Dr. Dean send me a letter and a preliminary proposal of not more than five pages. Make sure he includes a half or so page abstract and for goodness sake make sure he includes a budget. I must know how much the project will cost (ball park at least). Have him send it to my attention at NCI — you have my address. Who knows it might be good? Thanks for calling Tom, I will be looking forward to seeing you at the Gordon Conferences next month. Give my very best to your dear wife Sonja — goodbye."

Mad as fire, he taxied to the hotel and made ready for his trip back to the West Coast. He was determined not to let this defeat him but when questioned after his return to the campus he did say he kicked the hotel waste basket a few times and muttered a few obscenities under his breath and cursed the damn bureaucrats.

CASE STUDY COMMENTS

It is quite common for an author to justify a case study by giving what is generally called the *school solution* or *authors analysis*. Unlike the conventional approach, the authors feel that the case study should be analyzed and conclusions made by the reader in whatever role the reader has placed himself. (See beginning of Case Study for instructions).

The following questions are included to precipitate thought. They are not intended to influence judgement. Should the reader wish to alter any procedure or behavior which took part by any of the characters in the case study —somewhere in one or more places in the text are ideas, procedures and solutions which will fit in a number of different situations.

Questions for Thought —

- WAS THE TRIP WORTHWHILE?

- WAS THE TRIP A COMPLETE FAILURE?
- WHAT SHOULD THE VISIT WITH SENATOR REKAF HAVE PRODUCED?
- COULD ONE EXPECT MORE FROM THE SENATOR THAN WAS GIVEN?
- WAS COMMUNICATION ADEQUATE BETWEEN THE CLOUD RE-SEARCH FOUNDATION AND THE SUN UNIVERSITY RELATIVE TO THE FUNDING OF PROJECTS?
- DID DR. SMYTHE IN HIS CAPACITY DO ALL THAT COULD BE EXPECTED?
- IN ANY OF THE VISITS TO THE AGENCIES COULD MORE HAVE BEEN ACCOMPLISHED BY DR. DEAN?
- IF YOU WERE DR. DEAN AND IN THE SAME SITUATION, WOULD YOU HAVE DONE ANYTHING DIFFERENT? IF SO ELUCIDATE THE DIF-FERENCES IN DETAIL AND STATE HOW AND WHY.
- DO YOU BELIEVE THIS CASE STUDY IS EXAGGERATED? IS THIS CASE STUDY POSSIBLE OR PLAUSIBLE TO HAVE ACTUALLY TAKEN PLACE IN TODAY'S SOPHISTICATED ENVIRONMENT?
- DOES ANY ONE CENTRAL THOUGHT COME THROUGH AS BEING MORE IMPORTANT THAN ANOTHER IN THIS CASE STUDY?
- DO YOU FEEL SUN UNIVERSITY DID ALL THEY COULD TO MAKE THIS TRIP WORTHWHILE?
- IF YOU WERE SITTING AT DR. AYP'S DESK WOULD YOU HAVE ASKED ANY QUESTIONS OR DONE ANYTHING DIFFERENT RELATIVE TO IFASS FUNDING THAN THAT OF DR. DEAN?
- WAS DR. DEAN A VICTIM OF CIRCUMSTANCES OR SHOULD HE HAVE BEEN EXPECTED TO DO MORE THAN WAS DONE?
- WHAT SHOULD BE THE ROLE OF THE PRINCIPAL INVESTIGATOR (DR. DEAN) — BEFORE, DURING AND AFTER THE TRIP?
- WHAT SHOULD BE THE ROLE OF RESEARCH VICE PRESIDENT DR. SMYTHE — BEFORE, DURING AND AFTER THE TRIP?
- SHOULD DR. DEAN HAVE BEEN ALLOWED TO GO ON THIS TRIP ALONE — IT WAS HIS FIRST TRIP TO WASHINGTON, D.C.? SHOULD DR. DEAN HAVE GONE AT ALL? SHOULD DR. DEAN HAVE HAD SOMEONE REPRESENT HIM?
- WHAT DETAILED FOLLOW-UP SHOULD BE TAKEN BOTH BY DR. DEAN, SUN UNIVERSITY AND THE CLOUD RESEARCH FOUNDATION?

ESTABLISHING A DIALOGUE WITH POTENTIAL FUNDING SOURCES

The methods of communicating with a funding agency are the telephone, telegram, letter or in person. The methods may be directly by the project director or by an inter-mediary person representing research, graduate studies, extramural funding, sponsored projects or federal pro-grams etc.

Before any contact is made, the important fact to keep in mind is the reason why the contact is being made in the first place. Do not make contact just for contact sake. Have something (abstract, talking paper, preliminary proposal or proposal) ready to go.

An abbreviated version of preliminary proposal is called a *talking paper.* Some refer to the *talking paper* as *discussion* or *position papers.* Where a preliminary proposal numbers approximately five pages the length for a talking paper should not exceed three pages. The preliminary proposal normally is not sent blind but with some advance dialogue. The talking paper can be sent as an initial contact with an accompanying letter.

The talking paper can serve to assist the institution and the potential principal investigator by establishing initial contact and future dialogue with a person at a particular agency and program. The covering letter should indicate the wishes of the principal investigator, particularly if comments are to be returned either of a positive or negative nature.

Some agencies and programs use the talking paper as their first screening procedure and encourage or discourage further dialogue with the agency.

The same talking paper may be used as a basis of establishing a working relationship with a selected agency representative. If a visit is planned indicate in the covering letter that the talking paper has been sent in advance of a scheduled visit. Attempt to obtain an appointment so that you do not barge in to an office unannounced.

The talking paper is a distinct advantage for the intermediary to hand carry to various funding sources. The talking paper is sufficiently short not to impose on the action officer and yet sufficiently long to establish discussion and determine interest. A highly recommended approach for the institution that has an experienced dean, vice president or official is to carry these papers on regular trips to potential sources. Where this service is not available, it is wise to develop the dialogue with the preliminary proposal.

Although this comment has been made in other Chapters of this book, the responsibility is clearly on the potential principal investigator to write the proposal and defend the technical aspects. The Dean or Vice President or whatever the title of the administrative unit overseeing the principal investigator is clearly responsible for assisting and expediting processes. **This point cannot be over stressed. The research administrator cannot be held responsible for writing proposals.**

WHY RESEARCH GRANT APPLICATIONS ARE TURNED DOWN

Dr. Donald Lisk in his paper *Why Research Applications Are Turned Down* gives in an indirect way cogent reasons and items to include and not include in the talking paper, preliminary proposal and formal proposal.[1] In the communication with the funding source his point of view will be of major assistance.

Donald J. Lisk

By permission. From Bioscience. *21*,1025-26 (1971) ©

A major portion of academic research is presently supported by grant awards from various government agencies. The decision of approval and priority or disapproval depends largely on the content of the grant proposal. The proper preparation of it is therefore crucial.

There is apparently the gross misconception in some quarters that submitted applications are hastily scanned, the only notations being the name of the investigator or the number of his publications with judgment resting wholly on this information. Rather, it should be known that each proposal is closely scrutinized by several reviewers who are working in, or familiar with, the proposed research area, who can judge the required training and number of investigators and auxiliary staff truly needed to perform the study, who are aware of the limitations and prices of various equipment requested, and so on. Reviewers serving on a particular study section may simultaneously include medical doctors, pharmacologists, biochemists, analytical chemists, organic chemists, ecologists, etc. When necessary, a proposal may also be sent to outside reviewers who may be specialists in the applicant's field.

An interesting fact soon becomes apparent to a reviewer. It is that applications are not disapproved or poorly rated for innumerable reasons but rather for a fairly manageable number of recurring ones. It is therefore not too difficult to organize and assemble these to serve as a guide to prospective applicants. One might logically begin by listing typical parts of a research application in sequence and presenting, by questions, faults which lowered the adjudged quality of past proposals.

Introduction (Rationale, Significance)

Does the introductory presentation indicate that the principal investigator (PI) crystallized his ideas as a result of a logical and thorough review of the literature rather than having put together something which might work as a result of a superficial survey, a chance or isolated observation, or a number of unauthenticated personal communications?

Is it obvious that the research proposed simply resulted because the PI has a favorite analytical (or other) technique or skill that he strongly wants to use in a study which is not particularly important or sound?

Have certain pertinent literature references been ostensibly omitted which would refute or weaken the justification for the study or which would expose the study as mere duplication?

In describing his related work, does the PI truly describe studies which *are related* to the proposed research?

From a knowledge of the PI's past aptitudes and intentions and the nature and quality of the proposal, does its submission appear to have been initiated by the PI or as a result of administrative pressure upon him? It should be noted that this latter type of information is not officially sought after but often is general knowledge owing to unsolicited publicity by the investigator and colleagues which seems to accompany preparation and submission of grant proposals or site visits.

Is the claimed practical significance of the research extremely remote or farfetched?

Investigator

From a knowledge of the past record and accomplishments of the PI and the nature of the project, is it evident that he will likely originate the research ideas or will he rather simply serve as a figurehead?

Has the PI published research papers in well-regarded scientific journals? Are his publications instead largely semi-technical or review articles, book chapters, abstracts, or a raft of manuscripts in preparation?

Is it obvious that the PI, although accomplished in a particular discipline, has hastily entered a new field and prepared the application without proper scientific preparation through literature survey, personal communications, and so on?

If the PI is not competent in the proposed research, are others included to provide the needed expertise? Are there other competent scientists located nearby who would be peculiarly suited to provide this expertise as consultants but who are not included in the proposal?

Has the PI listed another scientist as a cooperator without the latter's knowledge?

As a result of a site visit, is it obvious that the PI lacks the leadership qualities to properly direct the project and to provide and maintain the needed cohesiveness among the participants?

Is the percentage of time to be devoted to the program by the PI too small? Are many small percentages of his total time already committed to each of several other projects?

Is the investigator noted for "annual job hopping"?

Is the success of the project pivotal on securing a specialist such as a competent electron microscopist, the available number of whom are very scarce?

Is it obvious from the background and age of an investigator or co-worker that claims made concerning his competence may be in doubt? An example might be that of an individual described as a "seasoned electron microscopist" who is only 24 years old and simply used the instrument for part of his thesis research.

Is the PI truly aware of the auxiliary personnel needed to accomplish the objective? For example, if the true "fate" of a toxicant is to be studied in a biological system, isotopic techniques are usually necessary. Thus has the PI arranged for outside synthesis of the tagged compound and expected metabolites? If not, is an organic chemist requested to accomplish this? If gas chromatographic analyses are necessary, has the PI included an operator who is clearly experienced?

Will the research result in graduate students being trained or are technicians solely requested to perform the experiments even though students would be available?

Does the PI obviously dodge the issues or seem reluctant when asked to provide additional information for an application?

Have titles for investigators been contrived to appear expedient when considering a current type of research which is politically popular? An example might be, John Doe, "molecular ecologist."

Budget

Is the study satisfactory in most respects but simply too large in scope to accomplish with the manpower and in the time requested?

Is support requested for too long a time when technology and concepts in the particular field of study are changing at an explosive rate and thus may rapidly outmode the proposed research approach?

From a knowledge of the true instrumental needs for the research and the extensive number of items requested, is it probable that the proponent is "just out to equip a laboratory"? Would less expensive apparatus suffice?

Is equipment requested which is known to already exist as available and underused equipment in the same department or reasonably nearby? This information can be obtained, for instance, from recent graduates of the PI's department.

If a first proposal was rejected or not funded because of low priority, was it resubmitted in a very perfunctory manner and containing nothing new? Has the cost of certain items strangely and sharply risen for no apparent reason?

Is an exorbitant amount requested for publication costs which might lead one to infer that the PI is to be extremely productive but which his past publication record does not support?

Methods of Procedure

Is one part of the proposal sound but many more experiments appear to be simply included or briefly mentioned for enticement or to pad the proposal? This is known as the "goodies for everybody" approach.

Is it obvious from the procedural description that the investigator truly possesses the ability to design a crucial experiment?

Is the proposal replete with descriptions or mentions of what "should" be done, leaving the reviewer wondering what really "will" be done?

Does the PI allude to certain problems which he expects may arise but then offers no approach to their solution?

Is the proposal replete with glowing or naive predictions of success which are largely unwarranted?

Does the PI go to great lengths to describe in minutest detail the proposed methods which are already known to be routine or accepted to divert attention away from other uncertain experimental procedures which are only mentioned and not described?

Has new information appeared in the literature since the time of application which would require a new research approach by the applicant?

Is the proposed research already underway elsewhere? Is a commercial firm already engaged in the proposed study?

Although the experiments proposed are important, is the experimental design unrealistic when related to practical problems? For instance, in a toxicological study are the dosage levels of toxicants designed to literally "knock 'em dead" in hopes of eliciting the desired or hypothesized effect or to obviate the later analytical difficulties of isolation and identification of trace amounts of metabolites, etc.

If a living species is chosen for a toxicological study, is it simply a favorite of the investigator and perhaps not as desirable from a public health point of view (i.e., the observations may be quite difficult to extrapolate as to their effects on humans than if another species were chosen)? Are "in vitro" studies to replace "in vivo" studies just as a matter of convenience?

Does success in the whole proposal rest solely on development of a single crucial analytical technique early in the study? If the method is not developed, are alternative methods available and proposed? In this regard, it is often advisable to seek grant support for method development alone first and reapply later to use the method is a desired investigation.

Are the chances for success virtually nil because of the unavailability of special chemicals or equipment or the extreme difficulty in synthesis or construction of these?

Will the insolubility, etc., of a compound or its method of addition to a living system introduce other objectionable artifacts?

Have sources of error or artifacts such as bacterial contamination or the effects of temperature and light, etc., been overlooked.

Will representative control samples be available?

In the case of renewal applications, does the applicant only briefly describe his planned research and approach, leaving the impression that he feels he has "his foot in the door" as a result of having had a number of previous proposals approved and expects a "blank check"?

In a renewal application, was certain of the work, previously proposed, truly never studied for no apparent reason? Was real progress, or at least effort, shown under the first grant award?

In summary, preparation of a grant application or for a site visit should never degenerate into a battle of wits in which an adroit literary ability or the verbal gymnastics of the PI are pitted against the acumen of reviewers. In the vast majority of cases the reviewers' side will win. It is therefore folly for researchers to compose shrewd or popular answers to anticipated questions prior to a site visit. It is similarly pointless for the PI to go to great lengths to properly prepare an application if he himself is not properly prepared or qualified to direct the research. If you haven't got the goods, don't apply. An application submitted following a previously related but disapproved one is scrutinized ever more closely.

For a general recommendation in preparing grant proposals one might best borrow an expression from our younger generation, "Tell it like it is!" If there is anything which impresses reviewers favorably it is sincerity. Reviewers are after one thing, and that is facts, clearly and concisely presented. Give them precisely that.

For further information on this subject the reader is referred to the literature (Allen, 1960; Hunt et al., 1959).

References

Allen, E. M. 1960. Why are research grant applications disapproved? *Science*, **132:** 1532-1534.

Hunt, G. H. 1959. Research grant program of the National Institutes of Health. *Geriatrics*, **14:** 396.

The author is at the Pesticide Residue Laboratory, Department of Entomology, Cornell University, Ithaca, New York 14850.

CONCLUSION

Communications with funding sources require careful planning. Plunging — is not the usual practice that should be followed. The case study in this Chapter illustrated many *faux pas*. Perhaps, those errors will not be as obvious to one reader as to others. The key to successful communications with sources that provide support for extramural activities is **to be prepared** when the communication does take place. Do not make contact just for the sake of making contact. Know what you are going to talk about in advance. The communications whether they be written or oral should be completely honest. Do not exaggerate. When funding officials speak or write — listen.

Chapter Six

EXAMPLES OF COMMUNICATIONS

- **INTRODUCTION**
- **LETTERS OF ENCOURAGEMENT**
- **LETTERS OF AWARD**
- **LETTERS OF DENIAL**
- **CONCLUSION**

INTRODUCTION

In previous Chapters of this book the methodology described for communicating with funding sources was discussed in general terms. The importance of both composing and sending letters to funding agencies is only one-half of the picture. It is essential to understand what is being said in the letters sent to you as a project writer as well as those to the institution. All that can be said about the project will not always be committed to writing. Particularly in the Federal sector, the number of approvals required from superiors before a letter is dispatched would stagger the imagination. Thus, the very controversial letter is seldom sent.

Examples of communications given in this Chapter have been disguised so that they are not readily traceable. The basic content of each letter or "extract" is from an actual case. Attention should be directed to the content of the letter and "extracts" rather than to the format.

LETTERS OF ENCOURAGEMENT

The most appealing letter other than an award is referred to as a *Letter* of *Encouragement*. Normally after a proponent funding agency receives a preliminary proposal an internal review process takes place. *Letters of Encouragement* may also come as a result of unusual reviews for formal proposals. In Figure 7 is an example of a formal proposal which went through the entire review process and was "encouraged" but at a different funding level than was originally requested. This is not uncommon — and particularly true of projects which will yield a great impact.

A trend which is increasing in frequency may be unfamiliar to many of the readers. Instead of requesting a formal or preliminary proposal which is the most common, a request for an abstract will be made. Those abstracts which appear to be interesting to the agency will result in a request for a formal proposal or a more detailed preliminary proposal. Another trend which is quite new is requesting only the title of projects. Interesting titles will be matched against the interests of the agency making the request and when titles are found to fit the interests, the writers will be contacted and either an abstract or preliminary proposal will be requested. This new approach to request for titles of projects has been used by the United States Department of Agriculture.

Do not plan to spend the money when a letter of encouragement has been received. There is a *very* long way between the encouragement and the actual award.

Many factors influence the outcome. Some of these factors are: National economy; upcoming Congressional elections (changes National priorities); and the manpower needs of a particular segment of our population. These are normally referred to as *"external pressures"* and may be a facet of the process which causes the denial of a project even when the quality of the proposal is excellent. The action officer will normally communicate this to you but not in writing — should quality and excellence be present. He will probably not tell you of the *"external pressures"* if the project was evaluated as mediocre or marginal in any way.

In the example shown in Figure 7, the National Solar Foundation asked for a revised proposal by a certain date. In all cases this courtesy will not be extended. If no date for return is included, the best procedure to follow is to reply immediately and say the proposal will be revised and that meetings are being arranged with administrative officials to discuss the alternatives. Also tell the agency that by a certain date the Agency will receive the revised proposal. This is quite important. It is for two reasons that this *"instant"* reply is used. One, it lets the funding agency know of the intentions of the proposed funded project. Second, it alerts the agency to watch out for the receipt of the proposal. Do this without delay.

LETTERS OF AWARD

Awards are made to an institution with the principal investigator (project director) serving as an agent to conduct the project. Sample awards letters are found in Figures 8, 9 and 10.

The president is the only one person authorized to accept an award for a college or university. He or she may delegate this responsibility and authority. Normally, but not always the funding agency sends the formal

NATIONAL SOLAR FOUNDATION
SOLAR BOULEVARD
SOLAR, COLORADO 56789

Office of the Director   January 31, 1976

Dr. Sam Y. Ghoetel
Energy Coordinator
The University of Energy Study
Cape Harvard - Yale, Florida 36764

Dear Doctor Ghoetel:

This letter is in response to your proposal number 45678 sent to the NSF on July 3, 1975. Your proposal was read and reviewed by the staff of the NSF and by two independent panels consisting of up to fifteen total members.

Each of those who read your proposal agreed that in principle, the content was both innovative and quite worthwhile. I personally, found the interface between the nuclear facilities in Arkansas and the fossil fuel facilities in Mississippi fascinating.

Your proposal was just a bit above the average in scoring, but because of the innovation and the interface with industry with two forms of energy along with solar energy each of the nineteen persons who read your proposal suggested that it be funded if certain criteria were met.

The original proposal was for five years duration and at a level of $500,000. If you and your institution are willing to accept an award for $100,000 for a twelve month period, and can revise the content to show that the project can be piloted in that twelve month period, the staff of the NSF will reconsider the amended proposal without outside review. At the end of the one-year period your project will be reevaluated for an additional two year funding.

We at the NSF hope that you will consider rewriting the proposal and justify the piloted period of one year. Because of stringent funding, your proposal in the revised form must reach the Foundation no later than February 15, 1976.

Sincerely,

J.H. Frederlewer, Ph.D.
Deputy Director

copy: President Lewelleyn Yourter-House

Figure 7   •   LETTER OF ENCOURAGEMENT

letter of award to the president and an information copy to the principal investigator. Some agencies (private and Federal) state that the award is contingent upon formal acceptance by the president of the organization or university.

Clauses in Letters of Award — Clauses are becoming more common in communications from funding agencies. For example, an award may be made but one sentence may read. . . . *"expenditures under the provisions of this grant may not be made until after July 1, 1976."* The award letter may be dated January 1, 1976. Another clause might be. . . . *"this grant is being made for three years, however, funds are being allocated only for one year — every effort will be made to fund this project but due to stringent funding pressures, funds for succeeding years will have to be based upon the availability of funds and the results of reexamining program priorities".* This means the principal investigator had better *produce* during the first year or multiple funding will *not* result.

Make very sure that you read the award letter with much care. There is a tendency to become elated during the time an award letter makes an appearance. Note that the clause cited above awards a grant but with no funds to begin until after July 1. This is a six month period without support.

From the clause given relative to multiple year funding, one should construe a site visit is certain at the end of the first year — that is if all goes as planned according to the project plan. The progress reports during the first year should be clear and concise — reports that are able to communicate the whole story. Under the pressure that such a clause gives to the project operation — whether or not progress reports are requested, take the initiative to prepare a summary report every three months. If no standards or format are required, make sure the report does not exceed three typewritten pages. Agencies and their action officers appreciate it when you keep them informed.

NATIONAL TECHNOLOGY FOUNDATION
Washington, D.C. 20559

October 26, 1975

Dr. Robert Bee, President
State University of Wyoming and Systems   Grant: ILY-2
Stillwaters, Wyoming 47070   Proposal No. TXS-2U

Dear Doctor Bee:

It is a pleasure to inform you that $87,000 is granted to State University of
Wyoming and Systems for support of the 1976 Summer Institute as outlined
in the above numbered proposal. This project is under the direction of
Professor John Love.

The funds provided by this grant are intended to support the project in
accordance with the attached budget summary. The grant will expire on
September 30, 1976.

The indirect cost rate shown in the attached budget summary is a fixed,
predetermined rate which is not subject to adjustment.

The provisions of "Grants for Education in Technology" (NTF 92-9) and
the "College Professors Programs-Guide for Preparation of Proposals and
Operation of Projects" (Z-92-Z-89), copies of which have been sent to your
Business Office and Project Director, are applicable to this grant.

Sincerely yours,

Charles Friendly
Grants Officer

Enclosures

Figure 8   •   LETTER OF AWARD

STATE ARTS AND HUMANITIES COUNCIL
City, State 83119

January 29, 1976

Dr. Howard Harrold
Head, School of Arts and Humanities
State University of New Hampshire
Nashua, New Hampshire 79012

Dear Doctor Harrold:

The State Arts and Humanities Council has voted to assist the Humanities Forum scheduled for June 19-20, 1976, in the amount of up to $16,750 as per approved budget, based on actual deficit incurred at the conclusion of the project.

Information, terms and conditions of the grant are outlined on the enclosed pages. Please read these pages carefully to avoid possible delay.

In particular, may we call your attention to the requirement that reference be made to the *Humanities Task Force of the State* in all publicity and printed material. Failure to comply with this grant condition could seriously affect this and future grants.

Thank you for your prompt response to these conditions and best wishes for a most successful project.

Sincerely yours,

I.M. Pleased
Executive Director

Enclosures

Copy: President Arjay Jose III

Figure 9 • *LETTER OF AWARD*

THE PRIVATE FOUNDATION, INCORPORATED
NEW YORK PLAZA
New York, New York 10016

February 3, 1976

Dr. James Courtland Zee-Allen
Department of Sociology
University of Utopia
Anywhere, USA 39909

Dear Doctor Zee-Allen:

We are glad to report that the Staff of the Associate Programs has approved your request in the amount of $46,450 from the Associates Projects Fund for your proposal.

Our check in the above amount will be sent to your President in the Spring of 1976, as you requested for your use in carrying out this project.

Sincerely,

A.P. Nartec Smith
Program Secretary
Private Foundation Associate
Programs

Copy: President Gordon Dreamawhyle

Figure 10 • *LETTER OF AWARD*

LETTERS OF DENIAL

In the next several pages actual samples of letters of denial and "extracts" of specific reasons for denial have been included. Figures 11, 12, 13, 14 and 15 illustrate various funding sources and a variety of disciplines seeking funds. Paragraphs have been taken out of context from other denial letters and are likewise included.

Extracts of Specific Reasons for Denial—

....."Thank you for your recent request for a critique of the above referenced proposal to the (Blank) Agency. It is our policy to provide such information to the person responsible for the content of the proposal (i.e., the proposed Principal Investigator) so that the proposer may have the benefit of an objective review as he or she considers future plans. We shall be happy to release this information upon receipt of written permission from the proposed Principal Investigator or from the academic officer who countersigned the proposal on behalf of the institution."

....."After carefully studying your proposal and the comments of the reviewers, we are unable to relate any significant weakness to you. The major reason that the (Blank) Agency did not support your project was our lack of funds to provide for all of the proposals judged to have substantial scientific and educational merit. Again this year, only proposals which ranked very high could be granted ½ of the 1976 proposals received, 510 resulted in grants. We make every attempt to maintain objective grading standards, but when the competition is so keen, decisions clearly favor proposals which strike some special spark of interest in the reviewers."

....."Actually there was nothing "wrong" with your proposal, and consequently, I really cannot offer any suggestions as to how you might improve it. Our limited funds enabled us to support only proposals that were in the highest merit categories ½ those that struck some special spark of interest in the reviewers. We are at a complete loss as to how to tell you in what way you might add this indefinable something to your project. You can guess our regret over having to deny proposals as substantial as your own, and over our inability to offer any really constructive advice."

....."In studying the staff and outside reviewers' comments, I note that your proposal was assigned to a generally meritorious category, but not to the high priority group. Several basic points appear to have prevented its receiving a higher rating. (List of specifics would follow)...."

....."In your proposal, some items of scientific equipment requested appeared to cover basic needs of your department, as contrasted to that needed to implement a specific course improvement. Such requests compete poorly, since in them it is difficult to maintain focus on the particular curricular developments intended, and on the relationship of each item of equipment to these improvements."

....."Apparatus which tends to duplicate equipment already on hand must be especially carefully justified, since the natural assumption is that it relates primarily to enrollment pressure or obsolescence. Specifically, the following items in your proposal were questioned by the reviewers. (The specific items would follow)...."

....."With regard to your request for library materials, I should like to suggest that you consider another funding source. The United States Department of Libraries administers Title 987 of the Post Secondary Education Act of 1977. Title 987 offers assistance to institutions of higher education and private research libraries of library materials, microfiche equipment and readers which are needed for expanded responsibilities in research. You may find that Title 987 and its programs will be more applicable to your needs."

....."While the reviewers know the basic capabilities of most scientific equipment, it is incumbent upon proposers to make clear the correlation between their plans for the research and the equipment they request   to state quite specifically how they plan to utilize the equipment in their project. In many cases it is wise to outline the new experiments which the requested equipment would make possible. Several reviewers felt that your proposal was deficient in this area, a sample comment reading, "(Blank)." (A comment would be taken out of context but verbatim from the proposal reviewers' file)...."

....."In summary, the "ideal" proposal in this program is one which (a) critically defines some deficiency in a research sequence; (b) presents a sound plan for the correction of this deficiency; (c) gives evidence of sufficient expertise in the present faculty to carry out the project; and (d) presents a list of equipment that is precisely correlated to the planned research, and that is appropriate in terms of its level of precision and sophistication."

The following pages represent sample letters of denial. One must understand in large programs the numbers of project denials preclude being very personal and individual. However, whenever you receive a denial, and it is very clear that no specifics of your project are included, write the agency and request specific reasons for the denial of your project. Do it in a positive spirit and ask for a reply at the convenience of the agency. This will be very valuable for future projects you write.

AGENCY FOR AEROSOL RESEARCH
Arlington, Virginia 20333

January 31, 1976

Professor Mary-Richards Tyler-Moore
University Research Center
Bowie, Maryland 20715

Re: Grant Proposal: Zeta-RUT-106

Dear Professor Tyler-Moore:

The above referenced proposal submitted by you has been reviewed. I am sorry to inform you that it has been rejected for funding by the Agency.

Two principal criticisms were made. They were: (1) the proposal did not clearly express the investigator's knowledge of the complex problems involved in relating atmospheric behavior of the aerosol size distributions and pollutants. Serious gaps were left in the discussion of aerosol physics; (2) the dependence on other investigators for the basic data. In relation to the latter, it would have been helpful if the necessary coordination had been undertaken beforehand so that assurances could have been given that this data would be available when needed.

Your interest in the research problems in air pollution is deeply appreciated.

Franklin P. Size
Director

Copy: Dr. Zebulon Zee-Zady
Director, University Research Center

Figure 11 • LETTER OF DENIAL

DEPARTMENT OF INSTRUMENTS
Washington, D.C. 20120

Re: 92/Y50-7321

January 31, 1976

Department of Curriculum Improvement
My State University
Yourez, North Dakota 77745

Dear Doctor Ellizer:

In response to a request from Dr. Chares Whitehed, Director of Research, we have prepared a critique of your proposal to the Department of Instruments.

With three programs to conduct, the staff has had to schedule its work very carefully. While delayed, this response will reach you in good time to be considered in relation to your plans for 1977.

In the present extremely competitive situation, successful proposals are those which convince your peers that:

(a) the local faculty has identified a significant deficiency in their existing curriculum;

(b) the proposer has formulated a remedy that is reasonably up-to-date, and is both scientifically and pedagogically sound in terms of the presentation methods and the adequacy and balance of the content of the revised course;

(c) the prescribed remedy is suited to the student audience to whom it is addressed; and

(d) the gains (both in terms of relative improvement and of the number of students affected) justify the cost of the project.

Not until these basic points are satisfied do evaluators turn attention to the instruments request itself.

In assigning your project a rating that fell below this year's uncomfortably high cut-off point, reviewers remarked,

"Improvement program worthwhile but total department commitment not evident."

"No basic science prerequisite to the project is mentioned. To get maximum benefit from the instruments requested, some basic understanding would be helpful. Otherwise, becomes knob-spinning."

I hope that the Department's inability to reward your efforts has not brought progress to a halt, nor occasioned you any great discouragement. Should you decide to enter the FY 1977 competition, I hope that the result will be a happier one.

Sincerely yours,

Alexander Frouwnhoust
Deputy Director

Copy: President Merel Cummerbunder

Figure 12 • LETTER OF DENIAL

ENDOWMENT FOR THE THEATRE
Capitol City Complex
Columbia, Maryland 20716

February 22, 1976
Ref. Application 7654

Professor Euling Volks
University of Romance Study
Mountain View Top, Colorado 83210

Dear Professor Volks:

I am sorry to inform you that your application for support from the Endowment for the Theatre has not been approved.

Since the Endowment's funds are very limited, and the National competition for those funds is intense, often we find ourselves having to choose between applications all of which have merit.

To help insure that our judgements are informed and objective, the Endowment required that every application be carefully reviewed by the panel of outstanding persons in the humanities and other appropriate fields. The National Council of Theatre, an advisory group of distinguished private citizens appointed by the President of the United States must also, by Law, review and make recommendation on each application. I recognize that this cannot allay your disappointment or my regret, but at least I can assure you that your application received full, careful attention.

We appreciate the opportunity to learn something of your work, and we are grateful for the interest that led you to apply for our support. We hope that other means of carrying out your project will be available.

Sincerely,

Robert Hargis Looktoburner, Jr.
Chairman

Copy: Dr. Bill Jones, President

Figure 13 • *LETTER OF DENIAL*

DEPARTMENT OF OPERA AND MUSIC
Washington, D.C. 20203

January 31, 1976

Re: Proposal No. 75-043

Dr. Robert L.T. Mood
Professor of Opera
University of Sunshine
Cloud, Oregon 55512

Dear Professor Mood:

We regret that the Office of Opera and Music is unable to support your proposal referenced above.

A number of factors were considered in evaluating each proposal submitted to the Department. Careful consideration is given to the National educational and social significance, soundness of the rationale and design, procedure or plan, adequacy of personnel and facilities, and economic efficiency. The review procedure makes support decisions a matter of selection rather than rejection of proposed projects. The problem of selecting the most meritorious projects is illustrated by the fact that out of 108 proposals officially transmitted to the Program in response to the September 6, 1975 deadline, the Department is supporting only seven.

Although we cannot support your request, we encourage your continuing interest in music research. If you wish further details about the evaluation of your proposal, please contact me by letter or telephone.

Sincerely yours,

Honorable Harvey Singer
Secretary

CC: President Thomas Xavier Zilch

Figure 14 • LETTER OF DENIAL

THE UNITED STATES GOVERNMENT CENTER
FOR SPACE RESEARCH

Greenbelt, Michigan 33333

January 31, 1976

Dr. Gloria Robinson Redster
Space Research Department
State University of Florida
Atares, Florida 37540

Dear Dr. Redster:

Your Research Proposal No. 7506312 entitled, "Improvement of Measurement of Atmospheric Electricity on Jupiter" has now been evaluated by the CSR staff and independent referees.

In the allocation of our research funds, several factors are considered: scientific merit, relevance to CSR, contribution to CSR's high priority scientific goals, compatibility with the overall field experiment, etc.

Although this proposal obtained good ratings in several areas, it has been rejected because the CSR's program in atmospheric electricity will not be implemented in Summer, 1976. As the program develops, the Director of CSR plans to devote a greater effort in this area, and at that time, contributions from the universities will be sought and considered.

Thank you very much for your interest in participating in the National Research Experiment.

Very truly yours,

John Moongloe
Chief Scientist, CSR

Copy: Dr. Charles Glow, Director
Space Research Department

Figure 15 • LETTER OF DENIAL

CONCLUSION

Communications from potential funding agencies and organizations require discernment and understanding to determine the exact messages being sent. Letters received may include those of encouragement, award, and denial. Examples of all types have been provided to give indications of the possible variations and nuances. Each example in the book and those actually received by proposal writers should be studied with care and used as learning mechanisms for the improvement of future endeavors.

Chapter Seven

THE REVIEW PROCESS

INTRODUCTION

One of the most misunderstood and little known procedures which ultimately decides the fate of a proposal submitted for funding is the *Review Process*. Much has been written in magazines, periodicals, books and the literature in very general terms. But little has been written about the review process in detail. This Chapter will be devoted to such coverage in detail of the various processes used throughout the proposal funding community. In general, this will cover the Federal government, private industry, private foundations and contracted review groups. The Chapter cannot in all cases deal with specifics because of limited space; however, wherever and whenever possible detailed descriptions will be given.

The basic review scheme used today is called the *peer review*. With mechanical modifications of the peer review we have the mail review, panel review and council review. This system has been under fire for the past two years with pressures being exerted by the United States Congress on the National Institutes of Health and the National Science Foundation. Phillip Boffey in the lead line of his recent article in the *Chronicle of Higher Education* said, *"Scientists Fear 'Sacrosanct' System Of Making Federal Grants May Be In Peril."*[1] More discussion pertaining to the *peer review system* will appear throughout this Chapter and remarks relative to the current attacks on the *peer review system* will be made.

PEER REVIEW

In general, all proposals sent to a proponent funding agency are reviewed by professional peers representing a particular profession or specialty. Review procedures differ in mechanics but seldom differ in principle. The funding agency whether it be a private foundation, an industrial entity or a Federal agency, prior to convening or mailing a proposal to an expert, sets specific criteria and reporting forms — which in essence assigns quantitative values to each proposal that agency has received.

A mechanism at each college, university, corporation or organization should be instituted so that preliminary proposals can undergo the scrutiny and be evaluated in a similar fashion. Also found in this Chapter are examples suitable for adoption in your own particular individual environment.

Funding agencies normally assign one person to supervise a fundable program. Titles vary for these individuals.

Examples are, *program manager, project manager, program director, branch chief, executive officer, program officer* or *action officer.* This person behind the scenes is one of the *most important* persons in the funding process. More often than not this person in the position of action officer holds a doctorate in his specialty. The office he or she may occupy may not be the posh office with the expensive furniture and decor of others in the organization you visit. A look in the *American Men of Science, Who's Who in America, Who's Who of American Women* and similar biographies of notables will probably reveal this person's name and background. His or her educational background will probably include a professorship, research papers, a department chair or perhaps a deanship or vice presidency. Of course, some action officers have slipped in without the background either through *the buddy buddy system* or politics. By-and-large this is a minority number and we should be thankful for that.

The action officer may be the initial person choosing the reviewers, setting up the panels, recommending the proposal for funding or recommending a proposal for denial. The action officer is responsible for the cut-off point for the proposals to be funded from those not to be funded. It is well to know the individuals who will be involved in handling your proposal— whether it be a preliminary (informal) or a formally submitted proposal. It is folly to send a proposal to an agency to be funded without doing a considerable amount of homework. The homework should include finding the individual desk or person who will review and act upon the proposal. The proposal when submitted should adhere to the *guidelines* which are published by the funding agency. Always obtain *guidelines* when available. If the *guidelines* are in transition at the time you are submitting a preliminary proposal refer to the last previously published *guidelines* as your source of procedures.

The reviewers are given the same *guidelines* the prospective grantee receives along with verbal instructions which amplify points not delineated in the *guidelines*. It would be impossible to include, if they were available, samples of all instructions given to reviewers. To illustrate some of the points covered, examples which affect the broadest reader population are included.

PANEL REVIEW

The panel review is part of the peer review system. This methodology involves convening a group or several groups of technically qualified people from universities (more often than not), from industry, private foundations and Government (Federal, State and Municipal), etc. The procedure varies, but most of the agencies send advance material for study to the reviewers which includes the *program guidelines* and the requirements for conducting the review of the proposals. In addition, information is included as to the location of the scheduled meeting, travel information, and specific instructions not given to the writer of the proposal to assist in the review process. If the funding agency's action officer has done the necessary homework, a statistical breakdown of the proposals received will be included in the packet. Fellow reviewers are not usually identified until the first general meeting takes place at the site of the evaluation. Depending upon the number of proposals and the intent of the funding agency, one city will be chosen for the review meeting. Private foundations often choose New York City. This is probably because of the large number of foundations headquartered in New York City. New York, Chicago, Dallas, Atlanta and Los Angeles are also common choices for these activities — mainly because of the ease of getting in and out by air travel. For the Federal agencies, Washington, D.C. usually wins out.

Typically the action officer will speak first welcoming the group and assuring each present how fortunate they were to be among the few hand-chosen for this exercise. In fact, one should consider himself fortunate if chosen to be a reviewer. Those who have served or are serving in this capacity are exposed to more of the pitfalls of proposals and the reasons why proposals are accepted or rejected for funding. Thus, it would stand to reason with such exposure, one should become more proficient when the reviewer returns home to write his or her proposal as a result of this experience.

The next part of the discussion from the podium will cover the grading system and how it will be employed. The program officials will identify to the audience who the chairpersons will be for each group of panelists. Those chosen for this task have no doubt served on that or similar programs several times. Chairpersons will not be determined by vote of each panel — the chairperson was designated well in advance of the panel meeting. Some agencies send a different packet of material to those chosen to serve as chairpersons. Panelists will be told that the Agency will do everything in its power to protect the names of the reviewers under the limitations of the Freedom of Information Act (5 U.S. Code 552).[2]

Instructions will be given how to complete the answer sheets. The reviewer will be asked only to make *many comments* and not place a numerical grade on the answer sheet. The *kiss of death* to a future review panel experience is not to write comments on the answer sheets. This is a sure way to insure never to be reinvited. The narrative comments are what the action officer and his staff must use to separate borderline cases. It is wise to pay close attention to the podium for what they are telling the reviewers are the important breakdowns in the system and how to avoid being caught by them. The speech from the podium may appear extemporaneous but it is not. The speech probably was written twenty-five times and approved by an equal number of people. If the panel is conducted in more than one city — the identical words will be spoken in the other cities whether it be by the same person or other staff members.

Other points not found in writing will be discussed. They can be called items referring to *ethics*. The panelists will be told not to arrive at grades based upon known politics existing at an institution but *only on the merits of the proposal itself*. The project itself, and the ability of the individual to perform as stated in the proposal, should be the basic and the only criteria for consideration. The reviewers will be told not to right social injustices, internal institutional politics, and mere opinions —these are outside the arena of the panelists. The panelists will be asked, if proposals from their own institutions happen (by error) to come to their panel, to merely step outside the room during the judging and wait to be recalled by the chairperson or another member of the group should it be the chairperson's institution. Reviewers will also be reminded that they are professionals and that as panelists they are not permitted to talk about proposals at meetings in the hallway or lunch or at any future time — this is particularly true pertaining to individuals who may have submitted proposals. Lastly, the reviewers are asked not to accidentally take any proposals when they are ready to return to their homes.

MECHANICAL MIX OF PANELISTS — An ideal mechanical mix is a panel consisting of five members (4 plus a chairperson) with a variance of expertise which covers the gamut of that particular discipline being reviewed. In addition, the same proposals would be examined and graded by a second panel of equally qualified persons from similar backgrounds. The second panel is not known to the first panel. The proposals are read first by each individual on a particular panel. He or she according to the grading scheme employed would place on the grading sheet comments and arrive at a numerical grade. After each of the panel members completed either one or several in this manner (as decided by the chairperson) the chairperson would ask each panelist on a rotating basis to defend and summarize each proposal outlining the strengths and weaknesses. At that time each panel member would have the opportunity to contribute reactions and evaluations on the proposal. On a separate grading sheet the individual assigned to conduct the major discussion for the particular proposal or the chairperson records all of the comments given by the panelists on the summary sheet. The numerical grades are likewise posted on the summary sheets and a consensus letter grade is assigned. Commonly the letter grades used are **"D"**, **"M" and "H"**. The letters meaning, **"D"** for **"disaster"**, or **"disallowed"** or **"denial"**; **"M"** for **"mediocre"**, **"middle of the lot"** or **"marginal"**; and **"H"** for **"highly meritorious"**, **"high value"** or **"high"**. One common numerical scheme used is **"D"** equal to **1, 2 or 3**; **"M"** equal to **4, 5, 6, or 7**; and **"H"** equal to **7, 8, 9 or 10.** When the action officer reviews the results of the two panels letter combinations may be: **HH; HM; HD; MM and MD.** It should become obvious at this point that the two panels have served as discriminators for the group of the proposals submitted. The action officer is also provided with raw numerical scores for each panel representing the individual panelists' experience and point of view. These numerical scores are totaled and also serve as discriminators. Two five-person panels could give the same proposal the grade of "HH". However, the total raw score of Panel One was 45 and the total raw score of Panel Two was 40 or a grade of "HH" 85. The total possible points for two five panel grades would be (by the system elucidated in this example) "HH" 100. "HD" grades are resolved in many ways. If enough time is given and this is detected before the panels break up, the "HD" proposals are given to a third panel.

Often the resolution is made by the staff members of the funding agency. Sometimes a proposal marked *"D"* in an *"HD"* situation holds and in other cases it is resolved to an *"M"* or *"H"* and ends up as a fundable project.

When agencies employ economy and use one panel, it can be readily seen that the probability of bias being introduced is increased. Another shortcoming is introduced when the panel is drastically cut to two or three members. The former has happened in some instances. This could be the result of poor planning by the action officer. It could be from poor backing and the lack of support by his superiors. Whatever, it reflects poor planning and management in general. The planning must take into consideration scheduled events. For example, one would not like to have projects which require the expertise of astronomers scheduled for evaluation on the day of an announced eclipse. Do not laugh — it actually happened. It is strange to see proposals evaluated with members standing at the window behind a shade made of aluminum foil fastened to the window with masking tape and a pin hole made in the foil for observation.

To illustrate the types of documents distributed to reviewers for panel evaluation of proposals the following samples have been used by the National Science Foundation for the Instructional Scientific Equipment Program. *Figures 16 and 17 illustrate the PROPOSAL EVALUATION and the CONSENSUS REPORT SHEETS used by panelists.*

INSTRUCTIONS TO PANELISTS

NOTE: EXPERIENCED PANELISTS ARE PARTICULARLY CAUTIONED TO NOTE THAT SEVERAL SIGNIFICANT CHANGES FROM PAST OPERATIONS IN GRADING PROCEDURES AND PHILOSOPHY ARE DESCRIBED IN THESE INSTRUCTIONS.

The Instructional Scientific Equipment Program of the National Science Foundation provides assistance to academic units of institutions that propose to improve the quality of their undergraduate science education, and need assistance in acquisition of equipment in order to implement their improvement plans. Proposals are

PACKET_____ PANEL_____ | PROPOSAL NUMBER

PROPOSAL EVALUATION SHEET

SCORE
10 HIGH; 1 LOW

INSTITUTION: _____

1.   Is the institution following its own established priorities in selecting this particular course (or sequence of courses) for improvement? (Is the need for the project apparent? Will it affect a significant body of students? Does this project "make sense" in its institutional and departmental context?)

2.   Are the projected improvements well conceived in terms of their science content? (If implemented, will they facilitate an **adequate** and **balanced** presentation of the **significant** concepts in the field?)

3.   Are the projected improvements educationally well conceived? (Are they clearly designed to deliver a stronger, more modern course to the students? Do they provide for adequate "hands-on" experience? Are they well suited to the student audience in question?[1] Are the proposed teaching techniques efficient in comparison with other available teaching methodologies? Are there beneficial side effects in terms of imaginative teaching methodology? Is desirable flexibility given adequate attention?)

---

[1] NB. Courses for technician training, science for humanities majors, junior college students, pre-service teachers and other non-science majors are as eligible for support as courses for students majoring in the disciplines.

Figure 16 • PROPOSAL EVALUATION SHEET

4.   Is the equipment requested **necessary** and **appropriate** to carrying out the stated aims of the project? (Does it effectively supplement current holdings? Is the cost per student affected reasonable? If the request is overly modest, indicate here what upgrading or additions would strengthen it. If the request is extravagant, note in #5.)

5.   Does any of the equipment have only marginal value to the aims of the project? (Note here any items ineligible under the guidelines, possible reductions where an excessive number of a given instrument is requested, cases where less sophisticated models would be equally effective substitutes for the more expensive models requested, and items which could be eliminated outright without seriously impairing the project.)

6.   Are the project director and other faculty members associated with this project likely to mount an effective attack on the existing weaknesses, and do they appear to be technically competent to produce significant course improvements? (Faculty expertise need only be adequate to the project — not necessarily outstanding in absolute terms.)

7.   Other comments:

_____

PANELIST (PLEASE PRINT LAST NAME)

Figure 16 • *PROPOSAL EVALUATION SHEET, Continued*

CONSENSUS REPORT

	CONSENSUS GRADE*
CHAIRMAN:	
PANEL :	
Director : _____	
Institution : _____	

PANELIST'S INITIALS						TOTAL
INDIVIDUAL PANELIST'S RATINGS (10 HIGH, 1 LOW)						

General Recommendations and Comments (especially desirable):

*H - HIGHLY MERITORIOUS
M - MERITORIOUS
D - OF DOUBTFUL MERIT

Figure 17 • CONSENSUS REPORT SHEET

selected for award on the basis of their scientific and educational merit. Therefore, as a PANELIST you are asked to provide the Foundation with wise counsel in selecting those proposals that offer the greatest promise of relative local improvement.

Panelists' comments on proposals under review by this program are solicited and received in confidence by the National Science Foundation, an agency of the U. S. Government, and will be given maximum protection from disclosure permitted under applicable laws, including 5 U.S.C. 552 (THE FREEDOM OF INFORMATION ACT).

It should be emphasized that the program aspires to support proposals offering the promise of greatest relative qualitative improvement in their undergraduate science curriculum. While panels should not concern themselves with the relative affluence or poverty of a given institution, they should bear in mind that it is relative improvement (not absolute level of quality) that is to prevail in the evaluation. HOWEVER, THERE MUST BE A SUFFICIENT BASE OF STRENGTH AND PROFICIENCY DESCRIBED IN THE PROPOSAL TO ASSURE THAT THE PROJECT FOR IMPROVEMENT CAN BE CARRIED OUT WITH A REASONABLE CHANCE OF SUCCESS.

The curricular improvement proposed should involve an updating or upgrading in the subject-matter content of the undergraduate program at the institution. Such improvement takes priority over improvement in the instructional efficiency (i.e., the efficiency with which the present curriculum is taught) of an institution. In addition, normal expansion of an institution or increases in enrollment are not suitable justification for an award. Of course, such expansion or enrollment increase may trigger a reevaluation of the curriculum and consequently changes in the content of a curriculum — as this is often the case, a proposal should not be discredited because of COINCIDENTAL quantitative increases. Similarly, no penalty should be exacted for coincidental improvement in instructional efficiency in a good proposal.

There are now several programs in several Federal agencies through which it is possible to obtain scientific equipment, although the justification in each case is markedly different. In the evaluation of proposals to this program, the possible suitability of the proposal to another program should NOT enter into the evaluation; it will be sufficient to judge the proposal on its merits, provided that the objectives are coincident with those of the Instructional Scientific Equipment Program.

Proposers have been asked to provide information on the following items:

1. the particular curricular pattern to be improved,
2. the way in which the requested support will lead to improvement,
3. the competence of the staff to carry out the improved program as well as the improvement,
4. recent changes in the unit seeking support,
5. current holdings of major equipment items that are directly related to the proposed project, and

6. the specific desired purchases and their relationship to the planned improvement.

You should expect proposals to contain at least information relevant to the above six topics, and any other information necessary for you to make an informed judgement. Proposals must demonstrate that informed, realistic planning has ALREADY TAKEN PLACE and that the improvement proposed lacks only the equipment for full implementation. In judging the OVER-ALL MERIT of each proposal, the following broad characteristics should be carefully examined:

1. the scientific and educational soundness of the objectives of the proposed project,
2. the detailed plans for the use of the equipment to meet the objectives of the project,
3. the ability of the proposer as measured by both staff and physical facilities to carry out the project, and
4. the propriety of the equipment selected for the project.

With regard to the last of these characteristics, the equipment requested should be of a design and quality appropriate to the project proposed. It should be borne in mind that current undergraduate science programs often utilize a broad range of equipment, from very simple to very complex. Therefore no TYPE of equipment is AUTOMATICALLY ineligible for support by this program — the level of sophistication of the proposed project should be the guide to the propriety of a particular item.

In general, the size of the dollar request or the numbers of items requested should NOT be of concern during the evaluation of a proposal. However, there may occur instances in which it is felt for various reasons that the fiscal aspects of an otherwise sound proposal affect its merit. The accompanying document, GRADES AND GRADING PROCEDURES, includes procedures to be followed in the event that your consideration of the proposal's budget becomes appropriate. Because your counsel on the substantive aspects of the proposals is valuable to the Foundation, we ask that you follow carefully the recommendations on the "GRADES AND GRADING PROCEDURES" document concerning fiscal matters; PLEASE DO NOT LET SUCH MATTERS INTERFERE WITH THE MORE IMPORTANT EXAMINATION OF THE SCIENTIFIC CONTENT OF A PROPOSAL. Of course, separating consideration of academic matter from budgetary factors does NOT preclude your judging the competence of the staff on the basis of the logic displayed in their preparing the proposal's budget.

Subsequent to panel review, proposals will be read by the Foundation staff to provide additional opinion on the merit of the proposals and especially to check on matters of adherence to regulations and policies of the program. Therefore, consideration of program policy, institutional eligibility, etc., should NOT affect your evaluation of a proposal. However, your comments concerning a possible question of policy or other consideration on your evaluation sheet would be valuable in calling the staff's attention to possibly important considerations.

Proposers are specifically requested to prepare their proposals so sufficient information is provided to permit an effective evaluation. Therefore, panelists should NOT read into a proposal what may appear at first glance to be an obvious omission. Of course, your knowledge of certain facts pertinent to a given proposal will enter into your evaluation even though that knowledge may not be described in the proposal; please be certain, however, that if such facts affect the evaluation they are described in your comments on the pink evaluation sheet. Furthermore, proposals should be examined with the Instructional Scientific Equipment Program objectives AS THEY ARE in mind.

The Foundation solicits your opinion on the objectives of the program, and would appreciate any suggestions, written or oral, that you care to make to the program staff.

GRADES AND GRADING PROCEDURES

GRADES: Two types of grades are used. Each panelist assigns an individual numerical grade and each panel assigns a consensus letter grade. The letter grades are defined as follows:

> H = Highly Meritorious, eminently worthy of support;
> M = Meritorious, sound and supportable if funds are available; and
> D = Of Doubtful Merit, recommended denial.

The individual numerical grades range from 1 (low) to 10 (high). A relationship between the individual numerical grades and the consensus letter grades may be expressed as follows:
> H = 8, 9, or 10;
> M = 4, 5, 6, or 7; and
> D = 1, 2, or 3.

BASIC GRADING PROCEDURE:

Each panel member is requested to express his evaluation of each proposal by assigning an individual numerical grade. The accompanying document, "Instructions to Panelists," enlarges on the criteria to be examined during this evaluation. This grade should reflect the individual panelist's judgment of the proposal.

After each panelist has assigned a numerical grade to a proposal, the panel should during its discussion of the proposal arrive at a consensus that may be expressed by one of the three letter grades. PLEASE NOTE THAT IT IS NOT NECESSARY FOR THE PANEL LETTER GRADE TO BE CONSISTENT WITH THE AVERAGE OF THE INDIVIDUAL PANEL SCORES. By the same token, a panelist may make an observation during the discussion of the proposal that he had earlier overlooked; if this observation prompts him to change his numerical score, he may do so. PLEASE DO NOT ASSIGN PLUS OR MINUS SIGNS TO EITHER LETTER OR NUMERICAL SCORES. ONE SUCH SIGN IS USED AS A SPECIFIC SIGNAL AS DESCRIBED BELOW.

BUDGETARY CONSIDERATIONS:

You may have noticed that no mention has been made of the fiscal aspects of a proposal; the evaluation has been concerned with only the academic and scientific aspects of the proposal. The letter and numerical scores thus obtained reflect the panel's evaluation of the proposed idea and the soundness of the idea's implementation.

After (and only after) such a judgment has been made, the panel may observe that certain budgetary factors deserve attention. For example, it may be felt that the objectives of the project are attainable at a lower cost, or the proposal may contain one or a few items that appear to be unjustified for an otherwise excellent project. An asterisk should be appended to the panel consensus letter grade of such a proposal. The panel must then record on the yellow comment sheet specific recommendations which, if effected, would eliminate the minus sign. PLEASE DO NOT CHANGE EITHER THE NUMERICAL OR THE LETTER GRADE AS A RESULT OF BUDGETARY CONSIDERATIONS.

MISCELLANEOUS SUGGESTIONS:

In grading a proposal, IT IS MOST IMPORTANT THAT YOU PROVIDE BRIEF WRITTEN NOTES of your consideration on both the individual proposal evaluation sheets and the consensus report form.

Please be certain that the individual numerical scores are correctly entered on both the individual panelist's pink sheet and in the proper box on the chairman's yellow sheet.

If specific questions arise which require additional information before a grade can be assigned, please request an immediate consultation with a Foundation staff member during the panel session.

STUDY SECTION REVIEW

George N. Eaves of the Division of Research Grants at the National Institutes of Health presents the NIH story in his paper published in 1972. Because of the importance and the content of his paper, it was felt that the meaning would be diluted if the entire article were not included.[3]

WHO READS YOUR PROJECT — GRANT APPLICATION TO THE NATIONAL INSTITUTES OF HEALTH?

GEORGE N. EAVES

Executive Secretary, Molecular Biology Study Section,
Division of Research Grants, National Institutes of Health, Bethesda, Maryland

By permission. From Federation Proceedings, 31, 3-9 (1972)

EFFECTIVE COMMUNICATION of scientific information requires that an author have a reliable knowledge of his readers. An author who is preparing a manuscript for publication in a primary journal has no difficulty in imagining his readers; but many authors of research grant proposals are not sure for whom they are writing. To them, the National Institutes of Health (NIH) is a giant, impersonal machine into which a research grant application is inserted at one end and from which a decision emerges at the other. If these authors knew more about the NIH review process, they would have a clearer idea of their audience and might therefore write better proposals. My purpose in writing this article is to describe the process and provide the helpful insight.

The NIH consists of ten Institutes, one Bureau, an International Center, the National Library of Medicine, and six research and service Divisions.[1] The Division of Research Grants exists as a service to the Institutes and other awarding units and to grantees. A primary function of this Division, through its Research Grants Review Branch, is the responsibility for the operation of the Study Sections, which are committees of nongovernment scientists in about 50 different areas of scientific research that provide the peer-group review of applications for research grants. This Division is also responsible for the assignment of applications to Study Sections for scientific review and to Institutes or other awarding units for administration and for possible funding.

ASSIGNMENT OF APPLICATIONS

A project-grant application, duly approved and signed by the appropriate official in the applicant investigator's institution, is submitted to the Division of Research Grants, where scientists read the application and assign it to the Institute or other awarding unit that has responsibility for support of research in that scientific area. Sometimes the proposal overlaps the interests of more than one Institute. In such cases, the application may be assigned to two Institutes.[2] Simultaneously, the application is assigned for scientific appraisal to the Study Section whose members have expertise in the area of the proposed research. When an application is clearly not appropriate to any of the established Study Sections, it may be assigned to an ad hoc Study Section, which will be formed from a group of consultants selected on the basis of their knowledge in the particular field of the application. An application that is not relevant to the institution that submitted it, with a letter of explanation.

The scientist administrators in the Division of Research Grants who assign applications are in no way connected with the Institutes or with their programs. Consequently, applications are objectively assigned to awarding units solely on the basis of approved guidelines that define the areas of research that a particular Institute or other awarding unit may support through research grants.

Who are the scientists who assign the applications? They are Executive Secretaries of Study Sections, with several years of experience in that capacity, who also serve as Referral Officers. A Referral Officer has responsibility for assigning an application to one of five or more Study Sections that together represent a broad scientific discipline. The Referral Officer is familiar with the scientific discipline through his own background and training. As the applications are received from the applicant investigators, the Assistant Chief for Referral, Research Grants Review Branch, or his deputy scans the proposal and makes an initial determination as to its general category. The application is placed on the desk of the Referral Officer with responsibility for that category who first reads and then assigns it to a Study Section and to an awarding unit. If it is not appropriate to any of the Study Sections in the category for which the Referral Officer has responsibility, he will ask the other Referral Officers to read the application and assist in determining the most appropriate assignment.

REVIEW BY STUDY SECTION

The Study Section review for scientific merit is the first step in a dual-review process. The second step is the review by the National Advisory Councils. As far as the preparation of the research grant application is concerned, the initial review is the critical one.

The Study Sections are public advisory committees with 10 to 15 highly qualified consultants, who serve terms of up to 4 years. These members are selected on the basis of their recognized competence and achievements in their respective research fields, and they provide the NIH with the kind of peer judgment that is essential for the most competent scientific review.[3] Each Study Section is served by an Executive Secretary who is a Health Scientist Administrator on the professional staff of the Division of Research Grants. The names of all consultants and Executive Secretaries are listed in NIH Public Advisory Groups: Authority, Structure, Functions, Members,[4] which is issued twice yearly and distributed to the offices of those individuals in universities, colleges, and other nonprofit institutions who are authorized to sign an application for the grantee.[5]

The Executive Secretary is responsible for coordinating and reporting the review of each application assigned to his advisory group. He carefully reads each application and determines whether additional information should be obtained from the investigator. At the same time he determines which two or more members are the best qualified to judge the application in detail. The proposal and any accompanying materials are then mailed to these members, each of whom prepares a detailed written critique of the proposal and sends a copy to the Executive Secretary in advance of the formal meeting of the Study Section. The members receive the applications 6-8 weeks before the meeting date. During each of three annual meetings, each of which lasts 2-3 days, most Study Sections review 50-100 applications. Thus, each member usually reviews 10-20 applications in detail. In addition, each member is expected to read, without preparing a detailed critique, all of the applications to be reviewed during the meeting.

The Executive Secretary is the intermediary between the applicant investigator and the reviewers of the application. Study Section members never contact an applicant investigator directly, but request any information or explanations through the Executive Secretary. Likewise, an applicant investigator never contacts the members in relation to the research grant application; if he wishes to provide additional information he does so through the Executive Secretary. Indeed, the scientist administrator is required to do what he can to ensure that each application to be reviewed is presented to the investigator's best possible advantage and is as complete as possible. The Executive Secretary's experience permits him to recognize those parts of the proposal that may cause difficulties in the review process. Consequently, his request for additional information to be submitted without delay is an attempt to help the investigator avoid those difficulties.

Before the formal meeting of the Study Section, the investigator should feel free to contact the Executive Secretary for answers to questions that he may have. Inquiries may be sent to the same address to which the application was mailed. The letter will reach the appropriate Study Section more rapidly if the investigator's full name, his institution, and the title of the research grant proposal are provided.

The knowledgeable investigator would never rely on a scientist administrator to advise him about the scientific content of the proposal, nor would he merely attempt to meet a submission deadline by providing a minimal amount of information with the anticipation that the remainder would be requested. Many Executive Secretaries and members of Study Sections consider the way an application is written and presented to be a valuable indicator of the investigator's competence and of his attitudes toward the research problem, or to science in general. The investigator is therefore well advised to submit as complete an application as possible; after all, he is, or should be, the best judge of what information is most pertinent to the appraisal of his own research.

STUDY SECTION MEETING

During the formal meeting of the Study Section, each application is discussed individually. The Chairman, who is a member of the Study Section and who presides at the formal meeting, calls first on those members who wrote detailed reviews to present their critiques. Then, the other members are given the opportunity to ask questions or to present their views and opinions.

Study Sections review applications on the basis of scientific merit, which also includes an assessment of the importance of the proposed research problem; the originality of the approach; the training, experience, and research competence or promise of the investigators; the adequacy of the experimental design; the suitability of the facilities; and the appropriateness of the requested budget to the work proposed. The final recommendation of the Study Section, which is made by majority vote of the members, is for one of three options: approval, disapproval, or deferral.

For each approved application, each member privately records a numerical score based on his opinion of scientific merit relative to the "state of the art" of the particular research area. After the meeting the arithmetic means of these scores are computed by the Study Section staff and entered into the computer system of the Division of Research Grants. The scores resulting from this meeting are then merged with the scores from the two previous meetings of the Study Section. This composite distribution is linearly transformed (normalized) to a specified mean and standard deviation that is common to all Study Sections. The priority scores serve as a guide to the National Advisory Councils and the awarding units in their final decisions concerning the order in which approved applications would be funded. These scores are meaningless if considered out of the context of all the approved applications of an awarding unit and without consideration of the program interests of an Institute. Hence, priority scores are treated as confidential.

Councils may not change priority scores; however, some Councils occasionally recommend that an approved application be placed in a category to be funded or in one not to be funded. This classification is based not on scientific merit but on high or low "program relevance." Nevertheless, even when program interests dictate the appropriateness of financial support for a highly relevant project, the priority score guides the final decision about funding.

Immediately after the Study Section meeting, all recommendations on each application are summarized in detail by the Executive Secretary. The summary statements are based on a combination of the reviewers' written critiques and the discussion during the meeting. They also include notations of any special points, such as a split vote or a potentially hazardous experimental procedure, and a recommended budget based on the investigator's requested budget. These summary statements are then transmitted to the appropriate National Advisory Councils, which meet within 6-8 weeks after the meetings of the Study Sections.

Usually, the recommendation of the initial review group for approval or for disapproval of an application is transmitted directly to the National Advisory Council(s) of the Institute(s) to which the application was assigned, but sometimes an application may be deferred for consideration at the next meeting of the Study Section. Deferral for additional information or for a project site visit is recommended for only a few applications, and then only when it is necessary for the review group to obtain additional information for which the need could not be anticipated in advance or when it is necessary, for example, for representatives of the group to observe a special technique or to ascertain the adequacy of an investigator's facilities.

When the initial review of an application is deferred, the requested starting date for a new project could be delayed 4-6 months. An application submitted for any particular deadline (3), however, is reviewed at the Study Section and Council meetings associated with that deadline, regardless of the requested starting date. Consequently, the chances of delaying a new project could be avoided if the application could be submitted for an earlier review.

REVIEW BY NATIONAL ADVISORY COUNCIL

The second and final step in the dual-review process is the Council review. Each grant-awarding unit in the NIH has a National Advisory Council or an equivalent group that must review and recommend approval of an application before it can be awarded. These Councils consist of 12 individuals who are leaders in such fields as the fundamental sciences, medical sciences, education, or public affairs. A member of a National Advisory Council is appointed for a term of 4 years by the Secretary of the Department of Health, Education, and Welfare on the advice of the particular Institute concerned. Half of the appointed members must be authorities in scientific and health fields directly related to the program interests of the Institute; the other six are lay members who are noted for their interest or activity in national health problems.[6]

The National Advisory Councils receive the Study Sections' recommendations on applications for grants and review the proposals against a rather broad background of responsibilities that include, in part, a determination of the needs of the NIH and the missions of the individual Institutes, the total pattern of research in universities and other institutions, the need for the initiation of research in new areas, the degree of relevance of the proposed research to the missions of the Institutes, and other matters of policy. The Councils usually accept a Study Section appraisal with regard to scientific considerations, but they may have occasion to modify the recommendation in relation to one or more of the factors just mentioned.

After the review by the National Advisory Councils the Study Sections no longer have any authority or administrative responsibility for any aspect of the research grant application. Each Institute has professional staff members who provide the further and continuing administration of the applications, as well as of grants. Indeed, it is one of the Institute's staff who will notify the applicant investigator of the final decision on his proposal. It is to this same person that the investigator can direct his request, in writing, for the bases on which the final action regarding his application was taken by the awarding unit. Sometimes an investigator will call the Executive Secretary to learn how his application is faring. Unfortunately, such requests are a waste of the investigator's time, for there is absolutely no information available in the interim between the Study Section and the Council review. In the first place, the NIH review has not been completed at that point. Second, if a Council recommendation differs from that of a Study Section, which occasionally happens, premature notification might lead the applicant into unwise actions on the basis of erroneous expectations. Even when an application receives approval by a National Advisory Council, there is no guarantee that an award can be made; there may be more approved applications than funds available. The investigator is notified of the final recommendation within a few weeks after the meeting of the National Advisory Council.

GRANTEE REVIEW

The foregoing discussion has focused on the NIH review of research grant proposals, but an application is also reviewed by the submitting institution before it is sent to the NIH. Frequently, the institutional review is concerned only with budgetary matters, although in view of the number of unrealistic requests that are not funded, it appears that even in examining the financial aspects of the application some institutions are lacking in the rigor of their review. There is also a type of institutional review that is optional, but extremely valuable: the scientific review of grant proposals by local committees. If employed, scientific review by the applying institution would, I believe, result in greatly improved proposals with far better chances of being reviewed favorably by the NIH. I am not advocating a complex system of miniature study sections or even committees that would necessarily conduct formal meetings, but that perhaps two or three individuals could be requested to review applications in their general areas of specialty. The procedure would have to be informal and fast, for obvious reasons. Of course, an investigator may ask one or more of his colleagues to read the application and provide suggestions for its improvement, just as he is expected to do before he submits a manuscript for publication[7]—and this is certainly a worthwhile practice and a perfectly reasonable alternative. It could be expected that institutions would consider such assistance an obligation to the principal investigator. After all, the grant is awarded to the institution, which is the "grantee," not to the principal investigator.[8]

Most institutions that apply for research grants have a number of experienced investigators whose constructive criticism would be of considerable value to their colleagues, especially to the beginning investigator. In presenting possible explanations for differences in acceptance rates of scientific reports submitted for publication, Zuckerman and Merton (4) discuss the high scientific quality of certain papers in relation to more demanding standards of a department or an institution for manuscripts to be submitted and to the likelihood that the authors had their papers exactingly appraised by competent colleagues before submission for publication. The counsel implied here pertains as well to institutions that submit grant applications to the NIH.

PREPARATION OF A RESEARCH GRANT APPLICATION

An investigator who prepares a research grant application will realize, in the light of the foregoing discussion, that he is writing for his peers, just as he is when he writes a manuscript for publication. Indeed, the preparation of the research grant application involves essentially the same principles as does the preparation of the scientific publication.

From my experience as an Executive Secretary, I have concluded that there are two important rules that an investigator is well advised to follow when he is preparing a research grant application. First, read the instructions provided with the application forms carefully and follow them exactly. Second, never assume that the reviewers are already acquainted with any aspect of the proposal — and this includes the methods being used or that would be used in the proposed research. Additional important rules that should be followed during the preparation of the application are equally applicable to the preparation of a manuscript for publication: search the literature thoroughly and thoughtfully; state explicitly what gap remains to be filled or what extension of established lines of research make the proposed investigations important and worthy of support; formulate a title that is accurate and informative; write an abstract of the proposed research that outlines accurately and specifically the objectives and methods; include well-designed tables and figures when they would enhance the point being made; and make the application as easy as possible to comprehend through the use of a logical presentation of ideas. I would also add that one should avoid attempts to artificially adapt the purpose and significance of the proposed research to meet the stated, implied, or suspected objectives of any of the granting components of the NIH.

INSTRUCTIONS FOR COMPLETING THE APPLICATION FORM

Over the years, the general instructions for the preparation of an application for research grant support from the NIH have been continually revised, by scientists, in response to deficiencies in proposals that have been noted during the review process. The major sections of the current instructions are related to the budget, the biographical sketch, and the research plan.

Budget. A portion of the budget section that should be straightforward but is often incomplete relates to personnel. The investigator is instructed to list *all* participants — professional and nonprofessional — by name and position, or by position only if not yet employed, whether or not salary is requested, and to give his best estimate of the percent of time and effort on the project for each professional. Yet many principal investigators do not list themselves! Many others who do list themselves fail to indicate the percentage of time or effort that they would give to the proposed project. The reviewers must be able to determine whether the amount of time that would be devoted to the proposed project is realistic and appropriate to the stated goals.

Another frequently overlooked, or perhaps misinterpreted, item is the instruction to justify any item of equipment for which the need may not be obvious. As a wise precaution, it would be best for the investigator to justify all expensive equipment requested whether he thinks it obvious or not. Furthermore, the equipment category should be closely related to the later discussion of "Facilities Available." Imagine the fate of a requested, but unjustified, item of equipment such as an ultracentrifuge when the list of available facilities included two ultracentrifuges!

A third area of the budget section that is often explained incompletely is the budget estimates for future years of requested support. The instructions state that the applicant should explain the basis for any increases requested for personnel in future years and justify amounts requested for equipment and for any unusual increases in other categories.

Although the information requested in the budget section is explained in the instructions, many investigators are unfortunately using obsolete instructions. Since policies and requirements change, old instructions are now usually inadequate, if not misleading. Therefore, the investigator should always make sure that he has a copy of the latest instructions, which may be obtained by requesting an application kit from the Division of Research Grants. Preparation of a proposal on the basis of obsolete instructions can lead to untoward delays while consideration of the application is postponed.

Biographical sketch. One section that unexpectedly causes problems is the biographical sketch. In this section, the applicant is instructed to provide for each professional participant in the proposed project a chronological list of all or the most representative of his publications. Probably as a result of the concept that equates accomplishment with quantity of publication, many investigators submit bibliographies which they clearly hope will be impressive, artificially lengthened by the inclusion of elaborate references to manuscripts "in preparation" or "to be submitted for publication." When such manuscripts are only contemplated, which is frequently the case, it is a distinct disadvantage to the applicant investigator for him to list them, since it is predictable that he will be requested to submit copies of these manuscripts in support of his proposal. If the manuscripts have indeed been completed, even in draft form, a copy should be included with the research grant application; if the manuscript would be relevant if completed, but is not yet written, the data can and should be incorporated into the text in the section entitled "Background."

It is also helpful if the beginning investigator includes in the biographical sketch the names of his mentors for the doctoral research program and for any postdoctoral research experience. The reviewers of the application can usually determine much more about the potential of a beginning investigator if they know the details of his background and training.

The biographical sketch should also contain mention of any plans for leave of absence from the applicant institution during the period that the application is being reviewed. It is not uncommon to find that the principal investigator of an application that has been deferred for a project-site visit is out of the country for the year. Unfortunately, the decision on his proposal would have to await his return. (Here, again, the delay could be avoided if the investigator were able to submit the application for an earlier deadline.) In addition, much time can be saved in requesting additional information before the Study Section meeting if the Executive Secretary knows the whereabouts of the principal investigator.

The final recommendation of the Study Section includes an opinion about the amount of time (project period), as well as of money (budget), that would be required for the investigator to complete the research project proposed. Since the reviewers must be able to estimate whether the requested project period, the percent of time or effort that would be devoted to the research, and the requested budget are reasonable, they must have an accurate indication of the total research activities and grant support of all the professional personnel associated with the proposed project. Thus, the instructions specify that all research support — current, pending, anticipated, and regardless of source — is to be listed in the biographical sketch. The specific information requested for each item of support listed is described in the instructions(3).

Research plan. In accordance with the major rule that the author of an application should never assume that the readers of his proposal are already familiar with the research program proposed, the instructions for presenting the research plan state that complete information should be included so that each application can be reviewed without reference to previous applications. Of vital importance is the stark reminder that the reviewing groups will consider the information provided as an example of the investigator's approach to a research objective and as an indication of his ability in the proposed area of research. This concept applies particularly to the methods section, where many investigators make the mistake of assuming that the reviewers need little information. The reviewers are indeed quite familiar with current methodology and with the most potentially fruitful use of available methods, but they have no way of knowing that the investigator has the same familiarity unless he tells them. Merritt (2) has emphasized that the description of methods is one part of the application where nothing should be left to the imagination and that the most successful requests are those that contain a well-defined problem with a well-defined approach. Since the methods section will contain much of the real scientific substance of the application, the instructions for preparing it are worth repeating: "Give details of your research plan, including a description of the experiments or other work you propose to do; the methods, species of animals, and techniques you plan to use; the kinds of data you expect to obtain; and the means by which you plan to analyze or interpret the data to attain your objectives. Include if appropriate a discussion of pitfalls you might encounter, and of the limitations of the procedures you propose to use. Insofar as you can, describe the principal experiments or observations in the sequence in which you plan to carry them out and indicate, if possible, a tentative schedule of the main steps of the investigation within the project period requested" (3). The key word in these instructions is "details." In a recent proposal for an investigation of a subcellular process, neither the type of cell nor the animal from which the cells were to be obtained was ever mentioned. It is also wise to describe alternative approaches that would be utilized in the event the preferred approach to any given step in the experimental sequence should prove inadequate. Similarly, if the preferred approach is not the easiest or the most direct, the reason for choosing it over the more obvious approach should be explained.

All of the foregoing discussion is as applicable to the renewal application as to the new application. An applicant investigator should never assume that any of the same individuals who reviewed the original application would be involved in the review of the renewal application. The composition of the Study Sections is constantly changing. Moreover, the directions of the original research program may have changed to the extent that the renewal proposal would be reviewed more appropriately by another Study Section. The only practical distinction between new and renewal applications, in terms of preparation, is the requirement for a comprehensive progress report for the renewal. The importance of this report cannot be overly emphasized. The fate of the renewal application lies almost as much with past progress as with future plans.

When preparing the abstract and the title for the application, the author should remember that the first people to examine the application will be interested initially in the broad disciplinary category into which the application can be classified. An accurate title and an indicative abstract can greatly facilitate assignment to the most appropriate review group and therefore ensure the most knowledgeable review.

Why did I include an admonition that the investigator should avoid attempts to artificially adapt the purpose and significance of the proposed research to meet the stated, implied, or suspected objectives of any of the granting components of the NIH? Primarily because such manipulations frequently obscure the simplicity and directness that is so vital to the communication of one's intentions and goals. For example, an application was disapproved because the principal investigator proposed to utilize an experimental system with which he was clearly not familiar in an investigation that was peripheral to his own specialty. When he was subsequently notified of the reasons for the disapproval action, he replied that he had selected the research topic because he thought that the awarding unit which had supported his research in the past had a particular interest in that area of research. Even without the recognition that an investigator must successfully pass the initial review for scientific merit before his research can be considered eligible for support, the irony of this situation was made more dramatic by the fact that the awarding unit had no such interest. Since the initial review of a research grant application is for scientific merit only, an applicant can gain nothing by distorting his actual intentions in anticipation of the program interests of the Institutes or other awarding units. The strongest applications are those that are the most honest and straightforward representation of an investigator's own unique interests, competency, and abilities. Indeed, the Council of Biology Editors' manual on the teaching of scientific writing (1) states that authors of research project proposals "should not allow a feeling of false modesty to lead them into affected circumlocutions, but should maintain the same clean scientific style — brief, simple, and direct — throughout the proposal. Deviousness of any kind is to be avoided, and the applicant's best chance of success, here as in all kinds of scientific writing, lies in honesty and clarity of purpose."

COMMON REASONS FOR DISAPPROVAL OF APPLICATIONS

One of the questions most frequently asked of an Executive Secretary is "What are the most common reasons for disapproval and for marginal approval?" This question is extremely difficult to answer, because there is rarely a single reason for the final recommendation. A few expressions recur frequently, however, and can provide the basis for valid overall impressions. Although the specific reasons for disapproval are available only to the principal investigator, it may be helpful to paraphrase, in general terms, some of the common reasons for disapproval. It will be seen that the reasons for the failure of the application may frequently be related to many of the ambiguities and inaccuracies associated with poor scientific writing.[9] For example, one application was disapproved because the proposed experiments were based on apparent misconceptions of the current status of the field and on misinterpretation of the pertinent literature. Furthermore, the principal investigator did not appear to have the necessary background and experience to conduct such difficult studies. How much of the misinterpretation of the literature may have been related to the author's careless use of words in conveying his interpretation to the reviewers? Did the principal investigator appear not to have the necessary background for the proposed investigations merely because he failed to devote sufficient attention to the "biographical sketch"? In a similar case, the reviewers recognized that most of the proposed procedures required special training and experience. Yet there was little to suggest that the principal investigator had the training and experience necessary to direct the project into the complex areas proposed. Was the investigator overly modest or had he left too much to the imagination of the reviewers?

In another case, the reviewers had serious reservations about the reliability of the data produced so far, and they felt that many of the proposed studies repeated previous work reported by the author. Did the investigator fail to impress the reviewers because he did not present complete and unambiguous data analyzed by appropriate statistical methods? Had he indeed little to propose in the way of future work, or had he merely failed to convey how the proposed work differed from and extended what had been completed?

In a fourth case, the application was disapproved because the reviewers felt that in terms of present knowledge and methodology the proposed study did not have a sufficiently firm foundation to warrant investigation. Had the author searched the literature thoroughly and thoughtfully, and had he attempted to explain what gap his research would fill in this area? In a contrasting case, however, the author certainly searched the literature thoroughly — but apparently not thoughtfully. Here, the reviewers considered the review of the field to be well written and informative, but the research plan was confused and scattered, and it appeared to be based on the acceptance of unproven claims. Furthermore, the direction of the research was not made clear and no one aspect of the proposed research was described in enough detail to make clear the thought processes of the investigator. If even one aspect had been selected for detailed and critical study, a worthwhile research program might have been constructed, but neither the application nor the relatively uncritical published work of the investigator led the reviewers to believe that this was likely.

The following examples illustrate the importance of a well-organized presentation. In several applications the experimental design was so poorly presented that it was not possible to discern a logical sequence for the steps that would be taken. Unfortunately, it is not unusual to find poorly written and unfocused applications in which the proposed experiments have not been sufficiently defined to provide answers to any of the questions asked. There have also been massive and ambitious proposals in which none of the key requirements for success in any one of the vast number of experiments proposed had been considered in sufficient detail.

The importance of the comprehensive progress report in proposals for continued support and of carefully prepared tables and figures is exemplified by an application that was seriously weakened by a disappointing progress report. Numerous errors were found in the charts and in the description of the tabular data. It was clear in several instances that the investigator had drawn conclusions that were not warranted and that he had failed to apply appropriate statistical tests to much of the data. The total effect of the tabular data and the investigator's statements about them raised serious doubts about the whole endeavor.

Although lists can be misleading because of their implied exclusivity, it may be helpful to itemize some of the more common reasons that may apply singly or in combinations for disapproval of an application:[10]

    an apparent lack of new or original ideas;
    a diffuse, rambling, superficial, or unfocused research plan;
    a lack of understanding of published work in the field, as reflected in large part by the
        presentation and treatment of the pertinent literature;
    a lack of background and experience in the essential methodology;
    uncertainty concerning the future directions that the research could take;
    an experimental approach that involves questionable reasoning;
    the absence of an acceptable scientific rationale;
    an attempt to conduct an unrealistically large amount of work;
    a lack of sufficient experimental detail; and
    an uncritical approach.

In addition to the foregoing, renewal applications may be disapproved because of

    a lack of new ideas for continued investigations; and
    a lack of sufficient productivity during the previous years of the grant, as reflected by the
        progress report and any materials accompanying it.

For purposes of impact, I have emphasized reasons for negative recommendations. Actually, more applications are approved than are disapproved. But the members of the Study Sections spend more time discovering what is good in a proposal than ought to be necessary. The long hours spent in reviewing applications in preparation for the formal meetings of the initial review groups are unremunerated. The work is especially arduous because all of the consultants are intensely concerned about making the right decision and about serving the best interests of the investigators and of science. Indeed, the success of the peer-review system, and therefore much of contemporary science, depends on the help provided by the numerous scientists who serve on NIH public advisory groups. These men and women are willing to give their valuable time because they recognize that the quality of science in this country depends on constant surveillance and guidance by the scientists themselves. They also recognize the probable consequences were they not afforded the opportunity for active participation in the policies and decisions related to the public support of research. Thus, they are keenly aware of the magnitude and importance of their responsibilities. An author cannot, then, in good conscience do less than his best in attempting to prepare a complete and lucid application that will serve his own interests as faithfully as his peers serve him.

BIBLIOGRAPHY

Available from the Office of Information, Publications and Reports Branch, Office of the Director, National Institutes of Health, Bethesda, Maryland 20014:

U. S. Department of Health, Education, and Welfare, Public Health Service, National Institutes of Health. *A Guide to Grant and Award Programs of the National Institutes of Health.* PHS Publication No. 1067, Rev. 1970.

U. S. Department of Health, Education, and Welfare, Public Health Service, National Institutes of Health. *NIH Almanac 1971.* (Offers in one volume all important historical data and other reference material; revised annually.)

U. S. Department of Health, Education, and Welfare, Public Health Service, National Institutes of Health. *NIH Public Advisory Groups: Authority, Structure, Functions, Members.* Issued biannually.

U. S. Department of Health, Education, and Welfare, Public Health Service, National Institutes of Health. *NIH Publications List.* Issued biannually.

For sale by the Superintendent of Documents, U. S. Government Printing Office, Washington, D. C. 20402:

U. S. Department of Health, Education, and Welfare. Catalog of HEW Assistance. Providing Financial Support and Services to: States, Communities, Organizations, Individuals. August 1969. Price $5.50.

Office of Economic Opportunity, for the Executive Office of the President. *Catalog of Federal Domestic Assistance.* April 1970. (A description of the Federal government's domestic programs to assist the American People in furthering their social and economic progress. Explains nature and purpose, specifies major eligibility requirements, tells where to apply, and lists printed materials available.) Price $6.75.

REFERENCES

1. Council of Biology Editors. Committee on Graduate Training in Scientific Writing. *Scientific Writing for Graduate Students, A Manual on the Teaching of Scientific Writing.* edited by F. P. Woodford. New York: The Rockefeller University Press, 1968, p. 148.
2. Merritt, D. H. *Clin. Res.* 11: 375, 1963.
3. U. S. Department of Health, Education, and Welfare, Public Health Service. *Information and Instructions for Application for Research Grant, Form PHS 398,* Instruction Sheet Rev. 3-70.
4. Zuckerman, H., and R. K. Merton, *Minerva* 9:66, 1971.

FOOTNOTES

[1]The organization chart for the Public Health Service is available from the Information Office, Westwood Building (Room 435), Division of Research Grants, National Institutes of Health, Bethesda, Maryland 20014.

[2]Assignment of an application to two Institutes, or other awarding units, means that the first, or primary, Institute to which the application is assigned has the prerogative for funding; it may relinquish this privilege to the second Institute.

[3]For a discussion of the selection and appointment of members of technical advisory committees, see *The Research Grant Programs of the Public Health Service. Issues and Considerations Relating to the Ninth Report of the House Committee on Government Operations,* February 1968, U. S. Department of Health, Education, and Welfare, and the *Bulletin of the Association of American Medical Colleges,* Volume III, Number 3, Supplement, March 8, 1968, which may be ordered from the Publications Division, Association of American Medical Colleges, 1 DuPont Circle, N. W., Suite 200, Washington, D.C. 20036.

[4]For information on how to obtain a copy of *NIH Public Advisory Groups: Authority, Structure, Functions, Members* see BIBLIOGRAPHY, which also lists other useful documents that should be available in every institution that is eligible to receive Public Health Service grants.

[5]See item 10 on page 1 of the NIH research grant application, form PHS-398, Rev. 3-70.

[6]See *NIH Public Advisory Groups: Authority, Structure, Functions, Members* for information concerning the legal authority for the Councils, their specific missions and functions, the presiding official, the current membership, and the terms of office of the members.

[7]At least one journal, *Science*, requires that manuscripts submitted for consideration for publication be accompanied by a letter of transmittal that gives the names of colleagues who have reviewed the paper (The Editors, *Science* 171: xv, 1971).

[8]The *grantee* is the "university, college, hospital, public agency, or nonprofit research institution which submits an application and receives a grant for support of research by a named principal investigator" and the *principal investigator* is the "individual designated by the grantee and approved by the Public Health Service who is responsible for the scientific and technical direction of the project." (U. S. Department of Health, Education, and Welfare, Public Health Service. *Public Health Service Grants for Research Projects Policy Statement* (Rev. July 1, 1967), PHS Publication No. 1301.)

[9]F. P. Woodford, Chapters 1-10 in reference 1.

[10]While the reasons for disapproval listed or stated by example were encountered in a single Study Section, they include most of the 26 shortcomings found in 605 disapproved research proposals reviewed by all Study Sections in the spring of 1959 (E. M. Allen, *Science* 132: 1532, 1960).

PROGRAM REVIEW

Program review is the process a proposal undergoes when it is reviewed within the funding agency. Both formal and informal preliminary proposals are program reviewed although each is treated somewhat differently. The formal proposal usually receives outside evaluation and undergoes a program review before an award is made. This is especially true in marginal proposals for which the borderline must be judged within the funding agency. Budgets are likewise adjusted accordingly. The program review can determine the recommended level of funding although it may be different from the original request. The program review is universal and is used both by the private and public sector of the funding community.

The preliminary proposal is not ordinarily sent to reviewers in the same manner as a formal proposal. In the case of Federal agencies, particularly in the Washington, D.C. area, the preliminary proposal may be sent to three up to 15 specialists within the Federal government for comments and reactions. Because proposal review procedures are somewhat universal, we recommend that the writer adopt similar procedures before taking the draft proposal to final copy. The simplest method is to ask several trusted colleagues to critically review the proposal. Those who are chosen may have had this experience with private or public funding agencies — if so, all the better.

MAIL REVIEW

The mail review is the least expensive of the evaluative techniques used by funding agencies. Simply, it is sending the proposal(s) to selected reviewers and asking them in the leisure of their office or home to evaluate the merits of a particular proposal. In some cases very specific rules are given to the reviewer, and in other cases only reactions and comments are solicited.

The method allows the funding agency to arrive at a decision with a relatively large number of reviews. As previously stated, this is an inexpensive process. The reproduction and postage are the basic costs, thus the action officer will naturally seek a large number of reviewers.

THE SITE VISIT

In the proposal-award life cycle an important component not often discussed is the site visit. The site visit is an official visit by members of the funding agency and outside consultants. The visit may be conducted for one of several reasons. The proposal may be of such interest to the funding agency that there is question without seeing the facility and talking to the people who will conduct the project the evaluation cannot be fair and impartial. Another common reason is the project is up for renewal and there is doubt whether or not the project will be funded for another period. Whatever the reason may be there are certain rules and procedures that should be followed in preparation for the site visit.

The site visit team normally has been picked before the telephone call or letter informing the prospective grantee of the upcoming visit. At this time attempt to gather all of the information that the agency will give about the visit such as the members of the team, full names and affiliations. The purpose is to look up all of the members in advance and brief your staff and administration.

Most important of all are planning for the visit and organizing the substantive part of the project. What is meant is simple. The project plan, and what has happened to it from the time the project proposal was originally written will be of importance to the visiting team. A one hour briefing should be prepared with details and visuals. The briefing should be practiced several times before critical audiences. The material whether it be scientific, humanistic or otherwise should be brought up to date. If the area is scientific be sure to have cleared up any ambiguities or weak spots in the plan before the visitors arrive.

What might one expect to be asked at a site visit? Depending upon the nature of the project and the amount of dollars involved, it is possible that fiscal and administrative questions will be asked. Alert those people in advance and have them stand-by. Facilities and equipment will be inspected by the team — have appropriate personnel ready on a stand-by basis. If graduate students are involved with the project or support for graduate students was requested, it would not be uncommon to expect the visitors to interview the students without the presence of the principal investigator and his staff.

What should be the posture of the principal investigator during a site visit? Simply be honest and do not try to put anything over on the team. More often than not team members are seasoned at site visiting and can tell when one is trying to impress the site visitors.

PEER REVIEW CONTROVERSY

John Conlan *(R. Arizona)* in the 1975 Congressional Hearings made accusations that the peer review system at the National Science Foundation is not the very best it should be. He called it an *"old boy's system."*

Basically the peer review system is excellent. To be sure there are "flukes" and what system would not have these? The action officer is very important in the overall integrity of the peer review system. Should an action officer wish to bury a project for reasons only known to him — a simple way to do this is to choose the reviewers that have similar prejudices. He may also purge the file of good reviewers (qualified and knowledgeable) for selfish personal biases — none of which bear on the integrity of the scientist.

So Mr. Conlan in some respects what you are saying is true — but it is not the peer review system *per se* that is wrong, it is just that a very few people abuse the system. The abuses to the system if investigated and eliminated in those perpetrating the abuses would cleanse the peer review system.

THE REVIEW PROCESS

The National Science Board (NSB) and the policy-making body of the National Science Foundation (NSF), took this action at its 174th meeting June 20, 1975 at the Scripps Institution of Oceanography at La Jolla, California. The NSB said it believes the new policy will improve the information exchange with scientists and allow the scientific community to better understand the reasons behind NSF decisions. The NSB said the peer review process should be conducted with as much openness as is consistent with the effective administration of the decision process.

**RESOLUTION ADOPTED BY THE NATIONAL SCIENCE BOARD
AT ITS 174th MEETING ON JUNE 20, 1975
ON PEER REVIEW INFORMATION**

The National Science Board has examined the use of peer review in the National Science Foundation decision process on grant awards and declinations. The Board intends the peer review process to aid the effective evaluation of proposals with the fairest possible treatment of each individual proposal and the broadest possible participation of qualified scientists and other appropriate persons. The Board intends that the review process be conducted with as much openness and information to proposers as possible consistent with effective administration of the decision process. To these ends the National Science Board RESOLVED that:

1. The Foundation will publish annually a list of all reviewers used by each Division;
2. Program officers should seek broadly representative participation of qualified individuals as reviewers;
3. Verbatim copies of reviews requested by the Foundation after January 1, 1976, not including the identity of the reviewer, will be made available to the principal investigator/project director upon request. The question of including the identity of the reviewer will be considered further by the National Science Board;
4. The Foundation, upon request, will inform the principal investigator/project director of the reasons for its decision on the proposal.

All reviews requested prior to January 1, 1976 will continue to be governed by earlier policies since those reviews will have been solicited with a commitment on the part of the National Science Foundation to the confidentiality established by that earlier policy.

The Board believes this new policy will serve to improve the information exchange with the scientific community and allow it to better understand the reasons behind National Science Foundation decisions.

CONCLUSION

Every proposal which serves to seek funds for the accomplishment of research or creative endeavor will be subject to the review process. The review process serves to select the most qualified proposals from among those submitted. The researcher should accept as a *fact of life* that there is never enough money at any level to fund all proposals which minds can create. Variations of the peer review process are used for both intramural and extramural funding. Researchers, if denied, can use peer review remarks to improve proposal preparation skills.

Chapter Eight

TYPES
OF AWARDS

INTRODUCTION

When seeking funds from private sources such as foundations, the most common way funds are disbursed are in the form of grants. However, when seeking funds from the governmental sector, funds are obtained under the umbrella of two instruments, the grant and the contract. The later is a genera with many subdivisions. As stated previously in *Chapter Three, The Proposal,* the governmental sector, namely the Federal government, is moving very rapidly toward contracts and away from grants. It then becomes necessary for the prospective awardee (grant or contract) to have a speaking familiarity with terms surrounding grants and contracts.

GRANTS

The grant is the preferred instrument for support of basic research with institutions of higher learning. Some agencies are limited by Statutes to give grants only to non-profit organizations of higher education and/or non-profit organizations whose primary purpose is to conduct scientific research. A grant is an agreement by a funding agency to award, and by the grantee to accept and use those funds to support an identified activity. Ordinarily, this agreement is based upon the grantee's proposal and contains a minimum number of expressed conditions by the grantee. Grants are made normally from one to three years. In past years up to five years was quite common. Quite often, stipulation for additional year funds (second, or third year support) is made upon the contingency of the "availability of funds." The latter is termed a *"moral obligation"* or *"moral agreement"* and is not legally binding on the funding agency offering support. Grants may be revoked in whole or in part, at any time after consultation with the grantee.

The National Science Foundation defines a grant instrument as consisting of five parts. (1) The grant letter and any numbered amendments thereto; (2) The grant budget, which indicates the amounts, categories of expense, on which NSF has based its support; (3) The proposal referenced grant letter; (4) A standardized enclosure, identifying the basic conditions applicable to that type of NSF grant; and (5) Such other documents as may be referenced in the grant letter. The basic conditions contained in a standardized enclosure is more fully explained in Chapters II through VI of the "Grant Administration

Manual". The "NSF Grant Administration Manual" consists of 55 pages and an Appendix.[1]

The Office of Management and Budget (OMB), Executive Office of the President of the United States is responsible for the overall cost principles associated with grants and contracts. OMB Circular A-21 Revised, provides the cost principles and policy guides to be applied by Federal agencies supporting research and development, training and other educational services under grants and contracts with educational institutions.[2] Because of the importance of this document and the few principal investigators that have familiarity of its contents, the Circular A-21 has been included in the Appendix. Those associated with State and local governments need to become familiar with OMB Circular A-87.[3] In addition University and non-profit organizations need to be familiar with OMB Circular A-88.[4]

When the reader examines Circular A-21, many unanswered questions soon will be cleared. Indirect costs,[5] consultants fees, travel, computer charges, contracts with consortia, costs of operating specialized facilities, printing, stipends, books and periodicals, etc., are covered in detail in this document. The more important reason to become familiar with Circular A-21 is the inclusion of principles and details of allowable expenditures. When planning the budget of a new proposal — Circular A-21 should be referred to.

CONTRACTS

Contracts in the past were few and not commonplace to the University environment. Today, contracts are becoming commonplace and several agencies use this as their preferred "modus operandi". Contracts vary from cost-plus a percentage cost, cost-plus an award fee, cost-plus-a-fixed fee, cost-plus incentive fee, cost-reimbursable, *fixed-price, firm-fixed-price* and many others. Contracts involving government agencies fall under the controls of *"Federal Management Procurement Regulations"* (FMPR) (all agencies of the U.S. Government); U.S. Atomic Energy Regulations (now Energy Research and Development Administration (ERDA) and Nuclear Regulatory Commission (NRC); and Department of Defense (Armed Services Procurement Regulations) (ASPR).[6]

The authority of the United States Government to enter into contracts although inherent in its sovereignty is not expressly granted by the Constitution of the United States or by its Statutes. In 1831, The Supreme Court of the United States held in its ruling that the United States Government could enter into contracts. In 1947, The United States Congress passed the *Armed Services Procurement Act* which authorized the services to reach agreements upon the performance of procurement functions. From this, the *Armed Services Procurement Regulations* was born. Today the *Armed Services Procurement Regulations (ASPR)* is the bible of those who deal with any organization of the armed services. For example, if one is planning to submit proposals to the Office of Naval Research — *ASPR'S* are followed.

ARMED FORCES PROCUREMENT REGULATIONS (ASPR)

What does this compendium of regulations cover? The *ASPR'S* cover: principles and policies; procedures; advertising methodology and standards; negotiation; special methods of procurement; foreign purchases; contract clauses; termination of contracts; patents, licences; copyrights; bonds; insurance; taxes; labor; government inspection; government acceptance; contract principles and procedures; forms; Charter and Rules for Armed Services Board of Contract Appeals; etc.

When dealing with a potential source of funds from a unit of the Department of Defense, one must have an understanding of *ASPR*. It is recommended that a complete set of *ASPR'S* be in every research administration office or library.

NEGOTIATION

Although the term *negotiation* is used to describe all of the Department of Defense procurements from private industry, all contracts which involve the Federal government require negotiation. The common belief is that negotiation is unilateral and is only used when the Federal government wishes to bargain or arbitrarily reduce the amount of the request for dollars. This is only one small portion of the negotiation process. One can negotiate the use of equipment from a Federal facility; the rights to patent and copyright; and a host of other items inherent to the details of the contract.

USE OF CONTRACTS

Those who write and negotiate contracts must be skilled and experienced people. The Federal government and private industry use highly trained personnel for both executing and negotiating contracts. Many are attorneys, and many are not. A contract negotiator for a union contract must be very skilled and we would expect that. So must the person designated to negotiate with the funding source be equally skilled when it comes to contracts which involve city, state and municipal governments and colleges and universities. In industry, particularly aerospace, computer and electronics industries, this group of industries have large staffs of experts in grants, contracts and proposal design. Many industries maintain Washington, D.C. offices and branches. Those who do maintain such offices are normally headed by a senior corporate official such as a vice president or senior vice president. Some universities emulating the industrial model likewise have set up Washington offices. The State University of New York System has a large staff and a suite of offices in Washington, D.C. as does others.

Many universities especially those referred to previously in this text as *"biggies"* have experienced and skilled contract negotiators on their staff. That does not mean the smaller or medium size institution should not have some chance at the same trough. Perhaps there is more fear associated with trying, than the lack of knowledge associated with the process. Each year the Department of Defense generates approximately fifteen million separate purchase actions. Should not this be a reason for seeking funds through DOD agencies?

GENERAL CONSIDERATIONS

Government contracts are classified according to the form they take and the pricing terms they include. Contracts fall into three major categories: the letter contract; the definitive contract; and the purchase order. The later one, the purchase order, has been used by the National Institutes of Health. An interesting way to avoid payment of indirect costs. Project directors and administrators should be very cautious when accepting a purchase order in lieu of a contract.

THE LETTER CONTRACT — This is defined as a preliminary contractual instrument. In some, but not in all cases, the letter contract specifically states that an award has been made and that funds may be drawn upon the contract. In other cases, the letter contract may be very specific when funds may be drawn upon the contract. Do not accept the contract unless the original terms and plans for executing the contract coincide.

THE DEFINITIVE CONTRACT — This is defined as a contract in which all terms and conditions of the contract are agreed upon and expressed in full.

PURCHASE ORDER — A purchase order is defined as a simplified contractual instrument for the rapid means of purchasing small quanities of standard materials. Author's Note: In recent years, the purchase order definition has been stretched to include what might be expected to be a contract.

Although non-profit organizations such as universities and foundations have to define what is cost very carefully — inherent in the *ASPR'S* and governmental regulations in general pertaining to contracts, is a cognizance that profit is "the basic incentive of business enterprise."

TYPES OF CONTRACTS

FIXED-PRICE — In a fixed-price type of contract, the contractor agrees to produce an item or perform services for a price that is either specified in the contract or calculated from its terms. There are four types of fixed-price contracts. They are as follows: firm fixed-price; fixed-price with escalation; fixed-price incentive; and fixed-price-*redeterminable*. Each member of the fixed-price contract family limits the price for the total effort undertaken. Each allocates the element of risk and incentive in a different manner. Suggestions for further reading will be found at the end of the Chapter.

COST REIMBURSEMENT TYPE OF CONTRACTS — During the 1950's the Nation experienced a surge of technological advancement. By necessity, the Department of Defense took the lead to adapt the technology to military needs. The U.S. Congress gave the blessing to allow maximum flexibility in contractual agreement. The reader may question why emphasis is on the Department of Defense. The reason is simple. All agencies of the Federal government have taken the procurement approach for research and development which was originally adopted by DOD in the 1950's. There is still a great question in the minds of many scientists and educators whether or not the same rules can apply for the acquisition of end-items such as ball bearings compared to that of conceptual basic research. Nonetheless, the DOD philosopy has spilled over to almost every agency within the Federal bureaucracy.

The industrial and defense communities both understand the importance of cost-reimbursement contracts. They are simply derived because of the unknowns of transformation of ideas and concepts to research and development to the ultimate acquisition of hardware. In essence one may say the more unknowns in the completion of a contract, portend the cost-reimbursable route as opposed to the fixed price route. Cost-reimbursable contracts fall into several categories. The simplest is called the *cost-contract*.

COST-CONTRACT — This is defined as a contract in which the contractor receives no fee, but the Federal government agrees to reimburse the contractor for allowable costs as governed by the procurement regulations and the terms of the contract. This type of contract usually is used for facilities or for research and development activities which involve educational and other types of non-profit institutions.

COST-SHARING CONTRACT — This type of contract is defined as a cost-type in which the contractor receives *no fee* and is reimbursed only for an agreed portion of his allowable costs. This contract classification recognizes that the contractor may benefit in ways other than profit from the performance of a Federal government contract. Authors Note: Often times faculty and administrators get caught short in these kinds of contracts. The over zealous principal investigator desiring the award may be one reason. The most common is the *"cost-effectiveness"* of the award was not considered in advance of the decision to accept the award became an ex-post facto exercise.

COST-SHARING — In itself is most complex. *Office of Management and Budget Circular A-21 should be studied carefully. Circular A-21 is found in the Appendix of the text.* Cost-sharing accounts are required in the accounting methods and procedures. Cost-sharing in days gone by was interpreted as an in-kind type of contribution. In-kind is a thing of the past. Any activity, person or item of equipment, etc., must be accounted for and documented. Cost-share uses real monies and real resources. Records are required for all personnel efforts made on a contract or grant. Total effort must not exceed 100 per cent. Effort must match performance and all documents must be placed on file for future audits.

COST-PLUS-FIXED-FEE CONTRACT — The cost-plus-fixed-fee contract provides for reimbursement to the contractor for the allowable costs of performing the contract, along with payment of a fixed-fee based upon estimated costs. Authors Note: It is this type of contract that the famous columnist Jack Anderson has mentioned on several occasions in the Washington Post as being the most abused of all the governmental contracts.

Basically the *cost-plus-fixed-fee type of contract* places the cost burden on the Federal government and is not conducive to economical use of labor and facilities. Accountability is the watchword of administration and managers today. The Federal government in this type of contractual agreement pays the costs and guarantees profit.

COST-PLUS-INCENTIVE-FEE CONTRACT — This is a cost-reimbursable type of contract which pays the contractor

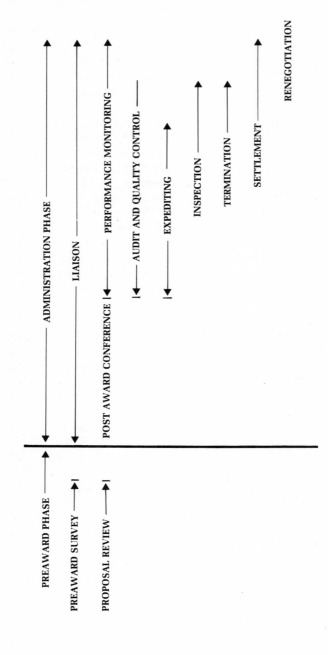

Figure 18 • *TYPICAL STEPS IN CONTRACT ADMINISTRATION*

allowable costs incurred in the performance of the contract. This is necessary when uncertainties involved in the contract performance are of such a magnitude that cost of performance cannot be estimated with a degree of certainty to warrant the award of a fixed-price contract of any type.

COST-PLUS-AWARD-FEE CONTRACT — A variation of those described above. This type of contract was introduced because of the need to cover such services as architectural design, programming, and engineering. It does indeed resemble the cost-plus-incentive-fee contract in many ways. This type of contract insures that a periodic re-evaluation upward or downward of the fee takes place.

CONCLUSION

Funds are awarded through two types of instruments: grants and contracts. Each funding source has variations from other agencies in its requirements for grants and contracts. The essential differences between the two instruments lie in the initiation of the request and the requirements for completion of the project. The proposal for a grant is initiated by the researcher within guidelines established by the source. The proposal for a contract is generated in response to a request of the source. The request specifies what is desired in rather specific terms. At the conclusion of a grant, the researcher establishes that he or she has done what was originally proposed. At the termination of a contract, the researcher must confirm that he or she has accomplished what was desired by the funding source. Currently Federal agencies are shifting strongly from the awarding of grants to the contract. The type of award should be carefully studied by the researcher and implications of each type thoroughly understood by research administrators.

SELECTED READING LIST

Armed Services Procurement Regulations, Department of Defense, Superintendent of Documents, Government Printing Office, Washington, D.C. 1975 *(Updated with supplements periodically).*

Contractors Guide, No. 0-333-12, United States Army Materiel Command, Department of Defense, Washington, D.C. 1974.

Grants Administration Manual, NSF No. 73-26, National Science Foundation, Washington, D.C. 1973.

Gromfine, I.J. and Edwards, J.D., "Termination After World War II," *Law and Contemporary Problems,* Volume 29, No. 4 (1944).

Government Contracts, *Law and Contemporary Problems,* Volume 29, No. 1 (1964).

Laurent, F.W., *Legal Aspects of Defense Procurement,* University of Wisconsin, Law School, Madison, Wisconsin, 1962.

National Security Management, "Procurement," Industrial College of the Armed Forces of the United States, Washington, D.C. 1968. *(100 references on the subject of procurement).*

Staats, E.B., "The General Accounting Office, Long Range Plans for Military Audits," *Armed Forces Comptroller,* April, 1967.

Title 6, Civil Rights Act of 1964, Public Law 88-352, Superintendent of Documents, Government Printing Office, Washington, D.C. 1964.

Title 45, United States Code of Federal Regulations, Part 666, National Science Foundation, Superintendent of Documents, Government Printing Office, Washington, D.C.

United States Congress Hearings, 93rd Congress, House, Subcommittee on Committee on Appropriations, Department of Defense Appropriations, 1975.

United States Department of Defense, *Polaris Management — Fleet Ballistic Missile Program.* Superintendent of Documents, Government Printing Office, Washington, D.C. September, 1962.

Chapter Nine

USE OF CONSULTANTS

INTRODUCTION

A Chapter pertaining to consultants has been included in this book because of the large number of Federal agencies and private foundations allowing and encouraging consultant services. Today there are many grant programs which require a certain percentage of effort coming from outside expertise. Consulting and consultant services cover a wide range. The term consultant in grants and contracts may be applied to a local physician overseeing a project involving human subjects experimentation; a revision of an entire teaching program with team of outside experts giving input to the project; and environmental impact study; a five year plan, etc. The material herein described can serve as information and reference should expertise not be available from your indigenous organization. Another important consideration which gives credence to the need for consultants is the national trend of funding agencies moving from traditional granting mechanisms to the awarding of contracts. This trend not only changes requirements and content of proposals, it places an added burden on the applying group or groups of expecting local expertise to complete the complex documents required for contracts.

GENERAL DISCUSSION

Every organization at one time or another exhibits the quality of a lack of direction. Research and sponsored programs administration are no exception. Within an organization's heirarchy of management someone may recognize that there is a need which cannot be met from within. The need may arise from one or a combination of sources or reasons. The *status quo* may be so entrenched, movement of ideas and implementation of change would be impossible. The organization has never come to the realization that its managerial and operational philosophies are completely antiquated. The growth of the college, university, State or Federal agency was too rapid and with growth a number of *people problems* have emerged. Formal objectives have not been communicated to the organizational staff or what has been communicated has been diffuse and unclear. These are just a few of the more common reasons why assistance may be sought.

When assistance is needed, whether it be substantive problems in a research project, or the overall management of a research program, such assistance may be performed by a consultant.

The term expert may be appropriate for those within the organization; however, because of internal conflicts those persons with the expertise would pose a threat and be virtually useless to the problem-solving process. The *fresh look* accomplishes many purposes. The main one being, problems can be solved. Alternative methods to solving problems are also given. The opinion or opinions are generally unbiased, and the outsider does not purport as great a threat to the group as would be if the "expert" were utilized from within the organization.

WHAT IS A CONSULTANT?

Webster's New World Dictionary defines a consultant *as a person who consults with another or others . . . an expert who is called on for professional or technical advice or opinion.*[1]

WHO USES CONSULTANTS?

Almost every endeavor of the business, professional, governmental and educational world uses consultants. The lawyer seeks professional assistance from scientists and engineers regularly. The courts seek consultants and call these people "expert witnesses". The medical profession seeks other opinions in controversial and difficult cases involving surgery or other procedures. These people are not usually called consultants by this profession — they are called "specialists". The specialists give opinions. The Federal Government uses consultants in numerous ways. One person may be called in for advice and consultation for a 120 day maximum per year. The reader of research proposals at a peer review panel is a most common use of consulting. Serving on councils and commissions is another way. Reorganization of an agency, program, or formulating policy also requires consultants. Development of a management information system. The evaluation of one piece of hardware over another. The list can grow longer and longer.

INDUSTRY — It is not always cost effective to hire individuals or groups of individuals on a permanent basis to perform a task, evaluate a system, develop personnel, conduct seminars, etc. Therefore it is becoming commonplace for nearly all industrial organizations to bring in from time to time or have on a retainership a specified number of experts at the company's disposal. Another reason is cost-effectiveness. The costs of overhead, salary, fringe benefits and payment of taxes required of permanent personnel are not a problem with consultants. One of the most cogent reasons for using consultants is to obtain another view of a problem or situation. Consultants by-and-large are persons with great expertise and possess the quality and experience to objectively evaluate problems.

COLLEGES AND UNIVERSITIES — This sector is also realizing that it cannot do everything for itself. A problem associated with governance of universities and colleges which plagues administrators is the threat of collective bargaining or unionization. Yet, only a few institutions of the 3000 listed in the *Education Directory-Higher Education* published by the Department of Health, Education and Welfare are doing something about the problem. The way most higher education administrators attempt to solve the problem is to appoint a committee. As a result of the *"committee syndrome"*, many colleges and universities today have faculty in a full time role serving in faculty governance. Faculty should be teaching, engaging in research or another creative activity and constantly re-evaluating and improving the curriculum. A *schism* now exists between faculty and administrators. This is called the *"we-they"* syndrome. As a result of this emergence, a new breed of consultant has been born. This is the *collective bargaining agent, unionizer or negotiator.* To be sure this is not new to industry but new to higher education. This will have a marked effect on research and research administration. The effect can be both to the substance of the proposal as well as the time the project will be completed. Some say this can be a death blow to creativity and motivation. Time will tell.

CASE STUDY — COMPUTER

An interesting case took place during the writing of this Chapter relative to college and university consulting.[2]

A university located in the Southeastern part of the United States was about to purchase a new configuration of hardware to update its computer center at a cost of just under $2,000,000. The design for the center was essentially that used by many other universities and industries. It was to be a million bytes, with remote job entry and virtual memory. Because of the number of other successful users with the same design, it was felt that this was a safe and sane manner to travel. The finances would be taken from some of the newly planned programs, maintenance of buildings, and anticipated revenues from indirect costs for extramural funds. In addition each budget in the academic and non-academic area would be charged for the use of the computer plus a surcharge to pay for the computer. The decision recommendation was to buy the computer and pay the additional service contract charges.

The maintenance program of this university left a great deal to be desired. Painting, rotten wood trim and many of the sidewalks within the complex required repair and/or replacement. The acquisition of the $2,000,000 facility would place the maintenance in a deferred mode for at least two years assuming no crisis would befall the university and enrollments would remain the same or increase. Otherwise it would not be unreasonable to assume up to five years of deferred maintenance. In addition, the $2,000,000 expenditure would also defer purchase of much needed undergraduate and research equipment. The deferment would include the maintenance contracts which would be contracted for equipment coming off manufacturers warranty.

The study committee which recommended purchase of the new computer recommended that the existing computer equipment be junked because it dated back to the 1960's, although it was working well. The precipitant to this thrust for a new computer was made through the manufacturer of the currently owned university equipment when they announced that no maintenance contracts would be available in two years because of the age of the computer. One of the people in a leadership position either the Vice-President for Academic Affairs who was a physical scientist or a Trustee who was an executive in a chemical processing industry made the suggestion that a consultant be brought in to affirm the current plan and see whether or not this was the best route or if alternate routes should be taken with the idea of not sacrificing quality or performance only price.

A recommendation was made after several days on the campus followed by a two week period for a written report. The report did not affirm the configuration recommended by the university committee. The consultant recommended another configuration for the computer center which nearly rocked the foundations of the campus. It was advised in the carefully written and documented report that the "Mega-Mini"[3] concept be adopted either as an outright purchase or lease-buy contract. The comparable system (in a sufficient number of ways) could be purchased for approximately $900,000.

At a special meeting called by the Trustees of the University, the spokesman for the consulting firm said, "...for approximately the cost of my firm's services

($13,000) we can save over $1,000,000."

The "piece de resistance" is the fact the consultant firm found a buyer for the university's second generation solid state computer which it had been committed to junk. The yield in dollars for the sale of the old computer minus the consultant's costs still resulted in a savings to the University of $1,100,000.

CASE STUDY COMMENTS

Indeed, not always do the stories turn out this way, but they can if one remembers much homework is required before asking the consultant to visit. The consultant cannot be expected to be the *oracle of Nostradamus* or a *genie* who by the stroke of a wand can change things the way they should be or the way the client would like them to be.

Another methodology of using consultants which is fast becoming popular is placing the consultant on a retainer much like that of an attorney. This has many advantages. The main one is, the consultant becomes more familiar with the client's needs, talents, and resources within the client's organization. A dollar figure is normally arrived at and either paid in advance or installments of half in advance and the remainder in 30, 60 or 90 days into the life of the contract. The contract life should be one year with an optimum of eighteen months. This gives both parties an opportunity to see results. The contract should have a renewable option along with an evaluation period to ascertain actual performance. This should be at the beginning of the last quarter of the contract period. The contract should also specify the number of visits to the campus or to other sites. The consultant's vita should be carefully examined so that an experienced consultant is assigned to the client. If the retainership philosophy is adoped, one should expect advice and counsel throughout the planning process. If the latter were the case it may not have been necessary to spend nearly a year in committee deliberation for the almost $2,000,000 computer.

STANDARDS FOR PROFESSIONAL CONDUCT

Standard and Ethics serve both the client as well as the consultant. The client is served by at least matching the list of standards against the consultant and the particular problem or area the consultant is operating. The consultant benefits by having exposed himself or his firm to what the client may expect. In essence the mystique which might have existed — no longer exists.

The Association of Consultant Management Engineers developed a list of *Standards for Professional Conduct in 1963.*[4]

- We believe that the principal objective of the profession of management consulting is to help . . . nonprofit organizations analyze and solve management and related operating and technical problems.
- We will further the public interest by contributing through research and competent counsel on management problems to the development and better understanding of the art and science, practice and role of management in the economic and social systems of the free world.
- We will publicize our firm or services only in a manner upholding the dignity of the profession. We will present our qualifications to prospective clients solely in terms of our ability, experience, and reputation.
- We will accept only those engagements we are qualified to undertake and which are in the best interests of the clients.
- We will charge reasonable fees which are commensurate with the nature of the services performed and the responsibility assumed, and which, whenever feasible, have been agreed upon in advance of the engagement.
- We will guard as confidential all information concerning the business and affairs of clients coming to us in the course of professional engagements.
- We will not serve clients under terms or conditions which tend to interfere with or impair our objectivity, independence, or integrity.
- We will negotiate for possible work with a client where another firm is currently engaged only when we are assured that there is no reason for conflict between the two engagements.
- We will serve two or more competing clients at the same time on problems in a sensitive area only with their knowledge.

- We will not make direct or indirect offers of employment to employees of clients.
- We will make certain that the members of our professional staff, in order to insure their continuing objectivity, shall under no circumstances use a consulting engagement as a means of seeking new employment for themselves.
- We will not use data, technical material, procedures, or developments originated by other consulting firms but not released by them for public use, without their written permission.
- We will review for a client the work of another consulting firm currently employed by him only with the other consultant's knowledge.
- We will not make direct or indirect offers of employment to consultants on the staffs of other consulting firms.
- We will administer the internal and external affairs of our firm in the best interests of the profession at all times.
- We will endeavor to safeguard clients, the public, and ourselves against consultants deficient in moral character or professional competence.
- We will strive continually to improve our knowledge, skills, and techniques, and will make available to our clients the benefits of our professional attainments.

TEN REASONS FOR USING CONSULTANTS

In his book *Data Systems and Management,* Alton R. Kindred gives the following ten reasons for using outside consultants:

1. UNIQUE AREA OF EXPERTISE. Consultants can afford to specialize to a degree not practical in a typical systems department.
2. LIMITED ONE-TIME USE OF SPECIALIZED SKILLS. Often the need for a special body of knowledge is limited to a very small phase of the systems study. The outside consultant can provide this in such areas as computer software, data communications, market planning, etc.
3. COMPANY WAGE SCALE. Often a firm can justify a high-priced person on a short-term basis where it is not feasible to bring in a regular employee on a regular salary.
4. UNAVAILABILITY of SKILLS IN THE PRESENT MARKET. The consultant may be able to devote his specialized talent over the entire country or a large section of the country, thus bringing expertise to many users who might not be able to find such skills as a part of their permanent staff.
5. OBJECTIVITY. The outside consultant presumably will bring a less-biased viewpoint to his study of an organization than the person working among his close friends and personal acquaintances.

6. **ACCESS TO OUTSIDE SOURCES.** The consultant may himself often employ other consultants where he needs additional support and professional knowledge.

7. **MULTIPLE EXPOSURE TO ALTERNATE SOLUTIONS.** The outside consultant presumably has encountered frequently problems that are being faced in the current organization. They should be able to propose solutions that have been applied successfully in other institutions.

8. **RESPECT OF TOP MANAGEMENT.** It is sometimes unfortunate but nevertheless true that outsiders have easier access to the ear, as well as the respect, of top management. A man away from home becomes the expert. Recommendations coming from a consultant frequently carry more weight than equally good recommendations coming from a member of the organization's own staff.

9. **AVAILABILITY OF EXECUTIVE TIME.** Even where the company executives have the knowledge and ability to devise systems and procedures for new applications, they often do not have time to do so because of the press of their other duties. They might therefore bring in consultants to tackle specific jobs on a short-term basis.

10. **MANAGEMENT TRAINING AND EDUCATION.** Because consultants must deal with a variety of clients, many of whom have similar problems, the consulting firm is likely to have well established techniques, good documentation, adequate staff for charting, coding, and writing procedures, as well as methods of training the customer's personnel. It would be an extremely well organized, well-funded systems department that would be able to perform all of these functions within a single organization.[5]

Kindred has touched upon many requirements for a consultant. He of course focused primarily in the area of his expertise which is computers. Academic organizations have also found that a "fresh look" and analysis of their functions would be a wise investment.

CASE STUDY — SYSTEMS PLANNING

A very common practice now being used by most colleges and universities when planning a new campus site, the addition of a medical, dental, pharmacy or law school is to bring in a consulting company to prepare the plans. The hard look of ten to twenty years into the future is becoming a necessity for survival. Consultants worth their salt can use new and modern simulation techniques to determine parameters for such new ventures as a new college or university or adding schools at a new site. The same principles would apply to a Federal agency relocating to a new site; a new agency setting up a laboratory type or research facility; a new industry choosing from one or more sites to expand facilities or relocate and consolidate facilities at a new location. Those in the category who have not made the investment to carefully analyze all of the new techniques now available have found that many mistakes could have been avoided. The literature cites many of these cases where millions of dollars and untold numbers of hours have been wasted.

Recently, a consultant was asked to assist in the development of a student record system. The university had already estimated that in the past three years it had committed and spent over $300,000 of its own funds and the "SYSTEM" just was not getting off the launching pad. Frustrations as well as tempers flaired by students, faculty and administrators over codes and domains. The consultant was asked to examine and discuss a plausible system with cognizant university officials. After the first visit, the chaos was so obvious to the consultant that the report submitted read as follows: ". . . . XYZ Consultants have examined and evaluated the progress made to date of your internally designed student record system. For the number of reasons elucidated on pages three through ten of our report we are convinced that your system as currently designed will not perform as expected. We recommend that a new system be designed. XYZ Consultants possess sufficient experience in systems design to assure you sample models will be demonstrated ninety days after the contract has been signed and will place the university on line twelve to eighteen months after the contract has been executed."

After much discussion and dickering, the university signed a contract and work began. Sample models were completed before time some sixty days after the contract was awarded. Eleven months to the day the systems were operating and the editorial page of the student newspaper said all that could be said. "As Editor of the Beacon_____ and having spent almost four

years here at_____ University, the most exciting
experience I have had was registration for my last
semester. Having expected the usual, I was first in line
on Monday at 8:00 A.M. Expecting to spend the morning
at registration, I brought my hot coffee in a Thermos
and two sandwiches. To my surprise five minutes after
the registration line officially opened, I was registered
and on my way. Thank you, MIRACLE MAKER."

The old system was so much a "patchwork quilt"
that even the administrative officials realized what had
transpired in the past was just a plain loss. The University spent $75,000 for the finished job using outside
assistance. In the financial analysis submitted to the
Trustees of the University, the consultants uncovered
the actual expenses incurred. They were $300,000 for
the past three years; however, including the figures
since the student record system (1966), the nine year
period expenditures nearly reached the half million
dollar mark.[6]

CASE STUDY COMMENTS

Ironically, at another State university in the same State
less than 200 miles away, the sister University computer
center director and his staff were able to go on line with a
sophisticated computerized student record system one
year from the start date. The sister University used commercially available software. It can be done. Whether
it is a management information system, accounting system, library book record system or whatever. Ideas plus
dollars catalyzed by competent people or consultants
can produce the needed accessible information so that
good decisions can be made. Combinations of consultants
and commercial software are other dimensions of the
horrendous management information system problem.[6]
One caution — do not get caught in the "hardware quicksand". There are numbers of computer centers operating
inefficiently because of "hardware quicksand"; this being
the acquisition of hardware without real regard to what

the hardware can or cannot do. Because of this malady there are an inordinate number of computer centers operating with much too large budgets, enough at least to stagger the imagination. Too often an ICBM is used to shoot at a 12 inch balloon when an inexpensive 22 caliber dart gun will do the same job.

ACCOUNTING AND AUDITING FIRMS

Gordon B. Baty in his book, *"Entrepreneurship-Playing to Win"* speaks to the selection of an auditing firm. He refers to the *"Big Eight"* public accounting firms: Arthur Anderson & Co.; Coopers & Lybrand; Ernst & Ernst; Arthur Young & Co.; Haskins & Sells; Peat, Marwick, Mitchell and Co.; Price Waterhouse & Co.; and Touche Ross & Co.[7] These firms are all superb for the function of auditing financial records and making recommendations directly involved with that which is expected of a Certified Public Accountant. Occasionally, just as in all walks of life, members of an audit team become over zealous and seek to make recommendations for which they have no real substantive basis or background. This becomes obvious when reading the *"management letters"* or recommendations which accompany the financial reports. These letters are read by top management and in the university sector are normally sent to the governing board of the institution rather than to its president.

The audit of a graduate school or program, research program or office or academic programs in general should not be conducted by a public accountant, but by a team of experts in the subject area. Such consultants will pin point both the positive as well as the negative with objectivity. Conversely, one should not ask a graduate dean, research director or academic team to audit the financial records of the business office from a financial point of view. This is definitely the job of a Certified

Public Accountant.

Emphasis has been placed upon this subject because there is an increase in higher education encroachment by the business offices who for all practical purposes steer the audit teams to write up the recommendations as to which firms should be considered as the outside auditors. Too often the financial picture is examined without regard to the many other facets of the educative process. The reports thus become biased and do not tell the whole story. Consultants should be used when the resources for solutions are inadequate within the organization. Problems may range from simple to complex. They may include the reorganization of the entire organization or a smaller problem like a new accounting system. The consultant should not be used to pacify the current situation or *status quo*.

When considering any changes in management of people and ideas be sure to consider *records management* and *people volume*. (See Chapter Eleven Models of Research Administration). The computer has been mentioned a great deal and today the awe should be gone about computers. Just as an atmosphere of learning and research requires a library so does it require a computer. The computer may be used as a *number cruncher* or an *informational data base*.

CONCLUSION

It is rare that an individual researcher or even a research team has all of the skills for accomplishment of a project's objectives. In the past researchers chatted informally with colleagues. Today the process has been institutionalized into a system of consultation. The concept of consultants has been encouraged to give evidence of cooperative endeavors across discipline, departmental, institutional and geographic boundaries. The variety of information and services now available via the consultant route is enormous. Such availability and diversity indicate another area in which researchers and research administrators are required to acquire knowledge so that the concept of consultants can be legally, effectively and efficiently utilized.

Chapter Ten

RESOURCE ALLOCATION AND MANAGEMENT

- INTRODUCTION
- RESOURCES
- BUDGET
- EQUIPMENT
- COMPUTERS
- ANALYSIS OF NEEDS
- CONCLUSION

INTRODUCTION

The allocation and management of resources is critical to research in all ways. It is particularly important in the formulation of a good proposal. Resource allocation can be interpreted as the total of all requirements for conducting a project. It is the matching of the needs with resources which must be managed.

RESOURCES

Resources may be classified as *human, physical, facility* and *fiscal* in nature.

Human Resources — Human resources consist of faculty, consultants, graduate students, secretarial assistance, laboratory assistants, laboratory technicians, instrument repair technicians, interviewers, research associates, etc. The common denominator for resources is effort. Effort is measured in per cent and full time equivalents (F.T.E.) and translated into dollars.

Physical Resources — Physical resources consist of movable equipment, computers, specialized equipment and instruments, office furniture, office equipment, printing equipment, photographic equipment, etc. The common denominator for physical resources is output. Output is measured in percent usage and translated into dollars per unit time. A most common example would be the computer. I.e., an IBM 360/65 Computer using a fast-core may charge $600 per central processing unit (c.p.u.) hour for its use. A proposal budget submitted for funding requesting computer time should express computer usage in quantitative terms such as cost per c.p.u. hour.

Facilities Resources — Facility resources consist of buildings, special facilities, resource areas, laboratories, classrooms, conference rooms, libraries, etc. Facility resources differ from physical resources in that facility resources are fixed and are normally described as "brick and mortar". The common denominator for facilities resources is also output. It is not a simple matter to measure facility resources in conventional terms. Facilities usage is normally determined by a complex process of the computation of indirect costs. Indirect cost computation takes into consideration the use of all facilities used for research purposes. It also takes into consideration the percent use of any facility used in the support of the project. This could be a meeting room, office, library or any facility which supports the project in question. Computation of indirect costs is a cooperative venture. The input from the researcher and his staff must be accurate and detailed in cooperation with the business office which actually comes up with the computed figure. The work sheets and the iterations before the figure can be submitted for consideration by the DHEW Audit Agency can take as much as a year to assemble and compute. Some of the more important principles surrounding the computation of *indirect costs* can be found in the Appendix of this book under *"Federal Management Circular 73-8"* (formerly known as *Office of Management and Budget Circular A-21 Revised).*

BUDGET

Budget is the *key* to the operation of a research, developmental or demonstration project. Gordon Baty[1] defines a budget as: (1) a tool for implementing plans; (2) a tool for communication; (3) a tool for cost control; and (4) a tool for assessment of employee performance. Indeed, budget is a tool just as a library is for conducting a research project. Without either the probability of success would be questionable. The budget of a project connects the resources with the program phase. The program could be: laboratory experimentation; interviewing; writing tests; performing measurements; chemical analysis of foods; nuclear experimentation; or computer analyses. Regardless of whether the *research program* falls into the category of physical, biological, engineering or social sciences; or whether it be in music, humanities, arts, law or medicine; any *program* which is to be executed requires resources. Thus, the budget is not an entity by itself but a *connecting link* for the project.

Should a funding agency make a request or the need arise for the preparation of a budget without any guidance from within the organization or funding agency, the reader may turn to Chapter Sixteen for assistance.

Most agencies, particularly those in the Federal sector suggest and often require that the *exact* forms supplied with the *program guidelines* be used.

Allowances — The agency who has sent out the guidelines normally states the items which are considered *allowable* or *disallowable*. Do not skim these items — read them rather carefully. It may be shocking to find that no allowance is given for the salary of the principal investigator. This means a conference with the administration of your organization should be arranged immediately. Before considering submission of the project it is necessary to ascertain whether or not resources within the organization are available to support the percentage of *release time* needed to perform the project.

PROBLEM AREAS — Release-Time — Many readers will be under the apprehension that *release-time* does not cost actual dollars. Unfortunately, *release-time* is a real cost. It would be necessary for the proposing institution to transfer the percentage of funds which would be devoted to the project (an example would be 25%) to a *cost-share* account and reduce the load of the individual who would be the project director by 25 percent. Payment for remuneration would therefore be 75 percent from regular budget and 25 per cent from cost-share account. There are other ways to handle this kind of situation, but whatever way is used the principles remain the same. Either cost-share or whatever — the project still will cost the institution the 25 percent *release-time*. Some readers will say that an *"in-kind"* contribution will suffice and there is no cost involved. *"In-kind"* contributions for effort are a thing of the past — audits will not recognize such statements in a *post-grant-audit* without *personnel actions* to back it up. The *personnel actions* must conform with other Federal statutes — namely the *Fair Practices Labor Laws*. In the analysis of the project proposal when this kind of situation arises, it may be well for the project-writer to have prepared a defense of why his or her home institution should invest in the *release-time*. Does the overall improvement to the institution outweigh the cost of the "release-time"? One should remember that the competition for funds on the outside is also creating a similar competition in the internal organizations. Thus, the same care and effort should be exercised in convincing and justifying the need within the organization for supportive funds to conduct partially funded projects.

COSTING-OUT — *Costing-out* is a term which applies to analysis of each item in the budget. When requesting travel be sure that every consideration has been considered. Failure to specify jet-tourist and not first-class is one error. Travel without specifying both reason and location is also a common error. Requesting support for attending an unknown meeting is common. Publication costs without specifying the journal, the progress of the project toward publication and the nature of the proposed publication could be enough to kill the entire request.

EQUIPMENT

Whether it be physical measurement equipment or equipment to conduct a humanities project — the nature of the equipment is not important. The important factor to keep in mind is the use. Can the equipment requested be adequately justified in light of the proposed project.

There are problems associated with the advances in technology today. One such which plagues the researcher is the speed with which items of equipment undergo change. Some refer to this as obsolescence. In all cases this is not true — although claimed by many a project director. Many *"widgets"* undergo facial changes by competitive manufacturers. Indeed, there are many changes and with the micrologic in solid state electronics one just has to look at his pocket calculator to see what advances have been made in the short span of two years. Agency officials are just as aware of the technological changes as the project director is. One such approach which may avoid a great deal of turbulence is to add to the request based upon current prices and models after the detailed description the statement, *"or equivalent."* This often covers the internal requirements for competitive bidding, State purchasing requirements and the agencies' recognition that by the time a project may be funded a completely new generation of hardware may reach the marketplace.

Another aspect of equipment in grants, contracts and projects in general is the age old problem of how much will it be used? The percentage of usage or so called *"use factor"* is a critical one to consider if the equipment is expensive. Factors to consider are:

- Should the equipment be rented for the length of the project and paid for by the project?
- Should the equipment be purchased outright with only a portion of the dollars requested by the funding agency and the rest committed by the home organization?
- Should the equipment be purchased outright and all of the funds be requested by the home organization from the funding agency?
- Should a *lease-buy* (a lease with the option to buy and a percentage of the lease costs apply to the purchase price) be considered?

Because equipment costs are so high and very complex, funding agencies spend a great deal of time and effort in determining whether or not the items requested are justifiable. The number of analyses which may be performed in any given week or month will be taken into consideration. A project director of a proposal may receive a letter saying, ". . . . we have examined your proposal plan and would like to know why the samples cannot be sent to an outside laboratory for analysis at an expense of approximately $900 versus the outright purchase of equipment for $35,000?" This situation may not fit your particular case, but the example can be extrapolated to any piece of equipment in any discipline. Heed the *"use factor."* Try to answer the questions pertaining to your case as to purchase, lease, lease-buy or outright rental. One common error that costs investigators and their organizations losses is the omission of maintenance contracts for equipment which has gone out of warranty. Some warranties do not exceed ninety days and yet the additional years maintenance contract can run into several hundred dollars. A simple item like an office copier costs several hundred dollars a year for such protection; think what the maintenance costs would be for a computer, electron microscope, analytical instruments, nuclear magnetic resonance spectrometer, etc. The costs are very high and run into the thousands of dollars a year. Rental normally includes this kind of contract, lease also. Purchase presents a problem of maintenance contracts. Do keep these nuances in mind when writing a proposal and defending your project plan to your superiors.

COMPUTERS

The use of the computer has extended from the pure physical sciences to the social sciences and now into the humanities and arts. Projects of analysis and simulation have been conducted by music departments — an example of the wide usage the computer is receiving today. Because of this wide usage some thoughts surrounding the use of the computer are in order.

A bona fide request for computer time will not be considered by some funding sources. Some agencies consider computer time a cost which should be absorbed by the institution requesting the funding. The minicomputer for certain projects is considered a valid request. One caution should be exercised when writing proposals in which *"mini"*, *"micro"* or *"Megamini*ᴷ*"* type of computers are considered, and that is to be sure that there is compatibility with the requested items of hardware and the existing main frame. Also remember that the funding agency has at its disposal untold numbers of experts who will ask the same questions. When the questions are answered well in advance and in the proposal a much clearer chance of funds will result. Do mention the other items of a similar nature which exist on your home organization location.

ANALYSIS OF NEEDS

The preparation of a budget should not be done by taking a catalog and copying a list of items. In the funding agencies this is referred to as a *"Christmas stocking list"* and does not lead to favorable remarks. It is to the advantage of the writer to determine exactly what is needed to conduct the project. References and addenda with written justification for the use of items requested will serve to strengthen the project plan both at the writer's home institution and at the funding agency.

Travel requests should also be fully justified. Travel in general is given a great deal of scrutiny. Some cogent comments pertaining to travel were already cited earlier in this Chapter. A travel policy if it exists should be appended to the proposal. Almost all industrial organizations have printed policies as to what constitutes business and professional travel. Similarly many universities and private organizations have the same.It is this kind of policy which should be appended to the proposal especially when a large amount of travel is requested.

Publication costs are another sore place in the analysis of a proposal for potential funding. The variance in journal charges from over $75 to perhaps less than $10 a page requires explanation. The subject of page charges is sufficiently important to have been mentioned earlier in this Chapter.

CONCLUSION

Every step in the process of preparing a proposal may be described as important, but allocation of resources is the crux. To not carefully consider the human, physical, facility and fiscal resources which are requested or available can ultimately bring failure even after an award is received. To plan a sound budget and not manage the expenditure of funds received is self-defeating. A principal investigator and institution's research administration organization must work in cooperation from the point of initiation of an idea to the final post-audit. This will serve to insure the successful completion and implementation of the available resources.

Chapter Eleven

MODELS OF RESEARCH ADMINISTRATION ORGANIZATIONS

INTRODUCTION

Research administration means different things to different people. To some researchers it means red tape and to others it means assistance and support. Still to others it does not mean very much. If one were to query other administrators with the same question posed to active research personnel, similar answers would result. The reasons for the wide range of frustrations and opinions are many and varied. One of the most common reasons given is the lack of definition, mission, function, philosophy and purpose of the research administration organization. The authors intend to clarify definition,

201

mission, function, philosophy, purpose and to add the component commitment. Suggested models which are viable to any research organization will be discussed.

It should be understood that each model presented can be modified to suit a particular organization. Such modifications may be dictated by currently available personnel, pre-defined mission and goals of the organization, available budget and resources along with a host of other items.

One complex problem besetting research administration today is the multifaceted role that research administrators must play. They must impart information and give assistance to the how, why, where and when of proposal applications. Some refer to this phase as program development. Program development is a most important requirement for assisting faculty and staff. Another facet is acting as a monitor for Federal grants and contracts and their imposed requirements for approvals, signatures and reports. Pressure in the form of follow-up is often required to see that periodic reports are sent on time to the funding sources. Some administrators have voiced opinions that the roles of the research administrator are incompatible and it is this incompatibility which accounts for the wide range of opinion, frustration and confusion which may exist.

Compatibility can and must exist. Rapport can only be solidified when the roles and responsibilities of all parties have clear and defined written guidelines in which to operate. As a case in point, when an adversary atmosphere prevails, more often than not a standard operating procedure is absent or a very diffuse and unclear perception of responsibilities exists.

DEFINITION OF RESEARCH ADMINISTRATION

Research administration may be defined in the very

narrow sense as a functional organization serving to assist the principal investigator, project director, and/or the operating level of project management which seeks extramural and intramural funds, prepares informal preliminary and formal proposal plans, develops satisfactory and realistic budgets and assists in the typewriting, typesetting, duplication, printing and dispatch of the finished proposal. In addition, the research administration organization is responsible for the intervening activities in the life cycle of the proposal, from preparation to award through to the final report. In the broad sense research administration must be attuned to the needs, aspirations, plans, goals and resources of the overall organization it serves. The mere acquisition of extramural funds does not make up the full picture. Too often the influence of extramural funds has altered what might have been a healthy organization. It is essential that the entrepreneur be encouraged but not at the expense of the rest of the organization. Advanced planning with a knowledge of what requirements are developing and/or changing helps place the research administrator in a position of being an asset as well as a valuable source of information for executive planning and decision making.

IDENTIFYING RESEARCH ADMINISTRATORS

In a move stimulated by research administrators in Texas and the State of Washington, both the Society of Research Administrators and the National Council of University Research Administrators (national societies serving research administration) have committees examining ways to identify research administrators as professionals. Some thoughts which have been expressed concerning professionalism are to certify or license each research administrator. The area is quite controversial. Licensure usually is based upon the need to protect individuals or groups when health, life or limb is in jeopardy. From a legal point of view the research administrator does not seem to fall into that category. Certification although it sounds good on the surface is also not without its problems. The heterogeneity of the individuals who perform as research administrators adds to the complexity. Perhaps a well articulated Code of Ethics adopted by all of the societies concerned with research administration could answer the needs of *professionalism.*

There are no specific qualifications for becoming a research administrator. Some organizations for the reason of economy take recent college graduates and call them research directors or tack on a similar title without any rational reason. Others give the job to individuals who are experienced researchers with proven track records in research as well as administration. Still others just add duties to an individual who may or may not be qualified.

In the industrial community the research administrator is normally a very accomplished individual. The Lockheed Corporation uses these very accomplished individuals in a variety of tasks. Why should Lockheed be singled out? Simply because of their success. In 1975 they received $2.08 Billion in prime contracts from the United States Government. Formerly number one on the list, General Dynamics Corporation, now number six, received $1.3 Billion in contracts from the United States Government. Major corporations in contrast with other organizations have long recognized that top management is the place for research administration. SDS Xerox took a former engineering dean who became Assistant Secretary of Commerce and placed him at a senior vice presidential level.

The wish to better oneself and the image held by others is admirable and should not be looked upon lightly or discouraged. However, before one can be accepted as a professional there are some steps which must be taken. One must act as a professional and perform as a professional. Acceptance is not an instantaneous acquisition, it takes time. The tag of certification and/or licensure in itself will not accomplish the goal. There are other organizations and specialties which have gone this route. Noteworthy is the profession of the *"Health Physicist"* or *"Radiological Control Officer"*. This group used as its prime reason for certification, the need for standards because of the danger to health, life and limb.

In universities, colleges and academia in general, the range is very wide, the educational backgrounds and level of responsibilities are also quite varied. One may find research administrators with a background of strictly on-the-job training or no college training. Such people have spent a decade or so as administrative assistants, accountants, bookkeepers, receptionists, and many other jobs and have risen in their organizations. They also have acquired the jargon as well as the kinds of things principal investigators require. Others have been educated with one or two years of college, bachelor's degree and still others come into the position via the professorial route. Some with master's degrees have been entering the specialty after completing one career with the military. A careful study of the most successful in academia occupying this position indicates that the research administrator will be one who has gone through the *"chairs"* to full professor, has successfully served as a department chairman and later as a dean.

Salaries also range widely. They are from $10,500 to over $40,000. To be sure there are fewer at each end of the spectrum with the larger numbers hovering in between. The age of the active research administrator today ranges from twenty to the late sixties. Up until a very few years ago the profession was male dominated. Today and to the betterment of the profession — women are found in all levels and represent leadership positions in the professional societies.

In academia graduate deans, assistant, associate and full deans, assistant, associate and full vice presidents as well as non-academic administrative assistants serve as research administrators. Each or all may retain the same title of *Director of Research.*

RESEARCH ADMINISTRATION MODELS

BACKGROUND — In a college or university environment, whether it be large or small, church or non-church related, state or private controlled, the primary purpose for the existence of any academic institution is teaching, research and service. In the Land-Grant Colleges and Universities tradition, service is often called extension. Research is essential to the success and well being of instruction. It is the only true test that what is taught is both up to date and in accord with current thought.

Excellence pervades the atmosphere when methods and content of instruction are research based. It therefore becomes an important function in the academic environment to create, nurture, excite and serve the needs of research. It is this relatively new function, research administration within academic organizations, which serves the needs of research.

Research is not a separate and distinct entity. Research is but one of the components which make up the educative process. Too often research is treated separately and without regard to the other components of the process.

MODELS — Two questions posed by chief executives of universities whenever the subject of research administration is brought up are: what is the best organization for the program and which is the better approach, central or non-central control? There is no one answer to this compound question. One may be correct for one organization and incorrect for another. The authors are fortunate to have served under both models; however, no model will be given favor over the other. The reasons should be obvious. No two central or non-central models would be identical in all respects. What the reader can expect is an objective analysis of the two basic models with features that could and perhaps should be incorporated with whatever controls your organization uses. For example, later in this Chapter a great deal of detail will be given to the receipt of proposals and the conduct of a peer review system within your own organization. These are emphasized because of the importance of seeing that faculty, or staff (of academic, non-profit organizations, private research foundations and industrial entities) are given the tools to compete in the extramural funding world. The models given can fit either of the two — centralized or decentralized. Cost factors will be given for both the centralized and the decentralized which will be of value when choices are to be made.

FIRST COMMON ERROR — One of the most common errors made in developing, reorganizing and analyzing a research organization is first to construct on paper an organizational diagram fitting people and titles into blocks and *"wiring"* them to their co-workers and supervisors. This is definitely a backwards approach and should be avoided at all costs. *The organizational plan should precede the "wiring diagram" for the organization.* Although this may be the most commonly employed practice (drawing the diagram first), it yields the least efficacious route to success.

The most desirable approach is to decide on what the organization's mission shall be and evolve from the mission statement some realistic goals, specific objectives and finally programs and tasks. From this point the staffing can be objectively examined based upon expected functions rather than a table of organization.

The table of organization is necessary but only after the plan has been conceived, not before.

SECOND COMMON ERROR — Today in academic circles there are primarily two prevailing schools of thought as to how research should be funded and be administered. If one were fortunate enough to have looked at thousands of cover sheets of proposals submitted to Federal agencies they would note that the final approval signature was from one of three persons. Most infrequently it is the president of the institution, followed by the chief academic officer in order of frequency and finally the chief financial officer.

The function of the business manager, controller, comptroller or vice president for finance without question is important. The finance officer should never be allowed to administer research, graduate studies, or curriculum. The financial function is clearly service, maintaining current records with the most sophisticated systems available, financial accounting, requisitions, purchasing, payment of vouchers, financial audit and other areas of sound *fiscal* management.

Research and all of its tenets are academic, creative and instructional — fiscal management is repetitive, a necessary requirement and service oriented. Research administration also is truly academic. It is here the functions and services are focused toward the betterment of the entire academic community — students, faculty and academic administration. This is the healthy way and an assured road to success. The person chosen to head this organization should have the following qualifications:

- **EARNED DOCTORATE**
- **SUCCESSFUL RESEARCH ACCOMPLISHMENTS**
- **REASONABLE NUMBER OF PUBLICATIONS**
- **SUCCESS IN SECURING EXTRAMURAL FUNDS FOR HIS OWN RESEARCH**
- **SUFFICIENT ADMINISTRATIVE EXPERIENCE PREFERABLY AS DEPARTMENT HEAD, LATER AS DEAN**
- **DEDICATION TO EXCELLENCE IN RESEARCH**

- NO KNOWN BIASES FOR OTHER DISCIPLINES (THIS IS A FATAL FLAW)
- A TOUR AT A PRIVATE FOUNDATION OR FEDERAL AGENCY IN A GRANTING OFFICER'S CAPACITY.

Whatever structure the organization takes, similar qualifications follow for government, industry as well as academia. One argument against the qualifications above is *"it will cost too much."* Those who have hired the more experienced would answer, *"you get what you pay for."*

CENTRALIZED RESEARCH ADMINISTRATION

The centralized research administration model is one that normally operates directly under the president of a college, university, industrial organization, private foundation, or private research institute. The Federal government is excluded from this discussion because of the complexity of operations. In essence Federal government laboratories operate research in a dual mode. Industry by and large operates in a centralized mode and universities a combination of the two.

The ideal marriage between graduate studies and research has separated many of our academic institutions both substantively and organizationally. It really does not matter whether the institution is private or state controlled, some mechanism is necessary organizationally for receiving gifts, grants and contracts and submitting proposals for outside support and still maintain substantive integration within the institution.

Through the Research Management Improvement Program (RMIP)[1] which recently became defunct, studies have been made to improve research administration. There is a real question whether the $3.88 Million awarded will accomplish anything but place volumes of the required final reports on bookshelves or its reports remain in the National Science Foundation files. One study which has not been completed is examining research foundations and institutes. There are many colleges and universities which operate separate and distinct institutes and foundations. Some of the operations are separate corporations; others are separate organizations within the administration of the institution. No two appear to be the same. Fundamentally the best way to operate a research institute or corporate foundation for the administration of research and the receipt of funds is to insure that its prime purpose is for the improvement of the educational process.

One such organization is the Purdue Research Foundation. Through the wisdom and imagination of Purdue University's President, Frederick L. Hovde, the Purdue Research Foundation established a division of sponsored programs.[2] This organization which began in July, 1966 was succinctly charged with the review, approval and submission of proposals for research, instructional, and other externally sponsored programs. The officers of the Division of Sponsored Programs hold dual positions in the Research Foundation and the Graduate School. The personnel chosen to assume the responsibilities of proposals and extramural funds fit well into those qualifications elucidated earlier in the Chapter. Preliminary proposals and formal proposals are likewise handled by this group. Program development and ideas are channelled into the Foundation both from faculty, students as well as administrators. The system has undergone little modification since its inception and is quite accepted by the population it serves. The senior members of the Division of Sponsored Programs have discipline specialties which complement the various specialties on the campus. Rotating faculty also work within the organization, this keeps the blood flowing at all times and reduces the chances for stagnancy.

A centralized model with an interface with students, faculty and other administrators bridged closely with the graduate school helps develop priorities which ultimately serve the entire academic community rather than a few self-interest groups.

The normal procedure with this model is for the professor to engage in informal dialogue with his department head and dean and interact directly with the centralized research administration charged with program development. Program development should not be delegated to subordinates, the major development should be left to senior personnel. If this is done, when research or project ideas do not fit into the institutional process or setting the overall decision is made with full knowledge of the scope and purposes of the institution as a whole.

Services such as the preparation of final proposal for transmittal is one that few institutions have yet resolved. Industry accomplishes the completion of the proposal (typing and printing) in its word processing centers. Government follows a similar pattern. There are many Federal agencies which submit proposals for funding in a like fashion as do universities, industry and private non-profit organizations. For example, projects are funded for the military academies, other bureaus of the government, and the Department of Commerce, etc. Government likewise uses a standard format and the preparation of proposals is accomplished with automatic equipment at a central location.

Those who review proposals expect neat and easily readable copy. Because of this, some institutions have adopted the industrial approach and have proposals typed in a central location using standardized automatic equipment. Others have prescribed formats for each department within the institution to follow. Still others accept whatever is sent forward for dispatch and hold the originating department responsible for the typing and duplication of the proposal. Before hasty decisions are made in favor of adoption for central production, a cost analysis should be performed. The equipment which does outstanding work for proposal preparation is commercially available.

Rental versus purchase is another consideration. What will be the work load? Who will be held responsible for determining the priority of which proposal is to be prepared? With little imagination one can readily see that a great deal of material in proposal preparation is repetitive, such as: library holdings, history of the institution, computer charges, computer holdings, Civil Rights Compliance, travel policies, etc. All of the aforementioned examples could be retrieved from a cassette or magnetic card as needed. Faculty vitae could likewise be held on magnetic card or cassette compatible with the proposal producing equipment and revised annually on a rotating basis. It can be seen easily there are arguments for and against the centralized typing and duplicating approach. Which is best for your situation? Again make an analysis before you decide.

ORGANIZATION OF CENTRALIZED RESEARCH ADMINISTRATION — In the model given, the chief officer of research administration will be the vice president for research and graduate studies. The following will elucidate the responsibilities of key personnel involved in research administration and graduate research.

VICE PRESIDENT FOR RESEARCH AND GRADUATE STUDIES — The Vice President for Research and Graduate Studies reports directly to the President of the University. He represents the University's functions on the President's Cabinet. In addition he advises the President on University planning for research, graduate studies, physical facilities, equipment, computers, radiological safety, health and control, and academic salaries and tenure.

The Vice President is chairman of the University Research Committee and the Graduate Council and is

University Representative for research and the Graduate School at the annual meetings of the American Council of Graduate Schools, NCAR, NASULGC, NCURA and other organizations designated by the President.

The Office of the Vice President for Research and Graduate Studies is responsible for the creation, preservation and maintenance of an atmosphere conducive to creative activity, scholarly research and viable programs. The Office is expected to disseminate current information as to emerging programs, Federal and State regulations, applications for research and instructional programs and to be a place where the faculty can have hands-on access to reference material relative to programs leading to grants and contracts.

The Office shall disseminate abstracts of all proposals to the respective units of the University and to all members of the University Research Committee. The Office shall disseminate Standard Operating Procedures governing the use of research funds for intramural and extramural sponsored projects.

The Office shall assist faculty in the preparation of proposals for research and other educational projects. The Office shall assist the faculty in making contacts with potential funding sources.

The Office shall prepare for the President for distribution to the Deans of the Colleges periodic analyses as to the progress of the various units within the University by College and by department.

The Vice President for Research and Graduate Studies will maintain and/or establish progressive systems for the best standards for graduate theses. The office will establish and disseminate to all graduate students a copy of *"The University Standards for the Preparation of a Graduate Thesis."*

DEANS OF THE COLLEGES — The deans of the colleges have the responsibility for research activities of their faculty and for the allocation of research funds assigned to them. The dean's approval is required on each research proposal from his faculty for submission, whether it be for internal or external funds.

DEPARTMENT HEADS — The fundamental unit of the University for instruction and research is the department. It is in this environment where one finds both skills and similar academic backgrounds grouped together. Within the department both instructional and research objectives are borne, developed and coordinated.

VICE PRESIDENT FOR FINANCE — The Vice President for Finance and his office are responsible for all fiscal reporting to project leaders, certification of funds, completion of fiscal reports, sponsored funding account monitoring, budget control, billing, receipt of funds, disbursement of funds, accounting for funds, payroll operations, property accounting and internal audit.

CONTRACT NEGOTIATIONS — The person responsible for negotiation of contracts and grants is a member of the staff of the Vice President for Research and Graduate Studies. This person is responsible to see that all policies and procedures of the University and the outside sponsor have been adhered to. The contract negotiator will initially process all official papers before formally accepted by the Vice President for Research and Graduate Studies.

The Vice President for Research and Graduate Studies requires an interface with several groups in addtion to his close relationship and operations with the other vice presidents and the President. Depending upon the existing policies, procedures and faculty governance at your particular institution the formation and composition will vary from institution to institution. Examples of needed interface and dialogue follow:

- **ARTS AND HUMANITIES COUNCIL**
- **HEALTH SCIENCES COUNCIL**
- **SCIENCE AND ENGINEERING COUNCIL**
- **COMPUTER CENTER COUNCIL**
- **RESEARCH COUNCIL OR COMMITTEE**
- **CENTERS AND SPECIAL RESEARCH PROJECTS COUNCIL**
- **FACULTY RESEARCH AWARDS COUNCIL**
- **RADIOLOGICAL AND NUCLEAR SAFETY COUNCIL**
- **RESEARCH SAFETY COUNCIL**
- **PATENT AND COPYRIGHT COUNCIL**

DECENTRALIZED RESEARCH ADMINISTRATION MODEL

This model usually places the highest organizational level of responsibility at the level of the college dean. Some coordinating structure is usually present to oversee how the colleges are operating on a day to day basis in a monthly review council. The council is often headed by the academic affairs vice president or a dean elected from the council of deans for research.

A dean or a designated associate serves in a capacity similar to that of the vice president; however, operations are limited to one college. Each college operates somewhat independently of the others. The one exception is the articulation *vis-a-vis* the coordinator, and how strongly coordination is exerted dictates how much interaction will be among the colleges.

The rationale given for the decentralized model is that a maximum amount of interaction is enjoyed by the faculty with their research administrator. It is felt by those who favor decentralization that a greater closeness and trust emerges from this model than from the centralized approach. Indirect costs generated by the parent college are normally returned by some formula percentage derived for the operation of the research administration office. Some of the indirect cost funds are retained by the administration above the college level. The arguments in favor of or against one model versus another are many.

The authors are only reporting arguments made, not serving as commentators. The monitoring of research and graduate study is felt to be an advantage for this model. The chief academic officer of the college will argue that he has greater control and moral pursuasion at his command to excite change and alter road maps which will yield unsuccessful results.

A recent study conducted uy a private consulting firm determined the costs of two universities operating decentralized research administration organizations.[4] The figures have been disguised to protect the confidentiality of the institutions. In both institutions the faculty number less than one thousand, and the student body approximately 26,000. The operating costs of corresponding colleges in the two universities were astoundingly close. To allow for inflation and what the average institution pays for personnel, personnel costs have likewise been adjusted. To fit your situation adjust items which are not appropriate to your situation. **REMEMBER THE BUDGET SHOWN IS FOR ONE COLLEGE, NOT THE ENTIRE UNIVERSITY.** Comparable studies made for centralized research indicate between $500,000 and $750,000 for institutions of similar size for the entire university. The following decentralized **college** model represented a faculty of 490, a college budget for salaries of nearly $9 Million plus $2 Million in extramural research.[3]

1976 BUDGET SUN UNIVERSITY
(BLANK) COLLEGE RESEARCH ADMINISTRATION
(BLANK) COLLEGE RESEARCH ADMINISTRATION BUDGET ANNEX A

PERSONNEL

POSITION	TITLE	12 MONTHS
1. DEAN OF SPONSORED RESEARCH PROJECTS AND GRADUATE STUDIES AND PROFESSOR OF PSYCHOLOGY (1.0 FTE)		$38,000
2. ASSISTANT TO THE DEAN AND ASSOCIATE PROFESSOR OF BIOLOGICAL SCIENCES (ROTATING FACULTY MEMBER 0.5 FTE)		12,000
3. TECHNICAL WRITER (1.0 FTE)		10,500
4. CONTRACT ADMINISTRATOR ACCOUNTANT (1.0 FTE)		10,500
5. ACCOUNTANT I (1.0 FTE)		8,500
6. ASSISTANT ACCOUNTANT (1.0 FTE)		6,500
7. SECRETARY TO THE DEAN (1.0 FTE)		9,800
8. ELECTRONIC TYPEWRITER OPERATOR II (1.0 FTE)		8,000
9. RESEARCH OPERATIONS SUPERVISOR (1.0 FTE)		9,500
10. ELECTRONIC TYPEWRITER OPERATOR I-SECRETARY (1.0 FTE)		6,000
10 POSITIONS		**$119,300**
9.5 FTE	**FRINGE BENEFITS**	14,304
		$133,604

Table 1 • *SUN UNIVERSITY RESEARCH BUDGET "A"*

1976 BUDGET SUN UNIVERSITY
(BLANK) COLLEGE RESEARCH ADMINISTRATION BUDGET ANNEX B

EQUIPMENT

ITEM	QUANTITY	EQUIPMENT	EACH	TOTAL
1.	2 EACH	IBM CORRECTING SELECTRIC TYPEWRITERS MODEL II	$680	$1,360
2.	1 EACH	ELECTRONIC TYPING SYSTEM RENTAL CONTRACT FOR 12 MONTHS TO INCLUDE INSTALLATION CHARGES FOR IBM, XEROX, CMT, CPT, REDACTRON, ETC.	313.34/MO.	3,760
3.	ASSORTMENT	STARTER KITS AND AS-SORTED SUPPLIES FOR ELEC-TRONIC TYPING SYSTEM ITEM 2 ABOVE. DIABLO WHEELS, CASSETTES, COPY HOLDERS, AND CASSETTE TRAYS.		1,100
4.	10 ENSEMBLES	DESKS, TABLES, CHAIRS, FILE CABINETS AND FURNI-TURE FOR STAFF. (SHOWN PER PERSON AVERAGE)	490	4,900
				$11,120

Table 2 • SUN UNIVERSITY RESEARCH BUDGET "B"

1976 SUN UNIVERSITY
(BLANK) COLLEGE RESEARCH ADMINISTRATION BUDGET ANNEX C

MAINTENANCE BUDGET

ITEM	DESCRIPTION	AMOUNT
1.	TRAVEL: OUT OF STATE — $4,000 IN-STATE — 600	$4,600
2.	TELEPHONE-LONG DISTANCE	1,000
3.	COMPUTER SERVICES	1,000
4.	DUPLICATING SERVICES (XEROX, OFFSET ETC.)	2,500
5.	PAPER, MASTERS, ART SERVICES	1,800
6.	TYPEWRITER RIBBONS, ELECTRONIC TYPING SYSTEM SUPPLIES, ASSORTED EXPENDABLES	800 800
7.	OFFICE SUPPLIES AND STATIONERY	1,500
8.	POSTAGE, TELEGRAMS AND SHIPPING	1,400
		$14,000

Table 3   •   *SUN UNIVERSITY RESEARCH BUDGET "C"*

1976 SUN UNIVERSITY
(BLANK) COLLEGE RESEARCH ADMINISTRATION BUDGET ANNEX D
TOTALS

ANNEX	DESCRIPTION	AMOUNT
A	PERSONNEL	$133,604
B	EQUIPMENT	11,120
C	MAINTENANCE	14,000
	TOTAL AMOUNT	$158,724

Table 4   •   *SUN UNIVERSITY RESEARCH BUDGET "D"*

RESEARCH ADMINISTRATION MODELS

Philosophy of Decentralized Research Administration Model.

INTRODUCTION — As a component of the overall administration of the (Blank) College, research is an integral part of the academic functions of the college. The administration of the research component of the college must be managed through the same structure and utilize the same philosophy as all other components.

RATIONALE — The rationale and goals of research administration within (Blank) College includes the following:

- TO STIMULATE RESEARCH AND SCHOLARLY ACTIVITIES WHICH ARE PART OF THE EDUCATIVE PROCESS INVOLVING STUDENTS AND FACULTY AND WHICH FIT INTO PRIORITIES SET FORTH BY THE VARIOUS DISCIPLINES.
- TO COORDINATE RESEARCH PRIORITIES OF THE DEPARTMENTS AND PROGRAMS WITHIN THE MISSIONS OF SUN UNIVERSITY, AND THE PRIORITIES ESTABLISHED BY (BLANK) COLLEGE.
- TO UTILIZE THE RESOURCES OF (BLANK) COLLEGE AND SUN UNIVERSITY WITH REGARD TO FINANCES, EQUIPMENT, PERSONNEL, TIME AND SPACE IN THE BEST POSSIBLE MANNER.
- TO SEE THAT RESEARCH REQUESTS AND PROPOSALS WHICH FIT INTO THE UNIVERSITY FRAMEWORK ARE ALSO VIABLE TO THE NEEDS OF THE FUNDING AGENCY (WHETHER IT BE FEDERAL OR PRIVATE).

The mere production of proposals is not the prime purpose of research administration in (Blank) College. The purposes as noted are quality proposals fulfilling the mission of Sun University. The proposals developed should seek to generate sound research and support for graduate and undergraduate students and faculty, the development or the improvement of curriculum and the improvement in the visibility of Sun University in the State and Nation.

OPERATIONS — The research administration of (Blank) College is responsible for the following:

- FULL AUTHORITY FOR THE GENERATION AND DISTRIBUTION OF ALL PROPOSALS.
- DEVELOPMENT OF PROPOSAL BUDGETS FIRST APPROVED BY THE DEPARTMENT HEAD AND THEN BY THE COLLEGE.
- ASSUMPTION OF FULL AUTHORITY FOR FISCAL CONTROL OF ALL GRANTS AND CONTRACTS GENERATED BY THE COLLEGE.
- ASSUMPTION OF FULL AUTHORITY AND RESPONSIBILITY FOR GRANT AND CONTRACT NEGOTIATIONS. PROPERTY FROM ALL GRANTS AND CONTRACTS GENERATED BY (BLANK) COLLEGE IS ASSUMED BY THE COLLEGE.
- ASSUMPTION OF PREPARATION OF PROPOSALS. THE COLLEGE WILL TYPE PROPOSALS ON MAGNETIC MEDIA, COMPLETE THE FINAL DRAFT AND DUPLICATE THE PROPOSAL USING THE COLLEGE'S OFFSET PRINTING SERVICES.
- REGULAR REPORTING SCHEDULES WILL BE DEVELOPED FOR TRANS-MITTAL TO THE VICE PRESIDENTS AND THE PRESIDENT COVERING FISCAL RECORD MANAGEMENT AND PROPOSAL-GRANTS HISTORY. THE OFFICE WILL NOT DUPLICATE ANY BUSINESS OFFICE SERVICES AND COORDINATION WITH THE BUSINESS OFFICE WILL BE MAIN-TAINED TO INSURE THAT NO VIOLATION OF EXISTING UNIVERSITY POLICIES AND PROCEDURES TAKES PLACE.
- DISTRIBUTION OF REPORTS AND INFORMATION TO THE UNIVERSITY LIBRARY AND MEMBERS OF THE COORDINATING RESEARCH COM-MITTEE WILL BE INSTITUTED AND MAINTAINED.

STIMULATION OF FACULTY

Whether or not centralized or decentralized research administration models are adopted, it is of paramount importance that a system be developed and maintained for the stimulation of *seed* research. *Seed* research should encompass **ALL** disciplines. Monies should be allocated for both release time and summer salaries. Funds should not be made available on an *ad hoc* basis but only through the writing of proposals and a subsequent review process. It is folly to transfer monies without constraints and expect faculty to respond. The review process allows the faculty to learn the types of problems which will be encountered when seeking outside funds. It also gives the junior faculty the opportunity to participate as reviewers and to learn how to write good proposals early in their career. The entire procedure should be viewed as a faculty career development program.

Those opposed to such a system will throw up smoke screens. One such may be, *"It takes too much time,"* or *"The amount of monies awarded is so small it does not warrant that much energy"*. Neither of the excuses is valid. The atmosphere which is generated is positive and exciting. If this is bureaucratic nonsense, as a few will undoubtedly say, so are the procedures used by private, industrial and governmental agencies in their awarding of funds.

Outside sponsors' monies are essential to the health and well-being of research in institutions of higher education. Thus it follows, the faculty needs to know the system and learning the system takes time, energy and committment.

SAMPLE FACULTY RESEARCH AWARDS PROGRAM

The following program is applicable to a college, university, private foundation, research institute or federal agency. The geography need not be limited to the United States. With changes (very slight in most cases) the following program is adaptable to either centralized or decentralized research programs.

Sun University, (Blank) College are fictitious names given to the following Faculty Research Awards Program. The content is not fictitious. The material herein described has been successfully used and tested in a real environment over a two-year period.[3]

SUN UNIVERSITY
(BLANK) COLLEGE FACULTY RESEARCH AWARDS PROGRAM

Introduction

The purpose of the (Blank) College Faculty Research Awards Program is to provide faculty with an opportunity to engage and/or begin a research effort. Limited funds preclude long term commitments by the College. High priority will be given to those projects likely to generate support from non-university funds. In special cases where projects are unlikely supportable from outside sources, consideration will be given when a project is adequately justified. Proposals will be accepted from all departments in the College.

The intent of the Program is to provide "seed" research support to enhance research activities which are consistent with the goals, objectives and priorities within all disciplines and departments in the College.

Younger faculty members are encouraged to apply regardless of discipline or school within the College.

Eligible Items

1. Faculty release time for the Summer Semester 1976, Fall Semester 1976 and Spring Semester 1977.
2. Employment of technical assistants.
3. Travel for the collection of data and travel which is inherent in, and essential to the operation of the project. (Key questions: Does the travel required directly *focus* on the *objectives* of the research? Additional explanation with justification should be included with the application).
4. Duplication, offset printing and xerography are allowable charges to the project.
5. Computer time usage. Central Processing Unit time will be assigned to approved projects by the Department and/or School Head from the departmental and/or school's computer allocation. (Time for the Computer *will* be allocated by the Faculty Research Awards Program).
6. Computer Center Services are eligible items and are considered as "Direct Costs." Such costs will be funded under the category of "Maintenance," including services such as programming, card key punching, verifying, etc. Such costs are to be priced out separately and adequately justified with detailed explanation.
7. Page Costs. A maximum of $100 per funded project may be used for *defraying* the expense of publication page charges and/or reprints. (See detailed explanations regarding this category).
8. Equipment with an aggregate total of *less than* $300. (Specific justification is required).

Ineligible Items

1. Graduate Assistantships are *not* eligible for support under this program. (See detailed explanation regarding this category).
2. Equipment with an aggregate total of more than $300.
3. Travel to professional meetings.
4. (a) Purchases made without prior approval.
   (b) Purchases made without prior completion and processing of an approved requisition.

Figure 19 • *SUN UNIVERSITY RESEARCH AWARDS PROGRAM*

5. Computer Time (Central Processing Unit). Time for the University Computer. Allocations will be made from the departmental and/or school computer allocations.

Final Reports
1. Those persons receiving awards under the 1976 Research Awards Program will be required to submit a complete report with findings of the project prior to January 31, 1976 (See detailed explanations regarding this category).
2. Projects awarded for the 1976 Research Awards will be required to submit a Final Report (Dates for submission of Final Reports for the 1975 period will be announced at a later date).

Ineligible Applicants
1. Faculty working for advanced degrees at SUN UNIVERSITY or at another University may not apply for the Faculty Research Awards Program if any portion of the time and/or support will be used toward the completion of the degree.
2. Faculty not on a full time basis may not apply for the Faculty Research Awards Program.

Figure 19 • *SUN UNIVERSITY RESEARCH AWARDS PROGRAM*, Continued

GUIDELINES FOR THE COMPLETION AND SUBMISSION OF
AN APPLICATION FOR THE 1976 (BLANK) COLLEGE
FACULTY RESEARCH AWARDS PROGRAM

In order to process and review the large number of proposals which will be submitted for consideration with a reasonable efficiency, the following procedures will be of assistance to both the staff and those who evaluate the proposals. Your cooperation is appreciated.

Application

The application shall be submitted in original plus four copies, plus two additional copies of the completed cover page and two additional copies of the completed budget page. (Total of 5 Proposals, 2 Budget Pages and 2 Cover Sheets) Copies may be Xerographed, carbon copy or Ditto. Recognizing that some have limited facilities for the completion of the proposal, it will be judged on content and not on the copy. Care in the preparation and readability of the proposal (and copies) should nevertheless not be overlooked.

Each proposal shall consist of the following:

a. COVER SHEET — (provided for in the Proposal Packet).
b. PROPOSAL BODY — Up to seven typewritten pages or text according to the Format. (Suggested Format is provided for in Proposal Packet.)
c. BUDGET PAGE — (provided for in Proposal Packet).
d. HEAD OF DEPARTMENT CERTIFICATION — (provided for in Proposal Packet) This sheet is to be attached to the ORIGINAL copy only.
e. Fasten by stapling each proposal and cover packet, and bid all togehter with rubber band.

Due Date

The applications and all copies are to be transmitted to the Head of the Department or School. Applications are due in the Dean's Office no later than 5:00 P.M., January 31, 1976.

Announcement Dates

a. No specific date can be given at this time, however, every effort will be made to make the announcement of awards early in March.
b. Maintenance Funds will be announced shortly after the Official University Budget has been approved by the President.
c. Announcements will be made in writing and copies of the announcements will be sent to the respective Department Heads. Announcements for those who are successful as well as those who were not will be sent at the same time.

Review Procedures

1. Department Research Committee and/or Department Head.
2. The (Blank) College Research and Graduate Studies Advisory Committee.
3. Peer panel consisting of approximately five members.
4. Final screening by the Dean and his Executive Committee.

Please Note:

Each evaluation is kept PRIVATE and Confidential.
Reviewers will remain Anonymous.

Figure 20 • SUN UNIVERSITY GUIDELINES

SUN UNIVERSITY
(BLANK) COLLEGE 1976 FACULTY RESEARCH AWARDS PROGRAM
Suggested Research Proposal Body Format

1. NAME OF APPLICANT:
2. TITLE:
3. DEPARTMENT AND SCHOOL:
4. (a) NEW PROPOSAL (   )   4. (b) RENEWAL PROPOSAL (   )
   Check One Box Only
5. TITLE OF PROPOSED RESEARCH:
6. ABSTRACT OF PROPOSED RESEARCH (INCLUDE PROBLEM DEFINI-
   TION): (Abstract should not be over *one-half* to *three-quarters* of a typed
   page in length.)
7. PREVIOUS WORK ACCOMPLISHED BY THE APPLICANT AND/OR
   OTHERS IN THIS AREA OF STUDY: (Consider literature appropriate to
   the project.)
8. DESCRIPTION OF PROJECT PLAN AND METHODS AND PROCEDURES:
   (Be brief but specific in the coverage of this point.)
9. JUSTIFICATION OF PLANNED RESEARCH (AS PURE RESEARCH OR
   MISSION ORIENTED): (The general significance of the proposed research
   should be covered in this section along with justification.)
10. LIST OF OUTSIDE AGENCIES TO WHICH PROPOSAL(S) HAVE BEEN
    SENT WITHIN THE LAST TWO YEARS REQUESTING SUPPORT FOR
    YOUR RESEARCH. (Indicate preliminary proposals as well as formal
    proposals by project title and dollars (total) requested. If awarded please
    indicate. Indicate in parenthesis when listing awards what amount in %
    is salary for academic year and for summer salary. *Do not list in salary
    dollars.)*
11. PREVIOUS WORK (RELATED TO THIS REQUEST) ACCOMPLISHED BY
    PRINCIPAL INVESTIGATOR AND OTHERS:
12. IS THE RESEARCH HEREIN DESCRIBED SUITABLE FOR SUPPORT
    FROM AN AGENCY *OUTSIDE* THE UNIVERSITY? (If the answer is in
    the affirmative, specify the agency, program and reasons if known.)
13. SHOW PRIOR YEARS IN WHICH SUPPORT WAS RECEIVED FROM THE
    COLLEGE (IN THE LAST 3 YEARS) AND CITE RESULTS INCLUDING
    RESULTING PUBLICATIONS. (If none, state when first appointed to Sun
    University.)
14. INDICATE ON THE BUDGET PAGE CURRENT SALARY SUPPORT AS
    WELL AS REQUESTED SUPPORT. (Do not use dollars — only percent-
    ages.)

Figure 21 • *SUN UNIVERSITY FACULTY RESEARCH PROGRAM*

1976 RESEARCH PROPOSAL EVALUATION SHEET

1. CLARITY OF STATEMENT OF THE RESEARCH PROBLEM (10 Points)
   Has the principal investigator adequately described his or her research problem including the objectives and general utility of the proposed work?
2. REVIEW OF THE LITERATURE (20 Points)
   Has the principal investigator placed his or her ideas in proper perspective with the regard to the work of others (if any) in this area?
   Is the background literature coverage adequate?
3. METHODS AND PROCEDURES (20 Points)
   Will the experimental design allow the principal investigator to obtain data sought and thus permit proper interpretations?
   Are the methods of research, analysis of data and interpretation of results of sufficient merit and quality to yield a partial solution or completion within the time requested for the project? For renewals: Has adequate methodology been developed to indicate the proposed work can *now* be brought to fruition?
   Can the methods be applied with the resources available at Sun University or has the principal investigator made other arrangements elsewhere? (Equipment, space, etc.)
4. JUSTIFICATION FOR THE PROPOSED RESEARCH (20 Points)
   Regardless whether the proposed research is pure or mission oriented, has adequate justification been presented?
   If the proposal is a renewal, has sufficient evidence been submitted to justify renewal — and has the work that was performed been of sufficient quality to recommend more support? Has the *final report* been completed and attached to the proposal?
   If the proposal is a new proposal, what is the likelihood for completion?
5. POSSIBILITY OF OBTAINING OUTSIDE SUPPORT (20 Points)
   Have sufficient data been obtained to seek outside support?
   Has the research problem any relevance to non-university support — whether it be private or Federal sources?
   In the case of the non-sciences, has the project plan any relevance to others, such as a contribution to the professional discipline, enjoyment for others, learning experiences for others, etc.
   Has sufficient documentation been included in the proposed plan to show outside funds have been sought and proposals prepared and submitted?
6. BUDGET PREPARATION AND DEFENSE (5 Points)
   Has sufficient attention been given to the preparation of the Budget?
   Is the Budget realistic or blue sky?
7. GENERAL CRITIQUE OF THE PROJECT (15 Points)
   Will the research produce new data and concepts or confirm existing hypotheses or neither? Is the research likely to lead to publishable work? (For renewals, have publications resulted?) Are they attached? Give an overall appraisal of the significance of the work? If renewal, is the work sufficiently along the way to seek outside support — if yes, was this done? If no, was sufficient justification given?

Figure 22   •   SUN UNIVERSITY PROPOSAL EVALUATION SHEET

CONCLUSION

Within any organization of reasonable size which has research as a component of its mission, research administration should be given recognition by an established structure. The model chosen for research administration will depend upon the system of which it is a subsystem.

Each organization should identify its management policies which would make a centralized or decentralized model useful for accomplishing its mission. In whichever model implemented, research administrators are support personnel for researchers. They should not retard research, but assist researchers to gain skills, plan from ideas, and carry out research which has been funded. They work with the main line administration to provide a research base which fulfills the institution's purposes.

In summary, research administration, whatever its model, is an essential service function for research accomplishment in today's complex world of funding sources.

Chapter Twelve

EXCESS AND
SURPLUS PROPERTY

- **INTRODUCTION**
- **ACQUISITION OF EXCESS PROPERTY**
- **GENERAL USES AND ADVANTAGES TO RECIPIENTS OF EXCESS PROPERTY**
- **FEDERAL PROPERTY ASSISTANCE PROGRAM**
- **POLITICS OF EXCESS AND SURPLUS PROPERTY PROGRAM**
- **CONCLUSION**

INTRODUCTION

For many years the United States Government has allowed colleges, universities, industrial and private contractors access to items of equipment and property determined to be no longer useful to the Federal government. The program for the disposition of excess property is administered by the Personal Property Division, Property Management and Disposal Service of the General Services Administration. Public schools, civil defense agencies, and non-profit institutions are given access to property no longer useful to the United States Government by the Federal Property Assistance

Program administered by the Department of Health, Education and Welfare. The Federal Property Assistance Program is better known by its more popular older name, Federal Government Surplus Property Program.

Equipment of a scientific nature, heavy shop equipment, vehicles, furniture, office equipment, chemicals, medical, surgical and dental equipment, computers and a host of other classifications of materiel deemed *excess* and of no further value to the Federal government is disposed of by two basic mechanisms. The first and highest priority is through the General Services Administration; and the second, through the Federal Property Assistance Program. There are two terms about which much confusion centers — *excess* and *surplus.*

EXCESS PROPERTY — Excess property is that property found no longer useful to a particular agency of the United States Government. That property is then declared *excess* and listed in bulletins and catalogs published and distributed by the General Services Administration. The *eligible's* can be another Federal agency, government contractor, or university.

SURPLUS PROPERTY — Surplus property is that property no longer useful to the Federal government, (or in some cases, its contractor's property) which is released to the Department of Health, Education and Welfare, the DHEW Regional Offices and State Agencies for Surplus Property. There are infinitely more eligible organizations for *surplus* than for *excess property.* The Department of Health, Education and Welfare reported in 1975 that some 60,000 education, health and civil defense organizations were given access to surplus government property.[1] After *excess* and *surplus* have been *screened,* all items not taken by excess and surplus means are offered for sale by the General Services Administration Regional Offices by *"sealed bid"* to individuals and small businesses. The publications for this classification are distributed through the Regional Offices of the General Services Administration. (See Figure 23).

Because of the importance of excess and surplus property and the politics involved, additional explanation will be given at a later part of this Chapter relative to the power struggles now taking place.

ACQUISITION OF EXCESS PROPERTY

Excess Government Personal Property is the official name of excess property. Many become confused by its name and justly so. There is nothing personal about Excess Government Personal Property as the name implies. It is that new or used property which includes personnel equipment, instruments, hardware and materials (except consumable items such as drugs, paint, etc.) owned by the Federal government and no longer needed by the holding agency, but having additional useful life. Under regulations established by the General Services Administration (GSA), the Agency charged with operating this program, *Excess Government Personal Property* may be reported to, or requested from GSA and by other Federal agencies.[2] The process of declaring an item or items excess varies somewhat among Federal government agencies. This is essentially due to the different sizes of the various Federal establishments. The Department of Defense because of its huge size, scope and large budget allows other Department of Defense units and commands the opportunity of utilizing excess items of equipment and supplies by first transferring inventories within the DOD complex before listing items as excess with the General Services Administration.

WHO IS ELIGIBLE? — Grantees, contractors, other Federal agencies, and National Laboratories (eg. Brookhaven

IMPORTANT
This information **MUST** appear on lower ⎯➤ left hand corner of your Bid Envelope.

PAGE NO. 5	
SALE NO.	8FWS-76-75
OPENING	February 18, 1976

GENERAL SERVICES ADMINISTRATION

FEDERAL SUPPLY SERVICE

SALES LETTER

(No Deposit Required)

Region No.: 8 – Denver

Sale No. : 8FWS-76-75

Dear Sir

This piece is offering for sale the following property "as is where is" on a competitive bid basis. This offering is subject to the General Sale Terms and Conditions as Standard Form 114C January 1970 Edition, and Special Sealed Bid Conditions (Standard Form 114C-1, January 1970 Edition), which are incorporated herein by reference, and such other special Terms and conditions as may be contained herein. A copy of Standard Form 114C and Standard Form 114C-1 are on file and will be made available upon request.

ITEM	DESCRIPTION	QUANTITY
	ITEM 1 IS LOCATED AT THE VETERANS ADMINISTRATION CENTER, HOT SPRINGS, SD 57747. CONTACT: ARL ANDERSON; TELEPHONE: (605) 745-4101, EXT. 240.	
1.	X-RAY APPARATUS, dental, Ritter, Model F, acq. 1962, 11 to 15 MA cap., wall mtd. arm for tube head, S/N 8F2557 (Repairs Required) Used	1 Each
	ITEMS 2 & 3 ARE LOCATED AT THE VETERANS ADMINISTRATION HOSPITAL, BLDG. 46, FORT MEADE (STURGIS), SD 51741. CONTACT: M. D. BUTLER; TELEPHONE: (605) 347-2511, EXT. 225.	
2.	PIANO, upright, Weaver Spinet, acq. 1947, color red mahogany, size approx. 5' x 30" x 4', S/N 91714 (Repairs Required) Used	1 Each
3.	LOOM, weaving, J. L. Hammett, acq. 1960, floor type, foot operated, over 3 harnesses, natural wood color, S/N 3625-5752, (Repairs Required) Used . FOR ITEMS 3A THRU 3E SEE PAGE 10.	1 Each
	ITEM 4 IS LOCATED AT THE GSA PUBLIC BLDGS. SERVICE, 204 FEDERAL BLDG., US POSTOFFICE, FARGO, ND 58102. CONTACT: JAMES MEARS; TELEPHONE: (701) 237-5771, EXT. 453.	
4.	VACUUM CLEANER, Hoover, Model 913-01, upright, 115 VAC/DC, 7 ph, 60 cyc., S/N EE207282, (Repairs Required) Used	1 Each
	ITEM 5 IS LOCATED AT THE FEDERAL AVIATION ADMINISTRATION, GENERAL AVIATION DISTRICT OFFICE, HECTOR AIRPORT, FARGO, ND. CONTACT: MANAGER; TELEPHONE: (701) 232-8949.	
5.	AIR CONDITIONER, ZONER, VAN5344A, S/N 46G325701, (Repairs Required) Used	1 Each
	ITEMS 6 THRU 9 ARE LOCATED AT THE VETERANS ADMINISTRATION CENTER, FARGO, ND 58101. CONTACT: ROSE KNUDTSON; TELEPHONE: (701) 232-3241, EXT. 309.	
6.	MAX CART, Mobile Intensive Care and Emergency Life Support System, MAXX, acq. 1969, 115V, 750 watts, S/N 704, cart by Bucksco, complete w/cardio 2 external cardiac compressor and Luxo lamp, Used	1 Each
7.	DALLONS CARDIOSCOPE, Master Monitor, Model MM-11, acq. 1967, 115V, 50-60 cyc, .6 amp, S/N 1164, Used	1 Each
8.	REFRIGERATOR, mechanical, Whirlpool, Model GB11L0, acq. 1960, approx. 8 cu. ft., freezing unit across top, S/N 9L220237, Used	1 Each
9.	RANGE, elec., GE, acq. 1960, 4 hot plates w/1 large and 1 small oven, complete w/timers and clock, S/N 2871, (Repairs Required) Used	1 Each
	ITEMS 10 THRU 13 ARE LOCATED AT THE AGRICULTURAL RESEARCH SERVICE, HUMAN NUTR. LAB., 2420 - 2ND AVE. NO., GRAND FORKS, SD 58201. CONTACT: ROGER BOROWSKI; TELEPHONE: (701) 775-2545.	
	DESCRIPTION FOR ITEMS 10 THRU 13 NEXT COLUMN)	

ITEM	DESCRIPTION	QUANTITY
10.	STILL, Ultrapure, AMSCO, Model 10GPH, cat. #AF02-551, S/S, 208/220/440V, S/N 344716, w/1 additional unused top, (Repairs Required) Used	1 Each
11.	STILL, Ultrapure, AMSCO, Model 10GPH, cat. #AF02-551, S/S, 208/220/440V, S/N 344717, w/1 additional used top, (Repairs Required) Used	1 Each
12.	STILL, Ultrapure, AMSCO, Model 10 GPH, cat. #AF02-551, S/S, 208/220/440V, S/N 344718, (Repairs Required) Used	1 Each
13.	ALTERNATE BID: This item consists of all the property listed and described in Items 10 thru 12. Award under this item may be made only if the highest acceptable bid is equal to, or greater than, the total of the highest acceptable bids on the individual Items 10 thru 12. Used	1 Lot
	ITEM 14 IS LOCATED AT THE USDA - FARMERS HOME ADMINISTRATION, RM. 208, FEDERAL BLDG., THIRD & ROSSER, BISMARCK, ND 58501. CONTACT: STATE DIRECTOR; TELEPHONE: (701) 255-4011.	
14.	TYPEWRITER, electric, IBM, 1962, S/N 1525240, (Repairs Required) Used	1 Each
	ITEMS 15 & 16 ARE LOCATED AT THE FEDERAL AVIATION ADMINISTRATION, AIRWAY FACILITIES SECTOR, BISMARCK, ND 58501. CONTACT: S. WEST; TELEPHONE: (701) 255-4371.	
15.	SALVAGE AIR CONDITIONER, Gibson, Model 6520-29A, 20,000 BTU, window type, S/N 07551982, (w/o compressor) Used	1 Each
16.	SALVAGE AIR CONDITIONER, York, Model JN-2, 12,000 BTU, window type, Used	1 Each
	ITEM 17 IS LOCATED AT THE US FISH & WILDLIFE SERVICE, AUDUBON NATIONAL WILDLIFE REFUGE, RR #1, COLEHARBOR, ND 58531. CONTACT: REFUGE MANAGER; TELEPHONE: (701) 442-5474.	
17.	SHELVING, steel, 24" x 36", Est. 100 each, Used	1 Lot
	ITEM 18 IS WITHDRAWN	
	ITEM 19 IS LOCATED AT THE FEDERAL AVIATION ADMINISTRATION, SPO ARSB UNIT, ROCK SPRINGS AIRPORT, ROCK SPRINGS, WY 82601. CONTACT: UNIT DIRECTOR; TELEPHONE: (307) 362-3435.	
19.	SALVAGE CHAIR, Easy, recliner, Used	1 Each
	ITEM 20 IS LOCATED AT THE FEDERAL AVIATION ADMINISTRATION, FLIGHT SERVICE STATION, WORLAND, WY 82401. CONTACT: MANAGER; TELEPHONE: (307) 347-4122.	
	(DESCRIPTION FOR ITEM 20 NEXT PAGE)	

GSA - DC 2555-A

"WE URGE YOU TO INSPECT THIS PROPERTY"

Figure 23 • GOVERNMENT SALES LETTER

National Laboratory, Argonne National Laboratory —
both operated for the United States Government under
contract) are eligible to request excess property. The
eligibles are changing rapidly because of *politics.*
The simplest procedure for a grantee is to ask the project
officer overseeing the grant or contract as to eligibility
for participation in this program. The approved request
results in regular mailings to your place of business listing all of the available excess in particular materiel
classifications. This procedure is universal for the
excess property program.

The decision of eligibility is made by the agency conducting the contract or grant. The regular mailings will
come from the Federal Supply Service, Personal Property
Division of the General Services Administration. When
this has been accomplished, you are well on the way. A
verbal discussion either by telephone or in person with
your project officer will help determine the scope and
breadth of what items will be approved. The project
officer's signature is required before items will be released or your contract or granting agency will forward
such requests to GSA and the holding agencies for property release. Incidentally, the process of receiving the
Excess Property Catalogs is tantamount to authorization
to gain access to excess property.

GENERAL USES AND ADVANTAGES TO RECIPIENTS OF EXCESS PROPERTY

Excess property can range from one individual item of
equipment to the acquisition of an entire laboratory.
The following illustrations are actual situations where
excess property served to benefit both the recipients
and the spirit and intent of the Federal program.

The United States Navy recovered one of its sub-
marines sunk off the coast of California. Lead metal

used as ballast for the submarine was among the items declared excess by the Navy. A Federal grantee, doing nuclear research was given the virgin lead which was required for low background counting of nuclear events.[3] Upon receipt at the university, utilizing student labor and the university engineering shops, the entire shipment (two semi-trailer loads) was fabricated into a sophisticated low-background nuclear shield. The cost was miniscule except for that cost of shipping and fabrication which was under $1,000. After completion and later a publication, a commercial vendor offered to produce the identical shield for in excess of $50,000.[4] Another case was when an Army Service School wished to replace an entire scaler laboratory for counting radiological samples. The Army had let a contract for new and updated equipment. The entire laboratory was declared excess and offered to GSA for disposition. The university receiving the excess was able to set up a student laboratory with 24 stations at the cost of transportation and the installation of 24 electrical outlets.[5]

A small liberal arts college in the Eastern United States was awarded through excess an IBM 7040 Computer. The 7040 is still being used and serves the academic programs, research for undergraduate, graduate students, and the administrative requirements of the college. Another case was the closing down of a government contract on the West Coast.[6] The Federal government held title on a large laboratory which was designed for nondestructive testing. A Western university was given the holdings with the understanding they would pay shipping charges (crating and insurance) along with warehouse storage charges while the university renovated space for the nondestructive testing laboratory. The laboratory currently is providing undergraduate instruction, graduate research and service to the community and the State for specialized testing.[7]

MAILINGS — The General Services Administration distributes catalogs and mailings in great numbers but in irregular periodicity. When an item or group of items appears in the catalogs and there is reasonable assurance that the project officer will approve the acquisition, first call the telephone number in the Bulletin indicated for the *freeze* action and immediately thereafter call the telephone number indicated to ascertain the condition and history of the items under consideration. If the condition code is N, indicating new, the second telephone call is unnecessary. Following the above procedures, without delay, complete the Standard Form 122 (See Figure 24) and forward with appropriate institutional signatures to the project officer for processing. The project officer will see that the necessary actions are handled within his agency and forward the approved SF-122 to the holding agency and GSA for release of the declared excess property.

TITLE — Another area of confusion relative to acquired excess property is ownership. Title for property does not ever pass from the Federal government to the user in some agencies. This policy differs in different agencies. For example, the National Science Foundation normally passes title to the recipient after one year.[8] It is wise and prudent to ascertain this legal consideration before attempting to trade-in equipment acquired from excess or spending inordinate amounts of monies for repair and modification of excess property. Title of Ownership can make the use, repair, transfer and modification of hardware very complex.

CANNIBALIZATION — This term is associated with the use of excess property when one takes parts, components or units from one inventoried item of equipment and places parts, components or units into another ensemble. The common approach is to acquire several items of one

PREPARATION OF TRANSFER ORDER

WHEN ORDER IS SUBMITTED, GIVE ALL DATA SHOWN ON SAMPLE
TRANSFER ORDER BELOW

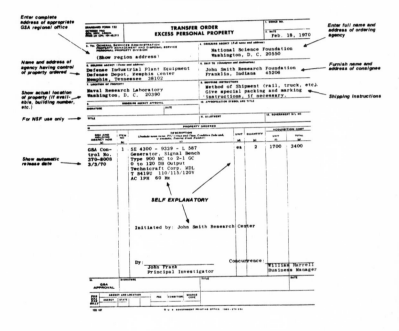

IMPORTANT

1. Make separate Transfer Order for each different property location and each GSA control number.
2. Furnish complete shipping instructions.
3. Place a freeze request with GSA or holding agency.

Figure 24   •   STANDARD FORM 122

model in hopes of having enough parts to complete one ensemble which will be in good working order. This practice is a common one. The privilege of *cannibalization* should be carefully and clearly understood in advance with the project officer and the principal investigator. A Memorandum of Record of the telephone conversation authorizing this procedure should be placed in the principal investigator's file and the official grants or contracts file for the institution. A better procedure is to place on the SF-122 a statement somewhat like this . . . "Parts, components and units will be used in other equipment and ensembles not inventoried or purchased under this contract or grant, thus the original identity of the inventoried units will not be preserved."

At a later date when the post-grant or post-contract audit takes place both the principal investigator and the institution are fully protected from the *cannibalization* process.

The Minuteman Ballistic Missile System was phased out by the Department of Defense for more advanced technology. Many hundreds of the missiles were deactivated and the military components separated from the non-military. The declassified military electronic components contained a mini-computer which was thought to have some value to knowledgeable persons in the computer area of higher education. A *"blue-ribbon"* group of scientists and engineers were convened by the DOD. As a result, the computers were declared excess and released both by Department of Health, Education and Welfare and the National Science Foundation through the Department of Defense. In 1971, 1972 and 1973 many colleges and universities were given title to Minuteman computers. The computers were not junked and the ingenuity of professors involved proved that much value could be obtained from them. All of the expertise was shared and a group was formed under the leadership of faculty from Tulane University. Today the modified Minuteman computers are driving analytical instruments such as infrared and ultraviolet spectrophotometers, atomic absorption apparatus, gas chromatography units and a long list of process control devices.[9]

PROJECT HOME-RUN — The code name *Home Run* was given to the project of shipping and distributing property much of which was brand new from Southeast Asia to the United States. The property declared excess was taken up by all eligibles to the excess program. Many universities and colleges watching the excess program carefully took advantage of their acquisitions — others unfortunately did not. *Project Home Run* essentially assigned a small figure which was to be paid to the United States Government for defraying shipping costs from Viet Nam, Cambodia and other sites in Southeast Asia. Computers, airplanes, boats, office furniture — almost anything that could be imagined filled the lists of *Home Run Bulletins* (See Figure 25). Some universities chartered aircraft and had officials waiting on the docks for the ships arriving on the West Coast. The acquisition of excess from *Home Run* did not help the stress between those in the *excess* eligible camp and those in the *surplus* camp. The condition code *N-1* was a most common condition code found on items of equipment, furniture and hardware. Vehicles and aircraft were very serviceable although not new. Ultrawave and unclassified radar equipment found their way to upgrading many electrical engineering laboratories. It was also welcome to see that the Office of Management and Budget sought to use *Home Run* in this way. At the close of World War II similar items of equipment, vehicles, aircraft and instruments were crushed by bulldozers and buried. Some in the European Theater, some en-route in Iceland and in other locations throughout the Continental United States. A waste which never should have been allowed or to ever be repeated.

PROJECT HOME RUN   E-X-T-E-N-D-E-D

Cond Code Quantity Control #	ITEM NO. & DESCRIPTION	UNIT ACQ. COST	UNIT RETURN COST
N2 25 EA BJ515B42	6110-787-8567 **Regulator** Volt, Mfg: Regohm, # 18528	66.00	3.96
N2 48 EA BJ515B43	4540-949-3067 **Lamp** Infrared, Mfg: General Electric, 120 volt, 8½" long	14.40	.86
N1 183 EA BJ515B44	5120-690-3766 **Wrench** Screwdriver, special type combination wrench, w/screwdriver O/A length 7"	1.95	.12
N2 38 EA BJ515B45	4510-684-7004 **Shower Head** 8" dia, with 1-3/4" female connector, Mfg: Speakman & Wilder, commercial type	15.20	.91
N2 13 EA BJ515B49	6115-956-6926 **Regulator Assy** Mfg: Tele-Craft Electronics, # 110360	92.00	5.52
N2 69 PKG BJ515B51	5120-234-8740 **Bender** Copper tubing ½", 6 ea per pkg	1.44	.09
N1 20 EA BJ515B55	5120-733-8953 **Replacer** Oil Seal, 7½" dia. 1-1/8" center hole, ½" thick	9.68	.58
N2 88 EA BJ515B56	4320-063-4789 **Impeller** Pump, Mfg: Deming, made of cast iron. 6" dia.	18.40	1.10
N2 54 EA BJ515B59	4820-592-0439 **Valve, Safety** Mfg: E. C. Kingston, size ½" set, 270 PSI cap. 157 CFM, Model 112C, Valve 3-3/8" long	10.90	.65
N2 12 EA BJ515B65	6105-752-2370 **Motor, DC** 26.4 volt, 2.25 AMPS, DC cycles, 10,000 RPM, .025 HP, Mfg: Indiana General	65.00	3.90
N2 30 EA BJ515B66	6220-772-3899 **Light** Signal marker, 24 volts, 28 volt, 0.23 AMPS, single contact bayonet	5.17	.31
N2 40 EA BJ515B70	5110-263-0316 **Handle** 13-7/8" long, complete w/holding blacket screw, 1-5/16" dia.	1.94	.12
N2 15 EA BJ515B71	6645-951-0682 **Timer** Interval, 220 volts, 60 cycles, 15 watts, Model CTD-5M, Mfg: Industrial Timer Corp., ⅓ HP, 10 AMPS, 125 VA, 115 or 230 volts. AC	25.00	1.50
N1 257 EA BJ515B75	4030-407-6512 **Hook, Guy** Hook 3-3/4" lg. 3/4" center hole, used to hold wire cable on line poles	26	.02
	LOCATION: PMD CENTER BATON ROUGE, LA		

Figure 25 • PROJECT HOME-RUN BULLETIN

FEDERAL PROPERTY ASSISTANCE PROGRAM

The Federal Property Assistance Program is administered through the Department of Health, Education and
Welfare, its regional offices, and the state agencies for
surplus property, which report to the Governors or State
Directors of Purchasing and Supplies and have the authority for distribution of property within each state. Each
state has established at least one distribution center,
and several states operate multiple centers. The states
also handle distribution of real estate for health and educational purposes. DHEW makes an attempt to coordinate
the needs of Federal government grantees for surplus
property by determining where these grants are located
and encouraging states to fulfill the needs of the grantees.
The Federal Property Assistance Program is organizationally under the Division of Administration, Office of
Surplus Property Utilization, Department of Health,
Education and Welfare, Washington, D.C. The program is
based on the recognition that the property which the
Federal government will dispose of is better returned to
the taxpayers for use than sold for minimal return. In
1975 the program disposed of $415 million worth of sur-
plus property to more than 60,000 eligible education,
health and civil defense organizations.

Several types of property may be designated as *surplus*. New property which has become available due to
changes in the needs of the Federal government; property
which is more costly to repair than replace; partially
useable items; and components of valuable base materials. To date, education has been the major beneficiary of the surplus property program. Approximately
three quarters of the total property distribution has been
for educational purposes. Higher education has received
about 40 per cent of the property.

Property under this program is found at State Surplus
Agency sites and payment is made to the State Agency

varying from two to ten cents on the dollar of the original *acquisition cost.* The acquisition cost is the original purchase cost to the Federal government not its value or condition as surplus property.

POLITICS OF EXCESS AND SURPLUS PROPERTY PROGRAMS

The eligibles are greater in number for *surplus* than *excess* property. The organizations for surplus property have grown to a formidable size. They consist of staff employees, supervisors and "screeners" of property. Both those in the DHEW and the State Agencies have been hard at work **encouraging** changes in legislation at the Federal level. The end product for the legislation sought by the surplus group is to take away from higher education the privilege of using excess property. Many of the State Agencies are under the superintendent of education for the respective state. The legislation sought would accomplish two things. First, not to allow acquisition of excess property for the higher education groups; and second, place the seat of power as to choice and distribution with the state agencies.

As stated earlier this is a very important area and has been discussed within the government and educational community on a National basis.[10] The authors feel that the reader is entitled to a more complete picture of this subject than is generally given in the news media. Thus, highlights of legislation, procedures and sample communications are included.

HISTORICAL — Appearing in the Federal Register, June 1, 1972 [Volume Number 37 (106) Pages 10959 and 10960] was a *Notice of Proposed Rule-Making* which directed the General Services Administration to change its Federal

Procurement Management Regulations to prohibit the use of General Services Administration and other Federal government sources of supply by recipients of Federal grants.[11] This very small size notice served to rock the very foundations of colleges and universities throughout the United States. Telegrams, personal visits, telephone calls and letters were composed and sent around the clock. The typical telegram sent to the Congress follows.

THE HONORABLE CARL B. ALBERT
SPEAKER OF THE HOUSE OF REPRESENTATIVES OF THE UNITED STATES
THE RAYBURN BUILDING - ROOM 2205
THE CAPITOL
WASHINGTON, D.C. 20515

MY DEAR MR. SPEAKER:

(BLANK) UNIVERSITY WISHES TO CALL TO YOUR ATTENTION THE FOLLOWING ITEM WHICH APPEARED IN THE JUNE 1, 1972 FEDERAL REGISTER, VOLUME NUMBER 37 (106) PGES 10959 AND 10960, A NOTICE OF PROPOSED RULE MAKING WHICH DIRECTS THE GENERAL SERVICES ADMINISTRATION TO REVISE THE FEDERAL PROPERTY MANAGE-MENT REGULATIONS TO PROHIBIT THE USE OF GSA AND OTHER GOVERNMENT SOURCES OF SUPPLY BY RECIPIENTS OF FEDERAL GRANTS.

IT IS OUR INTERPRETATION THAT THIS PROPOSED CHANGE WILL PROHIBIT (BLANK) UNIVERSITY FROM FURTHER UTILIZING THE SOURCES OF SUPPLY FROM GSA AND STOP THE ACQUISITION OF GOVERNMENT EXCESS PERSONAL PROPERTY FOR GRANTEES IN OUR UNIVERSITY. THE EQUIPMENT AND ITEMS OF PROPERTY ACQUIRED BY THESE MEANS CONSTITUTE A LARGE FIGURE IN THE UNIVERSITY'S BUDGET AND IF CURTAILED WOULD PRESENT A SIGNIFICANT BUDGET DEFICIT.

THIS MATTER IS OF VITAL IMPORTANCE NOT ONLY TO (BLANK) UNIVERSITY BUT ALL INSTITUTIONS OF HIGHER EDUCATION IN (BLANK) AND THE NATION.

WE HOPE THAT YOU LIKEWISE WILL CONSIDER THIS MATTER OF SIGNIFICANT IM-PORTANCE SO THAT IT MAY BE BROUGHT TO THE ATTENTION OF THOSE WHO CAN RESCIND THE PROPOSED REGULATION. BECAUSE OF THE JUNE 30, 1972 DEADLINE FOR PRESENTING OPPOSING VIEWS AND ARGUMENTS TO THE GENERAL SERVICES ADMINIS-TRATION, IT WOULD BE APPRECIATED IF SOME POSITIVE ACTION COULD BE TAKEN WITHOUT DELAY. I OFFER THE RESOURCES OF MY FACULTY AND STAFF FOR TESTI-MONY ON THIS MATTER BEFORE EITHER THE CONGRESS OR GSA HEARINGS.

YOUR CONSIDERATION TO THIS VERY IMPORTANT MATTER IS GREATLY APPRECIATED.
SIGNED: (BLANK)
PRESIDENT

Figure 26 • *TELEGRAM TO SPEAKER OF THE HOUSE*

The Congressional Record of the 92nd Congress, Session also reflected the pressures and the reactions of the higher education community.

CONGRESSIONAL RECORD

PROCEEDINGS AND DEBATES OF THE 92d CONGRESS, SECOND SESSION

VOL. 118   **WASHINGTON, FRIDAY, AUGUST 4, 1972**   **NO. 124**

SENATE

HON. WALTER F. MONDALE
OF MINNESOTA

By Mr. MONDALE (for himself, Mr. Javits, Mr. Kennedy, Mr. Pell, Mr. Williams, Mr. Humphrey, Mr. Church, Mr. Proxmire, Mr. Jackson, Mr. Hartke, and Mr. Stevenson):

S. 3882. A bill to amend the Federal Property and Administrative Services Act of 1949 to provide for the use of excess property by certain grantees. Referred to the Committee on Government Operations.

EXCESS PROPERTY

Mr. MONDALE. Mr. President, I would like at this time to inform my colleagues that I am introducing today S. 3882, a bill which would require the continuation of programs under which recipients of Federal grants may acquire Federal excess property at a reduced rate.

On this occasion, I want to outline the sequence of events which has led up to my introduction of the bill; and to provide for the record certain information concerning the operation of the program and the reasons I believed that it should be preserved.

I ask unanimous consent to have printed in the RECORD at this point a memorandum prepared for me by the Library of Congress. This document provides a clear, unprejudiced definition of the term "excess property"—which is often mistakenly confused with "surplus property"—and of the authority for the existing program.

There being no objection, the memorandum was ordered to be printed in the RECORD, as follows:

THE GSA PROGRAM ON EXCESS PROPERTY

1. The legislative basis for the GSA excess property program is the Federal Property and Administrative Services Act of 1949, as amended. Implementing instructions are delineated in the Federal Property Management Regulations. The salient features of the Federal Property and Administrative Services Act of 1949, are the following:

a. The Act makes a distinction between "excess property" and "surplus property". The former is any property under the control of a Federal agency which is no longer needed by *that* agency. Surplus property is any excess property not needed by *any* Federal agency, as determined by the Administrator of General Services.

b. The *Administrator* (GSA), to minimize expenditures for property, is given responsibility to prescribe policies and methods to promote the maximum utilization of excess property by Federal agencies. He makes provision for the *transfer of excess property* among Federal agencies. With the approval of the Director, Office of Management and Budget, he prescribes the extent of reimbursement for such transfers.

c. *Federal executive agencies* are responsible for surveying the property under their control to determine which is excess, reporting such property to the Administrator, GSA, and disposing of such property as promptly as possible, in accordance with GSA regulations.

d. Generally speaking, when excess property becomes *surplus property*, the Administrator, GSA, exercises supervision and direction over its disposition. Any agency authorized by the Administrator to dispose of surplus property may do so by sale, exchange, lease, permit, or transfer — for cash, credit or other property. Usually, disposals made or authorized by the

Figure 27 • *CONGRESSIONAL RECORD*

Administrator are made after publicly *advertising* for bids. However, disposals may be *nego-tiated* under regulations prescribed by the Administrator, GSA. Among the conditions which permit negotiation are the following: because such action may be necessary for the public interest in an emergency, promotion of the public health, safety or national security, because bid prices after advertising are not reasonable.

e. The Administrator is authorized to *donate surplus property without cost* (except for care and handling), for use in any State for educational, public health or research purposes. For surplus property under the control of the Department of Defense, the Secretary, DOD, determines whether it is usable for educational purposes which are of special interest to the armed forces (e.g., military preparatory schools). If found usable, he allocates it for transfer by the Administrator, GSA, to State agencies for distribution. If not usable for military education, the surplus property may be examined by Department of Health, Education and Welfare of Civil Defense for possible utilization by these activities.

f. Determination as to whether surplus property is usable for education, health or research is made by the Secretary of HEW, who allocates such property on the basis of needs for transfer by GSA to the States for distribution. The Civil Defense Administrator takes similar action for surplus property determined to be useful for Civil Defense purposes.

g. The Administrator, GSA, is authorized to assign to the Secretary, HEW, for disposal, such surplus *real* property that HEW recommends as needed for *education, health or research purposes.*

h. The administrator, GSA, is authorized to assign to the Secretary of the Interior, for disposal, such surplus *real* property needed for use as public parks or recreation area.

Mr. MONDALE. Mr. President, on May 16, 1972, Frank Carlucci, Associate Director of the Office of Management and Budget, wrote a letter to Rod Kreger, Acting Administrator of the General Services Administration, calling on GSA to "discontinue all authorizations and practices which now permit the use of Federal sources of supply or services by Federal grantees including "depots, stores, warehouses, contracts, excess personal property or other such sources."

At this point, I ask unanimous consent to have printed in the RECORD the letter from Mr. Carlucci to Mr. Kreger.

There being no objection, the letter was ordered to be printed in the RECORD, as follows:

Office of Management and Budget,
Washington, D.C., May 16, 1972.

Hon. Rod Kreger,
Acting Administrator,
General Services Administration,
Washington, D.C.

DEAR MR. KREGER: As you know, there has been increasing concern in the business community, the Congress and the executive branch regarding an authorization of the General Services Administration which permits Federal grantees to buy supplies and services directly from GSA and from other Federal sources of supply.

The provision at issue, as set forth in the Federal Property Management Regulations 41 CFR Sec. 101-33, authorizes other Government agencies to, in turn, authorize grantees of such agencies, to buy from GSA inventories and stores, and to order directly from manufacturers via Government contracts. Additionally, the authorization has been extended to the practice of allowing grantees to place orders with GSA regions or buying centers for direct purchase, and also allows grantees access to Federal sources of excess personal property.

The above authorizations are not consistent with the purpose of the Administration's policy of reliance on the private enterprise system and is particularly objectionable in this sense because the burden of GSA competition falls more heavily on small businesses throughout the country. To the extent that grantees are components of State or local governments, the authorizations are also not consistent with the intent of Congress as expressed in the Intergovernmental Cooperation Act and implementing regulations (Circular A-97) of OMB.

It is our conclusion, in view of the above, that GSA should discontinue all authorizations and practices which now permit the use of Federal sources of supply or services by Federal grantees.

I am requesting, therefore, that immediate steps be taken to propose an amendment to GSA regulations that would rescind all authorizations of GSA under which Federal grantees are permitted to use Federal sources of supply. The proposed regulation should, of course, be made available under OMB Circular No. A-85 for comment by State and local governments prior to issuance.

Upon issuance of the amendment, action should be taken to notify the agencies of the determination and request that they immediately advise their grantees that access to Federal sources, i.e., depots, stores, warehouses, contracts, excess personal property, or other such

Figure 27 • CONGRESSIONAL RECORD, Continued

sources is no longer authorized. Appropriate action consistent with the above should also be taken with respect to existing arrangements and unfilled requisitions.

As you know, studies of the Commission on Government Procurement have extended to all phases of supply support and the Commission's final report may include recommendations concerning grantee use of Federal supply sources. We will, of course, review the above conclusion in the light of any such recommendation which the Commission may propose.

Your cooperation and assistance in accomplishing the foregoing will be appreciated. Should you have any questions regarding this matter, we would be happy to discuss it further.

Sincerely,
FRANK CARLUCCI,
Associate Director.

Mr. MONDALE. Mr. President, in the Federal Register dated June 1, 1972, the following announcement appeared:

(General Services Administration — [41 CFR Parts 101 — 26, 101 — 33, 101 — 43])
USE OF GOVERNMENT SUPPLY SOURCES BY GRANTEES
NOTICE OF PROPOSED RULEMAKING

Notice is hereby given that the General Services Administration (GSA) is considering the adoption of revised rules prohibiting the use of GSA and other Government sources of supply by recipients of Federal grants.

The Office of Management and Budget has directed GSA to propose discontinuance of the authorization permitting Federal grantees to use Federal supply sources. Therefore, appropriate amendments to the Federal Property Management Regulations to accomplish this have been developed. However, cost-reimbursement type contractors will continue to be permitted to use GSA supply sources under the provisions of Subparts 1-5.5 and 1-5.9 of the Federal Procurement Regulations.

This notice is published pursuant to section 205(c), 63 Stat. 390; 40 U.S.C. 486(c).

Interested persons are invited to submit written data, views, or arguments regarding the proposed revision to the Commissioner, Federal Supply Service, General Services Administration, Washington, D.C. 20406, within 30 days after the date of publication of this notice in the FEDERAL REGISTER.

Dated: May 31, 1972.

M. S. MEEKER,
Commissioner.

I became aware of the appearance of this announcement more than a week later, when Minnesota grantees notified me that they stood to lose valuable and much-needed excess property if the rule change went into effect. Among the institutions and agencies in Minnesota alone which have since taken the trouble to inform me that they oppose the termination of the program are the following . . . .

After learning of the intention of GSA to terminate the excess property program, I wrote the following letter to GSA requesting information about the impact of the proposed change. The letter follows:

JUNE 15, 1972.

Mr. ROD KREGER,
Acting Administrator, General Services Administration, Washington, D.C.

DEAR MR. KREGER: It has recently come to my attention that GSA is considering the adoption of revised rules prohibiting the use of GSA and other government sources of supply by recipients of Federal grants.

I am most distressed to hear that such a policy change is under consideration. It is apparent that a wide variety of institutions in Minnesota, including vocational and technical schools and the University, would be adversely affected by the proposed change.

To my knowledge these institutions have received no explanation from GSA of the reasons for the proposed change. My staff has secured a copy of the letter from Frank Carlucci, Associate Director of the Office of Management and Budget, notifying you of the proposed change in regulations. This letter states that existing policy is not consistent with the purpose of the Administration policy of reliance on the private enterprise system and is particularly objectionable in this sense because the burden of GSA competition falls more heavily on small businesses throughout the country. This letter offers no documentation of the so-called "administration policy" referred to or any explanation as to what extent the present policy places a burden on small businesses throughout the country.

"In addition, my staff has been unable to secure from your agency an explanation of the potential impact of the policy change either nationally or in Minnesota.

I am very concerned about the possible effects of a change in the regulation on the quality of educational and other human service programs in Minnesota. But it is impossible

Figure 27 • *CONGRESSIONAL RECORD, Continued*

for me to address the substance of this issue without adequate information. For this reason, I request that complete answers to the following questions be forwarded to my office by the close of business on Thursday, June 20th:

1. Please list all Minnesota institutions which received excess property in FY 1971 and 1972, the value of the property acquired and which of these institutions would become ineligible under the proposed change.

2. Please indicate the dollar value of excess and surplus property received by each of the following types of institutions in each of the last five years:

(a) Minnesota institutions,
(b) Minnesota colleges and universities,
(c) Minnesota vocational and technical education institutions,
(d) all vocational education institutions nationally,
(e) all colleges and universities nationally.

3. Please list the dollar value of excess property disposed of throughout the United States in FY 1971 and 1972.

4. Please explain the difference between excess property and surplus property.

5. What agencies or other recipients will acquire or be eligible for acquisition of the excess property that would be unavailable to grantees under the proposed rule change? Please provide a general answer on the national situation and the specific list of eligible recipients in Minnesota.

6. Please explain in full "the Administration policy of reliance on the private enterprise system" with documentation of its origin and existence.

7. Please explain Mr. Carlucci's assertion that "the burden of GSA competition falls more heavily on small businesses throughout the country."

I am looking forward to your speedy reply.

Sincerely,
WALTER F. MONDALE.

Despite the repeated attempts of my staff to receive answers to these questions from GSA, none had been received by my office on June 29. The deadline for comments to GSA was imminent and I feared that the program would be terminated before Congress even had the chance to express its interest and concern. For these reasons, on June 29, I introduced an amendment to the legislation authorizing continuation of the excess property and supply sources programs for grantees.

The Senate approved the amendment. At this point, I ask unanimous consent to have printed in the RECORD a copy of the letter received in my office from GSA — after the amendment had already been approved by the Senate. I hope you will take note of the failure of GSA to answer directly virtually all of the questions I had submitted.

There being no objection, the letter was ordered to be printed in the RECORD, as follows:

GENERAL SERVICES ADMINISTRATION,
Washington, D.C., June 29, 1972.

Hon. WALTER F. MONDALE,
U.S. Senate,
Washington, D.C.
Dear SENATOR MONDALE: . . . .

. . . . In the event the proposed regulation is issued, Federal grantees in the State of Minnesota will no longer be able to acquire excess property. While we do not have available the names of these grantees, they are generally involved in programs concerned with education, manpower training and development, community action, antipoverty, local police training, and civil defense.

With respect to surplus property, it is allocated among the States by the Department of Health, Education, and Welfare, and approved by the General Services Administration for transfer to the States for donation for education, public health, and civil defense purposes. By law, distribution to eligible donees within the States is made by an agency established by each State for that purpose. In Minnesota, that agency is under the direction of Mr. Harold W. Shattuck, Supervisor, Surplus Property Section, Department of Administration, 5420 Highway 8, Arden Hills, New Brighton, Minnesota 55112. Therefore, data on the amounts donated to specific donees within Minnesota would be available only from the State agency.

In terms of original acquisition cost, during FY 1971 $751.2 million of excess property was transferred to other Federal agencies; for FY 1972 through May the amount was approximately $858.0 million.

The term "excess property" means any property under the control of any Federal agency which is not required for its needs and the discharge of its responsibilities, as determined by the head thereof. While in excess status, this property is only available for use by the Federal Government.

Figure 27   •   CONGRESSIONAL RECORD, Continued

The term "surplus property" means any excess property not required for the needs and discharge of the responsibilities of all Federal agencies, as determined by the Administrator of General Services. After being determined surplus, such property is made available first for donation to use within the States, after which any remainder is sold.

All agencies within the Federal Government which currently acquire excess property would continue to be eligible. However, the property would have to be acquired only for direct use or for use by their cost-reimbursement type contractors.

Since grantees would no longer be eligible, much of the excess property which Federal agencies acquire for such use would probably become surplus and donated for education, public health, and civil defense purposes. Consequently, grantees engaged in activities for other than those purposes would not be eligible for the donation of surplus property.

Since the quoted terms are extracted from the Office of Management and Budget letter of May 16, 1972, to GSA, we feel that OMB is better qualified to define their usage. Any such explanation should be obtained from the Office of Management and Budget.

Please let us know if we can be of further assistance.

Sincerely,
ROD KREGER,
Acting Administrator.

Mr. MONDALE. Mr. President, the amendment approved by the Senate was considered by the conference committee on the OEO bill. It was not included in the conference report, because the parliamentarian of the House of Representatives ruled that the amendment was not germane to the bill.

Apparently because of the high public interest and the volume of mail being received in response to the request for comments, GSA extended the comment period until July 31. In the meantime, Secretary of Health, Education, and Welfare Elliot Richardson unilaterally terminated the HEW excess property program on July 14. I ask unanimous consent to have printed in the RECORD here a copy of the document stating that the HEW program has been terminated.

There being no objection, the document was ordered to be printed in the RECORD, as follows:

MANUAL CIRCULAR — MATERIEL MANAGEMENT:
USE OF EXCESS PROPERTY ON GRANTS

1. *Purpose.* — This circular provides Department policy regarding the use of excess personal property by grantees.

2. *Background.* — It has been determined that the use of excess personal property by grantees will be discontinued inasmuch as the majority of HEW grantees are eligible for donation of personal property under the Department's surplus property donation program.

3. *Policy.* — It is the policy of HEW that the use of excess personal property by grantees not be authorized. Section 103 — 43.320 of the HEW Materiel Management Manual is in the process of being revised to reflect this polic...

4. *Accountability.* — Federally-owned personal property presently in the possession of grantees will continue to be accounted for in accordance with current regulations.

5. *Effective Date.* — This circular is effective immediately.

On July 28, I and 22 other Senators signed and sent a letter to M. S. Meeker, Commissioner of the Federal Supply Service, expressing our concern about GSA's intention to terminate the excess property and supply source programs without providing adequate documentation of the reason for the decision and without providing a hearing to those who would be affected by the change. A copy of the letter follows:

JULY 28, 1972.

Hon. M. S. MEEKER,
Commissioner, Federal Supply Services, General Services Administration, Washington, D.C.
DEAR MR. MEEKER: Please consider this letter a formal response to GSA's solicitation of comments on the proposed "adoption of revised rules prohibiting the use of GSA and other Government sources of supply by recipients of Federal grants", which appeared in the Federal Register on June 1, 1972.

We are deeply concerned to learn that GSA is considering terminating the excess property and GSA supply source programs for grantees. We believe that these programs are of considerable importance in keeping down the cost of government-supported projects to the tax-payers; and in maintaining the quality of service offered by many of these programs.

We have further been concerned to observe that GSA has not provided the Congress with a comprehensive analysis of the pros and cons of these programs as they exist; and of the specific reasons for the proposal to terminate them.

Any decision on the future of the grantee programs should be made only after complete information on its implications has been developed and provided to Congress and to affected parties. Further, we believe that GSA should make a decision only after calling a public hearing and receiving testimony from those affected parties who wish to testify.

Figure 27 • CONGRESSIONAL RECORD, Continued

In addition, we believe that GSA should notify HEW — which has unilaterally terminated its own program even before the period for comments has expired — and other executive agencies that they should continue to operate their programs until a general policy decision has been made.

We thank you for your serious consideration of these points and urge that you immediately announce a date for a hearing and provide the Congress with the documentation required to fully understand the implications of the proposed rule change.

Sincerely,

Walter F. Mondale, George McGovern, Vance Hartke, Fred Harris, Philip A. Hart, Claiborne Pell, Thomas Eagleton, Clifford P. Case, Edward W. Brooke, Robert Stafford, William Proxmire, Mike Gravel, Harold E. Hughes, Daniel Inouye, Harrison Williams, Hubert H. Humphrey, Frank Church, Gaylord Nelson, John Tunney, Robert Taft, Jr., Edmund Muskie, Edward M. Kennedy, and Jacob Javits.

And now today, I am introducing a bill which would require the continuation of the excess property program. I have more than one reason for believing that this legislation is necessary.

The first, and most obvious, reason is that I believe that the excess property program is the legitimate source of property that is strongly needed by and significantly improves the programs of many educational and other public service agencies. Representatives of the vocational schools, colleges and universities and community action agencies have testified over and over again to me in letters that they simply could not afford to acquire the same property at the market price. If they cannot get it under the excess property program, they often cannot afford to buy it at all.

Second, I believe that the excess property program saves the taxpayers money. Institutions and agencies do not have to pay market prices for certain property that they otherwise acquire under the program; and the costs associated with acquisition run less for excess property than they do for property secured under the surplus donation program.

My third reason for introducing this legislation is that I am appalled at the disregard of the administration and the executive agencies for the prerogative of Congress in this whole area of property transfer. No less an authority than the Constitution of the United States states — in the second paragraph of article IV:

The Congress shall have Power to dispose of and make all needful Rules and Regulations respecting the Territory or other Property belonging to the United States; and nothing in this Constitution shall be so construed as to Prejudice any Claims of the United States, or of any particular State.

The fact is that Congress was never consulted when the excess property program for grantees was initiated. And now that the program is threatened, now that the Government is trying to take away a privilege which it has previously granted, the attempt was again made to determine policy without the consultation of Congress. I am aware that Secretary Richardson wrote to Representative JACK BROOKS, chairman of the House Subcommittee on Government Activities, in June informing him that he expected to terminate the HEW program. But I am not aware that any member of the Labor and Public Welfare Committee, which oversees HEW programs, was notified that any such action was pending.

My fourth reason for introducing this bill today is this: while neglecting to work with and inform the Congress about the pending change in policy, the agencies involved have also completely failed to make their deliberations known either to the grantees who would be affected or to the general public. Notification of the proposed change proceeded in a most perfunctory manner giving rise to confusion and misinformation throughout the communities affected.

I strongly believe that we must put an end to secrecy in Government. I do not understand why a Senator who requests basic information concerning the impact of a proposed policy change which affects thousands of his constituents and cannot get an answer. I do not understand how an executive agency can make a policy change without being required to make public the reasons behind the proposed change.

It is apparent that not all of the executive agencies involved fully support the proposed termination of the excess property program. Phillip V. Sanchez, Director of the Office of Economic Opportunity, wrote to OMB Director Caspar Weinberger on June 23:

The annual utilization of excess federal property by OEO grantees is approximately $15 million. This excess property includes heavy equipment, many types of vehicles, shop equipment, furniture and other supplies and equipment that become excess to the many federal agencies. Loss of access to excess federal property will require commercial purchases whereas, the only cost for excess property is transportation.

And, Howard Matthews, Director of the Division of Manpower and Training of the Office of Education, wrote in a memo to the Director of the surplus property program at HEW:

Figure 27 • CONGRESSIONAL RECORD, Continued

We do have a strong program objection (to eliminating the excess property program for grantees), as hard core program savings reported by your regional excess property program coordinator exceeded $45 million in the last five years. These program savings reflect the utilization of Excess Federal Personal Property both in the consumable and major equipment categories in lieu of new procurement and represent savings of appropriated funds earmarked for the purchase of equipment and supplies for which excess Federal property was acquired and substituted. The monies saved have been used for program expansion and enrichment.

I see no justification for the high-handed, elusive treatment the public, interested parties and Members of the Congress have received in their attempts to learn about and have a part in decisions regarding the excess property policy.

At this time, I would like to make it clear for the record that the bill I am introducing and discussing here today concerns only the excess property program for grantees. It would not affect the access of grantees to Federal supply sources one way or the other. It is my belief that because these two programs were tied together in the announcement of a proposed rule change in the Federal Register, the public has been led to believe that the issues and the questions raised are inseparable. I think that the issues are different, and I am also introducing a completely separate bill that deals with the question of purchasing from GSA stores.

I am introducing the excess property legislation today in the hope that members of the Senate and House Committees on Government Operations will agree with me that the issues raised by the excess property policy are significant enough in themselves to warrant hearings and consideration by the Congress.

I am also pleased to note that Representatives, MICHAEL HARRINGTON, of Massachusetts, and DON FRASER, of Minnesota, and others are introducing in the House of Representatives a bill on excess property which is identical to mine.

I ask unanimous consent that the bill be printed in the RECORD.

There being no objection, the bill was ordered to be printed in the RECORD, as follows:

S. 3882

Be it enacted by the Senate and House of Representatives of the United States of America in Congress assembled, That section 202 of the Federal Property and Administrative Services Act of 1949, as amended (40 U.S.C. 483), is amended by adding at the end thereof the following new subsection:

"(i) Each executive agency shall furnish excess property to any grantee under a program established by law and for which funds are appropriated by the Congress if the head of that executive agency determines that the use of excess property by that grantee will (1) expand the ability of that grantee to carry out the purpose for which the grant was made, (2) result in a reduction in the cost to the Government of the grant, or (3) result in an enhancement in the product or benefit from that grant. Any determination under the preceding sentence shall be reduced to writing and furnished to the grantee involved. The Administrator shall prescribe regulations governing the use, maintenance, consumption, and redelivery to Government custody of excess property furnished to grantees under this subsection."

Figure 27   •   CONGRESSIONAL RECORD, Continued

The pressures exerted are in essence from three sources. The first was exerted by the Office of Management and Budget when they urged the General Services Administration to take steps to curtail excess property to grantees. This resulted in the Notice June 1, 1972. The second came from the wish of DHEW to take over the activity in its entirety from GSA. Finally, the third source was the state agencies themselves and the organized effort within the collective group of state agencies for surplus property. In addition, the third pressure point used the state departments of education under which many of the surplus agencies reside organizationally.

Immediately following the announcement, colleges and universities and professional societies placed much pressure on the United States Congress, The White House and the General Services Administration. The pressure exerted on the Office of Management and Budget was questionable. Representatives from the National Association of State and Land Grant Universities, American State Colleges and Universities, American Council on Education and other organizations sought audiences with OMB officials, but only perfunctory actions were afforded the visitors. The pressure of telegrams typical of the response is found in Figures 28 and 29, which were sent to the The White House and the General Services Administration. National societies provided a forum for disseminating information of the imminent change. Members of the news media, U.S. Congress representatives, university officials and others made up many of the debates which took place.[12]

TELEGRAM TO THE PRESIDENT OF THE UNITED STATES

JUNE 15, 1972

MR. RICHARD M. NIXON
THE PRESIDENT OF THE UNITED STATES
THE WHITE HOUSE
1600 PENNSYLVANIA AVENUE
WASHINGTON, D.C. 20500

DEAR MR. PRESIDENT:
      (BLANK) UNIVERSITY IS IMPELLED TO CALL TO YOUR ATTENTION A MATTER OF
SERIOUS CONCERN TO OUR UNIVERSITY IN PARTICULAR, AND ALL COLLEGES AND
UNIVERSITIES IN GENERAL. PUBLISHED IN THE JUNE 1, 1972 FEDERAL REGISTER, VOLUME
NUMBER 37 (106) PAGES 10959 AND 10960, IS A NOTICE OF PROPOSED RULE THAT THE
GENERAL SERVICES ADMINISTRATION REVISE THE FEDERAL PROPERTY MANAGEMENT
REGULATIONS TO PROHIBIT THE USE OF GSA AND OTHER GOVERNMENT SOURCES OF
SUPPLY BY RECIPIENTS OF FEDERAL GRANTS.
      AS WRITTEN MR. PRESIDENT, THE PROPOSED RULE WILL STOP THE UNIVERSITY
FROM SECURING GOVERNMENT EXCESS PERSONAL PROPERTY WHICH HAS BEEN A
LIFELINE TO THE UNIVERSITY BUDGET. THIS IS ESPECIALLY TRUE BECAUSE OF THE
TIGHTENING OF BUDGETS BOTH IN THE FEDERAL SECTOR AS WELL AS IN UNIVERSITIES.
      THE EQUIPMENT AND ITEMS OF PROPERTY ACQUIRED THROUGH THE GSA
AUTHORIZED SOURCES CONSTITUTE A LARGE FIGURE IN THE UNIVERSITIES' BUDGET
AND IF CURTAILED WOULD PRESENT A SIGNIFICANT DEFICIT. (BLANK) UNIVERSITY
REALIZES THAT ONE OF THE MORE SIGNIFICANT ASSISTANCES WHICH HAS COME OUT
OF THE WHITE HOUSE SINCE YOU HAVE BECOME OUR PRESIDENT, IS THE OPENING
UP OF GOVERNMENT EXCESS PERSONAL PROPERTY TO INSTITUTIONS OF HIGHER
EDUCATION.
      (BLANK) UNIVERSITY ASKS THAT YOU URGE MR. GEORGE P. SCHULTZ, DIRECTOR
OF THE OFFICE OF MANAGEMENT AND BUDGET TO RESCIND THE DIRECTIVE TO THE
GENERAL SERVICES ADMINISTRATION REQUESTING THAT MODIFICATIONS BE MADE IN
THE FPMR'S CLOSING OFF GRANTEE UNIVERSITIES FROM UTILIZING THE GSA SOURCES.
YOUR CONSIDERATION TO THIS VERY IMPORTANT MATTER IS GREATLY APPRECIATED.
                              SIGNED: (BLANK)
                                 PRESIDENT

Figure 28 • *TELEGRAM TO THE PRESIDENT OF THE UNITED STATES*

TELEGRAM TO THE COMMISSIONER OF THE PROPERTY MANAGEMENT
AND DISPOSAL SERVICE, GENERAL SERVICES ADMINISTRATION

MR. T. M. THAWLEY, COMMISSIONER
PROPERTY MANAGEMENT AND DISPOSAL SERVICE
GENERAL SERVICES ADMINISTRATION
GENERAL SERVICES ADMINISTRATION BUILDING
WASHINGTON, D. C. 20405

DEAR MR. THAWLEY:
THIS TELEGRAM SERVES TO EXPRESS OPPOSITION OF THE NOTICE OF PROPOSED RULE
MAKING PUBLISHED IN THE FEDERAL REGISTER, VOLUME NUMBER 37 (106) PAGES
10959 AND 10960 THAT THE GENERAL SERVICES ADMINISTRATION REVISE THE FEDERAL
PROPERTY MANAGEMENT REGULATIONS TO PROHIBIT THE USE OF GSA AND OTHER
GOVERNMENT SOURCES OF SUPPLY BY RECIPIENTS OF FEDERAL GRANTS. MEMBERS OF
THE STAFF OF (BLANK) UNIVERSITY ARE AVAILABLE TO PROVIDE PROFESSIONAL TESTI-
MONY TO SUPPORT OUR OPPOSITION. PLEASE INFORM ME AS TO DATES, LOCATION AND
TIME OF HEARINGS PERTAINING TO THIS MOST IMPORTANT MATTER.
SIGNED: (BLANK)
PRESIDENT

Figure 29 • *TELEGRAM TO GENERAL SERVICES ADMINISTRATION*

July 19, 1972, the Office of Management and Budget in a document released on August 2, 1972 entitled, "*USE OF FEDERAL SUPPLY SOURCES BY FEDERAL GRANTEES*" placed the events in chronological order.[13] Many of the issues were focused on the authority of grantees to purchase a variety of materiel and equipment through GSA and at GSA Price Schedules. One example that was not given by the OMB but well known throughout the Federal government was the pressure exerted by automobile dealers and other commercial organizations. A grantee could purchase an automobile much below state contract price at the Federal GSA Schedule from a local dealer. The OMB felt that this was a circumvention of free enterprise — and correctly so. This authority was absurd from the beginning and became a causative factor as well as a *smoke screen* for the real reasons the OMB wished to disband the excess property program for higher education. The document goes on and on and essentially states the purported intent of the document is to give all grantees the same access to surplus property such as the Boy Scouts, the local church, the common schools and civil defense. Another argument the OMB makes is the duplication of effort of *screeners* of useable property. In practice favorites in the state distribution systems obtain and hold items for specific individuals and/or institutions. There are cases when items of specialized equipment, photography equipment and sophisticated laboratory instruments have been given to non-qualified personnel. The justification process is not quite the same as for those grantees acquiring property from excess. In fact, there is no uniform procedure established for justification.

Take one simple example. A state agency has a list of requests for a walk-in vehicle from the following groups. The State University, School of Drama wishes to use it for a mobile theater and travel throughout the State and region. An excellent idea for both student and faculty involvement. On the same list is a request for a camping vehicle for the Boy Scouts, a student-Sunday school mission for the local church, five counties request a walk-in vehicle for civil defense units, three cities request the vehicle for the Fire department use and lastly the Civil Air Patrol requests two walk-in vehicles for emergency use. How shall the one vehicle be distributed? How shall the justification be met? The principles and the actual practices are quite far apart.

WHAT ARE THE POLITICS? — The politics of the excess versus the surplus property have been building up for a long time preceding the 1972 announcement in the Federal Register. The states are now well organized and constitute a **bloc.** The state surplus agencies are quite often under the superintendent of education or the department of education, **not higher education** but common schools. The employees of the agency likewise are loyal to the organization — properly so.

The argument made by the *surplus bloc* using the DHEW as their spokesperson is the gross unfairness of excess property being distributed to a chosen few with the priviledge of acquiring the property first, leaving the remains for the rest. The argument appears on the surface to make a great deal of sense but in actuality it is not valid. The majority of items in the excess category either awarded on an indefinite loan or by title transfer are specific in nature and serve only a very small population. Sophisticated instruments normally cannot be used by Vo-Tech schools, common schools and others on the long list of eligibles for surplus property. The lobby is clear. The DHEW personnel likewise want all of the action and this means the GSA would no longer be involved with property for grantees in higher education.

WHERE ARE WE NOW? — The 95th Congress has several pieces of legislation now under consideration which would dramatically reduce higher education's share of the total by adding additional organizations of *eligibles* and completely cutting off excess property to higher education. House Bill (HR 9152) has been referred to a Subcommittee of the House Committee on Government Operations which would lengthen the list of eligibles. Other legislation under consideration would end the excess property for higher education.

CONCLUSION

The excess property and the surplus property programs serve two separate and distinct purposes. Both programs should be maintained and the integrity of both programs preserved. The dedicated project officers in the several agencies authorized to release excess property have done yeoman's service to the program. Tight budgets and retrenchment facing higher education can be made less painful to the Nation by prudent use and careful distribution of excess property. The surplus property program likewise can produce libraries of volumes of cases supporting its use. The states by-and-large have done wonders with the equipment.

Chapter Thirteen

PRIVATE FOUNDATION FUNDING

Bruce Ketcham
Edited by Harold Zallen

- **WHAT IS A FOUNDATION?**
- **HISTORICAL BACKGROUND**
- **TAX REFORM ACT OF 1969**
- **CATEGORIES OF FOUNDATIONS**
- **UNIVERSITY FOUNDATIONS**
- **FLEXIBILITY OF FOUNDATIONS**
- **FOUNDATION STATISTICS**
- **FOUNDATION PRIORITIES**
- **ESTABLISHING AND CONDUCTING CONTACTS WITH FOUNDATIONS**
  CONCLUSION

WHAT IS A FOUNDATION?

Foundations are nongovernmental institutions that make grants. The source of their funds are usually from a single person or a relatively small group.[1]

†The contents of this chapter were presented at the April, 1973 Regional Meeting of the National Council of University Research Administrators, Oklahoma State University, Stillwater, Oklahoma, and later published in **Transactions,** 1973 Region V Meeting (136), April, 1973, Harold Zallen, Editor. Permission has been granted by the author.

257

HISTORICAL BACKGROUND

Philanthropic activity dates back to the establishment of Plato's Academy in the Fourth Century B.C. The Academy was endowed by the founder with farmlands and cattle and endured until the time of the Emperor Justinian 900 years later. Throughout the Middle Ages, the monastery and the established Church practiced a form of philanthropy. They received legacies and used their incomes for charitable purposes. With the break-up of the monasteries and the state-related Church in Tudor, England, private and secular philanthropists came into existence. For example, the Bodleian Library at Oxford, England was begun with a private bequest from Thomas Bodley in 1602. Private philanthropy existed in Early America from the founding of our Nation. Bequests of Benjamin Franklin to Philadelphia and Boston are still compounding interest today. One of the earliest foundations in America is the Magdalen Society of Philadelphia. It was established 1800, and is still operating today. It is known today as the White-Williams Foundation. The White-Williams Foundation was established to *"ameliorate the distressed condition of those unhappy females who have been seduced from the paths of virtue and are desirous of returning to a life of rectitude."* The foundation struggled for more than a century to survive in the face of a chronic insufficiency of unhappy females desirous of rectitude. In 1918, the controlling board voted to broaden its purposes.

In the Post-Civil War era great monopolies and trusts began to harvest profits beyond the opportunities of reinvestment. At this time in history there was no Federal Income Tax. This resulted in the era of the first great foundations in America. They were the Carnegie and Rockefeller Foundations which were based upon the founders' massed fortunes. It is noteworthy, that of the largest present day foundations, 5,436 have combined assets totaling over $25.2 billion. 4,911 were established after 1939; 2,546 during the 1950's and 1,231 in the 1960's.

Foundations have been subjected to various types of criticism throughout their history. During the 1930's the charge was against founders and managers who, the charges ran, perpetuated themselves and their power through the foundation. In the 1950's charges made seemingly were reversed (although misleading) when foundations were alleged to harbor vast communistic forces. In both cases, attacks were less upon the activity of the foundations than upon the men behind them.

During the 1960's Congressman Write Pattman of Texas began investigations to determine differences between genuine foundation and those foundations operating to perpetrate tax evasion. His investigations and reports resulted in formation of the Commission on Foundations and Private Philanthropy (The Peterson Commission, so called after its Chairman, Peter G. Peterson). The report of this Commission resulted in the Tax Reform Act of 1969.

TAX REFORM ACT OF 1969

The Tax Reform Act of 1969 is considered by legal and financial experts as a landmark piece of legislation. The Tax Reform Act of 1969 resulted in controversy and complaints from many of the diverse foundations from one part of the country to the other. William C. Archie, Executive Director of the Mary Reynolds Babcock Foundation estimated that $50 million is paid annually into the General Fund of the Treasury of the United States. Archie acknowledges that the greatest benefit of the Act is to reaffirm the only justification for the private foundation — that being for the good of the public. He further states that this is best assured through full public disclosure.[2] Merrimon Cunninggim, former president of the

Danforth Foundation, reports that this Law has not hurt the foundations seriously. There was a greater expectation that much more damage would have resulted by the Law than actually took place.[3]

SPECIFICS OF THE TAX REFORM ACT OF 1969 — This Act provides the following controls upon the private foundation:

- ABSOLUTELY FORBIDS DEALING WITH PERSONS RELATED TO IT.
- CURBS FOUNDATION OWNERSHIP OF CONTROLLING INTEREST IN A BUSINESS.
- PROHIBITS SPECULATIVE INVESTMENTS.
- REQUIRES PAYMENT TO THE GOVERNMENT FOR AUDITING COSTS OF FOUR PER CENT ON THE INVESTMENT INCOME.
- REQUIRES THAT THE FOUNDATION ANNUALLY SPEND ITS ANNUAL INCOME (OR AN AMOUNT EQUAL TO A CERTAIN PERCENTAGE OF THE VALUE OF ITS ASSETS) FOR CHARITABLE PURPOSES.
- PROHIBITS FOUNDATION ACTIVITY TO DIRECTLY INFLUENCE LEGISLATION OR A PARTICULAR ELECTION.
- RESTRICTS FOUNDATION SUPPORT OF INDIVIDUALS ALMOST TO THE POINT OF REQUIRING INSTITUTIONAL AFFILIATION.
- MONITORS THE ACTIVITIES OF CERTAIN TYPES OF GRANTS.
- REQUIRES THAT AN ANNUAL REPORT BE MADE PUBLIC, AT LEAST IN THE FORM OF THE U.S. INCOME TAX RETURN.

CATEGORIES OF FOUNDATIONS

The 26,000 foundations registered with the Foundation Center can be distinguished into five categories.[4]

THE GENERAL OR RESEARCH FOUNDATION — A general or research foundation is organized to promote the well-being of mankind throughout the world. Such a foundation does not serve to provide relief in emergency situations nor apply monies to short range types of problems. This type of foundation's aims are of an innovative or preventive nature. This category includes the major foundations such as Ford and Rockefeller.

THE SPECIAL PURPOSE FOUNDATION — This type of

foundation establishes priorities which are expressive of the donor's special interests. The operating philosophy is usually quite ordinary but occasionally they range to very narrow contraints to the ridiculous. An example of the special purpose foundation is the Casey Foundation in New York. The Casey Foundation projects are funded only when they deal with first voters. The Wenner-Gren Foundation also of New York devotes its funds to anthropology. The Presser Foundation in Pennsylvania supports only music projects. The Hayden Foundation in New York supports only projects involving boys and young men. There is a foundation in New Hampshire which uses all of its funds to stimulate interest in gravity. There is one in New York which provides funds for needy journalists and nothing more. A foundation in Ohio is devoted to scientific study of the arc welding industry. Foundations also may specialize in a *type* or *quality* of a project. The Portola Foundation in California funds only educational projects which are too radical and daring for anyone else to touch. Another foundation emphasizes projects which promote *positive thinking* as a tool to gain power.

COMPANY OR CORPORATE FOUNDATIONS — Corporate foundations are legally detached from the commercial enterprise, operated exclusively for giving, they are tax-exempt, and non-profit. The growth of company or corporate foundations has taken place largely since the end of World War II. This type of foundation attempts to generate and demonstrate good will. They usually concentrate on communities where the business is located or an area in close proximity. Company foundations may operate in any or all of the following areas:

- **GRANTS TO INDIVIDUALS IN THE FORM OF SCHOLARSHIPS, EDUCATIONAL LOAN PROGRAMS, COMPETITIVE FELLOWSHIPS, TEACHER RECOGNITION AWARDS AND WORK/STUDY PROGRAMS.**
- **GRANTS TO INSTITUTIONS IN THE FORM OF UNRESTRICTED FUNDS, ENDOWMENT, CAPITAL GRANTS, EQUIPMENT PURCHASES, SUPPORT**

FOR ACADEMIC CHAIRS, MATCHING PLANS, WORK/TEACHER PRO-
GRAMS, UTILIZATION OF RETIRED PERSONNEL, SUPPORT OF PROFES-
SIONAL ORGANIZATIONS, CONTRIBUTIONS TO FACULTY SALARIES,
ASSIGNED FELLOWSHIPS, RESEARCH GRANTS, DEPARTMENTAL
GRANTS, LIBRARY GRANTS, ALUMNI INCENTIVE AWARDS AND PRO-
GRAMS, PARTICIPATION AS ADVISORS AND TRUSTEES, THE EXXON
FOUNDATION IS AN EXAMPLE OF A COMPANY OR CORPORATE
FOUNDATION.

In 1967 a study was performed which revealed that
business corporation foundations provided $325 million
to higher education. Of 602 companies surveyed, the
following types of companies were found to have established foundations.

TYPE OF COMPANY	NUMBER OF FOUNDATIONS
Banks	33
Engineering and Construction	9
Finance Corporations	4
Insurance Companies	13
Manufacturers	216
Telecommunications	2
Transportation	8
Utilities	8
Miscellaneous	7

TOTAL: 280 OUT OF 602 WITH FOUNDATIONS

Table 5   •   COMPANY FOUNDATIONS

An additional questionnaire determined that 464 out
of the 602 foundations had a special educational committee to direct funds to institutions of higher education.
Four hundred and forty one of the 602 foundations had a
special officer in charge of educational grants.

FAMILY OR PERSONAL FOUNDATIONS — Foundations
of this type are established by living donors and generally
tend to be small. Some of these are quite good and operate
with a spirit and intent in conformity to the Tax Reform
Act of 1969. The majority of foundations criticized in the
public media and by the United States Internal Revenue
Service today fall into the category of *Family or Personal*

Foundations. It is this group which was most strongly affected by the *Tax Reform Act of 1969.*

COMMUNITY FOUNDATIONS — These are usually city-wide and act to pool gifts from a variety of sources. The purpose is to use those funds for the common cause of the community.

UNIVERSITY FOUNDATIONS

Foundations are a potential source of funds for university grants, to general fund, and to special projects in research and development, or student aid. The foundation offers some unique possibilities for university support for the following reasons:

- **THEY ARE NOT AFFECTED BY THE CURRENT FEDERAL CUTBACK OF RESEARCH FUNDING.**
- **THEY DO NOT TYPICALLY REQUIRE THE LENGTHY AND SOMETIMES COMPLEX REPORTING REQUIREMENTS WHICH ACCOMPANY FEDERAL GRANTS AND CONTRACTS.**
- **THEY HAVE THE FLEXIBILITY TO SUPPORT PROGRAMS WHICH ARE NOT ATTRACTIVE TO FEDERAL FUNDING AGENCIES.**
- **THEY OFTEN SERVE TO BYPASS THEIR STATE PURCHASING LAWS AND PROCEDURES AND EXPENDITURE REQUIREMENTS. THIS IS PARTICULARLY TRUE IN INSTITUTIONS FUNDED PRIMARILY WITH STATE FUNDS. (BECAUSE OF THIS, SEVERAL STATES HAVE CURTAILED THE PRACTICE OF SUCH METHODOLOGY BY INTRODUCING STRINGENT STATUTES REQUIRING THAT ALL FUNDS REGARDLESS OF SOURCE BE DEPOSITED THROUGH THE STATE TREASURY.)**[6]

FLEXIBILITY OF FOUNDATIONS

William C. Archie puts the foundation in perspective. He states, ". . . A Foundation, by virtue of the freedom of its privacy, has the opportunity — and thus the obligation — to seek unusual ways to be helpful. This will often mean that one is supporting an innovative project which may not pay off . . ." There is a logical explanation for the foundations' greater freedom.[5]

- FOUNDATION'S DO NOT HAVE TO RAISE ANNUAL FUNDS WHEN THEY ARE ENDOWED. THE FOUNDATION CAN OPERATE WITHOUT THE PRESSURE OF EXTERNAL FORCES WHICH GOVERN MUCH OF THE POLICY OF GOVERNMENT, UNIVERSITIES, AND CORPORATIONS.
- FOUNDATION DOLLARS ARE NOT COMMITTED TO BUILT-IN, ON-GOING ACTIVITIES WITHIN WHICH RESEARCH MUST FIT ITSELF. RATHER, THE FOUNDATION CAN CHOOSE TO FUND "X" IN 1976, "Y" IN 1977, AND "Z" IN 1978 AND THE FOUNDATION NEED NOT DE-MAND THE PRODUCTION OF FRUIT FROM ANY OF THESE UNTIL 1979.

FOUNDATION STATISTICS

SIZE AND CHARACTERISTICS — In 1970, private phi-lanthropy amounted to 2 percent of the Nation's Gross National Product which was $18.3 billion. This figure does not include the millions of man hours of donated time. The $18.3 billion breaks down as follows:

CONTRIBUTION OF INDIVIDUAL LIVING PERSONS	$14.3 BILLION	78%
FOUNDATIONS	$ 1.7 BILLION	9%
INDIVIDUAL AFTER-DEATH BEQUESTS	$ 1.4 BILLION	8%
CORPORATE GIVING	$ 0.9 BILLION	5%
TOTAL	**18.3 BILLION**	**100%**

Table 6   •   FOUNDATION STATISTICS

The Foundation Center lists 26,000 foundations in its 1976 edition. Of the 26,000, 20,000 are very small. This group contributes less than $25,000 annually in each of its grants made. Five thousand four hundred and fifty four foundations have assets totalling $25.2 billion and grant $1.5 billion annually. There are 3,275 foundations with assets of less than one million dollars. This group of foundations shows an average annual grant of $1,700. Of 1,830 foundations with assets between one and 10 million dollars, the average grant is $3,600. There are 331 foundations with assets of more than $10 million which yield an average size grant of $20,000. The largest 26 foundations hold one-third of the total foundation assets and account for $475 million in grants. This is slightly less than one-third of the total grants. The Ford Foundation is the largest. The Ford Foundation's assets are estimated at one-ninth of the total of all foundation assets.

FOUNDATION PRIORITIES

Based upon the analysis of what foundations are funding, the following is the best *guesstimate* of the distribution of priorities. Do note that the priorities can and change daily. Analyze one particular foundation before taking the step of submitting a proposal to that particular foundation.

EDUCATION	31%
HEALTH AND MEDICINE	21%
GENERAL WELFARE (I.E. UNITED WAY)	14%
CULTURAL	11%
RESEARCH, CONSERVATION AND INDIVIDUAL WELFARE	15%
RELIGION	4%
COMMUNITY SERVICES	4%
POLITICAL (LESS THAN 0.5% AND INCLUDED IN ABOVE)	
TOTAL	**100%**

Table 7 • *FOUNDATION PRIORITIES*

Of the 331 largest foundations, 38 per cent report interest in *innovative* or *controversial* proposals, dedicating 3 per cent of their grants to such projects. The smallest of the "biggies" indicate zero interest in innovative ideas, frequently citing the Tax Reform Act as being prohibitive.

One key to successful foundation proposals is having adequate information about the foundations themselves. Countless man hours and dollars can be and are being wasted every day by sending *en-masse* proposals to foundations who are really not interested in your subject area. Proposals are often sent to foundations which restrict grants to a specific geographical area. Or proposals are sent before initial inquiries are made. Watch carefully for specialized applications and suggested deadlines. Again, it can not be over emphasized, the process of gathering information is essential.

OBTAINING INFORMATION ABOUT FOUNDATIONS — Utilize as many information services and foundation publications as your budget can afford. In subscribing, consider both dollar cost and amount of resources (physical and human) available to fully utilize these sources. The published list of sources of foundation information normally indicate the range of services available along with the costs.

Address foundations directly for information. You may wish to broadly **canvas** a particular subject area or geographical location with a large number of mailings requesting information and copies of the foundation's annual reports. If so, use original letters. Do not send duplicated, xerographed or write-in quick reply types of forms. Xerox Electronic Typing System 800, Redactron, IBM Magnetic Card Executive, IBM Mag Card II, Savin, IBM MTST and other automatic typewriters are quite acceptable and produce excellent appearing **original** letters. The test to use, is the letter. It should look like an original when it is dispatched.

You may know enough about a particular foundation to be seriously considering them for a specific proposal. In this case, you should attract their attention by sending an original letter. In the initial letter elucidate your institutional strengths and the interests which parallel those of the foundation you hope to be sending the proposal. Generally, this type of request for information receives faster and more detailed response. An added bonus, the personal letter invites an individualized reply. Remember, that subsequent dialogue will be with **persons** and not organizations.

Maintain close contact with other university offices. Development, student aids, and alumni relations, also may be interested in foundations. The method for co-ordinating your efforts will vary from institution to institution, but there should be an understanding that one office or individual will maintain foundation information and that all data will be routinely routed to that office or individual. This is essential. Many Institutions have policies and practices dealing with foundations. Others, too few, however, have offices and officers which do nothing but handle foundations. The Ohio State University is a good example of this, many others operated in a like fashion.

FOUNDATION CENTRAL INFORMATION DATA BANK — There are manifold reasons why a *FOUNDATION CEN-TRAL INFORMATION DATA BANK OR INFORMATION SYSTEM* should be maintained. Departments can benefit from experiences of one another. The director of alumni relations often can introduce the research officer to a foundation trustee. Thus, a research project director may establish contact with a foundation interested in providing scholarships or fellowships which was unavailable from normal sources or government agencies. Departments can avoid multiple difficulties arising when a donor is approached with more than one proposal concurrently. The institution which provides itself with an internal information service through a single agent kept fully informed on needs and opportunities avoids difficulties. Publications and data services should receive maximum utilization through the one agent who is able to organize and synthesize information from multiple sources. The organization also should maintain a filing system which makes information easily accessible. The method adopted will depend upon the needs and resources of the particular institution. Ideally, faculty and department interests and needs can be filed in a computer bank which can be keyed to a file of foundation data.

This is not always possible — nor does the beginning effort always approach a work load to justify this approach. A dual-filing system might be considered as an alternative to the computer bank. To accomplish the dual-filing system with relative ease, a catalog is prepared. This catalog containing summaries of information concerning individual foundations is constantly updated. This file may include: name, address and telephone number; person to contact and major officers; priorities and brief notes regarding recent grants made; funding policies and size of grants; deadlines; a constant record of contacts with the foundation (proposals submitted, proposals denied, grants received, materials provided by the Foundation, etc.). This catalog should be indexed in terms of departmental needs.

The second file of the dual-filing system should contain actual materials, annual reports, correspondence, guidelines, proposals submitted and any other pertinent material.

ESTABLISHING AND CONDUCTING CONTACTS WITH FOUNDATIONS

Contact may be initiated in an early letter requesting information. If so, the initial personalized letter, on letterhead of course, (which we already have spoken at lengths about both in this Chapter and in other Chapters) should have provided a name and point of reference from which to begin when you have a specific project to discuss. Contact may begin with: a personal interview. Dermer's basic guide *"Where America's Large Foundations Make Their Grants"* is worthwhile to study for those foundations who prefer or at least allow interviews.[7] Generally local foundations should be approached by means of an interview. In other than the local situations one should contact the foundation with a written request for an interview. **DO NOT BARGE INTO THE FOUNDA-**

TION OFFICES WITHOUT PRIOR WARNING OR PER-MISSION. The letter should be very brief yet very specific to avoid burying the request for a meeting and to avoid conveying the impression that enough has been said to negate the need for an interview. Information in the letter should include the cost of the project planned, any support received to date from the home institution or other sources, the committment of the university to contribute and support the project both financially as well as morally. These items are important facets which should be included in the letter. Printed material such as the annual report of the university or a printed report of the research activities and finances likewise would be appropriate as an attachment to the letter. The written request for an interview can be followed-up in ten days to two weeks with a telephone call.

PERSONAL CONTACT TO OBTAIN AN INTERVIEW — There is nothing unethical to use friends, contacts, trustees, or local government officials to gain an interview. What must be avoided at all costs are pressure tactics. The foundation personnel may grant an interview under duress but if it is pro-forma due to pressure tactics — all will be lost. **IT IS UNWISE TO EXERT PRESSURE.** The nature of the interview itself is normally dictated by circumstances and cannot be 100 per cent pre-planned. However, there should be a fair amount of pre-planning and briefing prior to the actual interview. The principal investigator, university officers, or departmental representatives may appropriately attend. Do not bring a contingent so large that it will overwhelm the foundation staff.

Contact may begin with the submission of a full proposal. Although many foundations prefer the full proposal with the initial contact, this should be done only after thorough investigation of the foundation is complete. Indiscriminate mailings are costly and may endanger a later, more appropriate proposal. **IMPRESSIONS ARE IMPORTANT.** The cover letter should be brief, enthusiastic, but very businesslike. It should not attempt to fill gaps in the proposal itself. The proposal must be a good one. There is nothing to be gained by submitting a hastily conceived or poorly written proposal. Recognize, therefore, that no amount of professionalism in preparation and presentation can disguise a project that is poorly planned or conceived, that presents an unrealistic financial picture (too much or too little), or that is unjustifiable or unsuitable for foundation funding in general. The proposal must be written with the reader in mind. If the foundation review committee is highly specialized, the proposal may be presented in technical terms. Some foundations, private foundations are not as technically oriented as many of the governmental agencies. Here the technical writer can prove useful by translating technical terms to those clear to laymen. If technical writers are not available, try to use common sense. Talk to the investigator; keep talking until there is mutual understanding in what the principal investigator is going to do, why he needs funds, and how he plans to use the funds if he is successful.

ALL PROPOSALS SHOULD FOLLOW BASIC GUIDELINES — Present the most important data first. This will include length of the project, objectives, program methods, significance, and cost. **BE SPECIFIC AND CONCISE. IF YOU CANNOT BE SPECIFIC, THE PROJECT IS NOT READY FOR SUBMISSION.** The length should not exceed five typewritten pages. Reserve secondary data such as resumes, relevant publications, assurances and the like for the appendix.

Packaging the proposal should stress neatness coupled with simplicity. Foundations almost universally express distaste for elaborate covers, binding, etc. Follow through is an essential in the "foundation-game" as in golf or any other competitive exercise. If you are funded, express your appreciation. Keep your sponsor informed. Submit reports on time. If you are not funded, express your appreciation for the opportunity of being considered. The both parties concerned will have a better relationship for the future, when and if another proposal is to be submitted. It is not beyond the realm of possibility one foundation officer will leave his current position and join another foundation which is looking for exactly what you submitted earlier. This is a mobile society and it is no different in the fund disbursing area than in academe itself.

CONCLUSION

An area which is both tapped and untapped is the private foundation. The rules, guidelines and procedures are very similar to that of the Federal sector. Review procedures are likewise very similar.

The private foundation by-and-large dictates what the particular foundation wishes to fund. Just as insurance firms use actuaries and sophisticated analysis techniques so do the private foundations. The large private foundations to determine needs both nationally and internationally use library research, opinion polls, mail surveys and very sophisticated budget and program studies. The private foundations are interested in assisting in all areas imaginable. Those with announced programs like Ford and Rockefeller expect the guidelines to be followed as published. Others are looking for innovation and still others only assist in specified ways. Regardless what the pessimists say, the private foundations are worth pursuing.

Chapter Fourteen

LEGAL CONSIDERATIONS

- INTRODUCTION
- COPYRIGHTS AND PATENTS
- GOVERNMENT SPONSORED RESEARCH IN A UNIVERSITY
- CLINICAL RESEARCH
- PROTECTION OF HUMAN SUBJECTS
- CIVIL RIGHTS
- EQUAL OPPORTUNITY — AFFIRMATIVE ACTION
- NUCLEAR AND RADIOLOGICAL SAFETY
- OCCUPATIONAL SAFETY AND HEALTH ACT
- CONCLUSION
- SELECTED READING LIST

INTRODUCTION

This Chapter is intended to call to the attention of the proposal writer some of the items which are most commonly encountered. It is by no means a legal treatise. Many of the items are basic to the subject of *Contracts*. *Other items deal with copyrights and patents and a host of other items commonly found facing the principal investigator. Still other considerations fall under the* rubric of *administrative law* particularly when dealing with regulations pertaining to the conduct of a grant or contract.

Because of the complexity of research, development and demonstration projects and the discharge of the agreed terms of a grant or contract most organizations, colleges, universities, city and State governments, private foundations, private research institutes and industry retain professional legal counsel. Should any interpretation be required or anomalies which have not been adequately elucidated by the funding agency or any conflict result, professional legal personnel should be consulted. A most common procedure now used, is the routing of proposals, contracts and grants through a legal office at home institutions.

COPYRIGHTS AND PATENTS

COPYRIGHTS — The original Copyright Law dates back to 1909. Since 1964, there have been almost continuous hearings held in Washington, D.C. focused toward reform and change of the copyright laws. The reason underlying most of the requested changes stems from the fact the *electronic media* are virtually in a vacuum. *Section 24 of the United States Code, Title 17* (Copyright Law) provides a duration of 28 years of statutory protection.

Since 1962 four extensions have been made by the United States Congress. The current trend is to extend copyrights from 28 to 50 years. Complications to copyrights are very much misunderstood. *"Public Domain"* and the *"infringement"* are being very carefully examined.

As late as December 1, 1975, a Bill reforming the United States Copyright Law was reported in the United States Senate. The Bill, *Senate Bill 22*, allows **individuals** to make **single** copies of copyrighted works for their own use and permits libraries to photocopy materials for preservation. *Senate Bill 22* prohibits **multiple** copying of such materials either in response to individual requests or for routine distribution.

"*General Information on Copyright*,"[1] an eleven-page pamphlet, is of great assistance to the understanding of copyright and the protection copyrights give to authors. This is accomplished in very simple terms. Copyrights are issued by the Library of Congress, Copyright Office, Washington, D.C.

Most organizations, private and industrial have spelled out policies when it comes to claiming ownership of material, ideas, and research created while in the employ of a respective organization. Colleges and universities are not generally in this category. Notably few have definitive policies and it is unclear how and what happens to creative discoveries, copyrighted works and the like. It is hard to believe, but quite true, a most commonly debated subject in faculty governance circles is the copyright and patent policy on college and university campuses. There are policies very much worth examining. A few worth mentioning are: Auburn University; Purdue University; Northeastern University; Massachusetts Institute of Technology; and Pennsylvania State University. There are others. The examples cited are quite sophisticated and represent a tremendous amount of effort on the part of the writers.

The National Institutes of Health state, ". . . . *except as otherwise provided in the conditions of the award, when publication or similar materials are developed for work supported in whole or in part by the NIH, the author is free to arrange for copyright without approval. Any such copyrighted materials shall be subject to a* **royalty-free, non-exclusive and irrevocable license to the Government** *to reproduce them, translate them, publish them, use and dispose of them, and to authorize others to do so. . . .*"[2]

Other agencies are concerned in different ways with problems of copyright. If an agency funds writing of a textbook, or development of a course of study, obviously the problems and concerns are different. It is in the book writing and the curriculum writing that *Public Law 90-23, "The Freedom of Information Act"* becomes of great concern to funded projects. Be sure of what can and cannot be done relative to copyrights when working with a particular agency. Written policies should be examined and if there is doubt, discuss these matters with your research administration organization, the patents and copyrights committee (if one exists) and/or the legal office in your organization.

PATENTS — Patents are very important and *very, very* costly. They are often placed in the domain of the same committee with copyrights yet the execution of the two are diametrically opposite in complexity and requirements. Those who have undergone the cost and time for a patent search understand the problem at the outset. Some organizations have relegated patents to the Research Corporation and other such organizations and are content to let the problem just go away. Others have come to grips with the problem and look at it realistically. A patent for an invention is a grant by the Government to an inventor of certain rights. A patent is granted by the Government acting through the United States Patent Office. The subject matter of the patent is an invention. The person entitled to receive the patent grant is the inventor **(or his heirs or assigns).** The duration of a patent is 17 years. The right conferred by the patent grant extends throughout the United States its territories and possessions. The right conferred by the patent grant is, in the language of the statute and of the grant itself, *"the right to exclude others from making, using, or selling"* the invention. What is granted is not the right to *make, use or sell,* but the *right to exclude others from making, using, or selling* the invention.

PATENT LAWS — The first patent law was enacted in 1790. The law now in effect is a general revision which was enacted July 19, 1952, and which came into effect January 1, 1953. Currently there is an effort similar to that of the copyright groups to revise and update current patent laws. Several Bills have been written and the Judiciary Committee of the United States Senate is currently studying proposed ways to improve and update patent law. A list of references pertaining to patents and copyrights will be found at the end of this Chapter for the interested reader.

TRIPARTITE AGREEMENTS — In the case of the National Institutes of Health when a compound or system appears worthwhile to undergo tests limited disclosure of patent documents can be undertaken with the National Institutes of Health, the grantee or contract institution and an industrial firm. Since these arrangements are very *"tailor-made"* and very delicate in nature, each case stands on its own. Normally agreement is for one year or a given period awarded to the industrial entity to test the system or compound. Exclusivity and release require special expertise — a cooperative spirit needs to exist between the investigator, the administrative officers and the legal office.

TRADEMARKS — Trademark registration is handled by the United States Patent Office. The Copyright Office of the Library of Congress is often confused as the source of information and registration for Trademarks. Copyright registration cannot be made for names, titles, and other short phrases or expressions.

In general, the Federal Trademark statute covers trademarks, service marks, and words, names, or symbols that identify or are capable of distinguishing goods or services. When information relative to trademarks is required, contact the Commissioner of Patents, Washington, D.C.

INSTITUTIONAL PATENT POLICY — In the development of a patent policy it is essential that sufficient time be given to allow interested parties to give their point of view. Some of the essential items which should be part of a patent policy follow:

- **THE RIGHTS OF THE INVENTOR.**
- **RIGHTS OF THE SPONSORS.**
- **RIGHTS OF THE INSTITUTION.**
- **ALTERNATIVES FOR CARRYING OUT THE POLICY.**
- **MECHANISM AND POLICY FOR SETTING THE SIZE AND CLASSIFICATION OF AWARDS TO FACULTY INVENTORS.**
- **DETAILED SPECIFICATIONS FOR FACULTY-INSTITUTION AGREEMENT.**
- **MECHANISM AND POLICIES FOR OTHER STAFF AND STUDENT INVENTORS.**

GOVERNMENT SPONSORED RESEARCH IN A UNIVERSITY

When an analysis is made of sources of funds by classification, the State institutions receive most of their funds from the State and the Federal government. Most institutions of higher learning receive the majority of funds from a governmental source rather than an industrial entity. Many institutions have adopted and published conflict-of-interest policies to insure that company-consulting and involvement with government research in the university are fairly reimbursed for the use of its facilities.

One such policy, based upon a joint statement by the American Council on Education and the American Association of University Professors is included in the Appendix of this book. The content of the policy is self-explanatory and widely accepted.

CLINICAL RESEARCH

In 1964, the 18th World Medical Assembly adopted the

"*Declaration of Helsinki*," a series of recommendations which guide doctors (physicians) in clinical research. This took place in Helsinki, Finland. Three classifications in this Declaration evolved. Basic principles for clinical research, treatment of a patient coupled with clinical research and non-therapeutic clinical research. A copy of the "*Declaration of Helsinki*" is found in the Appendix of this book.

PROTECTION OF HUMAN SUBJECTS

In 1965, following the *Declaration of Helsinki,* The National Advisory Health Council sent to the Surgeon General of the United States the following resolution:

> **Be it resolved that the National Advisory Health Council believes that Public Health Service support of clinical research and investigation involving human beings should be provided only if the judgement of the investigator is subject to prior review by his institutional associates to assure an independent determination of the protection of the rights and welfare of the individual or individuals involved, of the appropriateness of the methods used to secure informed consent, and of the risks and potential medical benefits of the investigation.**

The Surgeon General in 1966 and again in 1969 established policies and procedures governing the use of human subjects for all recipients of contracts and grants from the United States Public Health Service. In 1971, the Department of Health, Education and Welfare (DHEW), in effect, extended the United States Public Health Service policies and regulations to all grants, awards and contracts funded by DHEW.

RESPONSIBILITY FOR PROTECTING HUMAN SUBJECTS — Safeguarding the rights and welfare of human subjects involved in activities supported by Federal funds is the responsibility of the institution applying for and receiving Federal funds. Human subject protection is widely discussed and the cause of much controversy. The requirements have been clearly elucidated in *Title 45, United States Code of Federal Regulations, Part 46.*

INSTITUTIONAL REVIEW COMMITTEE — Each institution must have an appropriate institutional review committee. No grant or contract involving human subjects shall be made unless the application for such support has been **reviewed and approved** by the institutional committee. The institutional committee shall determine that the rights and welfare of the subjects involved are adequately protected, that the risks to an individual are outweighed by the potential benefits to him or by the importance of the knowledge gained, and that informed consent is to be obtained by methods that are adequate and appropriate.

DEFINITION OF RISK — A human subject is considered to be *"at risk"* if he may be exposed to the possibility of harm — physical, psychological, sociological, or other. The determination of risk is a matter of the application of common sense and sound professional judgment to the circumstances of the activity in question.

INFORMED CONSENT — Informed consent is to be obtained from each subject. The basic elements of informed consent are:

1. A fair explanation of the procedures to be followed, including an identification of those which are experimental;
2. A description of the attendant discomforts and risks;
3. A description of the benefits to be expected;
4. A disclosure of appropriate alternative procedures that would be advantageous for the subject;
5. An offer to answer any inquiries concerning the procedures;
6. An instruction that the subject is free to withdraw his consent and to discontinue participation in the project or activity at any time.

Informed consent is customarily obtained in writing.

If strong cause exists, waiver of written consent or modification of the six basic elements above may be permitted by the Committee, but the reasons must be individually and specifically documented in the Committee minutes and signed by the chairman. Granting of permission to use modified consent procedures imposes additional responsibility upon the review committee to establish that the risk to any subject is minimum, that use of either of the primary procedures for obtaining informed consent would surely invalidate objectives of considerable immediate importance, and that any reasonable alternative means for attaining these objectives would be less advantageous to the subject.

DOCUMENTATION OF COMMITTEE ACTIVITIES — Committee activities must be documented. Files must include copies of all documents presented or required for initial and continuing review, and all transmittals on Committee actions. Meeting minutes, including records of discussions of substantive issues and their resolutions, are to be retained by the institution and be made available upon request to representatives of the DHEW.

ASSURANCE OF COMPLIANCE — Each institution performing DHEW funded human subject experimentation must provide written assurance that it will abide by DHEW policy. The assurance shall embody a statement of compliance with DHEW requirements for initial and continuing committee review of the supported activities; a set of implementing guidelines, including identification of the committee; and a description of its review procedures.

CIVIL RIGHTS

Grant programs of the Federal government must be administered in conformance with the *Civil Rights*

Act of 1964 and the United States Code of Federal Regulations Title 45, Part 80 issued pursuant thereto by the Department of Health, Education, and Welfare. Title VI of the Civil Rights Act of 1964 states: "No person in the United States shall, on the ground of race, color, or national origin, be excluded from participation in, be denied the benefits of, or be subjected to discrimination under any program or activity receiving Federal financial assistance." Every grantee organization is required to have an Assurance of Compliance (Form HEW 441) on file with the Office of Civil Rights, Office of the Secretary, DHEW, before a grant may be made to that institution. The assurance once filed is sufficient for all subsequent Federal financial assistance, insofar as compliance with Title VI of the Civil Rights Act of 1964 is concerned.

EQUAL OPPORTUNITY - AFFIRMATIVE ACTION

In days gone by a principal investigator would ask a few persons he chose to be on a particular project. This procedure is now illegal. Advance opportunities must be publicized for all positions whether they be on a research project or a permanent appointment. A somewhat detailed job description must be formulated and interviews made in earnest. The bridge which normally never existed between professionals and their personnel office needs to be brought closer together now more than in any days in the past.

Consideration as to what will be done in a 40 hour week is now the burden of the project director. Overtime and other abuses will not be tolerated under Federal statutes which oversee hiring and firing practices. Planning becomes more important for the project director because of the requirements of job descriptions. Ad hoc practices likewise cannot stand the test of the labor standards imposed.

Time and effort reporting cannot any longer be slipshod — accurate and carefully documented records will be required and are often a subject of audit in the extramural sponsored project arena. There are volumes devoted to the subject of affirmative action and equal opportunity. Be sure that the **fine print** is read and understood by the principal investigator and the institution applying for and receiving Federal support.

NUCLEAR AND RADIOLOGICAL SAFETY

At the close of World War II, it was realized that the peaceful use of *atomic energy* should be explored. The United States Atomic Energy Commission (AEC) was abolished on January 19, 1975, and the non-regulatory activities incorporated into the Energy Research and Development Administration, which was activated on that same date. The regulatory responsibilities formerly handled by the Division of Licensing and Regulation of the AEC are now handled by another new agency, the Nuclear Regulatory Commission. Both agencies oversee the nuclear field in the United States.

Nuclear and Radiological Safety is protected under *Title 10, United States Code of Federal Regulations, Atomic Energy.*[3] When handling *radionuclides (radioactive materials)* or devices capable of producing ionizing radiation whether by university; private foundation or institute; or by the Federal government, conformance to the many parts of *Title 10* must be adhered to. In some instances the regulatory agency is at the state level. This is because several states chose to become *agreement states.* An agreement state is one that has through its Governor signed an agreement with the Federal government to assume the responsibilities of licensure and inspection for *By-product Material* (radioisotopes).

Occasionally reviewers will find research proposals in which the capabilities of the instruments described will not serve the research elucidated in the proposal. Both the researcher and the research administrator must understand the requirements of *Title 10*. The proposal should specify that the principal investigator is licensed either by a *specific* or *broad* license. If under the institutional license — indicate that he or she is approved by the *Radionuclide Safeguards Committee*. The committee existence and approval are both *statutory*.

Several specifics in the proposal as to a diagram of the laboratory and a list of the specialized items of nuclear instrumentation which will be used in the project should be mentioned. A page or more should be devoted to experimental procedures and the health and safety methodology which will be applied to the study. When planning to use any radionuclide, radiation or any device or item capable of producing ionizing radiation, check first with the *radiological control officer* at your installation.

OCCUPATIONAL SAFETY AND HEALTH ACT

The Williams-Steigler Occupational Safety and Health Act of 1970 (OSHA)[4] applies to every employer engaged in a business affecting commerce. Government employees are excluded from coverage, but there are requirements of other laws which serve to effectively cover government employees. The *Act* serves to provide a safe working environment for all employees by stating that the duty of an employer is to furnish places of employment free from hazards. The familiar laboratory setting with the clutter in the aisles and the *"Rube Goldberg"* maze of pipes and connections covered with *"home-made"* electrical wiring can be reported by the employee as a potentially hazardous environment. If an employee reports an alleged hazard to the Occupational Safety and

Health Administration (OSHA), the employer is liable for a heavy penalty and a time deadline to correct the hazard.

Since the *Act* took effect in April, 1971, enforcement emphasis by the United States Department of Labor has centered on hazardous types and classifications of employment. Research organizations should not ignore the requirements of the *Act* because complaints have been filed by employees and actions have been taken at universities and hospitals. Employers must keep accident records and reports of exposure to toxic or hazardous substances. The employers must notify employees promptly of any excessive exposure. Employers must also inform employees of existing safety, health standards and regulations. In turn, employees have the duty to comply with the safety regulations.

CONCLUSION

Research and research administration is bound by a myriad of rules and regulations. It becomes increasingly apparent that participation in research or research administration requires a great deal of understanding of these rules and regulations. When the requirement is a patent — It is best to leave this to trained personnel. Patents require the counsel of a patent attorney. Decisions as to when and how to bring the patents to the attention of an attorney needs to be decided as a basic policy for each institution. The legal implications of rules and regulations can be quite costly. Adherence to rules and regulations are actually not impossible. It requires a close cooperation between the researcher and the research administration office. Legal problems are not necessary and can normally be avoided when both groups are fully aware of what is required by the sponsoring agency. Leaving requirements to chance is folly in the fund accepting business.

Copyrights are actually not as much of a problem to the funding agencies as they are to the institutions themselves. Some form of written policy is necessary for all institutions as to copyright and patents. So many organizations hedge on this matter and find in the end a large problem on their hands.

Safe handling of radionuclides is a must and the chief executive of an institution should be conversant about his program. Errors made in this arena are blown quickly out of proportion and panic ensues when the media is informed of an "accident."

SELECTED READING LIST

Patents

Thomas Registry of American Manufacturers, Thomas Publishing Company, Incorporated, New York, New York. (1975) Published annually.

Poor's Register of Corporations, Director's and Executives, Standard and Poor's Corporation, New York, New York. (1975) Published annually.

Calvert, R., Editor. Encyclopedia of Patent Practice and Management, Rheinhold Book Corporation, New York, New York. (1964).

Davis, A.S., Jr. "Putting Patents to Work", J. of the Patent Office Society, 36,713 (1954).

Eckstrom, L.J. Licensing in Foreign and Domestic Operations, Foreign Operations Service, Incorporated, Essex, Connecticut. (1964) Supplemented.

Smith, A.M. Patent Law Cases; Comments and Material, Overbeck. (1964).

Copyrights

Copyright Law of the United States of America, Title 17, United States Code, Revised. January 1, 1973.

An Act to Amend, Title 17, United States Code, Public Law 93-573.93rd Congress, S.3976, December 31, 1974.

Copyright for Books, Circular 60, Copyright Office, Library of Congress, Washington, D.C. 1974.

International Copyright Relations of the United States, Circular 38 A, Copyright Office, Library of Congress, Washington, D.C. 1974.

Protection of Human Subjects

Department of Health, Education and Welfare. *The Institutional Guide to DHEW Policy On Protection Of Human Subjects.* DHEW Publication No. (NIH) 72-102.

Department of Health Education and Welfare, *Grants Administration.* Chapter 1-40. Protection of Human Subjects. April 15, 1971.

Department of Health, Education and Welfare. "Protection of Human Subjects." *Federal Register,* November 16, 1963. *38,* (221) 31738-49.

Department of Health, Education and Welfare. "Protection of Human Subjects." *Federal Register,* May 30, 1974. *39* (10) 18914-20.

Nuclear and Radiological Safety

Atomic Energy, *Title 10, United States Code of Federal Regulations,* Superintendent of Documents, Government Printing Office, Washington, D.C. (Subscription with periodic supplements).
Part 2 — *Rules of Practice*
Part 7 — *Advisory Boards*
Part 8 — *Interpretations: Opinions of General Counsel*
Part 20 — *Standards for Protection Against Radiation*
Part 25 — *Access to Restricted Data*
Part 30 — *Licensing of By-Product Material*
Part 40 — *Control of Source Material*
Part 50 — *Licensing of Production and Utilization Facilities*
Part 55 — *Operators Licenses*
Part 70 — *Special Nuclear Material Regulation*

Chapter Fifteen

LITERATURE RELEVANT TO RESEARCH AND PROJECT FUNDING

- **INTRODUCTION**
- **PUBLICATIONS OF THE FEDERAL GOVERNMENT**
- **PRIVATE FOUNDATIONS**
- **ASSOCIATIONS**
- **REGISTERS, SYSTEMS AND FILES**
- **NEWSLETTERS**
- **MISCELLANEOUS PUBLICATIONS: TABLOIDS, MAGAZINES AND TRADE JOURNALS**
- **CONCLUSION**

INTRODUCTION

There is no dearth of literature dealing with funding. The problem is not the quantity available but the quality. It will take a very discerning group of individuals to decide whether the available literature is worthy of time and expenditure to acquire it. In relation to the following lists, wherever possible some commentary has been made about the item or items of interest. When the subject has been clearly described in the title, often no further comment will be made. When a reference or service is deemed as superior by the authors, that reference or service will be indicated in **bold type.**

A steady increase in costs has made it necessary to delete the prices of the various services and publications. Interested readers may contact the source as to price and availability.

PUBLICATIONS OF THE FEDERAL GOVERNMENT

PUBLICATIONS AVAILABLE FROM THE SUPERINTENDENT OF DOCUMENTS, United States Government Printing Office, Washington, D.C. 20402:

ARMED SERVICES PROCUREMENT REGULATIONS. Provides information necessary to carry on business with the agencies of the Department of Defense. Detailed information pertaining to the conduct of contracts is included. Supplements issued periodically.

FEDERAL PROCUREMENT MANAGEMENT REGULATIONS. Issued by subscription with periodic supplements. Covers the requirements of doing business with the Federal government in agencies other than the Department of Defense.

UNITED STATES GOVERNMENT ORGANIZATION MANUAL. A treatise which is used to determine where and who carry out the functions of the Federal government. Upgraded periodically.

SELECTED UNITED STATES GOVERNMENT PUBLICATIONS. A flier which is issued biweekly listing the most recent and some back-issued publications available through the Superintendent of Documents.

EDUCATION DIRECTORY. Issued in several volumes each by a different category. *"Higher Education"* lists all institutions with their respective officers of approximately 3,000 colleges and universities. Issued annually.

U.S. OFFICE OF EDUCATION SUPPORT FOR THE ARTS AND THE HUMANITIES. Publication No. DHEW (OE) 72-19. Detailed compendium of data relative to support given to the arts and the humanities.

CATALOG OF FEDERAL DOMESTIC ASSISTANCE. Published through the Executive Office of the President, Office of Management and Budget annually. Lists all Federal agencies and details programs which give support in the form of grants and contracts.

COMMERCE BUSINESS DAILY. Published through the Department of Commerce and contains information concerning proposed procurements, sales, and contract awards.

CONGRESSIONAL RECORD. A digest of all the happenings, Bills introduced and progress of legislation taking place in the United States Congress.

CONSUMER NEWS. Published through the Office of Consumer Affairs, Executive Office of the President. Periodical available on subscription basis.

FEDERAL FUNDS AND SERVICES FOR THE ARTS. Published through the U.S. Office of Education OE-50050, 1967.

FEDERAL REGISTER. The document is necessary to keep up with *Proposed Rule Making* **and administrative changes in the Federal government. Items which appear require action on the part of interested groups. Notice of location and hearings are found in the Register. Available on subscription basis.**

THE BUDGET OF THE UNITED STATES GOVERNMENT. Available in several volumes from an abridged version to the entire budget. Annually after the Budget has been submitted to the Congress by the President.

NATIONAL SCIENCE FOUNDATION ANNUAL REPORT. Issued at the close of the fiscal year illustrating grants and contracts awarded and directions the agency has taken during the previous fiscal year.

NATIONAL SCIENCE FOUNDATION GRANTS AND AWARDS. Issued annually at the close of the fiscal year. Grants are listed by State and institution.

DIRECTORY OF FEDERAL R & D Installations. A comprehensive, general reference to research and development establishments owned and directly controlled by the Federal government. Compilation was made in 1969 and 1970 at the request of Dr. L. A. DuBridge, Chairman, Federal Council for the Science and Technology by the National Science Foundation. Library of Congress No. 74-607546.

CONGRESSIONAL DIRECTORY. Issued each session of the United States Congress. Available in paperback, hardcover and thumb-index editions. Biographical, organizational and functional data of the Congress. Agencies with the principal officers in charge of the agencies within the Federal government are listed.

MOSAIC. Published through the National Science Foundation. A comprehensive look at the more promising research projects funded by the Foundation. Available on a subscription basis.

ARMY RESEARCH AND DEVELOPMENT NEWS MAGAZINE. Available on subscription for six issues annually. Covers the research and development within the United States Army. An informal communication covering all of the segments of the Army scientific community. Published bimonthly.

PUBLICATIONS AVAILABLE DIRECTLY FROM FEDERAL AGENCIES:

THE CHS SCENE. Community Health Service, Department of Health, Education and Welfare, Public Health Service, Rockville, Maryland 20852. Periodic information dealing with the important changes in community health.

GRANTS ADMINISTRATION MANUAL. Department of Health, Education and Welfare. Revised periodically.

GRANTS ADMINISTRATION REPORT. Office of the Assistant Secretary-Comptroller, Division of Grants Administration Policy, Department of Health, Education and Welfare, Washington, D.C. 20201.

HSMHA GRANTS-IN-AID. Office of Grants Management, Health Services and Mental Health Administration, 5600 Fishers Lane, Rockville, Maryland 20852.

HUMANITIES. National Endowment for the Humanities, Washington, D.C. 20506. Issued periodically giving the latest information as to the programs and the announcements of the Endowment.

LISTING OF OPERATING FEDERAL ASSISTANCE PROGRAMS COMPILED DURING THE ROTH STUDY. United States House of Representatives, Washington, D.C. 20515. A study conducted by Senator William V. Roth, Jr. (Delaware) listing the kinds of assistance various Federal agencies offered. House Document No. 91-177.

MANPOWER RESEARCH PROJECTS. U.S. Department of Labor, Manpower Administration, Washington, D.C. 20210. Periodic update of manpower studies.

NATIONAL SCIENCE FOUNDATION GUIDE TO PROGRAMS. National Science Foundation, 1800 G. Street N.W., Washington, D.C. 20550. Annually updated with a brief description of each program funded by the Foundation.

NATIONAL SCIENCE FOUNDATION DATA BOOK. 1800 G. Street, N.W., Washington, D.C. 20550. Annually updated to give timely information as to dollars and numbers of grants and contracts awarded. Pocket-sized compendium abridged for convenient size.

DRG/NIH NEWSLETTER. Office of Information, Division of Research Grants, National Institutes of Health, NIH Building, Rockville Pike, Bethesda, Maryland 20014. Published periodically giving current information relative to research grants.

FAR HORIZONS. United States Department of State, Office of External Research, Washington, D.C. 20520. Subscription basis telling about the far reaching programs conducted by the Department.

FOREIGN AFFAIRS RESEARCH: A DIRECTORY OF GOVERNMENTAL RESOURCES. Department of State, Washington, D.C. 20520. Updated periodically.

A GUIDE TO GRANT AND AWARD PROGRAMS OF THE NATIONAL INSTITUTES OF HEALTH. Department of Health, Education and Welfare, National Institutes of Health, Division of Research Grants, Bethesda, Maryland 20014. Updated periodically.

RESEARCH GRANTS INDEX. Department of Health, Education and Welfare, Public Health Service, Washington, D.C. 20202. Available in sets giving sources and programs. Updated periodically. Sold on a subscription basis.

HIGHER EDUCATION REPORTS. United States Office of Education, 400 Maryland Avenue, S.W., Washington, D.C. 20202. Periodic updates of the programs of the Office.

HUD NEWSLETTER. Department of Housing and Urban Development, HUD Building, 451 Seventh Street, S.W., Washington, D.C. 20410. Periodically updated flier bringing to the reader all updated information about personnel and programs of HUD.

LEAA NEWSLETTER. Department of Justice, Law Enforcement Assistance

Administration, Indiana Building, 633 Indiana Avenue, N.W., Washington, D.C. 20530. Periodically distributed newsletter with information as to programs and personnel within the LEAA.

CONTRACTOR'S GUIDE. Department of Defense, United States Army Materiel Command, Washington, D.C. 20315. A procurement guide which details the requirements for doing business with the United States Army and the many Laboratories under the AMC.

PRIVATE FOUNDATIONS

PUBLICATIONS OF THE PUBLIC SERVICES MATERIALS CENTER, 104 East 40th Street, New York, New York 10016

THE 1972-73 SURVEY OF GRANT-MAKING FOUNDATIONS WITH ASSETS OF OVER $500,000 OR GRANTS OF OVER $25,000. Provides information regarding application deadlines, personal interviews, authorized person to contact, and grants for operating budgets.

THE COMPLETE FUND RAISING GUIDE by Howard R. Mirkin. Information on conducting "virtually every kind of fund raising campaign."

HOW TO GET YOUR FAIR SHARE OF FOUNDATION GRANTS. Includes suggestions on how to research foundations, how to get appointments by telephone, how to interview with the foundations, how to write the proposal, how to follow-up the proposal, and the financial and program future of foundations.

HOW TO RAISE FUNDS FROM FOUNDATIONS by Joseph Dermer. (1968) Provides information on the history of foundations, techniques for "approaching and cultivating" foundations, and guidelines for writing presentations.

HOW TO WRITE SUCCESSFUL FOUNDATION PRESENTATIONS by Joseph Dermer. (1970) Directions for writing for an appointment, writing general purpose proposals and special projects, and writing letters requesting renewal.

WHERE AMERICA'S LARGE FOUNDATIONS MAKE THEIR GRANTS. Reports on 600 foundations throughout the United States with assets of $1 million plus.

PUBLICATIONS OF THE WASHINGTON INTERNATIONAL ARTS LETTER, 115 — 5th Street Southeast, Washington, D.C. 20003

AMERICA'S FIRST COMPREHENSIVE LISTING OF FINANCIAL AID TO INDIVIDUAL ARTISTS IN ALL ARTS. Library of Congress No. 70-11-2695.

GRANTS AND AID TO INDIVIDUALS IN THE ARTS. Arts Patronage Series. 1970. 1300 Sources of funds for creative work or education for it. Good directory for schools offering financial assistance to students of the arts.

MILLIONS FOR THE ARTS: FEDERAL AND STATE CULTURAL PROGRAMS. Library of Congress No. 72-78-232.

PRIVATE FOUNDATIONS ACTIVE IN THE ARTS. Vol. One. (1970) Arts Patronage Series. Provides alphabetical listing of foundations funding the arts, their addresses, brief description of policies and priorities. Also provides index by states.

LISTS PUBLISHED SINCE VOLUME I. Numbers 8, 9, 10, 11.

THE WASHINGTON INTERNATIONAL ARTS LETTER. Provides periodical data on grants awarded and foundation activity.

PUBLICATIONS AND SERVICES OF THE FOUNDATION CENTER, 888 Seventh Avenue, New York, New York 10019

THE FOUNDATION CENTER INFORMATION QUARTERLY. Provides updates with cross references to the *Directory*. Provides information on microfilm annual reports held by the Center (numbering 300 at present); a guide to Foundation Center services; bibliographies; updates on computerized Foundation Grants Data Bank which provides print-outs by subject matter.

THE FOUNDATION DIRECTORY, Edition 4. Marianna O. Lewis, Editor. (1971) Includes foundations with grants of $25,000 or assets of $500,000. Totals 5,454 entries. Provides address, data on establishment, names of donors, officers, trustees. Indicates priorities and general purposes, any specific limitations. For the most recent year, provides the assets, amounts of new gifts, total expenditures and grants, with number of grants made. Indicates person to address when known. Arranged alphabetically by states; cross-indexed by broad fields of interest and alphabetical listing. Also provides index of donors' names, trustees, and administrators.

FOUNDATION GRANTS INDEX. Removable pages within the *Foundation News* which update the *Directory*. Indicates all recent grants of $5,000 plus. Arranged alphabetically by state. Provides data on size, purpose, and recipient of grant. Also provides alphabetical list of recipients and an index of key words or phrases indicative of subject matter.

THE FOUNDATION GRANTS INDEX, 1970-1971. Lee Noe, Editor. Compilation of periodical listings. Provides a two-year cumulative listing of foundation grants, indexed by discipline and/or subject matter under broad categories of interest (Education, Health, Humanities, etc.).

THE FOUNDATION NEWS. Published bi-monthly by the Council on Foundations, Inc., in conjunction with the Foundation Center. Provides current data on internal activities of foundations and five to six articles on specific foundations, foundation policies, etc. Book reviews relevant to foundations.

REGIONAL FOUNDATION CENTER DEPOSITORY LIBRARIES. Contain information on smaller foundations, including IRS Forms 990 and 990-AR required of all philanthropic organizations filing as private foundations. These can be purchased on microfilm or paper copy. The Hogg Foundation for Mental Health, the University of Texas, Austin, Texas 78712.

PRIVATE INFORMATION SERVICES

Foundation Research Service, 1225 — 19th Street, NW, Washington, D.C.

20036. Provides a variety of services in various packages: data sheets with 4-5 pages of information on specified foundations; collected index; quarterly supplements; customized service based on program descriptions.

PUBLICATIONS OF COUNCIL FOR FINANCIAL AID TO EDUCATION INC., 6 East 45th Street, New York, New York 10017.

AID-TO-EDUCATION PROGRAMS OF SOME LEADING BUSINESS CONCERNS. Indexed by alphabetical name of participating companies, by field of business, and by categories of giving. 1968.

HANDBOOK OF AID TO HIGHER EDUCATION BY CORPORATIONS, MAJOR FOUNDATIONS, THE FEDERAL GOVERNMENT. Includes regular six-month supplements.

VOLUNTARY SUPPORT TO EDUCATION. Annual survey of gifts to educational institutions.

HOW CORPORATIONS CAN AID COLLEGES AND UNIVERSITIES. A study which includes consideration of corporate aid-to-education programs. 1972. Updated periodically.

EDUCATIONAL CONTRIBUTIONS BY PUBLIC UTILITIES AND OTHER REGULATED INDUSTRIES AS AN ALLOWABLE OPERATING EXPENSE FOR RATE MAKING PURPOSES. September, 1972.

MISCELLANEOUS PUBLICATIONS

THE BIG FOUNDATION by Waldemar A. Nielsen. Columbia University Press. 475 pp. Discusses 33 foundations with assets of $100 million plus. Includes history, strengths, and weaknesses of each.

COLLEGE MANAGEMENT, 22 West Putnam Avenue, Greenwich, Connecticut 06830. Monthly periodical, annual. Broad subject matter includes fund raising through private sources.

DIRECTORY OF EUROPEAN FOUNDATIONS. Editor Giovanni Agnelli Foundation. Basic Books, Inc., 404 Park Avenue South, New York City, New York 10016. 1969.

FOUNDATIONS, PRIVATE GIVING, AND PUBLIC POLICY: Report of the Commission on Foundations and Private Philanthropy. University of Chicago. 1970. Discusses various foundation problems, relationship of foundations to social problems and to government funding programs.

FUND-RAISING FOR THE PRIVATE SCHOOL: THE FOUNDATION APPROACH. Volume I. By Charles Cooley. Independent School Consultants, Cohasset, Massachusetts. (1964).

THE FUTURE OF FOUNDATIONS. Ed. Fritz Heimann. The American Assembly at Columbia University. Prentice-Hall, Inc. 1973. Articles involve the various problems of private foundations, including their relationship to political activism and public controversy, tax law, government funding programs. Also discusses internal policies and directions of foundations.

THE PHENOMENON OF AMERICAN LARGESSE: The Philanthropic Foundation. Published by The Fund Raising Institute, Plymouth Meeting, Pennsylvania 09462. Provides information concerning the history and policies of foundations along with psychological approaches and technical advice in preparation of presentations.

THE PHILANTHROPIC DIGEST. Published by Brakeley, John Price Jones, Inc. 6 East 43rd Street, New York City, New York 10017. Published sixteen times a year. The bulletins are arranged by broad area of interests and provide data on administrative changes in key university personnel, recent publications relevant to funding problems, current development campaigns in American universities, and current grants awards listing.

PHILANTHROPIC FOUNDATIONS IN LATIN AMERICA. By Ann Stromberg. Basic Books, Inc., 404 Park Avenue South, New York City, New York 10016. (1968)

PRIVATE FOUNDATIONS REPORTER. Commerce Clearinghouse, Inc., 4025 Peterson Avenue, Chicago, Illinois 60646.

PRIVATE MONEY AND PUBLIC SERVICE: THE ROLE OF FOUNDATIONS IN AMERICAN SOCIETY: By Merrimon Cunninggim. McGraw-Hill Publishers. 267 pp. Discussion includes the big foundations, family funds, community trusts. Information on a variety of foundation problems and policies.

THE ROLE OF FOUNDATIONS IN AMERICAN LIFE. By Dean Rusk. Claremont University Press. 1961.

SPONSORED RESEARCH IN AMERICAN UNIVERSITIES AND COLLEGES. Editor Stephen Strickland. American Council on Education. 1967. Broad subject matter including the role of research in the university and administration of research departments. Also devotes several chapters specifically to foundations and their role in support of university research and programs.

ASSOCIATIONS

AAC SPECIAL BULLETINS. Federal Advisory Service, Association of American Colleges, 1818 R Street, N.W., Washington, D.C. 20009.

FELLOWSHIP GUIDE FOR WESTERN EUROPE. Council for European Studies, 213 Social Sciences, University of Pittsburgh, Pittsburgh, Pennsylvania 15213. Available with updated editions.

GREEN SHEET. National Association of State Universities and Land Grant Colleges, One Dupont Circle, Washington, D.C. 20036.

HIGHER EDUCATION AND NATIONAL AFFAIRS. American Council on Education, One Dupont Circle, Washington, D.C. 20036. Annual subscription available.

NEWSLETTER. Council for the Advancement of Small Colleges,One Dupont Circle, Washington, D.C. 20036.

NEWSLETTER. National Council of Independent Colleges and Universities, One Dupont Circle, Washington, D.C. 20036.

OFP REPORTS. American Association of State Colleges and Universities, Office of Federal Programs, One Dupont Circle, Washington, D.C. 20036.

A SELECTED LIST OF MAJOR FELLOWSHIP OPPORTUNITIES AND AIDS TO ADVANCED EDUCATION FOR FOREIGN NATIONALS. National Academy of Sciences, Constitution Avenue and Twenty First Street, N.W., Washington, D.C. 20418.

CHEMICAL AND ENGINEERING NEWS. American Chemical Society, 1155 Sixteenth Street, N.W., Washington, D.C. 20036. Weekly organ of the American Chemical Society. Covers the trends and happenings of the chemical industry, and chemical education around the world. Special treatment is given to the legislation pending which might have an effect on any part of the industry. Available on subscription basis.

ENCYCLOPEDIA OF ASSOCIATIONS. Gale Research Company, Book Tower, Detroit, Michigan 48226. A listing of professional associations. Also indicates whether there are any sources of funds available for project support.

REGISTERS, SYSTEMS AND FILES

ANNUAL REGISTER OF GRANT SUPPORT. Academic Media Incorporated, 32 Lincoln Avenue, Orange, New Jersey 07050.

CCH COLLEGE AND UNIVERSITY REPORTER. Commerce Clearing House, Incorporated, 4025 Peterson Avenue, Chicago, Illinois 60646. Subscription with supplements weekly or within short time spans. Covers analysis of Federal programs, appropriative legislation with analysis and other timely information cogent to higher education in general.

THE COLLEGE BLUE BOOK: SCHOLARSHIPS, FELLOWSHIPS AND GRANTS. CCM Corporation, 909 Third Avenue, New York, New York 10022. Updated annually.

COLLEGE MANAGEMENT. The Management Publishing Group, 22 West Putnam Avenue, Greenwich, Connecticut 06830.

FEDERAL LAWS: HEALTH MANPOWER. The Science and Health Communications Group, 1730 Rhode Island Avenue, N.W., Washington, D.C. 20036.

FEDERAL RESEARCH REPORT. 104 South Michigan Avenue, Suite 725, Chicago, Illinois 60603.

GRANTS AND AID TO INDIVIDUALS IN THE ARTS. Washington International Arts Letter, 115 Fifth Street, S.E., Washington, D.C. 20003.

THE GRANTSMAN JOURNAL, 47 North Park Street, Mora, Minnesota 55051.

GRANTSMANSHIP NEWS. University Resources Incorporated, 160 Central Park South, New York, New York 10019.

THE GUIDE TO FEDERAL ASSISTANCE FOR EDUCATION. Appleton-Century-Crofts, Division of Merideth Corporation, 440 Park Avenue South, New

York, New York 10016. Monthly update for subscribers.

MANPOWER COMMENTS. 2101 Constitution Avenue, N.W., Washington, D.C. 20418.

MLA GUIDE TO FEDERAL PROGRAMS. Modern Language Association, 62 Fifth Avenue, New York, New York 10011.

NASA FACTBOOK. Academic Media, 32 Lincoln Avenue, Orange, New Jersey 07050.

NSF FACTBOOK. Academic Media, 32 Lincoln Avenue, Orange, New Jersey 07050.

REPORT ON EDUCATION RESEARCH. Suite G-12, 2430 Pennsylvania Avenue, N.W., Washington, D.C. 20037.

SCIENCE & GOVERNMENT REPORT. Science and Government Report, Incorporated, P.O. Box 21123, Washington D.C. 20009.

SCIENTIFIC INFORMATION NOTES. Trends Publishing Incorporated, National Press Building, Washington, D.C. 20004.

TIMES OF THE AMERICAS. Woodward Building, Washington, D.C. 20005. Weekly publication.

WASHINGTON AND THE ARTS: A GUIDE AND DIRECTORY TO FEDERAL PROGRAMS AND DOLLARS FOR THE ARTS. Associated Councils of the Arts, 1564 Broadway, New York, New York 10036.

WASHINGTON INTERNATIONAL ARTS LETTER. Allied Business Consultants, 115 Fifth Street, Washington. D.C. 20003.

WASHINGTON SCIENCE TRENDS. Trends Publishing Company, National Press Building, Washington, D.C. 20004.

AIR/WATER POLLUTION REPORT. P.O. Box 1067, Blair Station, Silver Spring, Maryland 20910.

BIOASTRONAUTICS REPORT. National Press Building, Washington, D.C. 20004.

EDP INDUSTRY REPORT. 60 Austin Street, Newtonville, Massachusetts 02160.

EDUCATION TRAINING MARKET REPORT. 4706 Bethesda Avenue, Washington, D.C. 20014.

ENVIRONMENT REPORT. National Press Building, Washington, D.C. 20004.

INNOVATION NEWSLETTER. Technology Communication, Incorporated, 265 Madison Avenue, New York, New York 10016.

OCEANOLOGY 1156 Fifteenth Street, N.W., Washington, D.C. 20005.

SPACE LETTER. P.O. Box 3751, Washington, D.C. 20007.

TAFT INFORMATION SYSTEM. Taft Products Incorporated, 1000 Vermont Avenue, N.W. Washington, D.C. 20005.

COMPUTERIZED RETRIEVAL SYSTEM FOR FEDERAL DOMESTIC ASSIS-

TANCE. Academic World Incorporated, P.O. Drawer 2790, Norman, Oklahoma 73069. Installation and assistance toward implementating the system.

ANNUAL REGISTER OF GRANT SUPPORT. Marquis Academic Media, Marquis Who's Who, Incorporated, 200 East Ohio Street, Chicago, Illinois 60611.

DIRECTORY OF PUBLISHING OPPORTUNITIES. Marquis Academic Media, Marquis Who's Who, Incorporated, 200 East Ohio Street, Chicago, Illinois 60611.

NEWSLETTERS

BEHAVIORAL SCIENCES NEWSLETTER FOR RESEARCH PLANNING. American Institute for Research in the Behavioral Sciences, 135 North Bellfield Avenue, Pittsburgh, Pennsylvania 15213. Weekly publication.

CHRONICA. The Research Foundation of the State University System of New York, P.O. Box 7126, Albany, New York 12224.

HUMAN ADAPTABILITY NEWSLETTER. United States International Biological Program, 513 Social Sciences Building, University Park, Pennsylvania 16802.

INNOVATION. St. Louis Research Council, 224 North Broadway, St. Louis, Missouri 63102.

NEWS REPORT. National Academy of Sciences, National Research Council, and the National Academy of Engineering, 2101 Constitution Avenue, N.W. Washington, D.C. 20418.

RESEARCH REPORTER. The Center for Research and Development in Higher Education, 1947 Center Street, University of California, Berkeley, California 94720.

MISCELLANEOUS PUBLICATIONS: TABLOIDS, MAGAZINES AND TRADE JOURNALS

BEHAVIOR TODAY, P.O. Box 2993, Boulder Colorado 80302.

CHANGE. The Magazine of Higher Learning. P.O. Box 2450, Boulder, Colorado 80302.

CHRONICLE OF HIGHER EDUCATION. 1717 Massachusetts Avenue, N.W., Washington, D.C. 20036. 38 Issues per year. Tabloid format with an excellent and full coverage of what is happening in higher education across the nation. One section of each issue devoted to awards made by both private and Federal sources. Legislative considerations are also included.

REGIONAL SPOTLIGHT. 130 Sixth Street, N.W., Atlanta, Georgia 30313.

WASHINGTON POST. Daily and Sunday Washington, D.C. newspaper. Congressional actions are detailed and the Federal government functions are well covered. Washington Post, 1150 Fifteenth Street, N.W. Washington, D.C. 20036.

WALL STREET JOURNAL. National Press Building, Washington, D.C. 20036. Business and Financial Newspaper. Federal trends and legislation also covered.

RESEARCH AND DEVELOPMENT. 1301 South Grove Avenue, Barrington, Illinois 60010. A must for the reader involved with research and development. Federal analysis of funds done very expertly. A monthly which covers not only the United States but implications of foreign R & D. Articles are written by experts and all subject matter is covered.

DATAMATION. 1801 South La Cienega Boulevard, Los Angeles, California 90035. One of the most complete coverages of the entire computer industry from educational to hardware and software. Legal implications are covered in each of the monthly issues.

CONCLUSION

There is no fixed and hard rule as to the efficacy of an item or items of literature in the funding arena. The error should not be made of only purchasing items from old-line firms. New things are happening and new groups are producing very excellent materials. Many new groups have become affiliates of the old-line firms because of the superior material they have been producing.

Some subscriptions cost several hundred dollars and others are virtually free. The information required to operate a large university research administration organization differs dramatically from that of a private research institute. It therefore is not possible to say categorically what one must have to cover the spectrum of funding. One rule to abide by is whatever your organization may be, the material and the services should be "all encompassing" for that specialty or group of specialties. The arts and humanities versus the physical sciences each have unique problems. The one requirement each organization should adopt is to subscribe to those documents and services which will cover the compliance of Federal Regulations.

Chapter Sixteen

USEFUL
SAMPLE FORMS

- **INTRODUCTION**
- **FORMS**

INTRODUCTION

A series of forms are included in this Chapter which represents the Federal sector; the college or university research administration office; an academic or program evaluation office reviewing proposals; and a legal or program development office within either an academic or non-governmental setting. Routing sheets, Cover sheets, planning charts, budgets represent a sample of the forms presented. The authors are aware that many of the readers will be quite familiar with many of these forms presented. On the other hand there may be some in the audience who can glean ideas and improvements for their current operations. It is admitted that it was difficult to cull some three hundred forms and come up with a representative sample for a wide audience.

II. **This is a new project.** My specific comments are as follows:

a. **Educational Suitability** — Is the proposed program compatible with the department's goals and capabilities?
Comments: Yes............ No............

b. **Staff Commitments** — Does it involve any long or short-term commitments requiring additional staff, professional, full-time or part-time?   Yes............ No............
Comments:

c. **Space Requirements** — Does it require space beyond that now used by this particular group?
Comments: Yes............ No............

d. **Students** — Will it result in an increase in the number of students registered in the Graduate School, Undergraduate School?   Yes............ No............
Comments:

e. **Facilities** — Does it require any special facilities, renovations, equipment, services and supplies not included in the proposal?   Yes............ No............
Comments:

f. **Curriculum Change** — Does it require any course or program change(s) at the departmental, divisional, or major faculty level (intra or inter)?   Yes............ No............
Comments:

g. **Inter-Departmental Involvement** — If another department is involved, has the proposal been reviewed and approved by that department? (If so, please attach written approval from the cooperating department).
Comments: Yes............ No............

h. **Summer Training Program** — Has space been reserved for necessary classroom, dining facilities, or housing for personnel attending programs?   Yes............ No............
Comments:

i. **Research on Human Subject** — Are humans involved as subjects in this research; if so, is a review by the Committee on Human Subjects recommended?   Yes............ No............
Comments:

NOTE: Required number of proposals (Number required by the sponsor, plus four (4) additional for administrative use) should reach the Coordinator of Sponsored Programs **two weeks prior to the sponsors deadline date.** (Special consideration will be given under extenuating circumstances).

— DO NOT WRITE BELOW THIS LINE —

Date Received by Coordinator:... Forwarded to:...

Date:...

Initials:...

Figure 31   •   ROUTING SHEET

Date _____

New _____ Renewal _____.   ROUTING SHEET   Recorded

Proposal _____ Acceptance _____

PART 1. A. _____   _____
              Name or Title of Project   Routing Number

         B. _____   _____
              Total Amount Requested   Total Amount Granted   Sponsor's Number

PART 2. (Check Appropriate Items)

Document Form	Source of Funding	University Function
☐ Contract	☐ Private Sources	☐ Resident Instruction	☐ Library
☐ Grant Award	☐ State Govt'l Agency	☐ Research	☐ Facilities & Equipment
☐ Grant-in-Aid	☐ Federal Agency	☐ Graduate	☐ Student Financial Aid
☐ Memo of Understanding	☐ Other _____	☐ Extension	☐ Other _____
☐ Modification	specify		specify

PART 3. Effective Period _____ to _____

PART 4. Sponsoring Agency or Enterprise (Name and Address)

PART 5. Comments and/or any special information which should be called specifically to the attention of the
         administration. _____

         _____

PART 6. THE UNDERSIGNED HAVE REVIEWED THE CONTENT OF THIS DOCUMENT AND
         RECOMMEND APPROVAL EXCEPT AS NOTED:

A. Principal Investigator _____ Project Leader _____ Coordinator_____

    _____ Date _____
                                              Department

B. _____ Date _____   _____
    Department Head

C. _____ Date _____   _____
    Dean and/or Director   Comments (Type)

D. _____ Date _____   _____
    Director of Internal Audits   Comments (Type)

E. _____ Date _____   _____
    Legal Counsel   Comments (Type)

F. _____ Date _____   _____
    Vice President   Comments (Type)

routing number to be assigned by responsible administrative office (6C above), according to University policy.

Proposals involving resources not available to personnel 6A, 6B and 6C must also be signed by 6D, 6E, 6F, and two informational copies
of the proposal submitted with routing sheet for Director of Internal Audits.

Proposals involving only funds available to 6A, 6B, and 6C must be signed only by these personnel, and two information copies of
the proposal submitted with routing sheet for Director of Internal Audits.

Acceptances of all grants and contracts by the University must be signed by all personnel, 6A through 6F, before submission to the
President for his signature, and two informational copies of the grant submitted with routing sheet for Director of Internal Audits.

Copies provided for: Principal Investigator, white; Department Head, green; Dean, goldenrod; Legal Counsel, canary; Director of Internal
Audits, pink; Vice President, white.

Figure 30 • ROUTING SHEET

Sponsored Funds Proposal Routing Sheet

Principal Investigator: .... Dept.: ....

Proposed Sponsor(s): ....

....

....

....

Title of Project: ....

Requested Support: Amount   Agency

....

....

....

....

(Check One)

New Project   Renewal   Continuation   Supplement   Revision

☐   ☐   ☐   ☐   ☐

Please indicate approval of the attached proposal by initialing below and forwarding to the proper person next presonsible, as indicated.

The attached proposal has my favorable recommendation as fulfilling all sponsor(s) guidelines, college goals and objective and regulations of the

1. Principal Investigator   4. Dean
   (or Project Director)   Initials   Date   Initials   Date

2. Department Chairman   5. Coord. of Spon. Programs
                           Initials   Date   Initials   Date

3. Division Director
   (if applicable)   Initials   Date

I. This is a renewal at approximately the same budget level of a previously approved project and no new comments are needed.   Yes   No

OR

Figure 31   •   ROUTING SHEET, Continued

Figure 32 • *CONTRACTS AND GRANTS SUMMARY FORM*

COVER SHEET FOR PROPOSALS

TITLE OF PROPOSAL

PRINCIPAL INVESTIGATOR OR PROJECT DIRECTOR | PROPOSAL TO WHOM (IF KNOWN)

ESTIMATE OF FUNDS NEEDED

OUTSIDE SOURCE | AMOUNT $

IS UNIVERSITY COST SHARING OR MATCHING INVOLVED | AMOUNT

SOURCE OF COST SHARING OR MATCHING, IF ANY | TOTAL $

DUE DATE, IF ANY, FOR PROPOSAL SUBMISSION | PROPOSAL PROJECT DATES | STARTING | TERMINATION

IS COMPUTER TIME INVOLVED?
☐ Yes ☐ No   If so, please attach the Computer Usage Form.

If the proposal involves instructional programs for academic credit or scholarship or fellowship support for students, use a separate sheet to name only other faculty members involved and to indicate the number of undergraduate and graduate students, if any, involved.

ENDORSE-MENT

PRINCIPAL INVESTIGATOR OR PROJECT DIRECTOR | DATE

CHAIRMAN OF DEPARTMENT | DATE

BUDGET DEAN | DATE

DIRECTOR OFFICE OF RESEARCH ADMINISTRATION (FOR RESEARCH PROPOSALS ONLY) | DATE

VICE PROVOST FOR RESEARCH (AS APPROPRIATE) | DATE

If proposal involves instructional programs for academic credit or scholarship or fellowship support for students, grants-in-aid, research participation, or construction of academic buildings:
PROVOST | DATE

FOR ALL PROPOSALS FINANCIAL REVIEW (as appropriate)

GRANTS AND CONTRACTS ADMINISTRATION | DATE

OFFICE OF RESEARCH ADMINISTRATION | DATE

VICE PRESIDENT | DATE

PROPOSAL SENT
☐ YES ☐ NO
SENT BY | DATE

REMARKS:

Figure 33   •   COVER SHEET FOR PROPOSALS

NATIONAL SCIENCE FOUNDATION	EDUCATION	Form Approved
Washington, D.C. 20550	GRANT BUDGET & FISCAL REPORT	OMB No. 99-RO168
		NSF Form 135, Apr. 71

Please read instructions on reverse side before completing this form.

'TUTION & ADDRESS	NSF PROGRAM		PROJECT PERIOD
			SUMMER ACAD. YEAR
	PROJECT DIRECTOR	19 ___	
		19 ___	
		19 ___	
PROPOSAL NUMBER GRANT NUMBER	GRANTEE ACCOUNT NUMBER	REPORTING PERIOD	
		FROM TO	

A. PARTICIPANT SUPPORT	RATE	NUMBER BUDGETED	NSF GRANT BUDGET	TOTAL # PAID	GRANTEE EXPENDITURES
10. Total Participant Support			$		$

B. OPERATING COST
SALARIES AND WAGES

		NSF GRANT BUDGET	TOTAL # PAID	GRANTEE EXPENDITURES
11.	Director (Administrative $_____ ; Instruction $_____		11	
12.	Staff		12	
13.	Assistants		13	
14.			14	
15.	Secretarial and Clerical		15	
16.	TOTAL SALARIES AND WAGES	$	16	$
17	Staff Benefits (When charged as direct costs)		17	
'8.	TOTAL SALARIES, WAGES AND STAFF BENEFITS (16&17)	$	18	$
19.	Guest Lecturers		19	
20.	Staff Travel		20	
21.	Field Trips		21	
22.	Laboratory and Instructional Materials		22	
23.	Office Supplies, Communications, Publicity		23	
24.	Fees		24	
25.			25	
26.			26	
27.			27	
28.	TOTAL DIRECT OPERATING COSTS (18 thru 27)	$	28	$
29.	INDIRECT COSTS		29	
30.	TOTAL OPERATING COSTS (28 & 29)	$	30	$

C. GRANT & EXPENDITURE TOTALS

31.	Total Granted by NSF (Participant Support (10) + Total Operating Costs (30))	$	
32.	Total Expenditures Charged to Grant (10 + 30)		$
33.	Unexpended Balance (31 – 32)		$

We certify that the expenditures listed above are properly chargeable to this Grant.

SIGNATURE OF BUSINESS OFFICER	TYPED OR PRINTED NAME & TITLE	DATE
SIGNATURE OF PROJECT DIRECTOR	TYPED OR PRINTED NAME	DATE

FOR NSF USE ONLY
Final Fiscal Report Accepted

Grant Closed _____ Remains Open _____

By _____ Date _____

Grants Administration Section, Area _____

FOR NSF USE ONLY

Organ. Code	F.Y.	Fund ID	Prog. Code	Ob.Class	O/Dres.	Award No.	Amd.	Inst. Code	Unexpended Balance	Trans.	Lot
									$		

Figure 34 • NSF EDUCATION GRANT BUDGET AND FISCAL REPORT

NATIONAL SCIENCE FOUNDATION Washington, D.C. 20550		RESEARCH GRANT BUDGET & FISCAL REPORT		Form Approved Budget Bureau No. 99-R0013	
Please read instructions on reverse side carefully before completing this form.					

INSTITUTION AND ADDRESS		NSF PROGRAM			GRANT PERIOD from to
					REPORTING PERIOD from to
GRANT NUMBER	BUDGET DUR. (MOS.)	PRINCIPAL INVESTIGATOR(S)			GRANTEE ACCOUNT NUMBER

A. SALARIES AND WAGES			NSF Funded Man Months			NSF AWARD BUDGET	CUMULATIVE GRANT EXPENDITURES *Do Not Round*
			Cal.	Acad.	Summ.		
1. Senior Personnel							
	a.	(Co)Principal Investigator(s)				$	
	b.	Faculty Associates					
		Sub-Total				$	$
2. Other Personnel (Non-Faculty)							
	a.	Research Associates—Postdoctoral					
	b.	Non-Faculty Professionals					
	c.	Graduate Students					
	d.	Pre-Baccalaureate Students					
	e.	Secretarial—Clerical					
	f.	Technical, Shop, and Other					
		TOTAL SALARIES AND WAGES				$	$
B. STAFF BENEFITS iF CHARGED AS DIRECT COST							
C. TOTAL SALARIES, WAGES, AND STAFF BENEFITS (A + B)						$	$
D. PERMANENT EQUIPMENT							
E. EXPENDABLE EQUIPMENT AND SUPPLIES							
F. TRAVEL 1. DOMESTIC (INCLUDING CANADA)							
	2. FOREIGN						
G. PUBLICATION COSTS							
H. COMPUTER COSTS IF CHARGED AS DIRECT COST							
I. OTHER DIRECT COSTS							
J. TOTAL DIRECT COSTS (C through I)						$	$
K. INDIRECT COSTS							
L. TOTAL COSTS (J plus K)						$	$
M. AMOUNT OF THIS AWARD (ROUNDED)						$	
N. CUMULATIVE GRANT AMOUNT						$	
O. UNEXPENDED BALANCE (N. BUDGET MINUS L. EXPENDITURE)							$

REMARKS: Use extra sheet if necessary

SIGNATURE OF PRINCIPAL INVESTIGATOR	TYPED OR PRINTED NAME	DATE

I CERTIFY THAT ALL EXPENDITURES REPORTED ARE FOR APPROPRIATE PURPOSES AND IN ACCORDANCE WITH THE AGREEMENTS SET FORTH IN THE APPLICATION AND AWARD DOCUMENTS

SIGNATURE OF AUTHORIZED OFFICIAL	TYPED OR PRINTED NAME & TITLE	DATE

FOR NSF USE ONLY

Organ. Code	F.Y.	Fund ID	Prog. Code	Ob. Class O/Ores.	Award No.	Amd.	Inst. Code	Unexpended Balance	Trans.	Lot
								$		

NSF Form 98, JULY 1971   *SUPERSEDES ALL PREVIOUS EDITIONS*

Figure 35   •   *NSF RESEARCH GRANT BUDGET AND FISCAL REPORT*

NIH GUIDE — for **GRANTS** and **CONTRACTS**

U.S. DEPARTMENT OF HEALTH, EDUCATION, AND WELFARE

Vol. 5, No. 1, January 30, 1976

IN THIS ISSUE:

PRIVACY ACT OF 1974

The Privacy Act of 1974 requires that a Federal agency advise each individual whom it asks to supply information of the authority which authorizes the solicitation, whether disclosure is voluntary or mandatory, the principal purpose for which the information is intended to be used, the uses outside the agency which may be made of the information, and the effects on the individual, if any, of not providing all or any part of the requested information. The article in this issue pertains to information requested in applications for NIH support in connection with the conduct of research and research training programs. Provision of the information requested is voluntary.   Page 1

TRAVEL BETWEEN U.S. AND CANADA

Correction of Chapter PHS: 1-510 with relation to travel between U.S. and Canada.   Page 2

AWARDING OF INDIRECT COSTS FOR NIH RESEARCH GRANTS

Minor revisions to No. 8, June 29, 1971, issue of the *NIH GUIDE FOR GRANTS AND CONTRACTS*.   Page 3

AVAILABILITY OF RESOURCE

The National Institute on Aging has established at the Institute for Medical Research, Camden, New Jersey, a repository for cultures of characterized mutant and normal cells for research on aging.   Page 4

The GUIDE is published at irregular intervals to provide policy and administrative information to individuals and organizations who need to be kept informed of requirements and changes in grants and contracts activities administered by the National Institutes of Health.

Supplements, printed on yellow paper, are published by the respective awarding units concerning new projects, solicitations of sources, and requests for proposals.

Figure 36 • NIH GUIDE FOR GRANTS AND CONTRACTS

NATIONAL SCIENCE FOUNDATION
WASHINGTON, D.C. 20550

ASSURANCE OF COMPLIANCE
with
NATIONAL SCIENCE FOUNDATION REGULATION
UNDER TITLE VI OF THE CIVIL RIGHTS ACT OF 1964

_____ (hereinafter called the "Applicant")

HEREBY AGREES THAT it will comply with Title VI of the Civil Rights Act of 1964 (P.L. 88-352) and all requirements imposed by or pursuant to the Regulation of the National Science Foundation (45 CFR Part 611) issued pursuant to that title, to the end that, in accordance with Title VI of that Act and the Regulation, no person in the United States shall, on the ground of race, color, or national origin, be excluded from participation in, be denied the benefits of, or be otherwise subjected to discrimination under any program or activity for which the Applicant receives Federal financial assistance from the Foundation; and HEREBY GIVES ASSURANCE THAT it will immediately take any measures necessary to effectuate this agreement.

If any real property or structure thereon is provided or improved with the aid of Federal financial assistance extended to the Applicant by the Foundation, this assurance shall obligate the Applicant, or in the case of any transfer of such property, any transferee, for the period during which the real property or structure is used for a purpose for which the Federal financial assistance is extended or for another purpose involving the provision of similar services or benefits. If any personal property is so provided, this assurance shall obligate the Applicant for the period during which it retains ownership or possession of the property. In all other cases, this assurance shall obligate the Applicant for the period during which the Federal financial assistance is extended to it by the Foundation.

THIS ASSURANCE is given in consideration of and for the purpose of obtaining any and all Federal grants, loans, contracts, property, discounts or other Federal financial assistance extended after the date hereof to the Applicant by the Foundation, including installment payments after such date on account of applications for Federal financial assistance which were approved before such date. The Applicant recognizes and agrees that such Federal financial assistance will be extended in reliance on the representations and agreements made in this assurance, and that the United States shall have the right to seek judicial enforcement of this assurance. This assurance is _binding on the Applicant, its successors, transferees, and assignees,_ and the person or persons whose signatures appear below are authorized to sign this assurance on behalf of the Applicant.

Dated _____   _____
                                        (Applicant)

                            By _____
                               (President, Chairman of Board, or comparable
                               authorized official)

_____
(Applicant's mailing address)

Figure 37 • ASSURANCE OF COMPLIANCE

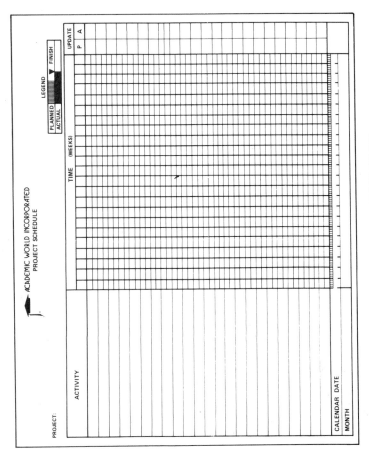

Figure 38 • *GANTT PLANNING CHART*

COLLEGE OF ARTS AND SCIENCES
1973 RESEARCH AWARDS PROGRAM
PANEL EVALUATION SHEET

Title of Project: _____

Proposal No. _____ Principal Investigator _____

1. CLARITY OF STATEMENT OF THE RESEARCH PROBLEM (10 points)
    Rating (number 10 highest score)

    1   2   3   4   5   6   7   8   9   10
                                                                        _____
                        (Circle Your Rating)   (your
                                                                        score)
                            (COMMENTS)

2. REVIEW OF THE LITERATURE (l0 points)
    Rating (number l0 highest score)

    1   2   3   4   5   6   7   8   9   10
                                                                        _____
                        (Circle Your Rating)   (your
                                                                        score)
                            (COMMENTS)

3. METHODS AND PROCEDURES (20 points)
    Rating (number 20 highest score)

    I 2 I 4 I 6 I 8 I 10 I 12 I 14 I 16 I 18 I 20
                                                                        _____
                        (Circle Your Rating)   (your
                                                                        score)
                            (COMMENTS)

Figure 39 • COLLEGE AWARDS PANEL EVALUATION SHEET

(COMMENTS CONT.)

4. JUSTIFICATION FOR THE PROPOSED RESEARCH   (20 points)
   Rating (number 20 highest score)

I 2 I 4 I 6 I 8 I 10 I 12 I 14 I 16 I 18 I 20
                        (Circle Your Rating)   _____
                                                                 (your
                            (COMMENTS)   score)

5. POSSIBILITY OF OBTAINING OUTSIDE SUPPORT   (20 points)
   Rating (number 20 highest score)

I 2 I 4 I 6 I 8 I 10 I 12 I 14 I 16 I 18 I 20
                        (Circle Your Rating)   _____
                                                                 (your
                            (COMMENTS)   score)

6. BUDGET PREPARATION AND DEFENSE   (5 points)
   Rating (number 5 highest score)

1   2   3   4   5
                        (Circle Your Rating)   _____
                            (COMMENTS)   (your
                                                                 score)

COLLEGE AWARDS PANEL EVALUATION SHEET, Continued

(COMMENTS CONT.)

7. GENERAL CRITIQUE OF THE PROJECT   (15 points)
    Rating (number 15 highest score)

    1   I   3   I   5   I   7   I   9   I   11   I   13   I   15

                        (Circle Your Rating)   *(your*
                                                                  score)

                        (COMMENTS)

TOTAL NUMBER OF POINTS __ _ _ _ _ _ _ _ _ _ _ _ _ _ _ _(   )

REVIEWERS LAST NAME PRINTED _____

GUIDE TO REVIEWER IN ASSIGNING POINT VALUES:

H=Highest Merit (Should be funded) 7, 8, 9 (grade of 10 very rare)
M=Meritorious (Funded if available--in second priority) 4, 5, 6
D=Disapproved (Project unworthy of support) 1, 2, 3

COLLEGE AWARDS PANEL EVALUATION SHEET, Continued

Proposal Number

CONFIDENTIAL

COLLEGE OF ARTS AND SCIENCES
1973 RESEARCH AWARDS PROGRAM
SUMMARY & CONSENSUS SHEET

LETTER	GRADE

GUIDE TO REVIEWER IN ASSIGNING POINT VALUES:

H=Highest Merit (Should be funded) 7, 8, 9 (grade of 10 very rare
M=Meritorious (Funded if available--in second priority) 4, 5, 6
D=Disapproved (Project unworthy of support) 1, 2, 3

Reviewer's Last Name In This Box							TOTAL
Numerical Score							

NOTE: If Reviewer Changes Score--Do Not Erase or Obliterate, merely cross out
with one line and place new score in box.

SUMMARY OF REVIEWER'S COMMENTS:

1.   Clarity of Statement of the Research Problem

2.   Review of the Literature

3.   Methods and Procedures

4.   Justification for the Proposed Research

5.   Possibility of Obtaining Outside Support

6.   Budget Preparation and Defense

7.   General Critique of the Project

_____   _____
Moderator's Printed Last Name   Moderator's Signature and Date

Form ASR 5 (3-73) Rev. 1.

Figure 40   •   COLLEGE AWARDS CONSENSUS SHEET

	SECTION I	Form Approved O.M.B. 68-R0249

DEPARTMENT OF HEALTH, EDUCATION, AND WELFARE PUBLIC HEALTH SERVICE

GRANT APPLICATION

	LEAVE BLANK	
TYPE	PROGRAM	NUMBER
REVIEW GROUP		FORMERLY
COUNCIL (Month, Year)		DATE RECEIVED

TO BE COMPLETED BY PRINCIPAL INVESTIGATOR (Items 1 through 7 and 15A)

1. TITLE OF PROPOSAL (Do not exceed 53 typewriter spaces)

2. PRINCIPAL INVESTIGATOR	3. DATES OF ENTIRE PROPOSED PROJECT PERIOD (This application.

2A. NAME (Last, First, Initial)	FROM	THROUGH

2B. TITLE OF POSITION	4. TOTAL DIRECT COSTS REQUESTED FOR PERIOD IN ITEM 3	5. DIRECT COSTS REQUESTED FOR FIRST 12-MONTH PERIOD

2C. MAILING ADDRESS (Street, City, State, Zip Code)	6. PERFORMANCE SITE(S) (See Instructions)

2D. DEGREE	2E. SOCIAL SECURITY NO.

2F. TELEPHONE DATA   Area Code TELEPHONE NUMBER AND EXTENSION

2G. DEPARTMENT, SERVICE, LABORATORY OR EQUIVALENT (See Instructions)

2H. MAJOR SUBDIVISION (See Instructions)

7. Research Involving Human Subjects (See Instructions)

A. ☐ NO B. ☐ YES Approved:

C. ☐ YES – Pending Review   Date

8. Inventions (Renewal Applicants Only - See Instructions)

A. ☐ NO B. ☐ YES – Not previously reported

C. ☐ YES – Previously reported

TO BE COMPLETED BY RESPONSIBLE ADMINISTRATIVE AUTHORITY (Items 8 through 13 and 15B)

9. APPLICANT ORGANIZATION(S) (See Instructions)

11. TYPE OF ORGANIZATION (Check applicable item)

☐ FEDERAL ☐ STATE ☐ LOCAL ☐ OTHER (Specify)

12. NAME, TITLE, ADDRESS, AND TELEPHONE NUMBER OF OFFICIAL IN BUSINESS OFFICE WHO SHOULD ALSO BE NOTIFIED IF AN AWARD IS MADE

10. NAME, TITLE, AND TELEPHONE NUMBER OF OFFICIAL(S) SIGNING FOR APPLICANT ORGANIZATION(S)

Telephone Number _____

13. IDENTIFY ORGANIZATIONAL COMPONENT TO RECEIVE CREDIT FOR INSTITUTIONAL GRANT PURPOSES (See Instructions)

14. ENTITY NUMBER (Formerly PHS Account Number)

Telephone Number (s) _____

15. CERTIFICATION AND ACCEPTANCE. We, the undersigned, certify that the statements herein are true and complete to the best of our knowledge and accept, as to any grant awarded, the obligation to comply with Public Health Service terms and conditions in effect at the time of the award.

SIGNATURES (Signatures required on original copy only. Use ink, "Per" signatures not acceptable)	A. SIGNATURE OF PERSON NAMED IN ITEM 2A	DATE
	B. SIGNATURE(S) OF PERSON(S) NAMED IN ITEM 10	DATE

NIH 398 (FORMERLY PHS 398)
Rev. 1/73

Figure 41 • GRANT APPLICATION NIH

SECTION 1

DEPARTMENT OF HEALTH, EDUCATION, AND WELFARE PUBLIC HEALTH SERVICE **RESEARCH OBJECTIVES**	LEAVE BLANK
	PROJECT NUMBER

NAME AND ADDRESS OF APPLICANT ORGANIZATION

NAME, SOCIAL SECURITY NUMBER, OFFICIAL TITLE, AND DEPARTMENT OF ALL PROFESSIONAL PERSONNEL ENGAGED ON PROJECT, BEGINNING WITH PRINCIPAL INVESTIGATOR

TITLE OF PROJECT

USE THIS SPACE TO ABSTRACT YOUR PROPOSED RESEARCH. OUTLINE OBJECTIVES AND METHODS. UNDERSCORE THE KEY WORDS (NOT TO EXCEED 10) IN YOUR ABSTRACT.

LEAVE BLANK

NIH 398 (FORMERLY PHS 398)
Rev. 1/73

Figure 42 • RESEARCH OBJECTIVES NIH

SECTION II — PRIVILEGED COMMUNICATION

DETAILED BUDGET FOR FIRST 12-MONTH PERIOD

FROM _____ THROUGH _____

PERSONNEL		DESCRIPTION (Itemize)		TIME OR EFFORT %/HRS.	AMOUNT REQUESTED (Omit cents)		
	NAME		TITLE OF POSITION		SALARY	FRINGE BENEFITS	TOTAL
			PRINCIPAL INVESTIGATOR				

CONSULTANT COSTS _____

EQUIPMENT _____

SUPPLIES _____

| TRAVEL | DOMESTIC |
| | FOREIGN |

PATIENT COSTS (See instructions)

ALTERATIONS AND RENOVATIONS

OTHER EXPENSES (Itemize) _____

TOTAL DIRECT COST (Enter on Page 1, Item 5) ————————————→

| INDIRECT COST (See Instructions) | DATE OF DHEW AGREEMENT: _____ % S&W* _____ % TDC* *IF THIS IS A SPECIAL RATE (e.g. off-site), SO INDICATE. | ☐ WAIVED ☐ UNDER NEGOTIATION WITH: _____ |

NIH 398 (FORMERLY PHS 398)
Rev. 1/73

Figure 43 • DETAILED BUDGET NIH

SECTION II — PRIVILEGED COMMUNICATION

BUDGET ESTIMATES FOR ALL YEARS OF SUPPORT REQUESTED FROM PUBLIC HEALTH SERVICE
DIRECT COSTS ONLY (Omit Cents)

DESCRIPTION		1ST PERIOD (SAME AS DETAILED BUDGET)	ADDITIONAL YEARS SUPPORT REQUESTED (This application only)					
			2ND YEAR	3RD YEAR	4TH YEAR	5TH YEAR	6TH YEAR	7TH YEAR
PERSONNEL COSTS								
CONSULTANT COSTS (Include fees, travel, etc.)								
EQUIPMENT								
SUPPLIES								
TRAVEL	DOMESTIC							
	FOREIGN							
PATIENT COSTS								
ALTERATIONS AND RENOVATIONS								
OTHER EXPENSES								
TOTAL DIRECT COSTS								

TOTAL FOR ENTIRE PROPOSED PROJECT PERIOD (Enter on Page 1, Item 4) ———▶ $

REMARKS: Justify all costs for the first year for which the need may not be obvious. For future years, justify equipment costs, as well as any significant increases in any other category. If a recurring annual increase in personnel costs is requested, give percentage. (Use continuation page if needed.)

NIH 398 (FORMERLY PHS 398)
Rev. 1/73

Figure 44 • BUDGET ESTIMATE (MULTIPLE YEARS) NIH

BIOGRAPHICAL SKETCH

*(Give the following information for all professional personnel listed on page 3, beginning with the Principal Investigator.
Use continuation pages and follow the same general format for each person.)*

NAME	TITLE	BIRTHDATE (Mo., Day, Yr.)

PLACE OF BIRTH (City, State, Country)	PRESENT NATIONALITY (If non-U.S. citizen, indicate kind of visa and expiration date)	SEX
		☐ Male ☐ Female

EDUCATION *(Begin with baccalaureate training and include postdoctoral)*

INSTITUTION AND LOCATION	DEGREE	YEAR CONFERRED	SCIENTIFIC FIELD

HONORS

MAJOR RESEARCH INTEREST	ROLE IN PROPOSED PROJECT

RESEARCH SUPPORT *(See instructions)*

RESEARCH AND/OR PROFESSIONAL EXPERIENCE *(Starting with present position, list training and experience relevant to area of project. List all or most representative publications. Do not exceed 3 pages for each individual.)*

☉ U. S. GOVERNMENT PRINTING OFFICE : 1974 564-253/3034

Figure 45   •   *BIOGRAPHICAL SKETCH NIH*

DO NOT WRITE IN THIS BOX   **REVIEWERS INFORMATION**

DATE _____

1. NAME

2. RANK

3. ADMINISTRA-
   TIVE TITLE
   (If Any)

4. COLLEGE OR UNIVERSITY

5. DEPARTMENT

6. CITY AND STATE

7. ZIP CODE

8. TELEPHONE: A. OFFICE
                 (Area Code)   (Extension)

                 B. HOME
                 (Area Code)

   SOCIAL SECURITY NUMBER   10. YEAR OF BIRTH

11. EDUCATIONAL HISTORY: INSTITUTION   LOCATION   DISCIPLINE   YEAR
                                                                          1   2

    A.   B.S.

    B.   M.S.

    C.   PH.D.   (See Reverse For Code)

    D.   POST DOCTORATE

    E.   OTHER DEGREE

12. DO YOU WISH TO SERVE ON OTHER NSF PANELS IN THE FUTURE?   (Yes)   (No)

    DO NOT WRITE BELOW THIS LINE

    PFS   NSF INSTITUTION CODE   A B C   E F
    4   5   6   7   8   9   0

    O. E. CODE   NSF FIELD OF SCIENCE CODE   II 2   II 3   II 4

                                                        NSF Form 428, December 1968

Figure 46 • *COMPUTERIZED REVIEWERS RESUME*

ISEP PROPOSAL EVALUATION SHEET

REVIEWER	PANEL	PROPOSAL NO.
		SCORE 10 HIGH; 1 LOW
INSTITUTION	PROJECT DIRECTOR	

FINDINGS OF FACT

DOES THE PROJECT CONFORM TO THE GUIDELINES:	YES	NO
1. IS THE PROJECT OBVIOUSLY DESIGNED TO IMPROVE THE CURRICULUM RATHER THAN BEING A RESPONSE TO FINANCIAL NEED OR INCREASED ENROLLMENT PRESSURES?		
2. IS THE EDUCATIONAL NEED FOR THE PROJECT APPARENT?		
3. WILL A SIGNIFICANT NUMBER OF STUDENTS BE AFFECTED?		
4. IS THERE ADEQUATE EVIDENCE OF INSTITUTIONAL SUPPORT OF THE COURSE(S) TO BE IMPROVED?		
5. DOES THE PROJECT "MAKE SENSE" IN ITS INSTITUTIONAL AND DEPARTMENTAL CONTEXT?		
6. IS THE EQUIPMENT TO BE PURCHASED FOR USE PRIMARILY BY UNDERGRADUATES?		
7. IS THE EQUIPMENT TO BE PURCHASED ADEQUATE IN QUALITY AND QUANTITY, WITHOUT BEING UNNECESSARILY SOPHISTICATED OR EXTRAVAGANT?		
8. IS THE FACULTY EXPERTISE (ESPECIALLY THAT OF THE PROJECT DIRECTOR) SUFFICIENT TO SUCCESSFULLY IMPLEMENT THE PROJECT?		

SUMMARY

ARE YOU SATISFIED THAT THE PROJECT MEETS THE REQUIREMENTS SET FORTH IN THE PUBLISHED ISEP GUIDELINES?

COMMENTS

EXPLAIN ALL NEGATIVE ANSWERS ABOVE AND CITE PAGE NUMBERS GERMANE TO EACH.

NSF FORM 145 (AUG. 1975)

Figure 47   •   PROPOSAL EVALUATION SHEET NSF

RATING SCALES (CHECK ONE BLOCK FOR EACH ITEM)	HIGH	MED	LOW	CAN'T TELL
9. WILL THE PROJECT IMPROVE THE ADEQUACY OF PRESENTATION OF SCIENTIFIC CONCEPTS?				
10. WILL THE PROJECT IMPROVE THE BALANCE OF PRESENTATION OF SCIENTIFIC CONCEPTS?				
11. IS THE PROJECT EDUCATIONALLY WELL CONCEIVED?				
12. IS THE PROJECT SUITABLE TO THE TARGET STUDENT AUDIENCE?				
13. WILL THE PROJECT HAVE A POSITIVE EFFECT ON TEACHING METHODS?				
14. WILL STUDENTS BENEFIT FROM A "HANDS-ON" EXPERIENCE WITH THE EQUIPMENT TO BE PURCHASED, OR IS DEMONSTRATION ONLY JUSTIFIED?				
15. IS EACH ITEM TO BE PURCHASED JUSTIFIED IN THE CONTEXT OF THE PROPOSAL?				
16. DOES THE EQUIPMENT TO BE PURCHASED PROVIDE ADEQUATE FLEXIBILITY FOR FUTURE USE IN UNDERGRADUATE EDUCATION?				
17. DOES THE EQUIPMENT TO BE PURCHASED SUPPLEMENT CURRENT HOLDINGS SO AS TO FACILITATE A SUCCESSFUL PROJECT?				
18. WHAT POTENTIAL DOES THE OVERALL PLAN DEMONSTRATE FOR IMPROVING SCIENCE EDUCATION OF THE DESCRIBED STUDENTS?				

COMMENTS AND JUSTIFICATION

19. RECOMMENDED DELETIONS (AND REASONS THEREFOR)

20. RECOMMENDED SUBSTITUTIONS (AND REASONS THEREFOR)

21. SUGGESTIONS FOR IMPROVEMENT

Figure 47 • *PROPOSAL EVALUATION SHEET NSF, Continued*

federal register

April 4, 1975—Pages 15063-15376

FRIDAY, APRIL 4, 1975

WASHINGTON, D.C.

Volume 40 ▪ Number 66

Pages 15063–15376

PART I

HIGHLIGHTS OF THIS ISSUE

This listing does not affect the legal status
of any document published in this issue. Detailed
table of contents appears inside.

Figure 48 • FEDERAL REGISTER

federal register

Phone 523-5240

Area Code 202

Published daily, Monday through Friday (no publication on Saturdays, Sundays, or on official Federal holidays), by the Office of the Federal Register, National Archives and Records Service, General Services Administration, Washington, D.C. 20408, under the Federal Register Act (49 Stat. 500, as amended; 44 U.S.C., Ch. 15) and the regulations of the Administrative Committee of the Federal Register (1 CFR Ch. I). Distribution is made only by the Superintendent of Documents, U.S. Government Printing Office, Washington, D.C. 20402.

The FEDERAL REGISTER provides a uniform system for making available to the public regulations and legal notices issued by Federal agencies. These include Presidential proclamations and Executive orders and Federal agency documents having general applicability and legal effect, documents required to be published by Act of Congress and other Federal agency documents of public interest.

The FEDERAL REGISTER will be furnished by mail to subscribers, free of postage, for $5.00 per month or $45 per year, payable in advance. The charge for individual copies is 75 cents for each issue, or 75 cents for each group of pages as actually bound. Remit check or money order, made payable to the Superintendent of Documents, U.S. Government Printing Office, Washington, D.C. 20402.

There are no restrictions on the republication of material appearing in the FEDERAL REGISTER.

FEDERAL REGISTER, VOL. 40, NO. 66—FRIDAY, APRIL 4, 1975

Figure 48 • FEDERAL REGISTER, Continued

Commerce Business Daily

U. S. DEPARTMENT OF COMMERCE
Rogers C. B. Morton, Secretary
OFFICE OF FIELD OPERATIONS
John P. Gleason, Jr., Acting Director

THURSDAY, NOVEMBER 6, 1975

A daily list of U.S. Government procurement invitations, contract awards, subcontracting leads, sales of surplus property and foreign business opportunities

U. S. GOVERNMENT PROCUREMENTS

Services

A   Experimental, Developmental, Test and Research Work (Includes both basic and applied research)- [EDTR].

A - - STRUCTURE-ACTIVITY STUDIES AMONG ANTICANCER AGENTS. Linear free energy relationships Organizations are being sought not affiliated with chemical and pharmaceutical industries, having capabilities and facilities for the study of structure-antitumor activity relationships among members of various classes of antitumor agents The approach to be applied in this particular project is the use of linear regression analysis to develop linear free energy relationships (LFER). The objective of the project is the use of the correlations developed to suggest structural modifications which will maximize antitumor activity and/or minimize toxic side effects within a series of congeners. The contractor selected will be expected to apply LFER techniques which are suitable to NCI chemical and biological data. It also will be expected to apply the synthetic and analytical techniques necessary to measure any required chemical and physical parameters, e.g. partition coefficients, electronic and steric constants, where they are not already available in the literature. The contractor selected will be expected to develop correlations within drug classes selected by the Project Officer. Anti-tumor data may be furnished by the Project Officer or be available from another source. When correlations are developed. The contractor will be expected to provide suggestions with respect to possible drug modifications. The Principal Investigator must have extensive experience in LFER structure activity correlations and substantial experience in the area of drug design together with evidence of the successful application of quantitative structure-activity techniques. It is anticipated that the total project will require two technical man years of effort per year—RFP will be available on or after 28 Nov 75, by request to the Division of Cancer Treatment, Contracts Section. Attn: W. T. Harris Requests for copies of solicitation will be honored if received within 20 calendar days after issuance date of 14 Nov 75. Requests received after this period will be filled on a first-come, first served basis until the supply is exhausted.—Job—RFP NCI-CM-67062—RFP due date 19 Jan 76.   (P307)
National Cancer Institute, Blair Building, Room 332, National Institutes of Health, Bethesda, MD 20014

A - - PROVIDE TECHNICAL ENGINEERING SERVICES IN SUPPORT OF THE GUNNERY IMPROVEMENT PROGRAM — In accordance with Specifications in the schedule — RFP N00024-76-R-7104 — (S) will be issued to Systems Consultants Inc., 1054 31st Street N. W. Washington D. C., 20007 since this is a continuation of work being performed by this firm under an existing contract See Note 49.   (P307)
Naval Sea Systems Command, Washington, D. C., 20362

━━━ BUSINESS NEWS ━━━

DESIGN TO COST-1976 PHASE II-IMPLEMENTATION

The American Institute of Aeronautics & Astronautics (AIAA) - Los Angeles Section in cooperation with the Department of Defense (DOD) announces the continuation of the series of summit conferences on Design to Cost and Life Cycle Costing. This year's program entitled, "Design to Cost-1976" will focus upon implementation. The conferences will be presented at the Newporter Inn in Newport Beach, California on 1-2 Dec 75 and at the Pier 66 Hotel in Ft. Lauderdale, Florida on 9-10 Feb 76.

Program Managers representing Navigation Systems, F-15, APN-209, AMST, FFG 7 (PF) and the XM-1 and officials from OSD will address the conference on problems faced and solutions found in implementing Design-To-Cost requirements, current trends and future directions.

Persons desiring further information, or those interested in registering for the conference should contact: AIAA Conference, 444 W. Ocean Blvd., Suite 1710, Long Beach, CA 91802, or call 213/437-7466.

HOW TO CONDUCT FOREIGN MILITARY SALES AND RELATED INTERNATIONAL LOGISTICS SUPPORT SEMINAR

This Seminar will be presented on 4-5 Dec 75 at the Marriott Twin Bridges, Washington, D. C.

Participating in this seminar will be representative of the Commerce, State and Treasury Departments who will discuss U. S. government policies and procedures and the Office Secretary of Defense and Military Services will present financial assistance and their future programs and the lessons they have learned from past and current programs.

Representatives of industry will present their experiences with, and methods of, conducting Foreign Military Sales. Of particular interest will be briefings by the Commerce and Defense Departments on opportunities in International Logistics Support and Follow-on Services.

A final session will include a panel discussion of questions and answers to afford the audience an opportunity for further communication with the participants.

Inquiries may be addressed to American Defense Preparedness Association, 819 Union Trust Bldg., 740 15th St., N.W., Washington, D. C. 20005; 202/347-7250 or Pasadena, CA 213/681-8021.

A - - ECONOMETRIC MODELLING AND FORECASTING TO 1990 OF DOMESTIC COMMERCIAL AIRLINE ACTIVITY AT 25 U. S. HUBS. Required capabilities are experience in econometric modelling and forecasting, and familiarity with CAB air activity definitions. Use of CAB Form 41 data is required. Standard Metropolitan Statistical Area income and population and coach fare data bases must be developed.—Job—RFP 210-0105-PK. See Note 24.   (P307)
US DOT, Transportation Systems Center, Kendall Square, Cambridge, MA 02142, Attn: Procurement Office, Code 8322.

❾ A - - A STUDY TO FORMULATE A SINGLE STANDARD SPECIFICATION that can be applied to NASA Standard Components. RFP 5-64244/053. Request copies Attn: C. Lerner.   (P307)

★ A - - LAUNCH OF ONE ROCKET PAYLOAD as additional work under NASS-20622. NASA/GSFC will issue RFP 5-90708-254 to the University of Michigan. See Note 46.   (P307)
NASA, Goddard Space Flight Center, Greenbelt, MD 20771.

★ A - - RESEARCH AND DEVELOPMENT ON TRI-AXIAL PIEZOELECTRIC ACCELEROMETER SYSTEMS and integrating into failing sphere pay loads to be negotiated with Accumetrics Corporation, Cambridge, MA, based on specifications reflected in their unsolicited proposal in support of the Air Force Cambridge Research Laboratories — PR FY71217603344, Sec Note 46.   (P308)
Procurement and Production, R&D Contracts Division, Laurence G. Hanscom Air Force Base, Bedford, MA 01731

A - - CANCELLATION - HMO MEDICAID ELIGIBILITY TURNOVER — RFP-SRS-75-17 previously issued in the Commerce Business Daily on 18 May 75 is cancelled.   (P307)
H.E.W., Social & Rehabilitation Service, Contract Branch, Room 4217, Switzer Bldg., (HEW South), Tel: 202/245-0271, 330 C Street, SW, Washington, DC 20201

★ A - - STUDY OF THE EFFECTS OF THE LEGAL ENVIRONMENT ON HOUSING MARKETS. Negotiations are being conducted with the University of California; 405 Hilgard Ave., Los Angeles, CA 90024 See Note 46.   (P308)
Department of Housing and Urban Development, Research and Demonstrations Div. (ACR-G), 451 Seventh Street, S.W. - Room B-133 (711 Building) Washington, DC

★ A - - XM 843 FLATBED, 4 Wheel, 5 Ton Trailers. Drawings—20 ea—Initial Spare & a Pocket Type Commercial Manual. Eidal International Corp., Albuquerque, NM. RFP DAAE07-76-R0026. See Note 46.   (P307)
Headquarters, U S Army Tank Automotive Command, Warren MI 48090

Content

Figure 49 • COMMERCE BUSINESS DAILY

The COMMERCE BUSINESS DAILY

ISSUE No. PSA-6443 DATE: Thursday, Nov. 6, 1975

SUBSCRIPTION INFORMATION

(Subscriptions accepted only for mailing to addresses in the United States, its territories and Possessions.)

Annual subscription $75.00, plus an additional $66.90 for airmail service. To order, send remittance with full mailing address to nearest Department of Commerce Field Office or to the Superintendent of Documents, Government Printing Office, Washington, D.C. 20402, Tel: 202/275-3050. Purchase order must be accompanied by payment. Make checks or money orders payable to Superintendent of Documents. Allow at least 30 days for delivery of first issue.

Expirations: Airmail subscriptions expire one year from date the mailing plate becomes active. **Regular mail** subscriptions expire last day of month of expiration. One expiration notice is mailed about 60 days before subscription expiration date.

Address changes: Send to Superintendent of Documents, GPO, Washington, D. C. 20402, with entire mailing label from last issue received.

Subscription sales, renewals and mailing are not handled by the Commerce Business Daily publishing office, Chicago, Illinois, but rather by the superintendent of Documents.

The mailing labels are produced and the mailing lists maintained by the Superintendent of Documents, Washington, D. C. This publication is printed and mailed by Government Printing Office, Chicago, Illinois.

The U. S. Dept., of Commerce (Commerce Business Daily) Room 1304, 433 West Van Buren Street, Chicago, Illinois 60607 is responsible for compilation and content only. (Telephone No. 312/353-2950).

GPO 810—882

Figure 49 • COMMERCE BUSINESS DAILY. Continued

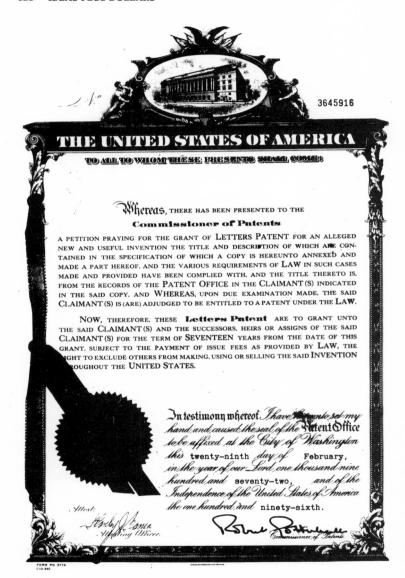

Figure 50 • SAMPLE PATENT

Certificate

Registration of a Claim to Copyright
in a published book manufactured in
the United States of America

FORM A

REGISTRATION NO.

DO NOT WRITE HERE

CLASS

A

This Is To Certify that the statements set forth on this certificate have been made a part of the records of the Copyright Office. In witness whereof the seal of the Copyright Office is hereto affixed.

Register of Copyrights
United States of America

1. Copyright Claimant(s) and Address(es):

Name ....

Address ....

Name ....

Address ....

2. Title: .... (Title of book) ....

3. Authors:

Name .... (Legal name followed by pseudonym if latter appears on copies) .... Citizenship .... (Name of country)

Domiciled in U.S.A.   Yes ......   No ......   Address ....

Name .... (Legal name followed by pseudonym if latter appears on copies) .... Citizenship .... (Name of country)

Domiciled in U.S.A.   Yes ......   No ......   Address ....

Name .... (Legal name followed by pseudonym if latter appears on copies) .... Citizenship .... (Name of country)

Domiciled in U.S.A.   Yes ......   No ......   Address ....

4. Date of Publication of This Edition:

.... (Month) .... (Day) .... (Year)

5. New Matter in This Version:

6. Book in English Previously Manufactured and Published Abroad: If all or a substantial part of the text of this edition was previously manufactured and published abroad in the English language, complete the following spaces:

Date of first publication of foreign edition .... (Year)

Was registration for the foreign edition made in the U.S. Copyright Office?   Yes ....   No ....

EXAMINER

If your answer is "Yes," give registration number ....

Complete all applicable spaces on next page

Figure 51   •   *COPYRIGHT APPLICATION*

NATIONAL SCIENCE FOUNDATION
Office of the Director
Washington, D.C. 20550

Notice No. 59   June 30, 1975

IMPORTANT NOTICE

TO

PRESIDENTS OF UNIVERSITIES AND COLLEGES
AND HEADS OF OTHER NSF GRANTEE ORGANIZATIONS

SUBJECT: **National Science Board Resolution on Peer Review Information**

The National Science Board has unanimously adopted a resolution that reemphasizes the need that proposals to NSF be evaluated as fairly as possible and that there be wide participation of qualified individuals in the review process. The Board reaffirms its belief that the review process should be conducted as openly as possible and with as much information to proposers as possible, consistent with the effective evaluation of proposals.

Following is the text of the resolution of the Board on peer review information:

1. The Foundation will publish annually a list of all reviewers used by each Division;

2. Program officers should seek broadly representative participation of qualified individuals as reviewers;

3. Verbatim copies of reviews requested by the Foundation after January 1, 1976, not including the identity of the reviewer, will be made available to the principal investigator project director upon request. The question of including the identity of the reviewer will be considered further by the National Science Board;

4. The Foundation, upon request, will inform the principal investigator/project director of the reasons for its decision on the proposal.

Items 2. and 4. of the resolution are procedures that have always been employed by the National Science Foundation; items 1. and 3. represent changes in prior practices. It is expected that these changes will lead to better communication between proposers and the National Science Foundation and, in general, help clarify the basis on which decisions are made. The peer review process has well served the scientific community and is the cornerstone for the management of much of the Federal support of science and technology in the United States; the Board's resolution strengthens the peer review process, thereby, insuring the continued vigor of research and development in the United States.

H. Guyford Stever
Director

Figure 52 • *IMPORTANT NOTICE NSF*

PROPOSAL COVER SHEET FORMAT

UNSOLICITED RESEARCH PROPOSAL SUBMITTED TO THE NATIONAL SCIENCE FOUNDATION

RESEARCH APPLIED TO NATIONAL NEEDS (RANN)

Name of Organization (including Branch title, if any)

Address of Organization

Title of Proposed Project

Amount Requested _____ Proposed Duration _____ Requested Starting Date _____

Name of Principal   Name of Project Manager if Other than
    Investigator _____   P.I. _____

    Social Security No. _____   _____

    Title _____   _____

    Telephone (w/area code) _____   _____

    Other No. _____   _____
        (where message can be left)

    Organizational Affiliation _____   _____

    _____   _____

    Address if Different from Above _____   _____

    _____   _____

For renewal requests, list previous Grant No. _____

                Endorsements   Other Endorsements   Approving Administrative Official
            Principal Investigator   (Formal Proposals Only)   (Formal Proposals Only)

Name _____   _____   _____

Signature _____   _____   _____

Title _____   _____   _____

Date _____   _____   _____

Figure 53 • PROPOSAL COVER SHEET NSF

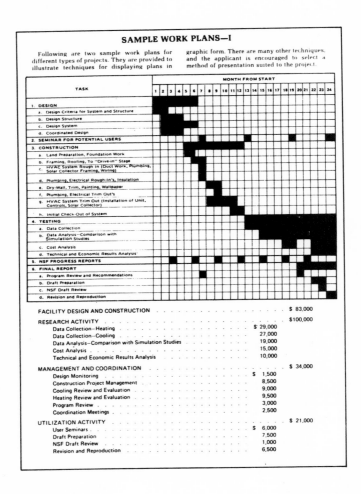

Figure 54 • SAMPLE WORK PLAN

References

CHAPTER ONE

1. Einstein, A. *"Report of the National Academy of Sciences,"* Washington, D.C. 1953.

2. Woolf, H.B., Editor-in-Chief, *"Webster's New Collegiate Dictionary."* G.C. Merriam Company, Springfield, Massachusetts, 1974.

3. Zallen, H. and Robl, R. *"Planning for Research and Sponsored Programs: A Guide and Resource Book."* Oklahoma State University, Stillwater, Oklahoma, 1973.

4. O'Hayre, J. *"Gobbledygook Has Gotta Go."* Superintendent of Documents, No. 0-206-141, U.S. Government Printing Office, Washington, D.C. 1966.

CHAPTER TWO

1. National Science Board, *"NSB Science Indicators, 1972,"* Report of the National Science Board, National Science Foundation, Superintendent of Documents, No. 3800-00146, U.S. Government Printing Office, Washington, D.C. 1973.

2. Sanders, R. and Brown, F.R., Editors, *"National Security Management: Science and Technology — Vital Assets."* Industrial College of the Armed Forces of the United States, Washington, D.C. 1966.

3. Beezer, R. *Personal Communication.* U.S. Office of Education, Washington, D.C. 1974.

4. Committee on Domestic Technology Transfer, *"Directory of Federal Technology Transfer."* Federal Council for Science and Technology, NSF No. 75-402, Superintendent of Documents, U.S. Government Printing Office, Washington, D.C. 1975.

5. Drucker, P.F. *"Management: Tasks, Responsibilities, Practices."* Harper & Row, Publishers, Incorporated, New York, New York. 1973.

CHAPTER THREE

1. National Science Foundation, *"Guidelines for Preparation of Unsolicited Proposals."* Research Applied to National Needs, NSF No. 75-21. National Science Foundation, Washington, D.C. 1975.

2. Zallen, H. *Personal Communication.* Academic World Incorporated, Norman, Oklahoma. No. 7-19. 1975

3. National Aeronautics And Space Administration. *"Basic Administrative Processes."* National Aeronautics and Space Administration, Washington, D.C. 1971.

CHAPTER FOUR

1. _____, *"Encyclopedia of Associations,"* Gale Research Company, Detroit, Michigan. 1971.

2. Gumm, R., Zallen, H. and Bahm, E. *"Computerized Retrieval System for Federal Domestic Assistance."* Computer Center, Oklahoma State University, Stillwater, Oklahoma. The computer program may be purchased from Oklahoma State University. Installation, training and implementation has been authorized to Academic World Incorporated.

CHAPTER FIVE

1. Lisk, D.J. *"Bioscience,"* *21,* 1025. 1971.

CHAPTER SEVEN

1. Boffey, P.M. "Scientists Fear 'Sacrosanct' System of Making Federal Grants May Be in Peril." *Chronicle of Higher Education, 10:* No. 14, 1. 1975.

2. Federal Register. "Freedom of Information Act." *United States Code, Title 5, Part 522.* 1971.

3. Eaves, G.N. *"Federation Proceedings,"* 31, 3. 1972.

CHAPTER EIGHT

1. National Science Foundation, *"NSF Grants Administration Manual,"* National Science Foundation, NSF No. 73-26, Washington, D.C. 1973.

2. Office of Management and Budget, *OMB Circular No. A-21 Revised.* OMB, Executive Office of the President, Washington, D.C. 1970. **(Authors' Note:** This document has been recently redesignated *Federal Management Circular (FMC) 73-8;* however, it is quite possible it will be redesignated an *OMB Circular* in the future.)

3. Office of Management and Budget, *OMB Circular No. A-87.* OMB, Executive Office of the President, Washington, D.C. 1968. **(Authors' Note:** This circular excludes institutions of higher education. It deals with Federal government awards to State and local governments.)

4. Office of Management and Budget, *OMB Circular No. A-88, and Attachment A.* OMB, Executive Office of the President, Washington, D.C. 1968. **(Authors' Note:** This document assigned to DHEW the authority for conducting *Indirect Cost Negotiations and Audits* at single educational institutions.)

5. National Institutes of Health, *"NIH Grants for Research Projects: Policy Statement."* U.S. Department of Health, Education and Welfare. Publication No. (NIH) 72-8. Washington, D.C. 1972.

6. Department of Defense. *"Armed Forces Procurement Regulations."* Superintendent of Documents, U.S. Government Printing Office, Washington, D.C. (Updated periodically — sold by subscription).

CHAPTER NINE

1. Guralnick, D.B., Editor-in-Chief, *"Webster's New World Dictionary, 2nd College Edition."* The World Publishing Company, New York, New York. 1970.

2. Zallen, H. *Personal Communication.* Academic World Incorporated, Norman, Oklahoma. No. 8-15. 1975.

3. *Megamini*®, Trademark, Interdata Corporation.

4. _____, *"Standards of Professional Conduct."* Association of Consultant Management Engineers, New York, New York. 1963.

5. Kindred, A.B. *"Data Systems and Management."* Prentice-Hall Company, Englewood Cliffs, New Jersey. 1973.

6. Zallen, H. *Personal Communication.* Academic World Incorporated, Norman, Oklahoma.

7. Baty, G.B. *"Entrepreneurship: Playing to Win."* Reston Publishing Company, a Prentice-Hall Company, Reston, Virginia. 1974.

CHAPTER TEN

1. Baty, G.B. *"Entrepreneurship: Playing to Win."* Reston Publishing Company, a Prentice-Hall Company, Reston, Virginia. 1974.

CHAPTER ELEVEN

1. Cutler, R.S. *"Summary of Awards, FY 1973-74-Research Management Improvement Program."* Presented at the 9th Annual Meeting, Society of Research Administrators, Las Vegas, Nevada. October 6, 1975.

2. Hovde, F.L. *"Executive Memorandum No. A-268."* Purdue University, Lafayette, Indiana. July, 1966.

3. Zallen, H. *Personal Communication.* Academic World Incorporated, Norman, Oklahoma. No. 10-6. 1975.

CHAPTER TWELVE

1. National Association of State Colleges and Land Grant Universities, *"Newsletter,"* NASULGC; pp. 30, No. 14, August, 1975.

2. General Services Administration, *"Federal Procurement Management Regulations 101-26.7."* GSA, Superintendent of Documents, U.S. Government Printing Office, Washington, D.C. 1971.

3. Zallen, H., Project Director. *U.S. Public Health Service Grant,* Division of Radiological Health, Auburn University, Auburn, Alabama. 1966.

4. Zallen, H. and Dixon, T.R. *"Isotopes and Radiation Technology."* 5, 207. 1968.

5. Zallen, H., Project Director. *U.S. Army Chemical School Grant.* Auburn University, Auburn, Alabama. 1966.

6. National Science Foundation. *Personal Communication.* Instructional Scientific Equipment Program, NSF, Washington, D.C. 1969.

7. National Science Foundation. *Personal Communication.* Instructional Scientific Equipment Program, NSF, Washington, D.C. 1970.

8. National Science Foundation. *"Important Notice No. 32."* NSF, Washington, D.C. 1970.

9. _____, *"Minuteman Computer Share Group."* Tulane University, New Orleans, Louisiana. 1970.

10. Greenberg, D., Hoffman, E., Zallen, H. et al. *"The Politics of Excess Property and Indirect Federal Dollar Support to Academic Science,"* Anton, I. Chairman. Presented at the 14th Annual Meeting, National Council of University Research Administrators, Statler Hilton Hotel, Washington, D.C. November 10, 1973.

11. Federal Register. *"Notice of Proposed Rule Making,"* General Services Administration. 37: 106, 10959. 1972.

12. United States Congress. *"Congressional Record, 92nd. Congress, 2nd Session."* 118: No. 124, S 12810. 1972.

13. Office of Management and Budget. *"Use of Federal Supply Sources by Federal Grantees."* OMB, Executive Office of the President, Washington, D.C. July 19, 1972.

CHAPTER THIRTEEN

1. Zallen, H., Editor. Transactions. National Council of University Research Administrators, Region V. Oklahoma State University, Stillwater, Oklahoma. April, 1973.

2. Archie, W.C. Annual Report, Mary Reynolds Babcock Foundation, New York, New York. 1971.

3. Cunninggim, M., *"Danforth Foundation Report."* St. Louis, Missouri. 1972.

4. _____, *"The Foundation Center Source Book, 1975-76.* Columbia University Press, Irvington, New York. 1975.

5. State of Oklahoma, Senate Bill 115. Oklahoma Legislature, State Capitol, Oklahoma City, Oklahoma. 1973.

6. Archie, W.C. Annual Report, Mary Reynolds Babcock Foundation, New York, New York. 1972.

7. Dermer, J., Editor. *"Where America's Large Foundations Make Their Grants."* Public Service Material Center, New York, New York. 1971.

CHAPTER FOURTEEN

1. U.S. Copyright Office. *"General Information on Copyright."* Library of Congress, Washington, D.C. 1974.

2. National Institutes of Health. *"NIH Grants for Research Projects: Policy Statement."* U.S. Department of Health, Education and Welfare. Publication No. (NIH) 72-8. Washington, D.C. 1972.

3. Nuclear Regulatory Commission. *"United States Code of Federal Regulations, Title 10, Atomic Energy,"* Superintendent of Documents, U.S. Government Printing Office, Washington, D.C. (Updated periodically — sold by subscription).

4. Occupational Safety and Health Administration. *"A Handy Reference Guide: The Williams-Steiger Occupational Safety and Health Act of 1970."* U.S. Department of Labor. Superintendent of Documents, No. 2915-0001, U.S. Government Printing Office, Washington, D.C. 1972.

Glossary

AUDIT — An audit is made to verify financial transactions and to determine whether grant funds were used in accordance with applicable laws, regulations, procedures and practices.

AUTHORIZED INSTITUTIONAL REPRESENTATIVE — The administrative official who is empowered to commit the proposing organization to the conduct of a project if a foundation, Federal, State or private agency agrees to support it and who, by his or her signature on the proposal, is responsible for the prudent administration of the grant, gift or contract by the recipient institution if that agency awards funds.

BUDGET — The plan for the expenditure of funds required for a research activity through support of designated services, materials and other allowable cost items.

BUDGET PERIOD — The interval of time (normally 12 months) into which the project period is divided for budgetary and reporting purposes.

BUSINESS OFFICER, VICE PRESIDENT FOR FINANCE — The financial official of the contract or grantee who has primary responsibility for the accountability for and reporting on the funds awarded.

EFFECTIVE DATE — The date the grant letter is signed by the agency unless some other effective date is specified therein. This date remains constant except under exceptional circumstances justifying a formal amendment to the grant letter. Allowable project costs normally may be charged against the grant on and after such a date.

EXPIRATION DATE — The date specified in the grant letter after which expenditures may not be charged against the grant except to satisfy obligations of funds to pay allowable project costs committed on or before that date. Granting agencies do not as a rule give "automatic grace periods" following the expiration of the grant period. The expiration date is normally the last day of the month.

GRANT — The mechanism by which an agency provides support for an approved research, development or demonstration project.

GRANTEE — The educational institution (university, college), hospital, public agency, or other organization (profit or non-profit) which submits an application in the form of a proposal and receives a grant for support of a project under the direction of a named Principal Investigator or Project Director. Some agencies restrict grants to the United States of America — others do not.

GRANT PERIOD — The grant period extends from the effective date through the expiration date. In some cases the grant period may be up to six months longer than the support period.

PRINCIPAL INVESTIGATOR (PI)/PROJECT DIRECTOR(PD) — The individual assigned by the grantee and approved by the agency awarding the funds who will be responsible for the scientific or technical direction of the project. The term *Principal Investigator* generally is used in basic research projects, while the term *Project Director* is used in development, demonstration and educational types of projects.

PROJECT — The activity outlined in the proposal and approved by the agency awarding the funds.

PROPOSAL — The application for support of a specific activity as outlined in the applicable brochure or program announcements by a funding agency, private foundation or industrial organization wishing to award funds.

RESEARCH — The systematic, intensive study directed toward a fuller scientific knowledge or understanding of the subject studied. Research may be classified as either basic or applied. In *basic* research the investigator is concerned primarily with gaining a fuller knowledge or understanding of the subject under study. In *applied* research, the investigator is primarily interested in the practical use for the purpose of meeting a required need.

SUPPORT PERIOD — The number of months (often called "duration") shown in a grant budget, during which the award amount is intended to support the project. In private and Federal government agencies, as a rule, the grant period and the support period are the same. There are exceptions.

Appendix

SIGNS USED IN CORRECTING PROOFS

Insert marginal correction at this point in line

tr Transpose; indicate by   in text

cap Capital; put 3 lines under letter or word

sc Small capital; put 2 lines under letter or word

lc Lower-case letter; put oblique line through letter

ital Italic; underline letter or word

rom Roman letter; circle letter or word

sp out Spell out; circle abbreviation

bf Boldface; underline letter or word with wavy line

wf Wrong font; circle letter or word

X	Defective letter	;/	Semicolon
⤒	Push down space	Ꮩ	Apostrophe
☉	Turn over	ꚛ or ꚛ	Quotation
ℓ	Take out	⧿	Hyphen
V	Space evenly	‖	Straighten lines
#	Insert space	⌊	Move left
⌣	Less space	⌋	Move right
⌢	Close up entirely	⬚	Em-quad space
⊙	Period	–⧸ₘ–	One-em dash
⋀	Comma	¶	Make paragraph
⊙	Colon	no ¶	No paragraph

**EXECUTIVE OFFICE OF THE PRESIDENT
OFFICE OF MANAGEMENT AND BUDGET
WASHINGTON, D.C. 20503**

September 2, 1970   **CIRCULAR NO. A-21**
                                          Revised

TO THE HEADS OF EXECUTIVE DEPARTMENTS AND ESTABLISHMENTS

SUBJECT: Principles for determining costs applicable to research and development and educational services under grants and contracts with educational institutions

1. **Purpose.** This Circular promulgates the two revised attachments containing principles for determining costs applicable to grants and contracts with educational institutions. The attachments are:

Attachment A — Principles for Determining Costs Applicable to Research and Development under Grants and Contracts with Educational Institutions

Attachment B — Principles for Determining Costs Applicable to Training and Other Educational Services under Grants and Contracts with Educational Institutions

Prior issuances of Circular No. A-21 are rescinded and superseded in their entirety by this revision.

2. **Changes.** In general, the changes are intended to clarify and refine the methods used in identifying, classifying, and distributing indirect costs, and to provide more definitive standards concerning the allowability of costs, both direct and indirect, applicable to Government grants and contracts with educational institutions.

3. **Additional copies.** Additional copies of this Circular may be obtained by sending requisitions directly to the Government Printing Office. These requisitions should be placed not later than October 1, 1970, in order that the total requirements of all agencies may be printed at the same time.

4. **Effective date.** The revised principles will be applied at the earliest practicable date.

GEORGE P. SHULTZ
Director

Attachments — 2

(No. A-21)

ATTACHMENT A
Circular No. A-21
Revised

**PRINCIPLES FOR DETERMINING COSTS APPLICABLE TO RESEARCH
AND DEVELOPMENT UNDER GRANTS AND CONTRACTS WITH
EDUCATIONAL INSTITUTIONS**

Executive Office of the President
Office of Management and Budget
September 2, 1970

ATTACHMENT A
Circular No. A-21
Revised

PRINCIPLES FOR DETERMINING COSTS APPLICABLE TO RESEARCH AND DEVELOPMENT UNDER GRANTS AND CONTRACTS WITH EDUCATIONAL INSTITUTIONS

TABLE OF CONTENTS

TABLE OF CONTENTS (Continued)

TABLE OF CONTENTS (Continued)

ATTACHMENT A
Circular No. A-21
Revised

PRINCIPLES FOR DETERMINING COSTS APPLICABLE TO RESEARCH AND DEVELOPMENT UNDER GRANTS AND CONTRACTS WITH EDUCATIONAL INSTITUTIONS

A.   **Purpose and scope.**

1. **Objectives.** This Circular provides principles for determining the costs applicable to research and development work performed by educational institutions under grants from and contracts with the Federal Government. These principles are confined to the subject of cost determination and make no attempt to identify the circumstances or dictate the extent of agency and institutional participation in the financing of a particular research or development project. The principles are designed to provide recognition of the full allocated costs of such research work under generally accepted accounting principles. No provision for profit or other increment above cost is intended.

2. **Policy guides.** The successful application of these principles requires development of mutual understanding between representatives of universities and of the Federal Government as to their scope, implementation, and interpretation. It is recognized that —

a. The arrangements for agency and institutional participation in the financing of a research and development project are properly subject to negotiation between the agency and the institution concerned in accordance with such Government-wide criteria as may be applicable.

b. Each college and university, possessing its own unique combination of staff, facilities and experience, should be encouraged to conduct research in a manner consonant with its own academic philosophies and institutional objectives.

c. Each institution, in the fulfillment of its obligations, should employ sound management practices.

d. The application of the principles established herein should require no significant changes in the generally accepted accounting practices of colleges and universities.

(No. A-21)

2

e. Cognizant Federal agencies involved in negotiating indirect cost rates and auditing should assure that institutions are generally applying the cost principles and standards herein provided on a consistent basis. Where wide variations exist in the treatment of a given cost item among institutions, the reasonableness and equitableness of such treatments should be fully considered during the rate negotiations and audit.

3. **Application.** All Federal agencies that sponsor research and development work at educational institutions should apply these principles and related policy guides in determining the costs incurred for such work under any type of research and development agreement. These principles should also be used as a guide in the pricing of fixed price contracts or lump sum agreements.

B.   **Definition of terms.**

1. **Organized research** means all research activities of an institution that are separately budgeted and accounted for.

2. **Departmental research** means research activities that are not separately budgeted and accounted for. Such research work, which includes all research activities not encompassed under the term *organized research,* is regarded for purposes of this document as a part of the instructional activities of the institution.

3. **Research agreement** means any valid arrangement to perform federally sponsored research, including grants, cost-reimbursement type contracts, cost-reimbursement type subcontracts, and fixed-price contracts and subcontracts for research.

4. **Other institutional activities** means all organized activities of an institution not directly related to the instruction and research functions, such as residence halls, dining halls, student hospitals, student unions, intercollegiate athletics, bookstores, faculty housing, student apartments, guest houses, chapels, theaters, public museums, and other similar activities or auxiliary enterprises. Also included under this definition is any other category of cost treated as "unallowable," provided such category of cost identifies a

3

function or activity to which a portion of the institution's indirect costs (as defined in section E.1.) are properly allocable.

5. **Apportionment** means the process by which the indirect costs of the institution are assigned as between (a) instruction and research, and (b) other institutional activities.

6. **Allocation** means the process by which the indirect costs apportioned to instruction and research are assigned as between (a) organized research, and (b) instruction, including departmental research.

7. **Stipulated salary support** is a fixed or a stated dollar amount of the salary of professorial or other professional staff involved in the conduct of research which a Government agency agrees in advance to reimburse an educational institution as a part of sponsored research costs.

C.   **Basic considerations.**

1. **Composition of total costs.** The cost of a research agreement is comprised of the allowable direct costs incident to its performance, plus the

allocable portion of the allowable indirect costs of the institution, less applicable credits as described in section C.5.

2. **Factors affecting allowability of costs.** The tests of allowability of costs under these principles are: (a) they must be reasonable; (b) they must be allocable to research agreements under the standards and methods provided herein; (c) they must be accorded consistent treatment through application of those generally accepted accounting principles appropriate to the circumstances; and (d) they must conform to any limitations or exclusions set forth in these principles or in the research agreement as to types or amounts of cost items.

3. **Reasonable costs.** A cost may be considered reasonable if the nature of the goods or services acquired or applied, and the amount involved therefor, reflect the action that a prudent person would have taken under the circumstances prevailing at the time the decision to incur the cost was made. Major considerations involved in the determination of the reasonableness of a cost are: (a) whether or not the cost is of a type generally recognized as necessary for the operation of the institution or the performance of the

4

research agreement; (b) the restraints or requirements imposed by such factors as arm's-length bargaining, Federal and State laws and regulations, and research agreement terms and conditions; (c) whether or not the individuals concerned acted with due prudence in the circumstances, considering their responsibilities to the institution, its employees, its students, the Government, and the public at large; and (d) the extent to which the actions taken with respect to the incurrence of the cost are consistent with established institutional policies and practices applicable to the work of the institution generally, including Government research.

4. **Allocable costs.**

a. A cost is allocable to a particular cost objective (i.e., a specific function, project, research agreement, department, or the like) if the goods or services involved are chargeable or assignable to such cost objective in accordance with relative benefits received or other equitable relationship. Subject to the foregoing, a cost is allocable to a research agreement if it is incurred solely to advance the work under the research agreement; or it benefits both the research agreement and other work of the institution in proportions that can be approximated through use of reasonable methods; or it is necessary to the overall operation of the institution and, in the light of the standards provided in this Circular, is deemed to be assignable in part to organized research. Where the purchase of equipment or other capital items is specifically authorized under a research agreement, the amounts thus authorized for such purchases are allocable to the research agreement regardless of the use that may subsequently be made of the equipment or other capital items involved.

b. Any costs allocable to a particular research agreement under the standards provided in this Circular may not be shifted to other research agreements in order to meet deficiencies caused by overruns or other fund considerations, to avoid restrictions imposed by law or by terms of the research agreement, or for other reasons of convenience.

5

5. Applicable credits.

a. The term applicable credits refers to those receipt or negative expenditure types of transactions which operate to offset or reduce expense items that are allocable to research agreements as direct or indirect costs. Typical examples of such transactions are: purchase discounts, rebates, or allowances; recoveries or indemnities on losses; sales of scrap or incidental services; and adjustments of overpayments or erroneous charges.

b. In some instances, the amounts received from the Federal Government to finance institutional activities or service operations should be treated as applicable credits. Specifically, the concept of netting such credit items against related expenditures should be applied by the institution in determining the rates or amounts to be charged to Government research for services rendered whenever the facilities or other resources used in providing such services have been financed directly, in whole or in part, by Federal funds. (See sections F.6., J.10.b., and J.37. for areas of potential application in the matter of direct Federal financing.)

6. Costs incurred by State and local governments.

Costs incurred or paid by State or local governments in behalf of educational institutions for certain personnel benefit programs such as pension plans, FICA and any other costs specifically disbursed in behalf of and in direct benefit to the institutions, are allowable costs of such institutions whether or not these costs are recorded in the accounting records of such institutions, subject to the following:

a. Such costs meet the requirements of sections C.1. through C.5.

b. Such costs are properly supported by cost allocation plans in accordance with Office of Management and Budget Circular No. A-87.

c. Such costs are not otherwise borne directly or indirectly by the Federal Government.

6

D. Direct costs.

1. **General.** Direct costs are those costs which can be identified specifically with a particular research project, an instructional activity or any other institutional activity or which can be directly assigned to such activities relatively easily with a high degree of accuracy.

2. **Application to research agreements.** Identifiable benefit to the research work rather than the nature of the goods and services involved is the determining factor in distinguishing direct from indirect costs of research agreements. Typical transactions chargeable to a research agreement as direct costs are the compensation of employees for performance of work under the research agreement, including related staff benefit and pension plan costs to the extent that such items are consistently treated by the educational institution as direct rather than indirect costs; the costs of materials consumed or expended in the performance of such work; and other items of expense incurred for the research agreement, including extraordinary utility consumption. The cost of materials supplied from stock or services rendered by specialized facilities or other institutional service operations may be included as direct costs of research agreements provided such items are

consistently treated by the institution as direct rather than indirect costs and are charged under a recognized method of costing or pricing designed to recover only actual costs and conforming to generally accepted cost accounting practices consistently followed by the institution.

E.   **Indirect costs.**

1. **General.** Indirect costs are those that have been incurred for common or joint objectives and therefore cannot be identified specifically with a particular research project, an instructional activity or any other institutional activity. At educational institutions such costs normally are classified under the following functional categories: general administration and general expenses; research administration expenses; operation and maintenance expenses; library expenses; and departmental administration expenses.

7

2. **Criteria for distribution.**

a. **Base period.** A base period for distribution of indirect costs is the period during which such costs are incurred and accumulated for distribution to work performed within that period. The base period normally should coincide with the fiscal year established by the institution, but in any event the base period should be so selected as to avoid inequities in the distribution of costs.

b. **Need for cost groupings.** The overall objective of the allocation and apportionment process is to distribute the indirect costs described in section F to organized research, instruction, and other activities in reasonable proportions consistent with the nature and extent of the use of the institution's resources by research personnel, academic staff, students, and other personnel or organizations. In order to achieve this objective, it may be necessary to provide for selective distribution by establishing separate groupings of cost within one or more of the functional categories of indirect costs referred to in section E.1. In general, the cost groupings established within a functional category should constitute, in each case, a pool of those items of expense that are considered to be of like character in terms of their relative contribution to (or degree of remoteness from) the particular cost objectives to which distribution is appropriate. Cost groupings should be established considering the general guides provided in c. below. Each such pool or cost grouping should then be distributed individually to the appertaining cost objectives, using the distribution base or method most appropriate in the light of the guides set out in d. below.

c. **General considerations on cost groupings.** The extent to which separate cost groupings and selective distribution would be appropriate at an institution is a matter of judgment to be determined on a case-by-case basis. Typical situations which may warrant the establishment of two or more separate cost groups (based on account classification or analysis) within a functional category include but are not limited to the following:

8

(1) Where certain items or categories of expense relate solely to one of the three major divisions of the institution (instruction, organized research or other institutional activities) or to any two but not the third, such

expenses should be set aside as a separate cost grouping for direct assignment or selective distribution in accordance with the guides provided in b. above and d. below.

(2) Where any types of expense ordinarily treated as general administration and general expenses or departmental administration expenses are charged to research agreements as direct costs, the similar type expenses applicable to other activities of the institution, must, through separate cost groupings, be excluded from the indirect costs allocable to those research agreements and included in the direct cost of other activities for cost allocation purposes.

(3) Where it is determined that certain expenses are for the support of a service unit or facility whose output is susceptible of measurement on a workload or other quantitative basis, such expenses should be set aside as a separate cost grouping for distribution on such basis to organized research and other activities at the institution or within the department.

(4) Where organized activities (including identifiable segments of organized research as well as the activities cited in section B.4.) provide their own purchasing, personnel administration, building maintenance or similar service, the distribution of general administration and general expenses or operation and maintenance expenses to such activities should be accomplished through cost groupings which include only that portion of central indirect costs (such as for overall management) which are properly allocable to such activities.

(5) Where the institution elects to treat as indirect charges the cost of the pension plan and other staff benefits, such costs should be set aside as a separate cost grouping for selective distribution to appertaining cost objectives, including organized research.

(6) The number of separate cost groupings within a functional category should be held within practical limits, after taking into consideration

9

the materiality of the amounts involved and the degree of precision attainable through less selective methods of distribution.

d. Selection of distribution method.

(1) Actual conditions must be taken into account in selecting the method or base to be used in distributing to applicable cost objectives the expenses assembled under each of the individual cost groupings established as indicated under b. above. Where a distribution can be made by assignment of a cost grouping directly to the area benefited, the distribution should be made in that manner. Where the expenses under a cost grouping are more general in nature, the distribution to appertaining cost objectives should be made through use of a selected base which will produce results that are equitable to both the Government and the institution. In general, any cost element or cost-related factor associated with the institution's work is potentially adaptable for use as a distribution base provided (a) it can readily be expressed in terms of dollars or other quantitative measure (total direct expenditures, direct salaries, man-hours applied, square feet utilized, hours of usage, number of documents processed, population served, and the like); and (b) it is common to the appertaining cost objectives during the base period.

(2) Results of cost analysis studies may be used when they result in more accurate and equitable distribution of costs. Such cost analysis studies may take into consideration weighting factors, population, or space occupied if they produce equitable results. Cost analysis studies, however, should (a) be appropriately documented in sufficient detail for subsequent review by the cognizant Federal agency, (b) distribute the indirect costs to the appertaining cost objectives in accord with the relative benefits derived, (c) be conducted to fairly reflect the true conditions of the activity and to cover representative transactions for a reasonable period of time, (d) be performed specifically at the institution at which the results are to be used, and (e) be updated periodically and used consistently. Any assumptions made in the study will be sufficiently supported. The use of cost analysis studies and periodic changes in the method of cost distribution must be fully justified.

10

(3) The essential consideration in selection of the distribution base in each instance is that it be the one best suited for assigning the pool of costs to appertaining cost objectives in accord with the relative benefits derived; the traceable cause and effect relationship; or logic and reason, where neither benefit nor cause and effect relationship is determinable.

3. **Administration of limitations on allowances for research costs.** Research agreements may be subject to statutory or administrative policies that limit the allowance of research costs. When the maximum amount allowable under a statutory limitation or the terms of a research agreement is less than the amount otherwise reimbursable under this Circular, the amount not recoverable under that research agreement may not be charged to other research agreements.

F.   **Identification and assignment of indirect costs.**

1. **General administration and general expenses.**

a. The expenses under this heading are those that have been incurred for the general executive and administrative offices of educational institutions and other expenses of a general character which do not relate solely to any major division of the institution; i.e., solely to (1) instruction, (2) organized research, or (3) other institutional activities. The general administration and general expense category should also include the staff benefit and pension plan costs applicable to the salaries and wages included therein, an appropriate share of the costs of the operation and maintenance of the physical plant, and charges representing use allowances and/or depreciation applicable to the buildings and equipment utilized in performing the functions represented thereunder.

b. The expenses included in this category may be apportioned and allocated on the basis of total expenditures exclusive of capital expenditures in situations where the results of the distribution made on this basis are deemed to be equitable both to the Government and the institution; otherwise the distribution of general administration and general expenses should be made through use of selected bases applied to separate cost groupings established within this category of expenses in accordance with the guides set out in Section E.2.d.

2. Research administration expenses.

a. The expenses under this heading are those that have been incurred by a separate organization or identifiable administrative unit established solely to administer the research activity, including such functions as contract administration, security, purchasing, personnel administration, and editing and publishing of research reports. They include the salaries and expenses of the head of such research organization, his assistants, and their immediate secretarial staff together with the salaries and expenses of personnel engaged in supporting activities maintained by the research organization, such as stock rooms, stenographic pools, and the like. The salaries of members of the professional staff whose appointments or assignments involve the performance of such administrative work may also be included to the extent that the portion so charged to research administration is supported as required by section J.7. The research administration expense category should also include the staff benefit and pension plan costs applicable to the salaries and wages included therein, an appropriate share of the costs of the operation and maintenance of the physical plant, and charges representing use allowance and/or depreciation applicable to the buildings and equipment utilized in performing the functions represented thereunder.

b. The expenses included in this category should be allocated to organized research and, where necessary, to departmental research or to any other benefiting activities on any basis reflecting the proportion fairly applicable to each. (See section E.2.d.)

3. Operation and maintenance expenses.

a. The expenses under this heading are those that have been incurred by a central service organization or at the departmental level for the administration, supervision, operation, maintenance, preservation, and protection of the institution's physical plant. They include expenses normally

incurred for such items as janitorial and utility services; repairs and ordinary or normal alterations of buildings, furniture and equipment; and care of grounds and maintenance and operation of buildings and other plant facilities. The operation and maintenance expense category should also include the staff benefit and pension plan costs applicable to the salaries and wages included therein, and charges representing use allowance and/or depreciation applicable to the buildings and equipment utilized in performing the functions represented thereunder.

b. The expenses included in this category should be apportioned and allocated to applicable cost objectives in a manner consistent with the guides provided in section E.2. on a basis that gives primary emphasis to space utilization. The allocations and apportionments should be developed as follows: (1) where actual space and related cost records are available or can readily be developed and maintained without significant change in the accounting practices, the amount distributed should be based on such records; (2) where the space and related cost records maintained are not sufficient for purposes of the foregoing, a reasonable estimate of the proportion of total space assigned to the various cost objectives normally will suffice as a means for effecting distribution of the amounts of operation and maintenance expenses involved; or (3) where it can be demonstrated that an area or volume of space basis of allocation is impractical or inequitable, other bases may be used provided consideration is given to the use of facilities by research personnel and others, including students.

4. **Library expenses.**

a. The expenses under this heading are those that have been incurred for the operation of the library, including the costs of books and library materials purchased for the library, less any items of library income that qualify as applicable credits under section C.5. The library expense category should also include the staff benefit and pension plan costs applicable to the salaries and wages included therein, an appropriate share of the costs of the operation and maintenance of the physical plant, and charges representing use allowances and/or depreciation applicable to the buildings and equipment utilized in the performance of the functions represented

13

thereunder. Costs incurred in the purchase of rare books (museum-type books) with no research value should not be allocated to Government-sponsored research.

b. The expenses included in this category should be allocated on the basis of population including students and other users. Where the results of the distribution made on this basis are deemed to be inequitable to the Government or the institution, the distribution should then be made on a selective basis in accordance with the guides set out in section E.2. Such selective distribution should be made through use of reasonable methods which give adequate recognition to the utilization of the library attributable to faculty, research personnel, students and others. The method used will be based on data developed periodically on the respective institution's experience for representative periods.

5. **Departmental administration expenses.**

a. The expenses under this heading are those that have been incurred in academic deans' offices, academic departments and organized research units such as institutes, study centers and research centers for administrative and supporting services which benefit common or joint departmental activities or objectives. They include the salaries and expenses of deans or heads, or associate deans or heads, of colleges, schools, departments, divisions, or organized research units, and their administrative staffs together with the salaries and expenses of personnel engaged in supporting activities maintained by the department, such as stockrooms, stenographic pools, and the like provided such supporting services cannot be directly identified with a specific research project, with an instructional activity or with any other institutional activity. The salaries of other members of the professional staff whose appointments or assignments involve the performance of such administrative work may also be included to the extent that the portion so charged to departmental administration expenses is supported as required by section J.7. The departmental administration expense category should also include the staff benefit and pension plan costs applicable to the salaries and wages included therein, an appropriate share of the costs of the

14

operation and maintenance of the physical plant, and charges representing use allowances and/or depreciation applicable to the buildings and equipment utilized in performing the functions represented thereunder.

b. The distribution of departmental administration expenses should be made through use of selected bases applied to cost groupings established within this category of expenses in accordance with the guides set out in section E.2.d.

6. **Setoff for indirect expenses otherwise provided for by the Government.**

a. The items to be accumulated under this heading are the reimbursements and other receipts from the Federal Government which are used by the institution to support directly, in whole or in part, any of the administrative or service (indirect) activities described in the foregoing (sections F.1. through F.5.). They include any amounts thus applied to such activities which may have been received pursuant to an institutional base grant or any similar contractual arrangement with the Federal Government other than a research agreement as herein defined (section B.3.).

b. The sum of the items in this group shall be treated as a credit to the total indirect cost pool before it is apportioned to organized research and to other activities. Such setoff shall be made prior to the determination of the indirect cost rate or rates as provided in section G.

G. **Determination and application of indirect cost rate or rates.**

1. **Indirect cost pools.**

a. Subject to b. below, indirect costs allocated to organized research should be treated as a common pool, and the costs in such common pool should then be distributed to individual research agreements benefiting therefrom on a single rate basis.

b. In some instances a single rate basis for use across the board on all Government research at an institution may not be appropriate, since it would not take into account those different environmental factors which

15

may affect substantially the indirect costs applicable to a particular segment of Government research at the institution. For this purpose, a particular segment of Government research may be that performed under a single research agreement or it may consist of research under a group of research agreements performed in a common environment. The environmental factors are not limited to the physical location of the work. Other important factors are the level of the administrative support required, the nature of the facilities or other resources employed, the scientific disciplines or technical skills involved, the organizational arrangements used, or any combination thereof. Where a particular segment of Government research is performed within an environment which appears to generate a significantly different level of indirect costs, provision should be made for a separate indirect cost pool applicable to such work. The separate indirect cost pool should be developed during the course of the regular distribution process, and the separate indirect cost rate resulting therefrom should be utilized provided it is determined that (1) such indirect cost rate differs significantly from that which would have obtained under a. above, and (2) the volume of research work to which such rate would apply is material in relation to other Government research at the institution.

2. **The distribution base.** Indirect costs allocated to organized research should be distributed to applicable research agreements on the basis of direct salaries and wages. For this purpose, an indirect cost rate should be determined for each of the separate indirect cost pools developed pursuant to section G.1. The rate in each case should be stated as the percentage which the amount of the particular indirect cost pool is of the total direct salaries and wages of all research agreements identified with such pool. For the purpose of establishing an indirect cost rate, direct salaries and wages may include that portion contributed to the research by the institution for cost sharing or other purposes. Bases other than salaries and wages may be used provided it can be demonstrated that they produce more equitable results.

3. **Negotiated lump sum for indirect costs.** A negotiated fixed amount in lieu of indirect costs may be appropriate for self-contained, off-campus, or primarily subcontracted research activities where the benefits derived

16

from an institution's indirect services cannot be readily determined. Such amount negotiated in lieu of indirect costs will be treated as an offset to total indirect expenses before apportionment to instruction, organized research, and other institutional activities. The base on which such remaining expenses are allocated should be appropriately adjusted.

4. **Predetermined fixed rates for indirect costs.** Public Law 87-638 (76 Stat. 437) authorizes the use of predetermined fixed rates in determining the indirect costs applicable under research agreements with educational institutions. The stated objectives of the law are to simplify the administration of cost-type research and development contracts (including grants) with educational institutions, to facilitate the preparation of their budgets, and to permit more expeditious closeout of such contracts when the work is completed. In view of the potential advantages offered by this procedure, consideration should be given to the negotiation of predetermined fixed rates for indirect costs in those situations where the cost experience and other pertinent facts available are deemed sufficient to enable the parties involved to reach an informed judgment as to the probable level of indirect costs during the ensuing accounting period.

5. **Negotiated fixed rates and carryforward provisions.** When a fixed rate is negotiated in advance for a fiscal year (or other time period), the over- or under-recovery for that year may be included as an adjustment to the indirect cost for the next rate negotiation. When the rate is negotiated before the carryforward adjustment is determined due to the delay in audit, the carryforward may be applied to the next subsequent rate negotiation. When such adjustments are to be made, each fixed rate negotiated in advance for a given period will be computed by applying the expected indirect costs allocable to Government research for the forecast period plus or minus the carryforward adjustment (over- or under-recovery) from the prior period, to the forecast distribution base. Unrecovered amounts under lump-sum agreements or cost-sharing provisions of prior years shall not be carried forward for consideration in the new rate negotiation. There must, however, be an advance understanding in each case between the institution and the congnizant Federal agency as to whether these differences will be considered in the rate negotiation rather than making the determination after the differences are known. Further, institutions electing to use this carryforward

17

provision may not subsequently change without prior approval of the cognizant Federal agency. In the event that an institution returns to a postdetermined rate, any over- or under-recovery during the period in which negotiated fixed rates and carryforward provisions were followed will be included in the subsequent postdetermined rates. Where multiple rates are used, the same procedure will be applicable for determining each rate. This procedure also applies to rates established for grants and contracts for training and other educational services, but does not apply to cost-type research agreements covering work performed in wholly or partially Government-owned facilities.

H.   **Simplified method for small institutions.**

1. **General.**

a. Where the total direct cost of all federally supported work under research and educational service agreements at an institution does not exceed $1,000,000 in a fiscal year (excluding direct payments by the institution to participants under educational service agreements for stipends, support, and similar costs requiring little, if any, indirect cost support), the use of the abbreviated procedure described in 2., below, may be used in determining allowable indirect costs. Under this abbreviated procedure, the institution's most recent annual financial report and immediately available supporting information, with salaries and wages segregated from other costs, will be utilized as a basis for determining the indirect cost rate applicable both to federally supported research and educational service agreements.

b. The rigid formula approach provided under this abbreviated procedure should not be used where it produces results which appear inequitable to the Government or the institution. In any such case, indirect costs should be determined through use of the regular procedure.

2. **Abbreviated procedure.**

a. Establish the total amount of salaries and wages paid to all employees of the institution.

18

b. Establish an indirect cost pool consisting of the expenditures (exclusive of capital items and other costs specifically identified as unallowable) which customarily are classified under the following titles or their equivalents:

(1) General administration and general expenses (exclusive of costs of student administration and services, student aid, student activities, and scholarships).

(2) Operation and maintenance of physical plant.

(3) Library.

(4) Department administration expenses, which will be computed as 20% of the salaries and expenses of deans and heads of departments.

In those cases where expenditures classified under 2.b.(1) and 2.b.(2) have previously been allocated to other institutional activities, they may be included in the indirect cost pool. The total amount of salaries and wages included in the indirect cost pool must be separately identified.

c. Establish a salary and wage distribution base, determined by deducting from the total of salaries and wages as established under 2.a. the amount of salaries and wages included under 2.b.

d. Establish the indirect cost rate, determined by dividing the amount in the indirect cost pool 2.b. by the amount of the distribution base 2.c.

e. Apply the indirect cost rate established to direct salaries and wages for individual agreements to determine the amount of indirect costs allocable to such agreements.

J.   **General standards for selected items of cost.**

Sections J.1. through J.46. provide standards to be applied in establishing the allowability of certain items involved in determining cost. These standards should apply irrespective of whether a particular item of cost is properly treated as direct cost or indirect cost. Failure to mention a particular item of cost in the standards is not intended to imply that it is either allowable or unallowable; rather determination as to allowability in

19

each case should be based on the treatment or standards provided for similar or related items of cost. In case of discrepancy between the provisions of a specific research agreement and the applicable standards provided, the provisions of the research agreement should govern.

1. **Advertising costs.** The term advertising costs means the costs of advertising media and corollary administrative costs. Advertising media include magazines, newspapers, radio and television programs, direct mail, exhibits, and the like. The only advertising costs allowable are those which

are solely for (a) the recruitment of personnel required for the performance by the institution of obligations arising under the research agreement, when considered in conjunction with all other recruitment costs, as set forth in J.32.; (b) the procurement of scarce items for the performance of the research agreement; or (c) the disposal of scrap or surplus materials acquired in the performance of the research agreement. Costs of this nature, if incurred for more than one research agreement or for both research agreement work and other work of the institution, are allowable to the extent that the principles in sections D and E are observed.

2. **Bad debts.** Any losses, whether actual or estimated, arising from uncollectible accounts and other claims, related collection costs, and related legal costs, are unallowable.

3. **Capital expenditures.** The costs of equipment, buildings, and repairs which materially increase the value or useful life of buildings or equipment, are unallowable except as provided for in the research agreement.

4. **Civil defense costs.** Civil defense costs are those incurred in planning for, and the protection of life and property against, the possible effects of enemy attack. Reasonable costs of civil defense measures (including costs in excess of normal plant protection costs, first-aid training and supplies, fire-fighting training, posting of additional exit notices and directions, and other approved civil defense measures) undertaken on the institution's premises pursuant to suggestions or requirements of civil defense authorities are allowable when distributed to all activities of the institution. Capital expenditures for civil defense purposes will not be allowed, but a use allowance or depreciation may be permitted in accordance with provisions set

20

forth in section J.10. Costs of local civil defense projects not on the institution's premises are unallowable.

5. **Commencement and convocation costs.** Costs incurred for commencements and convocations apply only to instruction and therefore are not allocable to research agreements, either as direct costs or indirect costs.

6. **Communication costs.** Costs incurred for telephone services, local and long distance telephone calls, telegrams, radiograms, postage and the like, are allowable.

7. **Compensation for personal services.**

a. **General.** Compensation for personal services covers all remuneration paid currently or accrued to the institution for services of employees rendered during the period of performance under Government research agreements. Such remuneration includes salaries, wages, staff benefits (see section J.39.), and pension plan costs (see section J.23.). The costs of such remuneration are allowable to the extent that the total compensation to individual employees is reasonable for the services rendered and conforms to the established policy of the institution consistently applied, and provided that the charges for work performed directly on Government research agreements and for other work allocable as indirect costs to organized research are determined and supported as hereinafter provided.

b. **Payroll distribution.** Amounts charged to organized research for personal services, except stipulated salary support, regardless of whether treated as direct costs or allocated as indirect costs, will be based on institutional payrolls which have been approved and documented in accordance with generally accepted institutional practices. Support for direct and indirect allocations of personal service costs to (1) instruction, (2) organized research, and (3) indirect activities as defined in section E.1., or (4) other institutional activities as defined in section B.4., will be provided as described in c., d., e., and f., below.

c. **Stipulated salary support.** As an alternative to payroll distribution, stipulated salary support amounts may be provided in the research agreement

21

for professorial staff, any part of whose compensation is chargeable to Government-sponsored research. Stipulated salary support may also be provided for any other professionals who are engaged part time in sponsored research and part time in other work. The stipulated salary support for an individual will be determined by the Government and the educational institution during the proposal and award process on the basis of considered judgment as to the monetary value of the contribution which the individual is expected to make to the research project. This judgment will take into account any cost sharing by the institution and such other factors as the extent of the investigator's planned participation in the project and his ability to perform as planned in the light of his other commitments. It will be necessary for those who review research proposals to obtain information on the total academic year salary of the faculty members involved; the other research projects or proposals for which salary is allocated; and any other duties they may have such as teaching assignments, administrative assignments, number of graduate students for which they are responsible, or other institutional activities. Stipulated amounts for an individual must not per se result in increasing his official salary from the institution.

d. **Direct charges for personal services under payroll distribution.** The direct cost charged to organized research for the personal services of professorial and professional staff, exclusive of those whose salaries are stipulated in the research agreement, will be based on institutional payroll systems. Such institutional payroll systems must be supported by either (1) an adequate appointment and workload distribution system accompanied by monthly reviews performed by responsible officials and a reporting of any significant changes in workload distribution of each professor or professional staff member, or (2) a monthly after-the-fact certification system which will require the individual investigators, deans, departmental chairmen or supervisors having first-hand knowledge of the services performed on each research agreement to report the distribution of effort. Reported changes will be incorporated during the accounting period into the payroll distribution system and into the accounting records. Direct charges for salaries and wages of nonprofessionals will be supported by time and attendance and payroll distribution records.

e. **Direct charges for personal services under stipulated salaries.** The amounts stipulated for salary support will be treated as direct costs. The stipulated salary for the academic year will be prorated equally over the duration of the grant or contract period during the academic year, unless other arrangements have been made in the grant or contract instrument. No time or effort reporting will be required to support these amounts. Special provision for summer salaries, or for a particular "off period" if other than summer, will be required. The research agreements will state that any research covered by summer salary support must be carried out during the summer, not during the academic year, and at locations approved in advance in writing by the granting agency. The certification required in section K will attest to this requirement as well as all others in a given research agreement. Stipulated salary support remains fixed during the funding period of the grant or contract and will be costed at the rate described above unless there is a significant change in performance. For example, a significant change in performance would exist if the faculty member (1) was ill for an extended period, (2) took sabbatical leave to devote effort to duties unrelated to his research, or (3) was required to increase substantially his teaching assignments, administrative duties, or responsibility for more research projects. In the latter event, it will be the responsibility of the educational institution to reduce the charges to the research agreement proportionately or seek an appropriate amendment. In the case of those covered by stipulated salary support, the auditors are no longer required to review the precise accuracy of time or effort devoted to research projects. Rather, their reviews should include steps to determine on a sample basis that an institution is not reimbursed for more than 100 percent of each faculty member's salary and that the portion of each faculty member's salary charged to Government-sponsored research is reasonable in view of his university workload and other commitments. The stipulated salary method may also be agreed upon for that portion of a professional's salary that represents cost sharing by the institution.

f. **Indirect personal services costs.** Allowable indirect personal services costs will be supported by the educational institution's accounting

---

system maintained in accordance with generally accepted institutional practices. Where a comprehensive accounting system does not exist, the institution should make periodic surveys no less frequently than annually to support the indirect personal services costs for inclusion in the overhead pool. Such supporting documentation must be retained for subsequent review by Government officials.

g. **General guidance for charging personal services.** Budget estimates on a monthly, quarterly, semester, or yearly basis do not qualify as support for charges to federally sponsored research projects and should not be used unless confirmed after the fact. Charges to research agreements may include reasonable amounts for activities contributing and intimately related to work under the agreement, such as preparing and delivering special lectures about specific aspects of the ongoing research, writing research reports and articles, participating in appropriate research seminars, consulting with colleagues and graduate students with respect to related research, and attending appropriate scientific meetings and conferences. In no case should charges be made to federally sponsored research projects for lecturing or preparing for formal courses listed in the catalog and offered for degree credit, or for committee or administrative work related to university business.

h. **Nonuniversity professional activities.** A university must not alter or waive university-wide policies and practices dealing with the permissible extent of professional services over and above those traditionally performed without extra university compensation, unless such arrangements are specifically authorized by the sponsoring agency. Where university-wide policies do not adequately define the permissible extent of consultantships or other nonuniversity activities undertaken for extra pay, the Government may require that the effort of professional staff working under research agreements be allocated as between (1) university activities, and (2) nonuniversity professional activities. If the sponsoring agency should consider the extent of nonuniversity professional effort excessive, appropriate arrangements governing compensation will be negotiated on a case-by-case basis.

24

i. **Salary rates for academic year.** Charges for work performed on Government research by faculty members during the academic year will be based on the individual faculty member's regular compensation for the continuous period which, under the practice of the institution concerned, constitutes the basis of his salary. Charges for work performed on research agreements during all or any portion of such period would be allowable at the base salary rate. In no event will the charge to research agreements, irrespective of the basis of computation, exceed the proportionate share of the base salary for that period, and any extra compensation above the base salary for work on Government research during such period would be unallowable. This principle applies to all members of the faculty at an institution. Since intra-university consulting is assumed to be undertaken as a university obligation requiring no compensation in addition to full-time base salary, the principle also applies to those who function as consultants or otherwise contribute to a research agreement conducted by another faculty member of the same institution. However, in unusual cases where consultation is across departmental lines or involves a separate or remote operation, and the work performed by the consultant is in addition to his regular departmental load, any charges for such work representing extra compensation above the base salary are allowable provided such consulting arrangement is specifically provided for in the research agreement or approved in writing by the sponsoring agency.

j. **Salary rates for periods outside the academic year.** Charges for work performed by faculty members on Government research during the summer months or other periods not included in the base salary period will be determined for each faculty member at a monthly rate not in excess of that which would be applicable under his base salary and will be limited to charges made in accordance with other subsections of J.7.

k. **Salary rates for part-time faculty.** Charges for work performed on Government research by faculty members having only part-time appointments for teaching will be determined at a rate not in excess of that for which

25

he is regularly paid for his part-time teaching assignments. Example: An institution pays $5,000 to a faculty member for half-time teaching during the academic year. He devoted one-half of his remaining time (25% of his total available time) to Government research. Thus his additional compensation, chargeable by the institution to Government research agreements, would be one-half of $5,000 or $2,500.

8. **Contingency provisions.** Contributions to a contingency reserve or any similar provision made for events the occurrence of which cannot be foretold with certainty as to time, intensity, or with an assurance of their happening, are unallowable.

9. **Deans of faculty and graduate schools.** The salaries and expenses of deans of faculty and graduate schools, or their equivalents, and their staffs, are allowable.

10. **Depreciation and use allowances.**

a. Institutions may be compensated for the use of buildings, capital improvements, and usable equipment on hand through use allowances or depreciation. Use allowances are the means of providing such compensation when depreciation or other equivalent costs are not considered. However, a combination of the two methods may not be used in connection with a single class of fixed assets.

b. Due consideration will be given to Government-furnished facilities utilized by the institution when computing use allowances and/or depreciation if the Government-furnished facilities are material in amount. Computation of the use allowance and/or depreciation will exclude both the cost or any portion of the cost of buildings and equipment borne by or donated by the Federal Government, irrespective of where title was originally vested or where it presently resides and, secondly, the cost of grounds. Capital expenditures for land improvements (paved areas, fences, streets, sidewalks, utility conduits and similar improvements not already included in the cost of buildings)

26

are allowable provided the systematic amortization of such capital expenditures has been provided, based on reasonable determinations of the probable useful lives of the individual items involved, and the share allocated to organized research is developed from the amount thus amortized for the base period involved. Amortization methods once used should not be changed for a given building or equipment unless approved in advance by the cognizant Federal agency.

c. Where the use allowance method is followed, the use allowance for buildings and improvements will be computed at an annual rate not exceeding two percent of acquisition cost. The use allowance for equipment will be computed at an annual rate not exceeding six and two-thirds percent of acquisition cost of usable and needed equipment in those cases where the institution maintains current records with respect to such equipment on hand. Where the institution's records reflect only the cost (actual or estimated) of the original complement of equipment, the use allowance will be computed at an annual rate not exceeding ten percent of such cost. Original complement for this purpose means the complement of equipment initially placed in buildings to perform the functions currently being performed in such buildings; however, where a permanent change in the function of a building takes place, a redetermination of the original complement of equipment may be made at that time to establish a new original complement. In those cases where no equipment records are maintained, the institution will justify a reasonable estimate of the acquisition cost of usable and needed equipment which may be used to compute the use allowance at an annual rate not exceeding six and two-thirds percent of such estimate.

    d. Where the depreciation method is followed, adequate property record must be maintained and periodic inventory (a statistical sampling basis is acceptable) must be taken to insure that properties for which depreciation is charged do exist and are needed. The period of useful service (service life) established in each case for usable capital assets must be determined on a realistic basis which takes into consideration such factors as type of

------

27

construction, nature of the equipment used, technological developments in the particular research area, and the renewal and replacement policies followed for the individual items or classes of assets involved. Where the depreciation method is introduced for application to assets acquired in prior years, the annual charges therefrom must not exceed the amounts that would have resulted had the depreciation method been in effect from the date of acquisition of such assets.

    e. Where an institution elects to go on a depreciation basis for a particular class of assets, no depreciation, rental or use charge may be allowed on any such assets that, under d. above, would be viewed as fully depreciated provided, however, that reasonable use charges may be negotiated for any such assets if warranted after taking into consideration the cost of the facility or item involved, the estimated useful life remaining at time of negotiation, the actual replacement policy followed in the light of service lives used for calculating depreciation, the effect of any increased maintenance charges or decreased efficiency due to age, and any other factors pertinent to the utilization of the facility or item for the purpose contemplated.

    11. **Employee morale, health, and welfare costs and credits.** The costs of house publications, health or first-aid clinics and/or infirmaries, recreational activities, employees' counseling services, and other expenses incurred in accordance with the institution's established practice or custom for the improvement of working conditions, employer-employee relations, employee morale, and employee performance, are allowable. Such costs will be equitably apportioned to all activities of the institution. Income generated from any of these activities will be credited to the cost thereof unless such income has been irrevocably set over to employee welfare organizations.

    12. **Entertainment costs.** Costs incurred for amusement, social activities, entertainment, and any items relating thereto, such as meals, lodging, rentals, transportation, and gratuities, are unallowable.

28

13. **Equipment and other facilities.** The cost of equipment or other facilities are allowable where such purchases are approved by the sponsoring agency concerned or provided for by the terms of the research agreement.

14. **Fines and penalties.** Costs resulting from violations of, or failure of the institution to comply with, Federal, State, and local laws and regulations are unallowable except when incurred as a result of compliance with specific provisions of the research agreement, or instructions in writing from the contracting officer.

15. **Insurance and indemnification.**

a. Costs of insurance required or approved, and maintained, pursuant to the research agreement, are allowable.

b. Costs of other insurance maintained by the institution in connection with the general conduct of its activities, are allowable subject to the following limitations: (1) types and extent and cost of coverage must be in accordance with sound institutional practice; (2) costs of insurance or of any contributions to any reserve covering the risk of loss of or damage to Government-owned property are unallowable except to the extent that the Government has specifically required or approved such costs; and (3) costs of insurance on the lives of officers or trustees are unallowable except where such insurance is part of an employee plan which is not unduly restricted.

c. Contributions to a reserve for an approved self-insurance program are allowable to the extent that the types of coverage, extent of coverage, and the rates and premiums would have been allowed had insurance been purchased to cover the risks.

d. Actual losses which could have been covered by permissible insurance (through an approved self-insurance program or otherwise) are unallowable unless expressly provided for in the research agreement, except that costs incurred because of losses not covered under existing deductible clauses for insurance coverage provided in keeping with sound management

practice as well as minor losses not covered by insurance, such as spoilage, breakage and disappearance of small hand tools, which occur in the ordinary course of operations, are allowable.

e. Indemnification includes securing the institution against liabilities to third persons and other losses not compensated by insurance or otherwise. The Government is obligated to indemnify the institution only to the extent expressly provided for in the research agreement, except as provided in d. above.

16. **Interest, fund raising, and investment management costs.**

a. Costs incurred for interest on borrowed capital or temporary use of endowment funds, however represented, are unallowable.

b. Costs of organized fund raising, including financial campaigns, endowment drives, solicitation of gifts and bequests, and similar expenses incurred solely to raise capital or obtain contributions, are not allowable under Government research agreements.

c. Costs of investment counsel and staff and similar expenses incurred solely to enhance income from investments are not allowable under Government research agreements.

d. Costs related to the physical custody and control of monies and securities are allowable.

17. **Labor relations costs.** Costs incurred in maintaining satisfactory relations between the institution and its employees, including costs of labor management committees, employees' publications, and other related activities, are allowable.

18. **Losses on other research agreements or contracts.** Any excess of costs over income under any other research agreement or contract of any nature is unallowable. This includes, but is not limited to, the institution's

30

contributed portion by reason of cost-sharing agreements or any under-recoveries through negotiation of flat amounts for indirect costs.

19. **Maintenance and repair costs.** Costs incurred for necessary maintenance, repair or upkeep of property (including Government property unless otherwise provided for) which neither add to the permanent value of the property nor appreciably prolong its intended life but keep it in an efficient operating condition, are allowable.

20. **Material costs.** Costs incurred for purchased materials, supplies, and fabricated parts directly or indirectly related to the research agreement, are allowable. Purchases made specifically for the research agreement should be charged thereto at their actual prices after deducting all cash discounts, trade discounts, rebates, and allowances received by the institution. Withdrawals from general stores or stockrooms should be charged at their cost under any recognized method of pricing stores withdrawals conforming to sound accounting practices consistently followed by the institution. Incoming transportation charges are a proper part of material cost. Direct material cost should include only the materials and supplies actually used for the performance of the research agreement, and due credit should be given for any excess materials retained, or returned to vendors. Due credit should be given for all proceeds or value received for any scrap resulting from work under the research agreement. Where Government-donated or furnished material is used in performing the research agreement, such material will be used without charge.

21. **Memberships, subscriptions and professional activity costs.**

a. Costs of the institution's membership in civic, business, technical, and professional organizations are allowable.

b. Costs of the institution's subscriptions to civic, business, professional, and technical periodicals are allowable.

c. Costs of meetings and conferences, when the primary purpose is the dissemination of technical information, are allowable. This includes costs of meals, transportation, rental of facilities, and other items incidental to such meetings or conferences.

22. **Patent costs.** Costs of preparing disclosures, reports, and other documents required by the research agreement and of searching the art to the extent necessary to make such invention disclosures, are allowable. In accordance with the clauses of the research agreement relating to patents, costs of preparing documents and any other patent costs, in connection with the filing of a patent application where title is conveyed to the Government, are allowable. (See also section J.33.)

23. **Pension plan costs.** Costs of the institution's pension plan which are incurred in accordance with the established policies of the institution are allowable, provided such policies meet the test of reasonableness and the methods of cost allocation are not discriminatory, and provided appropriate adjustments are made for credits or gains arising out of normal and abnormal employee turnover or any other contingencies that can result in forfeitures by employees which inure to the benefit of the institution.

24. **Plant security costs.** Necessary expenses incurred to comply with Government security requirements, including wages, uniforms and equipment of personnel engaged in plant protection, are allowable.

25. **Preresearch agreement costs.** Costs incurred prior to the effective date of the research agreement, whether or not they would have been allowable thereunder if incurred after such date, are unallowable unless specifically set forth and identified in the research agreement.

26. **Professional services costs.**

a. Costs of professional services rendered by the members of a particular profession who are not employees of the institution are allowable, subject to b. and c. below, when reasonable in relation to the

services rendered and when not contingent upon recovery of the costs from the Government. Retainer fees to be allowable must be reasonably supported by evidence of services rendered.

b. Factors to be considered in determining the allowability of costs in a particular case include (1) the past pattern of such costs, particularly in the years prior to the award of Government research agreements; (2) the impact of Government research agreements on the institution's total activity; (3) the nature and scope of managerial services expected of the institution's own organizations; and (4) whether the proportion of Government work to the institution's total activity is such as to influence the institution in favor of incurring the cost, particularly where the services rendered are not of a continuing nature and have little relationship to work under Government research agreements.

c. Costs of legal, accounting, and consulting services, and related costs, incurred in connection with organization and reorganization or the prosecution of claims against the Government, are unallowable. Costs of legal, accounting and consulting services, and related costs, incurred in connection with patent infringement litigation, are unallowable unless otherwise provided for in the research agreement.

27. **Profits and losses on disposition of plant, equipment, or other capital assets.** Profits or losses of any nature arising from the sale or exchange of plant, equipment, or other capital assets, including sale or exchange of either short- or long-term investments, shall not be considered in computing research agreement costs.

28. **Proposal costs.** Proposal costs are the costs of preparing bids or proposals on potential Government and nongovernment research agreements or projects, including the development of engineering data and cost data necessary to support the institution's bids or proposals. Proposal costs of the current accounting period of both successful and unsuccessful bids and proposals normally should be treated as indirect costs and allocated

---

33

currently to all activities of the institution, and no proposal costs of past accounting periods will be allocable in the current period to the Government research agreement. However, the institution's established practices may be to treat proposal costs by some other recognized method. Regardless of the method used, the results obtained may be accepted only if found to be reasonable and equitable.

29. **Public information services costs.** Costs of news releases pertaining to specific research or scientific accomplishment are unallowable unless specifically authorized by the sponsoring agency.

30. **Rearrangement and alteration costs.** Costs incurred for ordinary or normal rearrangement and alteration of facilities are allowable. Special arrangement and alteration costs incurred specifically for the project are allowable when such work has been approved in advance by the sponsoring agency concerned.

31. **Reconversion costs.** Costs incurred in the restoration or rehabilitation of the institution's facilities to approximately the same condition existing immediately prior to commencement of Government research agreement work, fair wear and tear excepted, are allowable.

32. **Recruiting costs.**

a. Subject to b., c., and d. below, and provided that the size of the staff recruited and maintained is in keeping with workload requirements, costs of "help wanted" advertising, operating costs of an employment office necessary to secure and maintain an adequate staff, costs of operating an aptitude and educational testing program, travel costs of employees while engaged in recruiting personnel, travel costs of applicants for interviews for prospective employment, and relocation costs incurred incident to recruitment of new employees, are allowable to the extent that such costs are incurred pursuant to a well managed recruitment program. Where the institution uses employment agencies, costs not in excess of standard commercial rates for such services are allowable.

b. In publications, costs of help wanted advertising that includes color, includes advertising material for other than recruitment purposes, or is excessive in size (taking into consideration recruitment purposes for which intended and normal institutional practices in this respect), are unallowable.

c. Costs of help wanted advertising, special emoluments, fringe benefits, and salary allowances incurred to attract professional personnel from other institutions that do not meet the test of reasonableness or do not conform with the established practices of the institution, are unallowable.

d. Where relocation costs incurred incident to recruitment of a new employee have been allowed either as an allocable direct or indirect cost, and the newly hired employee resigns for reasons within his control within 12 months after hire, the institution will be required to refund or credit such relocation costs to the Government.

33. **Royalties and other costs for use of patents.** Royalties on a patent or amortization of the cost of acquiring a patent or invention or rights thereto, necessary for the proper performance of the research agreement and applicable to tasks or processes thereunder, are allowable unless the Government has a license or the right to free use of the patent, the patent has been adjudicated to be invalid or has been administratively determined to be invalid, the patent is considered to be unenforceable, or the patent has expired.

34. **Sabbatical leave costs.** Costs of leave of absence to employees for performance of graduate work or sabbatical study, travel, or research are allowable provided the institution has a uniform policy on sabbatical leave for persons engaged in instruction and persons engaged in research. Such costs will be allocated on an equitable basis among all appertaining activities of the institution. Where sabbatical leave is included in fringe benefits for which a cost is determined for assessment as a direct charge, the aggregate amount of such assessments applicable to all work of the institution

---

during the base period must be reasonable in relatin to the institution's actual experience under its sabbatical leave policy.

35. **Scholarships and student aid costs.** Costs of scholarships, fellowships and other forms of student aid apply only to instruction and therefore are not allocable to research agreements, either as direct costs or indirect costs. However, in the case of students actually engaged in work under research agreements, any tuition remissions to such students for work performed are allocable to such research agreements provided consistent treatment is accorded such costs. (See section J.39.)

36. **Severence pay.**
a. Severance pay is compensation in addition to regular salaries and wages which is paid by an institution to employees whose services are being terminated. Costs of severance pay are allowable only to the extent that such payments are required by law, by employer-employee agreement, by established policy that constitutes in effect an implied

agreement on the institution's part, or by circumstances of the particular employment.

b. Severance payments that are due to normal, recurring turnover and which otherwise meet the conditions of a. above may be allowed provided the actual costs of such severance payments are regarded as expenses applicable to the current fiscal year and are equitably distributed among the institution's activities during that period.

c. Severance payments that are due to abnormal or mass terminations are of such conjectural nature that allowability must be determined on a case-by-case basis. However, the Government recognizes its obligation to participate, to the extent of its fair share, in any specific payment.

37. **Specialized service facilities operated by institution.**

a. The costs, including amortization by generally accepted accounting

36

practice, of institutional services involving the use of highly complex and specialized facilities such as electronci computers, including the cost of adapting computers for use, wind tunnels, and reactors are allowable provided the charges therefor meet the conditions of b. or c. below, and otherwise take into account any items of income or Federal financing that qualify as applicable credits under section C.5.

b. The costs of such institutional services normally will be charged directly to applicable research agreements based on actual usage or occupancy of the facilities on the basis of a schedule of rates that (1) is designed to recover only aggregate costs of providing such services over a long term agreed upon in advance by the cognizant Federal agency on an individual basis, and (2) is applied on a nondiscriminatory basis as between organized research and other work of the institution, including usage by the institution for interanl purposes. Commercial or accommodation sales of computer services will be charged at not less than the above rates; however, if the rates charged for these services are greater, the total amount of charges above the scheduled rates when significant may be considered in revising the schedule of rates. Further, within the constraints of this paragraph, it is not necessary that the rates charged for services be equal to the cost of providing those services during any one fiscal year.

c. In the absence of an acceptable arrangement for direct costing as provided in b. above, the costs incurred for such institutional services may be assigned to research agreements as indirect costs, provided the methods used achieve substantially the same results. Such arrangements should be worked out in coordination with the cognizant Federal agency in order to assure equitable distribution of the indirect costs.

38. **Special services costs.** Costs incurred for general public relations activities, catalogs, alumni activities, and similar services, are unallowable.

37

39. Staff benefits.

a. Staff benefits in the form of regular compensation paid to employees during periods of authorized absences from the job, such as for annual leave, sick leave, military leave, and the like, are allowable provided such costs are absorbed by all institutional activities, including organized research, in proportion to the relative amount of time or effort actually devoted to each. (See section J.34. for treatment of sabbatical leave.)

b. Staff benefits in the form of employer contributions or expenses for social security, employee insurance, workmen's compensation insurance, the pension plan (see section J.23.), tuition or remission of tuition for individual employees or their families (see section J.35.), and the like, are allowable provided such benefits are granted in accordance with established institutional policies, and provided such contributions and other expenses, whether treated as indirect costs or as an increment of direct labor costs, are distributed to particular research agreements and other activities in a manner consistent with the pattern of benefits accruing to the individuals or groups of employees whose salaries and wages are chargeable to such research agreements and other activities.

40. Student activity costs.
Costs incurred for intramural activities, student publications, student clubs, and other student activities, apply only to instruction and therefore are not allocable to research agreements, either as direct costs or indirect costs.

41. Student services costs.
Costs of the deans of students, administration of student affairs, registrar, placement offices, student advisers, student health and infirmary services, and such other activities as are identifiable with student services apply only to instruction and therefore are not allocable to research agreements, either as direct costs or indirect costs. However, in the case of students actually engaged in work under research agreement, a proportion of student services costs measured by the relationship between hours of work by students on such research work and total

student hours including all research time may be allowed as a part of research administration expenses.

42. Taxes.

a. In general, taxes which the institution is required to pay and which are paid or accrued in accordance with generally accepted accountting principles, and payments made to local governments in lieu of taxes which are commensurate with the local government services received are allowable, except for (1) taxes from which exemptions are available to the institution directly or which are available to the institution based on an exemption afforded the Government and in the latter case when the sponsoring agency makes available the necessary exemption certificates, and (2) special assessments on land which represent capital improvements.

b. Any refund of taxes, interest, or penalties, and any payment to the institution of interest thereon, attributable to taxes, interest, or penalties which were allowed as research agreement costs, will be credited or paid to the Government in the manner directed by the Government provided any interest actually paid or credited to an institution incident to a refund of tax, interest and penalty will be paid or credited to the Government only to the extent that such interest accrued over the period during which the institution had been reimbursed by the Government for the taxes, interest, and penalties.

43. **Transportation costs.** Costs incurred for freight, express, cartage, postage, and other transportation services relating either to goods purchased, in process, or delivered, are allowable. When such costs can readily be identified with the items involved, they may be charged directly as transportation costs or added to the cost of such items.Where identification with the materials received cannot readily be made, inbound transportation costs may be charged to the appropriate indirect cost accounts if the institution follows a consistent, equitable procedure in this respect. Outbound freight, if reimbursable under the terms of the research agreement, should be treated as a direct cost.

39

44. **Travel costs.**

a. Travel costs are the expenses for transportation, lodging, subsistence, and related items incurred by employees who are in travel status on official business of the institution. Such costs may be charged on an actual basis, on a per diem or mileage basis in lieu of actual costs incurred, or on a combination of the two, provided the method used is applied to an entire trip and not to selected days of the trip, and results in charges consistent with those normally allowed by the institution in its regular operations.

b. Travel costs are allowable subject to c. and d. below, when they are directly attributable to specific work under a research agreement or are incurred in the normal course of administration of the institution or a department or research program thereof.

c. The difference in cost between first-class air accommodations and less than first-class air accommodations and less than first-class air accommodations is unallowable except when less than first-class air accommodations are not reasonably available to meet necessary mission requirements, such as where less than first-class accommodations would (1) require circuitous routing, (2) require travel during unreasonable hours, (3) greatly increase the duration of the flight, (4) result in additional costs which would offset the transportation savings, or (5) offer accommodations which are not reasonably adequate for the medical needs of the traveler.

d. Costs of personnel movements of a special or mass nature are allowable only when authorized or approved in writing by the sponsoring agency or its authorized representative.

45. **Termination costs applicable to research agreements.**

a. Termination of research agreements generally gives rise to the incurrence of costs or to the need for special treatment of costs, which would not have arisen had the agreement not been terminated. Items

40

peculiar to termination are set forth below. They are to be used in conjunction with all other provisions of this Circular in the case of termination.

b. The cost of common items of material reasonably usable on the institution's other work will not be allowable unless the institution submits evidence that it could not retain such items at cost without sustaining a loss. In deciding whether such items are reasonably usable on other work of the institution, consideration should be given to the institution's plans and orders for current and scheduled work. Contemporaneous purchases of common items by the institution will be regarded as evidence that such items are reasonably usable on the institution's other work. Any acceptance of common items as allowable to the terminated portion of the agreement should be limited to the extent that the quantities of such items on hand, in transit, and on order are in excess of the reasonable quantitative requirements of other work.

c. If in a particular case, despite all reasonable efforts by the institution, certain costs cannot be discontinued immediately after the effective date of termination, such costs are generally allowable within the limitations set forth in this Circular, except that any such costs continuing after termination due to the negligent or willful failure of the institution to discontinue such costs will be considered unacceptable.

d. Loss of useful value of special tooling, and special machinery and equipment is generally allowable, provided (1) such special tooling, machinery, or equipment is not reasonably capable of use in the other work of the institution; (2) the interest of the Government is protected by transfer of title or by other means deemed appropriate by the contracting officer or equivalent; and (3) the loss of useful value as to any one terminated agreement is limited to that portion of the acquisition cost which bears the same ratio to the total acquisition cost as the terminated portion of the agreement bears to the entire terminated agreement

41

and other Government agreements for which the special tooling, special machinery, or equipment was acquired.

e. Rental costs under unexpired leases are generally allowable where clearly shown to have been reasonably necessary for the performance of the terminated agreement, less the residual value of such leases, if (1) the amount of such rental claimed does not exceed the reasonable use value of the property leased for the periodof the agreement and such further period as may be reasonable; and (2) the institution makes all reasonable efforts to terminate, assign, settle, or otherwise reduce the cost of such lease. There also may be included the cost of alterations of such leased property, provided such alterations were necessary for the performance of the agreement, and of reasonable restoration required by the provisions of the lease.

f. Settlement expenses including the following are generally allowable: (1) accounting, legal, clerical, and similar costs reasonably necessary for the preparation and presentation to contracting officers or equivalent of settlement claims and supporting data with respect to the terminated portion of the agreement, and the termination and settlement of subagreement; and (2) reasonable costs for the storage, transportation, protection, and disposition of property provided by the Government or acquired or proiduced by the institution for the agreement.

g. Claims under subagreements, including the allocable portion of claims which are common to the agreement and to other work of the institution, are generally allowable.

K.   **Certification of charges.** To assure that expenditures for research grants and contracts are proper and in accordance with the research agreement documents and approved project budgets, the annual and/or final fiscal reports or vouchers requesting payment under research agreements will include a certification, signed by an authorized official of the university, which reads essentially as follows: "I certify that all expenditures

42

reported (or payments requested) are for appropriate purposes and in accordance with the agreements set forth in the application and award documents."

ATTACHMENT B
Circular No. A-21
Revised

PRINCIPLES FOR DETERMINING COSTS APPLICABLE TO TRAINING AND OTHER EDUCATIONAL SERVICES UNDER GRANTS AND CONTRACTS WITH EDUCATIONAL INSTITUTIONS

TABLE OF CONTENTS

ATTACHMENT B
Circular No. A-21
Revised

PRINCIPLES FOR DETERMINING COSTS APPLICABLE TO TRAINING AND OTHER EDUCATIONAL SERVICES UNDER GRANTS AND CONTRACTS WITH EDUCATIONAL INSTITUTIONS

A.   **Purpose.** This Attachment extends the scope of Circular A-21 to cover the determination of costs incurred by educational institutions under Federal grants and contracts for training and other educational services.

B.   **Application.** All Federal agencies will use Circular A-21, including this Attachment, as a basis for determining allowable costs under grants and cost reimbursement type contracts with educational institutions for work performed under federally-supported educational service agreements.

C.   **Terminology.** The following definitions are to be used in determining the indirect cost of federally-sponsored training and other educational services under this Attachment:

1. **Educational service agreement** means any grant or contract under which Federal financing is provided on a cost reimbursement basis for all or an agreed portion of the costs incurred for training or other educational services. Typical of the work covered by educational service agreements are summer institutes, special training programs for selected participants, professional or technical services to cooperating countries, the development and introduction of new or expanded courses, and similar instructional oriented undertakings, including special research training programs, that are separately budgeted and accounted for by the institution.

The term does not extend to (a) grants or contracts for organized research, (b) arrangements under which the Federal financing is exclusively in the form of scholarships, fellowships, traineeships, or other fixed amounts such as a cost of education allowance or the normal published tuition rates and fees of an institution, or (c) construction, facility and exclusively general resource or institutional type grants.

2. **Instruction** means all of the academic work other than organized research carried on by an institution, including the teaching of graduate and

2

undergraduate courses, departmental research (see section B.2. of Attachment A) and all special training or other instructional oriented projects sponsored by the Federal Government or others under educational service agreements.

D. **Student administration and services.** In addition to the five major functional categories of indirect costs described in section F of Attachment A, there is established an additional category under the title "Student administration and services" to embrace the following:

1. The expenses in this category are those that have been incurred for the administration of student affairs and for services to students, including expenses of such activities as deans of students, admissions, registrar, counseling and placement services, student advisers, student health and infirmary services, catalogs, and commencements and convocations. The salaries of members of the academic staff whose academic appointments or assignments involve the performance of such administrative or service work may also be included to the extent that the portion so charged is supported pursuant to section J.2. The student administration and services category also includes the staff benefit and pension plan costs applicable to the salaries and wages included therein, an appropriate share of the cost of the operation and maintenance of the physical plant, and charges representing use allowance or depreciation applicable to the buildings and equipment utilized in the performance of the functions included in this category.

2. The expenses in this category are generally applicable in their entirety to the instruction activity. They should be allocated to applicable cost objectives within the instruction activity, including educational service agreements, when such agreements reasonably benefit from these expenses. Such expenses should be allocated on the basis of population served (computed on the basis of full-time equivalents including students, faculty, and others as appropriate) or other methods which will result in an equitable distribution to cost objectives in relation to the benefits received and be consistent with guides provided in section E.2. of Attachment A.

3

E. **Direct costs of educational service agreements.** Direct costs of work performed under educational service agreements will be determined consistent with the principles set forth in section D of Attachment A.

F. **Indirect costs of the instruction activity.** The indirect costs of the instruction activity as a whole should include its allocated share of administrative and supportive costs determined in accordance with principles set forth in section D above and in section F of Attachment A. Such costs may include other items of indirect cost incurred solely for the instruction activity and not included in the general allocation of the various categories of indirect expenses. Costs incurred for the institutions by State and local governments are allowable as provided for in section C.6. of Attachment A.

G.   **Indirect costs applicable to educational service agreements.** The individual items of indirect costs applicable to the instruction activity as a whole should be assigned to (1) educational service agreements, and (2) all other instructional work through use of appropriate cost groupings, selected
error   1
instructional work through use of appropriate cost groupings, selected distribution bases, and other reasonable methods as outlined in section E.2. of Attachment A. A single indirect pool may be used for all educational service agreements provided this results in a reasonably equitable distribution of costs among agreements in relation to indirect support services provided. However, when the level of indirect support significantly varies for work performed either on campus or off campus under a particular agreement or group of agreements, separate cost pools should be established consistent with the principles set forth in section G.1.b. of Attachment A. Where direct charges are provided for under educational service agreements for such things as commencement fees, student fees, and tuition, the related indirect costs, through separate cost groupings, should be excluded from the indirect costs allocable to the service agreements.

H.   **Indirect cost rates for educational service agreements.** An indirect cost rate shuold be determined for the educational service agreement pool or pools, as established under section G above. The rate in each case should be stated as the percentage which the amount of the particular educational service agreement pool is of the total direct salaries and wages of all

---

4

educational service agreements identified with such pool. Indirect costs should be distributed to individual agreements by applying the rate or rates established to direct salaries and wages for each agreement. When a fixed rate is negotiated in advance of a fiscal year, the over — or under-recovery for that year may be included as an adjustment to the indirect cost for the next rate negotiation as in sections G.4. and G.5. of Attachment A.

J.   **General standards for selected items of cost.** The standards for selected items of cost as set forth in sections J.1. through J.46. of Attachment A applicable to research agreements will also be applied to educational service agreements with the following modifications:

1. **Commencement and convocation costs (J.5.).** Expenses incurred for convocations and commencements apply to the instruction activity as a whole. Such expenses are unallowable as direct costs of educational service agreements unless specifically authorized in the agreement or approved in writing by the sponsoring agency. For eligibility of allocation as indirect costs, see section D.

2. **Compensation for personal services (J.7.).** Charges to educational service agreements for personal services will normally be determined and supported consistent with the provisions of section J.7. of Attachment A. However, the provision for stipulated salary support will not be used for educational service agreements. Also, charges may include compensation in excess of the base salary of a faculty member for the conduct of courses outside the normal duties of such member provided that: (a) extra charges

are determined at a rate not greater than the basic salary rate of the member; (b) salary payments for such work follow practices consistently applied within the institution; and (c) specific authorization for such cahrges is included in the educational service agreement.

3. **Scholarships and student aid costs (J.35.).** Expenses incurred for scholarships and student aid are unallowable as either direct costs or indirect costs of educational service agreements, unless specifically authorized in the educational service agreement or approved in writing by the sponsoring agency.

5

4. **Student activity costs (J.40.).** Expenses incurred for student activities are unallowable as either direct costs or indirect costs of educational service agreements, unless specifically authorized in the educational service agreement or approved in writing by the sponsoring agency.

5. **Student services costs (J.41.).** Expenses incurred for student services are unallowable as direct costs of educational service agreements unless specifically authorized in the agreement or approved in writing by the sponsoring agency. For eligibility of allocation as indirect costs, see section D.

GOVERNMENT-SPONSORED RESEARCH IN A UNIVERSITY

The following is a joint statement prepared by the Council of the American Association of University Professors and the American Council on Education, 1 Dupont Circle, Washington, D.C. 20026.

The increasingly necessary and complex relationships among universities, Government, and industry call for more intensive attention to standards of procedure and conduct in Government-sponsored research. The clarification and application of such standards must be designed to serve the purposes and needs of the projects and the public interest involved in them and to protect the integrity of the cooperating institutions as agencies of higher education.

The Government and institutions of higher education, as the contracting parties, have an obligation to see that adequate standards and procedures are developed and applied; to inform one another of their respective requirements; and to assure that all individuals participating in their respective behalfs are informed of and apply the standards and procedures that are so developed.

Consulting relationships between university staff members and industry serve the interests of research and education in the university. Likewise, the transfer of technical knowledge and skill from the university to industry contributes to technological advance. Such relationships are desirable, but certain potential hazards should be recognized.

A. CONFLICT SITUATIONS

1. *Favoring of outside interests.* When a university staff member (administrator, faculty member, professional staff member, or employee) undertaking or engaging in Government-sponsored work has a significant financial interest in, or a consulting arrangement with, a private business concern, it is important to avoid actual or apparent conflicts of interest between his Government-sponsored university research obligations and his outside interests and other obligations. Situations in or from which conflicts of interest may arise are the:

a. Undertaking or orientation of the staff member's university research to serve the research or other needs of the private firm without disclosure of such undertaking or orientation to the university and to the sponsoring agency;

b. Purchase of major equipment, instruments, materials, or other items for university research from the private firm in which the staff member has the interest without disclosure of such interest;

c. Transmission to the private firm or other use for personal gain of Government-sponsored work products, results, materials, records, or information that are not made generally available. (This would not necessarily preclude appropriate licensing arrangements for inventions, or consulting on the basis of Government-sponsored research results where there is significant additional work by the staff member independent of his Government-sponsored research);

d. Use for personal gain or other unauthorized use of privileged information acquired in connection with the staff member's Government-sponsored activities. (The term "privileged information" includes, but is not limited to, medical, personnel, or security records of individuals; anticipated material requirements or price actions; possible new sites for Government operations; and knowledge of forthcoming programs or of selection of contractors or subcontractors in advance of official announcements);

e. Negotiation or influence upon the negotiation of contracts relating to the staff members' Government-sponsored research between the university and private organizations with which he has consulting or other significant relationships;

f. Acceptance of gratuities or special favors from private organizations with which the university does or may conduct business in connection with a Government-sponsored research project, or extension of gratuities or special favors to employees of the sponsoring Government agency, under circumstances which might reasonably be interpreted as an attempt to influence the recipients in the conduct of their duties.

2. Distribution of effort. These are competing demands on the energies of a faculty member (for example, research, teaching, committee work, outside consulting). The way in which he divides his effort among these various functions does not raise ethical questions unless the Government agency supporting his research is misled in its understanding of the amount of intellectual effort he is actually devoting to the research in question. A system of precise time accounting is incompatible with the inherent character of the work of a faculty member, since the various functions he performs are closely interrelated and do not conform to any meaningful division of a standard work week. On the other hand, if the research agreement contemplates that a staff member will devote a certain fraction of his effort to the Government-sponsored research, or he agrees to assume responsibility in relation to such research, a demonstrable relationship between the indicated effort or responsiblity and the actual extent of his involvement is to be expected. Each university, therefore, should — through joint consultation of administration and faculty — develop procedures to assure that proposals are responsibly made and complied with.

3. Consulting for Government agencies or their contractors. When the staff member engaged in Government-sponsored research also serves as a consultant to a Federal agency, his conduct is subject to the provisions of the Conflict of Interest Statutes (18 U.S.C. 202-209 as amended) and the President's memorandum of May 2, 1963, *Preventing Conflicts of Interest on the Part of Special Government Employees.* When he consults for one or more Government contractors, or prospective contractors, in the same technical field as his research project, care must be taken to avoid giving advice that may be of questionable objectivity because of its possible bearing on his other interests. In undertaking and performing consulting services, he should make full disclosure of such interests to the university and to the contractor insofar as they may appear to relate to the work at the university or for the contractor. Conflict of interest problems could arise, for example, in the participation of a staff member of the university in an evaluation for the Government agency or its contractor of some technical aspect of the work of another organiuation with which he has a consulting or employment relationship or a significant financial interest, or in an evaluation of a competitor to such other organizations.

B. UNIVERSITY RESPONSIBILITY

Each university participating in Government-sponsored research should make known to the sponsoring Government agencies:

1. The steps it is taking to assure an understanding on the part of the university administration and staff members of the possible conflicts of interest or other problems that may develop in the foregoing types of situations, and

2. The organizational and administrative actions it has taken or is taking to avoid such problems, including:

a. Accounting procedures to be used to assure that Government funds are expended for the purposes for which they have been provided, and that all services which are required in return for these funds are supplied;

b. Procedures that enable it to be aware of the outside professional work of staff members participating in Government-sponsored research, if such outside work relates in any way to the Government-sponsored research;

c. The formulation of standards to guide the individual university staff members in governing their conduct in relation to outside interests that might raise questions of conflicts of interest; and

d. The provision within the university of an informed source of advice and guidance to its staff members for advance consultation on questions they wish to raise concerning the problems that may or do develop as a result of their outside financial or consulting interests, as they relate to their participation in Government-sponsored university research. The university may wish to discuss such problems with the contracting officer or other appropriate Government official in those cases that appear to raise questions regarding conflicts of interest.

The above process of disclosure and consultation is the obligation assumed by the university when it accepts Government funds for research. The process must, of course, be carried out in a manner that does not infringe on the legitimate freedoms and flexibility of action of the university and its staff members that have traditionally characterized a university. It is desirable that standards and procedures of the kind discussed be formulated and administered by members of the university community themselves, through their joint initiative and responsibility, for it is they who are the best judges of the conditions which can most effectively stimulate the search for knowledge and preserve the requirements of academic freedom. Experience indicates that such standards and procedures should be developed and specified by joint administrative-faculty action.

DECLARATION OF HELSINKI

RECOMMENDATIONS GUIDING DOCTORS IN CLINICAL RESEARCH

Adopted by the 18th World Medical Assembly, Helsinki, Finland, 1964

Reprinted from *World Medical Journal* — September, 1964

Introduction

It is the mission of the doctor to safeguard the health of the people. His knowledge and conscience are dedicated to the fulfillment of this mission.

The Declaration of Geneva of The World Medical Association binds the doctor with the words: "The health of my patient will be my first consideration" and the International Code of Medical Ethics which declares that "Any act, or advice which could weaken physical or mental resistance of a human being may be used only in his interest."

Because it is essential that the results of laboratory experiments be applied to human beings to further scientific knowledge and to help suffering humanity, The World Medical Association has prepared the following recommendations as a guide to each doctor in clinical research. It must be stressed that the standards as drafted are only a guide to physicians all over the world. Doctors are not relieved from criminal, civil and ethical responsibilities under the laws of their own countries.

In the field of clinical research a fundamental distinction must be recognized between clinical research in which the aim is essentially therapeutic for a patient, and the clincial research, the essential object of which is purely scientific and without therapeutic value to the person subjected to the research.

I.   Basic Principles

1. Clinical research must conform to the moral and scientific principles that justify medical research and should be based on laboratory and animal experiments or other scientifically established facts.

2. Clincial research should be conducted only by scientifically qualified persons and under the supervision of a qualified medical man.

3. Clincial research cannot legitimately be carried out unless the importance of the objective is in proportion to the inherent risk to the subject.

4. Every clinical research project should be preceeded by careful assessment of inherent risks in comparison to foreseeable benefits to the subject or to others.

5. Special caution should be exercised by the doctor in performing clinical research in which the personality of the subject is liable to be altered by drugs or experimental procedure.

II.   Clinical Research Combined with Professional Care

1. In the treatment of the sick person, the doctor must be free to use a new therapeutic measure, if in his judgment it offers hope of saving life, reestablishing health, or alleviating suffering.

2. If at all possible, consistent with patient psychology, the doctor should obtain the patient's freely given consent after the patient has been given a full explanation. In case of legal incapacity, consent should also be procured from the legal guardian; in case of physical incapacity the permission of the legal guardian replaces that of the patient.

3. The doctor can combine clinical research with professional care, the objective being the acquisition of new medical knowledge, only to the extent that the clinical research is justified by its therapeutic value for the patient.

III. Non-Therapeutic Clinical Research

1. In the purely scientific application of clinical research carried out on a human being, it is the duty of the doctor to remain the protector of the life and health of that person on whom clinical research is being carried out.

2. The nature, the purpose and the risk of clinical research must be explained to the subject by the doctor.

3a. Clinical research on a human being cannot be undertaken without his free consent after he has been informed; if he is legally incompetent, the consent of the legal guardian should be procured.

3b. The subject of clinical research should be in such a mental, physical and legal state as to be able to exercise fully his power of choice.

3c. Consent should, as a rule, be obtained in writing. However, the responsibility for clinical research always remains with the research worker, it never falls on the subject even after consent is obtained.

4a. The investigator must respect the right of each individual to safeguard his personal integrity, especially if the subject is in a dependent relationship to the investigator.

4b. At any time during the course of clinical research the subject or his guardian should be free to withdraw permission for research to be continued.

The investigator or the investigating team should discontinue the research if in his or their judgment, it may, if continued, be harmful to the individual.

Index

381

About the Authors

HAROLD ZALLEN, Ph.D., is Executive Vice President and Chief Executive Officer of Academic World Incorporated, a consulting firm. He has served as program officer for the U.S. Office of Education and the National Science Foundation. As an active researcher he has held grants from the U.S. Public Health Service, American Cancer Society, Elks Foundation, General Electric Foundation, International Business Machines and the Fairchild Instrument Corporation. As a graduate student, he was responsible for a U.S. Army research contract awarded to Purdue University. He has served as an academic department head, assistant dean, and associate vice president. He currently serves as President, Southern Section, Society of Research Administrators. He holds academic degrees from Northeastern University (B.S.); Boston University (Ed.M.); and Purdue University (M.S. and Ph.D.). He is listed in *American Men of Science* and *Marquis Who's Who in America* and *Who's Who in the World*. He is the author of many scientific papers and two additional books.

EUGENIA M. ZALLEN, Ph.D., currently serves as Associate Professor and Director, School of Home Economics, The University of Oklahoma. She is conducting research in the area of food storage and food habits and teaches a course in research methodology. Prior to coming to Oklahoma, she served on the faculty at The University of Maryland, and Auburn University. She holds degrees from Auburn University (B.S.); Purdue University (M.S.); and The University of Tennessee (Ph.D.). She is listed in *American Men and Women of Science* and *Marquis Who's Who of American Women*.

NOTES

NOTES

NOTES

NOTES

NOTES

NOTES

NOTES

NOTES

NOTES